W.O.

Bill Mitchell working on the manuscript of
Who Has Seen the Wind, *1945.*

W.O.

THE LIFE OF W.O. MITCHELL

BEGINNINGS TO *WHO HAS SEEN THE WIND*

— 1914-1947 —

BARBARA & ORMOND MITCHELL

M&S

Canadian Cataloguing in Publication Data

Mitchell, Barbara
    W.O. : the life of W.O. Mitchell : beginnings to Who has seen the wind
1914–1947

Includes index.
ISBN 0-7710-6107-2

1. Mitchell, W.O. (William Ormond), 1914–1998.   2. Authors, Canadian (English) – 20th century – Biography.   I. Mitchell, Ormond.   II. Title.

PS8526.19765Z727   1999   C813'.54   C99-931226-X
PR9199.3.M54Z78   1999

We acknowledge the financial support of the Government of Canada through the Book Publishing Industry Development Program for our publishing activities. Canadä

We further acknowledge the support of the Canada Council for the Arts and the Ontario Arts Council for our publishing program.

Typeset in Garamond by M&S, Toronto
Printed and bound in Canada

McClelland & Stewart Inc.
The Canadian Publishers
481 University Avenue
Toronto, Ontario
M5G 2E9

1 2 3 4 5 6   04 03 02 01 00 99

CONTENTS

In memory of our parents

PREFACE

Over his sixty-year writing career W.O. Mitchell wrote short stories, novels, magazine articles, radio and television plays, stage plays (including a musical), and film scripts. His work won numerous awards, including two Stephen Leacock awards, the Chalmers Canadian Play Award, and three ACTRA awards. Through his reading performances, he earned a reputation as one of Canada's favourite story-tellers. Perhaps no other Canadian writer has been so versatile, not only in art form, but in audience appeal. He is best known for his "Jake and the Kid" stories, dramatized in CBC's radio series in the 1950s and 1960s, and for *Who Has Seen the Wind*, a Canadian classic that has sold three-quarters of a million copies[1] and is taught in schools and universities across Canada.

In the early 1980s we began to collect information and to tape interviews towards a future biography on W.O. As close relatives we were able to tape conversations while living and travelling with our subject – play often overlapped with work. The biography grew at a leisurely rate as W.O. continued producing more work, including a novella, five novels, two stage plays, a collection of stories, and a collection of performance pieces. At times we wondered if we would ever catch up to him! Three of these novels were directly influenced by our biographical work with W.O. By 1994 our planned single-volume biography had grown into a two-volume project.

Our biography is composed of a number of narrative voices. The first is our shared voice, which attempts to document and appraise Mitchell's life and work in the tradition of the critical literary biography. Within this framing voice are woven a number of others, the most central of which is Mitchell's own. Using material from sixty-odd hours of taped interviews with him, we frequently let him tell his own story. There are also the voices of people Mitchell knew throughout his life, ranging from those very close to him, such as his wife, Merna, his children, and his brothers, to the more distant voices of acquaintances. Finally, there is a *memoir voice* (italicized in the text), sometimes Orm's alone and sometimes shared with Barbara, which recalls experiences with W.O. and reflects on his life in a more personal way.

At times we have used Mitchell's fiction and drama as a kind of wrecking yard from which bits and pieces of his autobiographical experience have been salvaged. He often described his fiction as compelling illusions largely composed of sensuous and emotional fragments of autobiographical experience: "Every bit's the truth, but the whole thing's a creative leap/lie."[2] One of our aims is to throw some light on the ways and the extent to which he used autobiographical experience in shaping his fiction and drama. Reading the life of a writer backwards from his work, however, can be a dangerous strategy for the literary biographer. As Mark Twain said in speaking of the relationship between his brother Henry and the fictional character Sid in *The Adventures of Tom Sawyer*, "[Henry] is Sid in *Tom Sawyer*. But Sid was not Henry."[3] We are wary of confusing the writer with his fictional characters.

Mitchell himself at times confused his own fictional embellishment with the "truth." As he put it, "you come to believe your own lie."[4] We all do this to one degree or another when we tell the stories of our lives. But the creative writer is perhaps more prone to this embellishment because he invests his own life so intensely in his characters. One of the problems with which we were faced in our taped interviews, as well as with salvaging autobiographical information from Mitchell's creative work, was to identify as accurately as possible the points at which Mitchell's instinct for exaggeration began to transform autobiographical "truth" into fictive illusion. Since we had lived with Mitchell's story-telling for a long time and were often witnesses to the events he turned into stories, we were able to differentiate fairly accurately between fact and fiction, to sense when Mitchell's memories of events in his life began to metamorphose into Jake Trumper tall tales.

In setting out to trace the growth and nature of Mitchell's imagination, to explore those forces that came together to make him a writer and performer, it became apparent that his childhood years in Weyburn were unusually significant. His philosophy about creativity, and about "how to be," were partially influenced by William Wordsworth's insight that "The Child is father of the Man,"[5] or as Mitchell said, "the man always retains in his magnitude the miniature boy."[6] Throughout his life he held fast to the belief that the channel to the imagination is through the senses, that it is essential to stay alive to sights, sounds, and smells with the freshness of childlike wonderment. There was nothing passive, however, about Mitchell's imaginative interplay with the world around him. He actively pursued the dramatic in life and welcomed – in fact, often created – what he called the "capsize quality" of life (*SD* 5). He retained all his life an irreverence, earthiness, immodesty, and enthusiasm, as well as a kind of immature solipsism. The child's consciousness and how the child's imagination is nurtured are primary concerns in his writing. The good guardians in his stories are those characters who have not suffered "complete amnesia for childhood" (*WW* 90).

The child's experience and prairie are central to *Who Has Seen the Wind* and the "Jake and the Kid" stories. Throughout his writing career, Mitchell returned to his early years in Weyburn as inspiration for his work. In his last novel, tentatively called "Brotherhood: True or False" and unfinished at his death, he had circled back to this landscape and era once again. But this circling back was not simply a nostalgia for a lost time and place – it was a continual exploration of the education of the imagination.

I

"A SPRING RITUAL"

ON A SUNDAY afternoon in mid-May of 1922, Margaret Lutecia Mitchell drove two of her four sons, Billie and Bobbie, to visit their father's grave in the cemetery six miles south of Weyburn, Saskatchewan. Her husband, Ormond Skinner Mitchell, had died just over a year before when Billie was seven. Many years later W.O. Mitchell recalled for us this first of many cemetery visits which had been engraved on his memory:

> She wanted to keep the memory of our father alive. Therefore, it was a spring ritual when the McLaughlin came down off the blocks and the water was put in the radiator to drive the six miles south of Weyburn to the cemetery and stand there. In those days the smell of death greeted us almost everywhere on the prairie, especially in the spring. It would be a lump-jaw steer or some critter that had been left and was just decaying. And one of the things that was vivid was an occasion with mother – probably when I would be about eight – in that Weyburn cemetery on the crown of the hill, and then just *zip* either direction, and the sound of the telephone wires. And Bobbie and I had been stepping over graves so we wouldn't tramp over top of people, and

reading all the things. And as I stood there, mother said, "Boys, come with me." And we stood with that great grey tombstone. And I looked up at my mother . . . and I do remember the tears were coming down and it just hit me in the guts as a child. And that's when I knew death – that it was the step that could not be retrieved or taken again. That there were things that happened to humans, that there was no turning back.[1]

This event was primal in Mitchell's memory. In 1940 he recalled it with such vivid immediacy that he was compelled to write it down in rough first-person recall, a kind of free-association or automatic writing which he later called "freefall." It was the first authentic writing he had done and was the beginning point for *Who Has Seen the Wind*. Although it is only a short scene in the novel, it carries within its images the symphonic structure of the novel – birth, then death, then birth again:

> Each Sunday Brian's growing sense of responsibility received impetus from visits to the cemetery. In spring and summer, Sean O'Connal would drive his old Ford into the town and take Maggie and her sons to the slight rise in the prairie a mile from town. They would stand together among the carven stone lambs and scrolls with the wind in the tall grass, now and then the song of a meadow lark, the squeak of a gopher. They would look down at the ground slightly raised, with everlasting flowers under a huge glass dome at the head of the grave. On such occasions Brian would think resolutely of his father, would caution Bobbie about walking over the tops of graves lost in prairie wool. (*WW* 288)

Mitchell drew on much of his own childhood experience for this novel, and the emotional impact of the death of his father is reflected through this novel's child hero, Brian Sean MacMurray O'Connal. Brian is just ten years old when his father dies following a gall-bladder operation. Like Brian, seven-year-old Billie Mitchell heard various mourners liturgically repeat, "He was a fine man," and, placing their hands on his head, tell him "he would have to be a brave boy now" (*WW* 275). As Brian watches his mother and the other mourners who have gathered at their home, he is concerned that he has not yet cried. He slips out of the house and sees his friend Fat, who suggests they go over to their hut and play rummy:

> They played silently and seriously a game that usually went with shouts and slapping down of cards. When they came to the end of the deck, Fat laid down his hand. The king of hearts, for which Brian had been waiting, was not there.
> "Where's the king of hearts, Fat?"
> "Must of been played."
> "No. I been waiting for it from the start. I needed it."
> (*WW* 277)

When he tells Fat that everybody at the house is "crying like anything" but that he has not, Fat says, "Maybe you'll bawl at the funeral" (*WW* 278). But at the funeral the following day he still does not cry. As Brian walks alone out onto the prairie, Mitchell, using the images and rhythms of the Book of Ecclesiastes, captures his inner thoughts and emotions:

> Forever and forever the prairie had been, before there was a town, before he had been, or his father, or *his* father, or *his* father before him. Forever for the prairie – never for his father – never again.
> People were forever born; people forever died, and never were again. Fathers died and sons were born; the prairie was forever, with its wind whispering through the long, dead grasses, through the long and endless silence. Winter came and spring and fall, then summer and winter again; the sun rose and set

again, and everything that was once – was again – forever and
forever. But for man, the prairie whispered – never – never. For
Brian's father – never. (*WW* 283-84)

Over the years Mitchell repeatedly pointed to his epiphanic
moment with his mother in the Weyburn cemetery as one of the
significant influences on his becoming a writer. Perhaps, in fact, its
symbolic value as the impetus for a career was heightened by
memory. Certainly, in the retelling of the scene, details that were not
in the original began accumulating, other details were discarded,
and death became the stronger force, laden not just with emotional
immediacy but with philosophic meaning. In 1979, when the
National Film Board (NFB) filmed him for a documentary on his
life, he said, "I started to write when I stood at that grave with my
mother"[2] and he gave this version of the scene:

> My mother would take us out and we would stand in the ceme-
> tery. I remember there was a gopher hole in front of that grey
> rock that said, "Loved by all who knew him. O.S. Mitchell." A
> gopher came out of that hole and I remember being outraged!
> What the hell right did that gopher have digging? Because my
> brothers and I were very careful when we were in the cemetery
> and we always stepped over – we wouldn't step on the sacred
> bones of the people under there. And here is a bloody gopher
> coming out of my father's grave. Then I looked up and saw my
> mother crying. What I am getting at is I think I discovered
> my own mortality around the age of eight or nine. Because
> when I looked up at my mother and the tears coming down her
> cheeks, I knew that death was the one irreversible step. That's
> all, there ain't no more.[3]

Perhaps the gopher hole was actually there on the first visit and only
in this retelling found a meaningful place. But, perhaps, it was imagined. The mother crying is now a fixture in the scene, and she is frequently described as pushing aside a tendril of hair as she wipes away

her tears. The carven lambs, actually present on a nearby gravestone, have disappeared from this version, as has the dome of artificial flowers. Interviews with Mitchell over a fifteen-year period show that some of his memories, told over and over again, were like four-bar themes in improvised jazz — with each retelling they were elaborated with different grace notes and runs.

Mitchell's imagination returned to and played with this scene because it held key elements that had shaped him: the loss of his father at a young age, the subsequent predominance of his mother, the burden of awareness of his mother's loss, the recognition of the need for human solidarity in the face of ultimate aloneness, and a combined love and fear of the prairie. His father's death and his familiarity with the prairie made him "really quite a mordant person, more than usually aware of the limit of man's days." This early and indelible awareness of death compelled him to persist in his efforts to be a creative writer: "I think you could look at almost all of my work — and I have even made the statement that death does stand behind any piece of art. Because art goes beyond survival and practicality. It has to be the one thing man does to assert he is not mortal. And I don't think without the energy of death you are going to get people who will stick the whole distance — they'll quit."[4]

— PRAIRIE —

Here was the least common denominator of nature, the skeleton requirements simply, of land and sky — Saskatchewan prairie. (WW 1)

In Mitchell's formative years, the impact of an absent father was mirrored by that of the prairie, a landscape of absence. Mitchell believed that prairie throws human consciousness back on itself, offering "so little on the outside, it shifts one's perspective inside." The prairie's minimalist landscape invites imaginative elaboration from the developing consciousness: "The Prairies are made to produce artists."[5] Wallace Stegner, an American novelist who had his beginnings in

Eastend, Saskatchewan, describes the distinctive effect of prairie landscape in *Wolf Willow*:

> You become acutely aware of yourself. The world is very large, the sky even larger, and you are very small. But also the world is flat, empty, nearly abstract, and in its flatness you are a challenging upright thing, as sudden as an exclamation mark, as enigmatic as a question mark.
>
> It is a country to breed mystical people, egocentric people, perhaps poetic people. But not humble ones.[6]

Like Mitchell, Stegner theorizes that the childhood years between five and twelve are an individual's most impressionable, and that when exposed to a particular environment at this susceptible time an individual will "carry [his] habitual and remembered emotions" and "will perceive in the shapes of that environment until he dies."[7] Mitchell frequently called these the "litmus years," the "most sensitively important years," in which the adult is forever marked by his childhood imprintings.[8]

Untamed prairie was only a block away from Mitchell's home. Even at the age of six Mitchell was aware of the enigma of the prairie landscape when he and his friends wandered out to play: "We must have started going out by at least the age of six – never alone but with several of us. As we walked over that empty prairie every one of us children knew that at one time this had once been the [home of] Plains Indians. It was almost impossible for us to accept that anyone could live in this flat emptiness."[9] As he "strolled on an immense prairie saucer with horizon rim," Billie felt "vulnerable under infinite sky."[10]

The prairie became even more significant when, because of health problems at the age of twelve, Billie was taken out of school for almost a year: "From nine until four, I was the only child alive on 6th Street, in Weyburn, in Saskatchewan, or in the world, and I used to wander into the prairie a great deal alone."[11] In rough freefall notes, written for a CBC talk, Mitchell described these lonely prairie excursions:

> — there is nothing sadder than a child wandering disconsolately about his neighborhood while all others are in school — there is nothing to do and black boredom descends upon him – a bitter-sweet sadness and a languor bringing with it an inward turning of the mind. On such days it became my habit to wander out our street to the prairie and there to idly stroll – with the wind in the grass – the sun warm and amorous on the nape of my neck — in winter — with my mother's snow shoes – out on full moonlit nights – to lie down on the snow – and look up into the dark face of the sky freckled with the fierce fire of white and blue stars ——12

Alone on the prairie, he started "to carry on more internal conversations" with himself and began "to pay more attention to what [his] senses were presenting [him] with."13

How I Spent My Summer Holidays, like *Who Has Seen the Wind*, draws on Mitchell's childhood experience in Weyburn and on the prairie. The seventy-year-old narrator, Hugh, revisits his childhood prairie haunts: "Now and as a child I walked out here to ultimate emptiness, and gazed to no sight destination at all. Here was the melodramatic part of the earth's skin that had stained me during my litmus years, fixing my inner and outer perspective, dictating the terms of the fragile identity contract I would have with my self for the rest of my life" (*SH* 10). Mitchell's own "fragile identity contract" was established through exposure on the prairie, through feeling "the total thrust of the prairie sun," or of the prairie night, on his "vulnerable head."14 Brian, in *Who Has Seen the Wind*, is pushed to the limits of vulnerability when he spends a night alone on the open prairie – significantly, the same night his father dies – and feels he "was being drained of his very self" (*WW* 271). However, he awakes the next morning to a new "vivid" awareness of himself, of his "apartness," and he experiences "a singing return of the feeling that had possessed him so many times in the past" (*WW* 272). A few days later, after his father's funeral, Brian walks out "into the prairie's stillness and loneliness that seemed to flow around him, to meet itself behind him, ringing him and separating him from the town" (*WW* 282). Now he realizes the finality of his father's death and now, as he thinks of the "dark well of his mother's loneliness" and her need for him, the tears come. He turns from the prairie and starts "for home, where his mother was" (*WW* 284).

Mitchell was "not by nature" a "loner."[15] Human community figured importantly in his life and in his fiction. His imaginative sensibility, made intensely aware of its own mortality and inescapable loneliness by prairie vacuum, may have been more prone to anaesthetize or fill the void of loneliness by making contact with others through art, as well as through the more usual ways of hanging together, such as love, family, and community. In a 1990 article, "Bridge Over Loneliness," Mitchell expressed this proposition:

> In my new world, at a very young age, I learned I was mortal, I could die; the end of Billie Mitchell. The humming, living prairie of old did not give one good Goddamn about that. My mother, my brothers and friends did and my grandmother; . . . When you learn you are going to die you truly understand that you are human. You have been then given a perspective that is very helpful in deciding what is important and what is unimportant, valuable, not valuable. A sense of mortality does make us examine our lives, to clarify priorities. Socrates said that the unexamined life is not worth living. . . . Man does not live by reason and common sense alone. The simply intellectual life is not worth living. This is the reason that humans build their bridges from lonely human self to lonely human self.[16]

One of the most important of these bridges for Mitchell was the writing and telling of stories, stories which often drew on those litmus years stained by the interior landscape of a child's consciousness and by the exterior landscape of prairie.

‑ RECONSTRUCTING THE KING OF HEARTS ‑

In the last filming session of the NFB documentary on Mitchell, the following exchange took place:

> NFB: Was your father's tombstone changed recently? 'Cause we went to see it and there's no carving on it, there's no "Loved by all who knew him" on it.
>
> MITCHELL: It is a great, solid granite, big, square thing, with the rough granite on the edges, and then across the front is . . . , and it couldn't be effaced, "Loved by all who knew him." What's happened?
>
> NFB: It has "O.S. Mitchell," and the dates. Maybe you imagined it.
>
> MITCHELL: Could be. You know there is a confusion you get [when autobiographical experience is used to create fiction]. . . . You do take creative leaps and that could be part of a creative leap that I assumed that "Loved by all who knew him" was on it. You get a little confused, you know, because when you are working on a novel, for about . . . five [years] was the instance with *Who Has Seen the Wind*, you come to believe your own lie as Eli Mandel said, or your own lies. Your own fictional people become real and as well known to you as lovers, children, brothers, sisters.[17]

"Loved by all who knew him," although not on the large upright marble gravestone, is chiselled into a smaller stone which lies flat on the ground, its edges buried in the grass. On it are O.S. Mitchell's name, his birth and death dates, and the epitaph. Mitchell had used his memory of the gravesite for his fictional father in *Who Has Seen the Wind*, whose headstone reads, "LOVED BY ALL WHO KNEW

COURTNEY MILNE

Bill's father's gravestone in Weyburn, Saskatchewan.

HIM. *Gerald Fitzgerald O'Connal* – 1892–1935."[18] Ironically, his memory was sharper than the NFB's camera, which missed the flat stone, perhaps because it had become overgrown with grass; the only mistake Mitchell made was in thinking the epitaph was on the large centre stone.

Nevertheless, Mitchell was quite ready to admit to a "lie" because creative embellishment of autobiographical experience was central to his story-telling. It may account for other details of the cemetery scene such as the gopher or his mother crying or the sound of wind in telephone wires. But both the fact of the epitaph engraved on Billie Mitchell's eight-year-old consciousness *and* Mitchell's later embellished details indicate the depth and intensity of his feeling for a father lost before he was really known and his desire to have known this man, so loved by others, as most sons know their fathers.

Mitchell's fictional imagination was often attracted to fatherless characters, some of whom have, or are searching for, father substitutes: Brian in *Who Has Seen the Wind*; the Kid in the "Jake and the

Kid" stories; David Lang and Keith Maclean in *The Kite*; Howard Arnold in *For Those in Peril on the Sea*; Jacob Schunk in *The Devil's Instrument*. In April 1946, Little, Brown, who were about to publish *Who Has Seen the Wind*, wrote Mitchell asking him for some biographical information. He wrote, "My father died when I was six [actually he had just turned seven]; Gerald O'Connal of the novel is what I imagine he was. My mother lives in Weyburn, Sask., completely surrounded by prairie and her son's stories."[19]

"Imagine" was all he could do, for Mitchell had very few actual memories of his father: "I was afraid of getting old when I was a kid on the prairies. The reason I think was that my father died when I was five [seven] so I never really knew my dad. I remembered him, and then I remembered remembering him and then I remembered remembering remembering him, so I guess he got paler and paler."[20] Although *Who Has Seen the Wind* is one of his most autobiographical works, he was not the "child who had a father with a relationship Brian had with Gerald."[21] Some of the details of Gerald and his relationship with Brian were invented and others came from Mitchell's observation of other father-son relationships. In *How I Spent My Summer Holidays*, Mitchell used memories of his relationship with his sons, particularly Hugh, for the fictional Hugh–father relationship. Both Brian and Hugh, in two scenes written more than thirty-five years apart, respond to the deaths of their fathers in similar ways. In *Who Has Seen the Wind* the ten-year-old Brian tries to reconstruct his dead father with remembered details:

> It was his father's gall-bladder that had made him die; he had been very sick; he had turned yellow. He was a big man like Uncle Sean, only no mustaches and gentler. He wore gold cuff links. His whiskers gritted. He recited "Casey at the Bat." Once he had helped him bury a baby pigeon on the prairie. He had a gold tooth in front. He brought stuff home from the store, once a fan with a Japanese girl on it. She had her hair piled high. It had been made of stretched silk. (*WW* 275)

In *How I Spent My Summer Holidays* twenty-five-year old Hugh resorts to the same incantatory process of evocation as he looks at the corpse of his dead father:

> It was not my father.
>
> My father was the bonfire smell of cigar smoke, cheek stubble male and harsh against the side of my face. . . . My father taught me to read at four. He pulled the leather laces snug on my skates, and he rubbed the circulation back into my aching feet after I had skated too long on the Little Souris ice. He tilted my chin in the bathroom and squeezed out the drops when I had pinkeye.
>
> This was not my father.
>
> My father bought me my first jockstrap on my thirteenth birthday. He clearly explained square root to me after Mr. Mackey had strapped me three times for refusing to get it right up at the board. He kept telling me, "Don't eat that Elmer," and he told Inspector Kydd to his face that Russian wolfhounds were stupid. He was the only one who always called me "Hugh." (*SH* 214-15)

Mitchell, using imaginative elaboration, was himself going through the same process as these sons, was on one level reconstructing his own father "as I imagine he was." This act of reconstructing what suddenly went missing when he was a child was not only an emotional and psychological response to loss. It was also a search for how to be, for how to live his life in the shadow of his father's and his own mortality. Perhaps this partly explains why Mitchell believed the "energy of death" lies behind the creative process, and that his writing is an assertion against mortality – in this instance not only his own but also his father's. If so, *Who Has Seen the Wind*'s dedication, "To O.S. MITCHELL, my father and my son," is particularly apt.

My father died on 25 February 1998, just sixteen days short of his eighty-fourth birthday. Federal buildings flew their flags at half-mast across the country for a man the media celebrated and mourned as Canada's "best-loved author." We had always known that W.O. had a special place in the hearts of those who read or heard him tell his stories. But we were not prepared for this outpouring of affection.

A few months before his death he said to Barbara, half question-ingly, half assertively, "I've had a pretty interesting life, haven't I,"[22] an understatement from a man prone to exaggeration and dramatic per-formance. His own full and adventuresome eighty-four years lie in sharp contrast to the premature death of his father at forty-six. In later life W.O. was often asked how he wanted to be remembered and his responses always came back to two things — to be remembered as a "loving-hearted human" and to be remembered through his children, and their children, and their children. . . .

So we begin an act of reconstruction — but with a difference, for our king of hearts was vividly present in our lives for many years. And I cannot remember not *knowing my father.*

2

THE GENETIC LITMUS BATH

— 1750s to 1906 —

IN THE LAST scene of *Who Has Seen the Wind*, Brian, now twelve years old, walks out onto the prairie on a cold winter afternoon. His grandmother has died two weeks before, and as he walks over the "spread and staring white of the land" where "no living thing moved," he struggles to understand what human mortality means:

> All kinds of people had died. They were dead and they were gone. The swarming hum of telephone wires came to him, barely perceptible in the stillness, hardly a sound heard so much as a pulsing of power felt. He looked up at rime-white wires, following them from pole to pole to the prairie's rim. From each person stretched back a long line – hundreds and hundreds of years – each person stuck up. (*WW* 342-43)

Brian here senses what Mitchell believed – that individuals gain a kind of immortality through the humming "wires" of genetic connection. In both his life and his writing Mitchell was drawn to relationships between the young and the old. This was partly a result of the close relationship he developed as a child with his Grandmother

McMurray. Following the death of her husband, just four months after Orm Mitchell's death, she moved in with her daughter and the four boys. With their strong sense of Scottish clan, these two McMurray matriarchs were largely responsible for Mitchell's keen interest in his family roots, for both women were determined to keep alive the memories of their dead husbands. Mitchell recalled family stories and his family tree with amazing accuracy. Although he last saw the McMurray family Bible in 1944 when he was working on *Who Has Seen the Wind* in Weyburn, the long list of five generations of births, marriages, and deaths inscribed on the flyleaf was imprinted on his memory with almost complete accuracy. When his mother died, he and his brothers inherited the family heirlooms, but the most significant inheritances for Mitchell were intangible ones — family tales, a gift for telling stories, and a strong sense of his Scots-Irish and Scots-Presbyterian heritage.

— THE EARLY MITCHELLS (1750S TO 1833) —

The stories that came down through the paternal side of the family, the Scots-Irish side, were less detailed and verifiable than those from the maternal side. Mitchell's paternal grandparents died in the early 1900s before he was born and he had no opportunity to hear about the Mitchell side of the family from his father. But the Mitchells were a family of "talkers" and "yappers," the latter term used by Mitchell to describe the more unreliable and boring story-tellers among them. Uncle Jim, his father's second-eldest brother, was one of the "talkers," and he told his nephew Billie some of the details of the family's Scots-Irish roots.

We know that Mitchell's great-great-grandparents, John and Elizabeth, were married on 2 August 1815 and settled down on what was by then the Mitchell family farm on Ballykeel Road in the parish of Rathfriland, County Down (five miles from the market town Rathfriland and about twenty-five miles south of Belfast). During the 1700s this area had been heavily settled by Scots Presbyterians. Mitchell recalled hearing as a child that David Mitchell, probably

Ancestors of William Ormond Mitchell

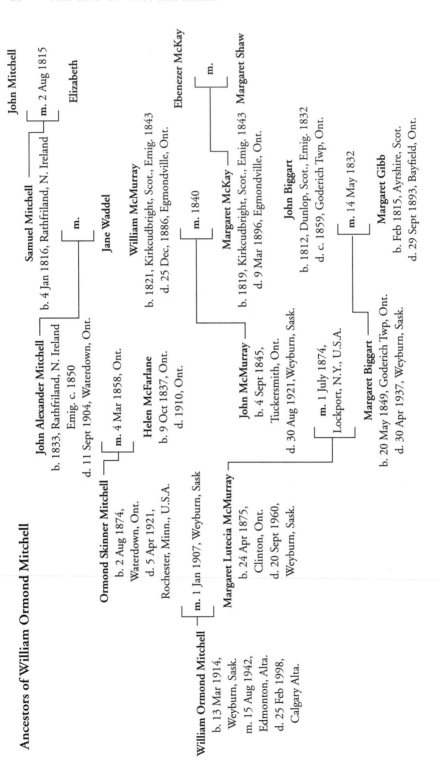

a great-great-grandfather of his grandfather John Mitchell, left Perthshire, Scotland, sometime in the mid-1700s to work for the Marquis of Downshire as a surveyor and that he was granted the Rathfriland farm for his services. It is likely that his son John Mitchell surveyed for the third marquis, Arthur Hill, who inherited the Downshire estates in 1809.[1]

In June 1997 we went to Ireland to learn more about W.O.'s Scots-Irish roots. We searched the public and church records at Belfast and Rathfriland and visited for a few days with Willie Mitchell (W.O.'s second cousin) and his son William, who, with his family, still works the Mitchell farm. The forty-acre farm is in a particularly beautiful area with green hills rolling out to the Mourne Mountains. The two-hundred-year-old white stone farmhouse has gained a modern addition. Across the fields can be seen an older rough grey stone cottage, the original farmhouse which, as one story goes, is the birthplace of John Alex Mitchell, W.O.'s grandfather. We wondered if this was the original David Mitchell cottage. It is now used as a barn but was at one time divided into two rooms. One side, with a high peaked roof, a glassed window, and a fireplace, was for the family, and the other side for the animals. We guessed that John's parents, Samuel and Jane, lived there, while their parents, John and Elizabeth, occupied the grander two-storey white house.

Our trip "back" to County Down to trace ancestral history had its highs and lows. It was wonderful to meet friendly and generous distant relatives in a landscape that redefined green for us. But Willie, like W.O., was bed-ridden and slowly withdrawing from the living. We visited with him for an afternoon tea, but he only occasionally surfaced to the family conversation which flowed around him. Both of us thought of W.O. back home. We were invited to stay that night and slept in what had been Willie and his wife's room – and Samuel and Jane's, John and Elizabeth's – in the old part of the farmhouse. Our search in the public and church records had turned up nothing, and we appeared to know more about the Mitchell history than Willie and his children did. They had never heard of David Mitchell but did recall having at one time some old surveying instruments. Our last hope was to check out the

cemetery of Ryan's Presbyterian Church, where the Mitchell family had
worshipped since 1826. But we found no clues here – the oldest grave-
stones in the cemetery dated back only to the late 1800s. One of the
Mitchell clan, who met us at the cemetery, explained that old graves were
reused. We left the cemetery thinking of Mitchell ancestors stacked like
cordwood, a family pyramid with David Mitchell and his forebears
somewhere on the bottom rows.

— JOHN ALEX MITCHELL (1833-1904) AND — HELEN McFARLANE (1837-1910)

John Alex Mitchell, Mitchell's grandfather, was born in 1833 and
raised on the Rathfriland farm. During the potato famine of the late
1840s, John and two of his brothers, like thousands of other Irish and
Scots-Irish at this time, emigrated to the New World. They sailed
out of Liverpool aboard the *Cultivator* on October 11 in 1849 or 1850.
Although they could afford passage on the upper deck, October was
a particularly stormy time of year for Atlantic crossings, so it was a
difficult journey. According to one family story, they were at sea for
five to six weeks.[2] Late in November the *Cultivator* docked in New
York, the brothers separated, and John made his way up to Ontario
to settle in Wentworth County in the District of East Flamborough,
near what is now the town of Waterdown.[3]

John Mitchell followed the pattern of many Irish emigrants to
Ontario in the first half of the nineteenth century. Settlers needed
150 pounds to establish themselves on one hundred acres. Thus,
many spent their first years as labourers on leased land trying to earn
enough to support themselves and save towards buying their first
hundred acres. John worked for a number of years as a farm labourer,
then became a "householder," leasing an acreage from a "freeholder,"
and finally purchasing his own farm. At some point he also began to
carry on the family profession of surveying and "was often called in
the East Flamborough areas as a fence viewer and settler of property
line disputes."[4] One of the grandsons recalled that some of John's
decisions led to further disputes in the local pub: "When they were

drinking in the kirk house there would be disputes and it is reputed that several times he threw people right out through the doors. So he must have been a real battler."[5] The minister who gave the tribute at John's funeral in 1904 gives us some idea of John's character and of what these settlers were faced with in the 1850s:

> About half a century ago he came here from Ireland. He was a mere youth then, but he was rich in good blood, and equipped with a good education and a fine fund of common sense. Needless to say, he witnessed many a change in East Flamboro. Where we now see fine houses and barns and cultivated fields, fifty years ago there was almost an unbroken forest, with here and there a settler's shanty. But the rich soil called for tillers and stroke by stroke the woods gave way to the flail and the sickle, and the sickle and flail to the self-binder and the steam thresher. Those early settlers were hardy men who knew nothing of fear and to whom labour was a delight.[6]

On 4 March 1858 John married Helen McFarlane in St. Paul's Church (Church of Scotland), just east of Waterdown. Helen's parents had emigrated from Scotland in the early 1830s. Between 1859 and 1879 John and Helen had ten children, six boys and four girls.[7] Their eighth child, Ormond Skinner Mitchell, born 2 August 1874, was W.O. Mitchell's father. Breaking with tradition, John and Helen named him after a doctor and friend of the family.

Over the next twenty-five years John and Helen farmed various acreages as tenants. During the winters the family would go up to northern Ontario to log, and on one of these trips their oldest son, William, was killed in a logging accident. They kept him frozen until they were finished that year's logging and then brought him home to bury him.[8] In 1885 John was able to buy his own farm. He was a successful farmer and developed a special interest in horticulture and in breeding and developing bloodlines in cattle and swine, talents which his second son, James, picked up. When the farm was sold in 1904, among the items listed to be sold in the auction of his farm property were breeding stock, including six "Pure Bred Short Horns, with Pedigree" and "20 Pure Bred Yorkshire, out of imported Stock."[9] In 1899 their son John took over the farm, and John and Helen moved to Mill Street in Waterdown.

John Mitchell's obituary in the *Hamilton Spectator* noted that he was a "Conservative in politics," "a life-long Mason," and "a *Spectator* reader for half a century."[10] This latter comment, noted twice, supports W.O. Mitchell's claim that his grandfather was not a descendant of "oatmeal savages," as one relative contended, but that he was an educated and literate man. As his pastor's tribute attests, John was a well-loved man with a talent for recitation:

> One delights in recalling memories of Mr. Mitchell. It does one good to think of his love for his family and of his attention to their wants. When he came home from market each child found out that he had been remembered. The very soil seemed to like him and yielded back its best in return for his labor. Or if we think of Mr. Mitchell at public entertainments, memory is still a delight, for he was a reciter of no mean order. Some of the finer selections from the poets took on a new meaning under his recitation. As a neighbor, Mr. Mitchell was one of the very best, ready as he was to help or to counsel or to cheer. There was nothing that he had that he would not gladly share. What he could he did and did gladly to relieve any who were in want.[11]

Recitations given by local amateurs and by professionals who travelled the circuit were standard entertainments at community gatherings. These were family occasions which also included debates and songs. John was probably a regular contributor to the weekly gatherings of the Waterdown Literary Society. By this time Bret Harte and Mark Twain had become widely known as professional readers who travelled throughout the United States and parts of Canada.[12] Popular "platform" short stories or tall tales, such as Mark Twain's "Acc't of Jim Smiley,"[13] often appeared on the front page of the *Hamilton Spectator*. John Mitchell collected some of these for his own repertoire and passed them on to his son Ormond, whose scrapbook includes many of the stories and poems he used later in his own recitations.

Also in this family scrapbook is a program for the Old Boy's Reunion in Millgrove (23-25 May 1903), which announces a "Recitation by Mr. John Mitchell" and a duet by Mrs. John Mitchell.[14] It would appear that the performing genes were running on both sides of Ormond Mitchell's family. Mitchell had almost no information about his grandmother except that she was born in Ontario of Scottish parents and died in 1910: "I did not know my grandfather or my grandmother Mitchell and remember only being told [by an older cousin Mildred] that my grandmother was a soft, gentle woman who, unlike my mother, did not run her household with an iron hand. She was particularly gentle with her youngest child, my aunt Elizabeth or Lizzie, who ended up crazy."[15]

John Mitchell died in 1904. According to the *Spectator* report he had a stroke while walking home from the post office and died a few days later. Mitchell, however, preferred to believe a more colourful, if macabre, version of his grandfather's death. At some point he had seen in his father's scrapbook the pastor's tribute to his Grandfather John and he could accurately quote from memory these lines: "Whatever his foibles may have been, however serious may have been any weakness that beset him, no one can charge him with meanness or selfishness, while those who knew him best pay tribute to his generosity, his kind heart and his honesty."[16] The pastor, who was also John's next-door neighbour in Waterdown, may have had first-hand knowledge of John's "foibles." Mitchell claimed that this was a subtle reference to Grandfather John's fondness for drink, and that it was drink which led to his death. According to this version, John arrived home late one evening from the local pub and went to bed. Having consumed a substantial amount, he soon had to get up and find his way to the outdoor privy. In his half-awake and intoxicated state, he forgot about the cistern he had been building by the back steps and fell ten feet to the concrete floor. We believe, however, that Mitchell confused Grandfather John's death with his son-in-law's. George Rohr, Mitchell's uncle, did fall into a cistern. On the other hand, it is possible that the actual details of John Mitchell's death were suppressed in the *Hamilton Spectator* obituary, and he too may have had a rather more interesting death. In any case, given his love for telling a good story, Grandfather John might have preferred his grandson's version.

‑ ORMOND SKINNER MITCHELL (1874-1921) ‑

In the 1891 census Ormond Skinner Mitchell, eighteen years old, is listed as "farmer." However, over the next twelve years he moved on to two other professions: druggist and professional reciter or "entertainer." After graduating in 1893 from Waterdown High School he apprenticed as a druggist in Hamilton and Toronto until September 1897. In 1898 he graduated from the Ontario College of Pharmacy, during which year he was class president. In October 1903 he obtained a certificate in Analytical Chemistry from the Faculty of Medicine, Trinity University. For a number of years he and his brother Alex managed the Gore Dispensary on York Street in Hamilton, and then the dispensary for Hawkins the Druggist, a drugstore chain, on King Street West.

While he was working in Hamilton, his business card announced him as both a "Druggist" and an "ENTERTAINER." He had by this time developed a reputation as a professional reciter in the Hamilton and Toronto area, and had even managed to finance some of his education expenses with his reading fees. A scrapbook, put together later by his wife, includes numerous announcements, programs, and reviews of his readings between 1893 and 1903 as well as many of the poems, anecdotes, stories, and monologues which he used for readings. He performed at "lawn socials" and "at homes," at festivals, church socials, annual meetings and banquets of business associations, community variety concerts, and literary societies. His readings included light verse (such as "Casey at the Bat" and "The Usual Way"), poems (Kipling's "The Mother Lodge" and "The Flag"), Black, Irish, and Scots dialect pieces ("Old Mose – A

Gettysberg Incident," "Mr. Dooley on the Irish Question," "The Heelan' Man's Prayer"), and monologues ("Riding a Bronco" and "St. Peter at the Gate").[17]

He was very popular, his audiences often demanding encores. On the program for the 3 February 1903 Hamilton Grocers Association banquet, Orm Mitchell is billed as an entertainer who is "as warm as the last half of his name." Most of the titles in his repertoire would suggest that his talent lay mainly in humour. However, according to Laura (Markle) Begg, an old friend of O.S., he was adept at working on the full range of his audience's emotions. She and her husband, Cameron, had been close friends of his while he was in Hamilton in the 1890s, and she recounted how the three of them were often on the same program at socials:

> So at garden parties, tea meetings etc. we were the programme
> – I would play the piano – Cameron a solo – then [O.S.]. . . .
> Now Orm always sat at a table, & he could really make them
> laugh and *cry* at one of his (tear-jerkers). I would play very softly
> on the piano & you would see the men folk reaching for the old
> *Red* Hkgf & the Ladies wiping their eyes – I remember one of
> his *encores* (*Good Bye Brother Watkins*) and his special closing
> number (*It's only an old Piece of Bunting*). I can still hear him say
> – (Its only an old tattered Rag) – O the memory of those days.
> They are very precious to me – I am only 97 years young –[18]

Orm would wear his formal elocutionist attire – suit, vest, white shirt with a high, stiff collar and bowtie – and with his full moustache and distinguished pose he looked very much the seasoned performer.

Mitchell said his father was a "professional Irishman" and that his favourite recitation was "Mr. Dooley says . . ."[19] The Weyburn house was full of "Irish stuff," including "flags with harps on them," "little wire-framed shamrocks which had exquisite threads of fluorescent green that made up the fabric," and a shamrock plant his father brought to Weyburn in the fall of 1904 after his father's funeral in Waterdown. This plant was said to have been brought over from Ireland by John Mitchell in 1850. "My father," said Mitchell, "must have been ecstatic that my brother Bob was born on the seventeenth of March." One of the family stories was what Billie said in grade one on St. Patrick's Day: "A teacher asked, 'Is there anyone here who is Irish?' I threw up my hand. She asked, 'Are you Irish?' I said, 'Well, not really but my brother is.' 'Oh, how could that be?' 'He was born on the seventeenth of Ireland.' To me there was nothing strange about my brother being Irish but not me!"[20]

When W.O.'s mother died in 1960, he brought home a division of the family shamrock and fifteen years later he gave us one. The three delicate heart-shaped leaves on each stem fold down on themselves at night and umbrella open in the morning. It is usually lush green and produces tiny pink flowers a couple of times a year. We are slightly sceptical that this *is truly a descendent of the plant that came across the ocean in 1850, but the story in itself is always a reminder of W.O.'s magic weavings of fictional history that knit us together. His other children, Hugh and Willa, received divisions from this plant as well and, we suspect, W.O. hoped that his grandchildren and their children would continue to perpetuate it. However, the significance of the shamrock plant for W.O. had more to do with ancestral connection than with Irish heritage. In a scene in W.O.'s greenhouse, shot for the 1980 NFB film, the interviewer, who has heard more than he cares to hear about W.O.'s passion for raising orchids, interrupts W.O. to ask him about a brown plant that looks moribund if not dead:*

> *Look at that. Isn't that a mess . . . this is a shamrock. It will come back. It is just like the grass. I've been away for a month and it has been allowed to dry out. . . . When my mother died, oh it's fifteen years ago, my sisters-in-law divided up the shamrock that I have always remembered and indeed have mentioned in* Who Has Seen the Wind. *My mother [put] it in the dining room. It was on a big brass urn, it was a beautiful thing. . . .*

*But it will come back beautifully. It is just as though I can
reach out and touch my father and my . . . grandfather John
Mitchell.*[21]

In spite of his father's Irishness, the Scots genes predominated
in Mitchell's sense of his ethnic background: "It's funny about the
Irish in the family – there really isn't any. Although great-great-
grandfather David lived in Ireland and my grandfather came over
from Ireland in around 1851, there was never any adulteration of
the Scottish-Presbyterian line. The Mitchells married Scots and
Protestants. My grandfather married a McFarlane; my father
married a McMurray."[22] It is, of course, a moot point whether or
not being born, like John Mitchell, into a family who had lived in
Ireland for eighty years makes one Irish. No doubt John Mitchell
and his family, like the Mitchells now living on the Rathfriland farm,
thought of themselves as Irish. John Mitchell retained his Irish
accent and some of the descendants recall that his second son, James,
had an accent but his eighth child, Ormond Skinner, did not. In any
case, while inheriting "a Scottish atavistic kind of thing"[23] from his
father's side, Mitchell inherited his Scots Presbyterianism first-hand
from his mother's side of the family tree.

⁓ WILLIAM McMURRAY (1821-1886) AND ⁓ MARGARET McKAY (1819-1896)

William McMurray, Mitchell's great-grandfather on the Scots side,
was born in Kirkcudbrightshire, Scotland, in 1821. Kirkcudbright,
southwest of Dumfries, is situated on Kirkcudbright Bay off the
Irish Sea. Here he met and married Margaret McKay in 1840.
William and Margaret, along with her parents, Ebenezer and
Margaret McKay, and two brothers and two sisters emigrated to
Tuckersmith Township in Huron County near Egmondville in 1843.

It was twelve more years before William and Margaret could
afford to buy a hundred-acre lot from the Canada Company for

110 pounds. The area "was almost an unbroken wilderness," but William soon established "a comfortable homestead" and was able to earn "a competency."[24] Certainly he did well enough to buy fifty additional acres in 1871, which he sold to his son John in 1875, and fifty more acres in 1880. In 1885 William and Margaret retired from farming and moved to a house in the village of Egmondville. He died the next year, on December 25, 1886; Margaret lived ten more years, until March 9, 1896.

~ JOHN BIGGART (1812-C. 1860) AND ~
MARGARET GIBB (1815-1893)

John Biggart and Margaret Gibb, Mitchell's other set of great-grandparents, were born, raised, and married in the parish of Dunlop in Ayrshire. Shortly after they married (14 May 1832) they emigrated to Canada. Mitchell remembered his Grandmother McMurray telling him about her mother's accounts of their voyage over in a sailing ship, "with little food, putrid water, crowded conditions, and cholera and typhoid running rampant."[25] Grandmother McMurray told Mitchell that the family owned stone quarries in Biggar, Scotland, and that she and her brother Robert were to inherit them. However, they were both so terrified of the Atlantic crossing that they never returned. But in 1932, when Mrs. McMurray heard that her grandson, Bill, was going to England for the summer, she urged him to go to Biggar "to claim those very considerable stone quarries."[26]

John and Margaret homesteaded in Goderich Township, Huron County, near Bayfield. They had five children, of whom Maggie, born 20 May 1849, was the youngest. She was only about ten when her father died in the late 1850s. Margaret, who apparently did not remarry, outlived him by more than thirty years, dying in Bayfield on 29 September 1893.

In our genealogical research, W.O.'s memory led us astray only once, and, in spite of our explanations and drawings of the family tree, he refused to believe us when we tried to correct him. He would rhyme off for us, "Maggie Gibb Biggart married John Ross Hannah and it is in the family Bible." He assured us many times that he recalled his grandmother Maggie (Biggart) McMurray describing John Ross Hannah as an important man in the community and remembered how she delighted him with the fact that "Hannah is spelled the same backwards as forwards."[27] This was his constant story. We discovered a John Ross Hannah who emigrated to the Tuckersmith area in 1827. He became one of the area's most successful farmers and was very active in community politics and affairs. One of his sons, John Hannah, was born in 1849 (the same year as Maggie McMurray), and more than one hundred years later in a newspaper article was said to be the oldest voter in the 1953 federal election. Mitchell saw this article and struck up a correspondence with this distant relative, who subsequently inspired the creation of his oldest-man-in-the-world character, Daddy Johnson.[28] All this was fodder for Mitchell's imagination: a successful emigration story, two remarkable ancestors in the family (one famous for his pioneering and community service, one for his longevity), and the memorableness of the name itself. However, the fact is that John Ross Hannah did not marry Margaret Gibb but (in 1844) married Catherine McKay, the sister of Margaret (McKay) McMurray. So John Ross Hannah was W.O.'s great-uncle by marriage, not his great-grandfather. It is ironic that, although we now know who married whom, we, like W.O., know more about John Hannah than we know about John Biggart.

～ JOHN McMURRAY (1845-1921) AND ～
MAGGIE BIGGART (1849-1937)

Mitchell's grandparents on his mother's side were first-generation Scots Canadians and were raised on homesteads in the adjoining townships of Tuckersmith and Goderich. The Biggarts' homestead was about six miles west and the McMurrays' about seven miles southeast of the village of Clinton (and the Hannahs were only a few miles from the McMurrays). Clinton was incorporated as a village in 1857, and with the building of the Buffalo and Lake Huron

Railway it became a busy manufacturing town. John and Maggie probably met at the school, church, and various community events in the town. On 21 July 1874 they were married in Lockport, New York, a popular honeymoon location.

John no doubt farmed the fifty acres he bought from his father in January 1875, but on the indenture he is described as a grain buyer living in Clinton. Their first child, Maggie Lutecia (Mitchell's mother), was born in Clinton on 24 April 1875. John bought a lot on Cutter Street in 1878 (which he sold to his mother-in-law three months later), and they built a two-storey frame house. Margaret Biggart lived there with her daughter and son-in-law. By the time of the 1891 census, John and Maggie McMurray had three children, Maggie, William, and Mary Josephine (Josie). John was listed as a warehouse man, which, according to Mitchell, meant he was a merchant of groceries.

In the late 1890s John got caught up in the Western migration fever. A 1906 advertisement for the Weyburn district illustrates the rhetoric that urged people like the McMurrays to come West: "Saskatchewan is a land of promise and opportunity. Saskatchewan – even the name has a wild free ring! The skies are so blue and the sunsets spectacular. People help one another and never expect to be paid, only for the kindness to be passed on."[29] In the spring of 1899 John, now fifty-three years old, and his nineteen-year-old son, Will, went out to what was then the North-West Territories to homestead just a few miles south of Weyburn. Weyburn at this time consisted of a railway station, general store, hardware store, livery, Massey-Harris dealer, carpenter's shop, lumberyard, post office, one doctor, and a population of one hundred.[30] The McMurrays were among the first to homestead in this area. Mitchell remembered his Grandmother McMurray telling him how his grandfather and Uncle Will located their homestead: "When they came there was no railroad line from Moosomin. They got off at Moosomin and then they came down in a buggy or a cart or democrat. And Grandma told me they tied a bandana on the wheel and then counted the revolutions of the wheel in order to find the place to drive their homestead stakes for that farm south of town."[31]

They built a sod house to live in while they prepared the land for farming and built a barn with a stone foundation. Dr. R.M. Mitchell, the first doctor in the area (and no relation to W.O. Mitchell's family), remembered that spring of 1899 as very cold and the summer as very wet. The mosquitoes that year were so bad "that many horses died . . . from exhaustion as the result of loss of blood." He describes winds of cyclone ferocity, prairie fires, and the beginning of typhoid fever which became an epidemic in the summer of 1900. The winter of 1900-1901 was mild but the summer was extremely hot and dry. There was a prairie fire which "cleaned up the whole south country from three miles south of town to the hills."[32] John and Will, living three and a half miles from town, must have lost their crops.

The usual pattern followed by prairie homesteaders was to live at first in a sod house and concentrate their time and resources on livestock and crops. Perhaps it was a good thing that it was hot and dry that summer, for it was said that when it rained outside for three days, it rained inside a sod house for ten. About a year later John McMurray brought out his wife and his daughter Josie from Clinton. Maggie, the oldest daughter, was in nursing training in New York at this time. The McMurrays built a frame house in the spring of 1906, and in 1909 they sold their farm and moved into Weyburn.[33]

⁓ MAGGIE LUTECIA McMURRAY (1875-1960) ⁓

Mitchell's mother, Maggie Lutecia McMurray, was determined to make a good life for herself. Apparently she was more interested in the social side of school, for although she managed to pass her high-school entrance exams in 1891, her marks were not good. She then spent nearly three years at the collegiate and left at the age of eighteen.[34] This would suggest that when she left the collegiate or high school in late 1893 or early 1894 she did not graduate with full credits.

Her autograph book with entries in it from 1888 to 1894 suggests that she was popular. In keeping with her Presbyterian upbringing most of the entries have moralistic messages:

To Maggie
Trust no future, howe'er pleasant!
Let the dead Past bury its dead!
Act – act in the living Present!
Heart within and God o'erhead!
      Your Friend
        Aurelia Plummer

            To Maggie
            May the golden gate of Heaven
            So far across the Sea
            Open wide enough dear Maggie
            To receive both you and me
                This is the sincere wish
                of your friend,
                  Mary

When you are old,
And cannot see
Put on your specks
And think of me

            It is not just as we take it,
            This mystical world of ours;
            Life's field will yield, as we make it,
            A harvest of thorns or flowers
                  Janet Wilson[35]

Most of these entries are addressed "To Maggie." At some point, however, perhaps after she left school or when she went to New York in September 1900, she decided that the diminutive "Maggie" was not refined enough, and she began to insist on being called Margaret.

After leaving school she spent a number of years in the Clinton, Goderich, and Bayfield area. According to Mitchell, who recalled some of his mother's accounts from this time of her life, she led the life of a debutante, waiting around for a husband. She probably spent most of this time living with her parents in Clinton, but apparently lived in Goderich for a period while taking singing lessons, and she stayed in a cottage in Bayfield in the summers. Here she went to picnics and balls and other social events. By the 1890s Bayfield, on Lake Huron, had become a popular summer resort area for the well-to-do from western Ontario and from the United States. It boasted four large hotels and a growing community of summer cottages, "inhabited by the wealthy citizens of inland towns and cities."[36] Margaret remembered with particular fondness the dances she went to at the River House Hotel.

For about five to six years Margaret led an active social life. She writes, with some pride, that she had the "pleasure of associating with the best people in the town."[37] She was a striking looking young lady, whose slightly elongated features, dark eyes and hair gave her a Pre-Raphaelite look.[38] As a child and young man, Mitchell never thought of his mother as beautiful, but when he recalled some of her earlier pictures he said, with her "thyroid eyes, which were very, very dramatic – and the nose, and the black hair – I guess she was one goddamned good-looking woman. And I don't think my dad would have gone for a woman who wasn't a good-looker."[39] She did attract a number of eligible young men during these Bayfield summers, one of whom, a successful prospector in the Yukon, gave her a bracelet of linked gold nuggets which has become a family heirloom. None of her suitors, however, measured up to her expectations and those who may have did not make her an offer.

It must have come as a disappointment to her when her father and mother decided to pull up stakes in Clinton and homestead near Weyburn in what was then called the District of Assiniboia. There would be fewer opportunities out there to meet the kind of husband she wanted. In October 1899, about six months after her father and brother had left for the West, she wrote to the New York Hospital asking to be accepted "for a probationary term." She said that she had always thought "hospital work would be very interesting," and, as she was "not really needed at home," this was the right time to take up an occupation.[40] She formally applied to the School of Nursing five months later and was accepted for the class of 1901. A notice in the local newspaper announced her departure on Saturday, September 22:

> Miss M. McMurray left on Saturday afternoon to become a professional nurse at the New York hospital. She will be greatly missed amongst her numerous friends here as she was an accomplished lady and was one of the favorites in social gatherings. Not only will the young people of Clinton miss her but Willis church choir loses its first soprano soloist. Her services were valuable and regret will be general with the congregation who highly appreciated her excellent singing.[41]

New York life and nursing training presented Margaret with some new experiences which shocked her Victorian sensibility. At first she adamantly refused to work with male patients but was finally convinced that if she wished to be a nurse she would have to overcome her delicate sensitivity to the male body. Mitchell was amazed when she told him that she would go on calls into the Bowery and other rough Manhattan areas wearing her nurse's uniform, cape, "Dutch Cleanser bonnet," and carrying her medical bag. When he commented on how dangerous it must have been for an unescorted woman to venture into these areas she said, "Oh no. Nobody would do harm to a nurse on an errand of mercy."[42]

Margaret's record sheet indicates that she spent most of her time in the surgical unit (which was separate from the operating room). Her record looks impressive, with some 9s, and with 10s achieved in "executive ability" and "tact and adaptability." In her final examinations she achieved 95 in Medicine and 98 in Surgery.[43] She graduated as a registered nurse in March 1904.

After graduation Margaret went to Weyburn to be with her family. She stayed about a year before returning to New York, where she began nursing at the New York Hospital and took on work as a private nurse for some well-to-do New York families.[44] Mitchell remembered his mother proudly telling him of her New York connections. She certainly knew, or perhaps nursed for, Mrs. Lucia Minturn's family, one of the established and wealthy families of New York.[45] She also bragged about her nursing classmates, Nell Vanstone (whose father was a furniture and organ manufacturer in London, Ontario) and Emma Rose (whose father was the King's Printer in Ottawa): "These were top-drawer ladies. That was what was important to my mother. Mother wasn't trying to be top-drawer – she knew she was."[46]

Her most interesting story was that she nursed Mark Twain sometime during her stay in New York. She claimed that Twain, to show his gratitude for her care, gave her a paperweight, a miniature cotton bale made of real cotton wrapped in burlap and bound with brass bands. Mitchell remembered his mother describing what a difficult and "cranky" man Twain had been. However, she prized this little gift which, as Mitchell remembered, was on display in her sitting room throughout her life. After doing research for his novel *Ladybug, Ladybug . . .*, in which the protagonist is writing a biography of Mark Twain, Mitchell thought it more likely that his mother was a private nurse for Twain's wife, Livy, during her final illness from 1902 to 1904.[47] Because Mitchell has often been called the Canadian Mark Twain (for his writing, his performances, and his appearance) this possible connection between his mother and Twain is intriguing.

Margaret stayed in New York until about the beginning of June 1906. By May of that year she had made the decision that her future lay in Weyburn rather than in New York.

3

ORM, MARGARET, AND THEIR FAMILY

~ 1904 to 1921 ~

IN 1902 AND 1903 Weyburn was booming. One commentator referred to 1902 as the "American Invasion,"[1] when a number of families from the states south of the border came to settle. In that year Weyburn became a village, its population having increased from about one hundred to three hundred and fifty. It was probably in this year that O.S. Mitchell first went out West on a scouting visit. He quickly realized that the many small towns, which were springing up to service the thousands of homesteaders arriving from the East and from the United States, afforded great business opportunities. Orm obviously liked what he saw. He went back to Ontario to convince his brothers James and Alex that this was a good place to settle. In 1903, "one of the most prosperous of the early years," Weyburn was officially designated a town, since its population had reached four hundred.[2]

In the fall of 1903 Orm returned to Weyburn. He formed a partnership with Dr. Bowman and oversaw the building of the drugstore. An advertisement in the *Weyburn Herald* announced the opening of "THE NEW DRUG STORE" on 5 December 1903 with "Mr. O.S. Mitchell, Phm.B." as manager.[3] As was common in those early days, O.S. set up his business in the front and two doctors, Bowman and Smith, had their offices in the rear of the building.

James and Alex had decided to come out to Weyburn with Orm. James with his wife, Sarah, and their eight children, bought land six miles south of Weyburn, where he established himself as a market gardener and a livestock breeder.[4] He also continued his obsession with building things in concrete.[5] The barn he built on his Weyburn farm was unique – its floors and walls, right up to the rafters, were cement. Even the kitchen floor of his farm house was poured concrete, much to the discomfort of Sarah, who suffered from varicose veins. Alex, now a doctor, settled with his wife, Mary, in Macoun, a village thirty-five miles from Weyburn. Orm had bought a drugstore there which Alex managed and from which he ran his practice. According to Mitchell, Alex and his family lived in the suite above the store, for which Orm refused to accept rent.[6]

In the spring of 1904 Margaret McMurray left New York after her graduation to visit with her family. Weyburn must have been a shock to her at first. It was a raw frontier town compared to Clinton or Bayfield, let alone New York. A photograph taken in 1904 shows Margaret and her sister, Josie, sitting sidesaddle on Montana ponies in front of the McMurray sod house.[7] Although it seems unlikely that the McMurrays were still living in this sod house after five years there (and it is difficult to imagine Margaret living in it for a year), we know of only one frame house, which was built in June 1906.

During this time Margaret did some nursing and, according to Jack Mitchell, the eldest son, Margaret and Orm met during one of Weyburn's yearly typhoid epidemics. Orm caught typhoid, but whether Margaret nursed Orm through his illness as Jack believed or they were just brought together because of Margaret's profession is not certain.[8] In any event, by the summer of 1905, Margaret had had enough of Weyburn and she went back to New York to live in a more civilized society and continue her search for a well-to-do husband.

In the spring of 1906, her parents were concerned that Margaret was working too hard. At the New York Hospital she worked the night shift, presumably twelve hours, and did some private nursing on the side. She wrote her parents indicating how busy and tired she was, but added, "Now don't say anything – if I find it is more than I can do I will stop."⁹ But the extra money was attractive: "I simply cannot afford to through [*sic*] a $1.50 a day aside. . . ." She was being paid a dollar-fifty for the hour or so of private nursing she was doing each day. One of the reasons Margaret was working so hard was to make payments on a parcel of farmland that she had purchased, probably jointly with her parents. Her parents each wrote letters urging her to give up nursing and come home. Her mother advised, "You must not work too hard. You know you are not accustomed to hard work and you must not over do yourself." The incongruity of the parents, aged sixty-one and fifty-seven, describing the hardships of their farm life and, at the same time, showing concern for their thirty-one-year-old daughter's work schedule in New York is hard to miss. Her mother reported that their hired man "gave us a nice doce" of lice, and the house had to be cleaned and sterilized (although the hired man apparently paid for the cleaning). "We are plodding along," she added, and "there was seeding and garden and burning old stacks, and cleaning up the yard, moving trees and Will is disking his farm and then there is the oats to weigh out. . . ." John was feeling tired and weak, probably because he was battling with the incessant prairie winds which had been particularly strong during this spring's seeding.¹⁰ And yet it looked as if Margaret's desire to be a high-society lady, exempt from any kind of menial work, was at least nourished if not planted by her parents.

There were other reasons Margaret's parents urged her to come home. A week after the San Francisco earthquake (18 April 1906), Margaret wrote,

Yes I have news reaching the papers concerning San Francisco – dreadful calamity. good thing for china town I guess[.] most awful place – beautiful white women found sold have not been seen or heard of for years[.] china town in San Francisco is much worse than in New York and this is bad enough. – I wish Weyburn would play tennis – it is way ahead of Basket Ball.[11]

It may have been the reference to the rough areas in New York that prompted her father to urge her to "strike for home." The McMurray letters also mention that Orm had been out to visit them at the farm and that he took Mrs. McMurray and Josie to a concert in Weyburn one evening. Neither of these letters suggested that he and Margaret were yet engaged. But the McMurrays must have realized that Orm was interested in their daughter and were likely anxious to get Margaret back to Weyburn where she could be wooed more effectively – and perhaps saved from a fate worse than death in New York City's white-slave trade.

Orm had become interested in Margaret during her visit to Weyburn, but he believed, probably quite rightly, that she had not been equally taken with him. However, he continued to court her by letter after she returned to New York and by May 1906 it appeared he had won her:

My dear Margaret,

This is the last day of May – so I am just writing to tell you I love you far better than I did last May. Tho' last May I would have loved you had I ever dreamed you cared. However, I do believe now you care & I am perfectly happy.

Darling I love to get your letters. Your last letter I have read over and over – and my dear Margaret you need not worry about whether I will ever drink or not. I am rather peculiar regarding that drink question and I feel very deeply for any one who have loved ones who are addicted to it. I do not believe that every body can become drunkards in acquir[ing] a desire for drink – nor yet do I believe it to be inherited. I do believe it to be the most foolish habit in the world and I cannot for the life of me understand why people become so silly as to get intoxicated. Now I do not intend to give a lecture on drink but will tell you all about it when I see you. Yes dear I believe we shall be very happy together – whether we will be fortunate enough to become very wealthy . . . I do not know. However we will make the best of the future and wait for it. Dearest I am glad to hear you express yourself as you have about it – and I love you more and more. Your idea is exactly the same as my own and I have often thought along the same line.

I believe we will have a bright future before us – and we must try and make all of it we possibly can. I feel much better since I got the partnership dissolved and am alone & you only for a partner. I will tell you all about it when you come. By the way dearest I gave the Methodist Church elders an option on my lot up near Mrs. Hilliar until the 10th June – they want it for a manse – price $400. I gave $125 last year for it.

I will buy several on the hill near the hospital in place of this one if I sell it. The surveyors are going to open up a number of lots in a week or so – and several of the good folks are going to buy together several lots so we will have some good houses & cut out the shanties. I will not tire you with more, but will close with all my love & Kisses. Your own Orm[12]

Orm had obviously prospered in the year and a half he had been in Weyburn. He bought out Dr. Bowman, so he owned as well as managed the Weyburn Pharmacy (which he renamed The People's Drug Store), he was doing well in real estate (a $275 profit on a $125 investment within one year is a considerable return), and he appeared to be moving in Weyburn's top social circles ("the good folks").

By this time, as Mitchell put it, Margaret McMurray had decided that she could not wait around any longer for a rich New York doctor and Orm certainly looked as if he was well on the way to establishing himself financially and socially. But she had clearly written him a letter in which, although expressing her love for him, she voiced some reservations about their future together. Wealth and social position ranked high on Margaret's list of priorities, and Orm seemed to be particularly concerned about reassuring her on these issues. He also tried to dispel her worries about drinking. In spite of his protestations to the contrary, he was not an abstainer – he may in fact have been as fond of a drink as his father had been.

Margaret appeared to be a very straitlaced woman who took her Presbyterian upbringing quite seriously. One senses from her April 27 letter that her world was overseen by a strict Presbyterian God who would punish wayward sinners, as evidenced by the San Francisco earthquake, which though a "dreadful calamity" may have been a "good thing," for it wiped out the Sodom and Gomorrah of San Francisco's Chinatown. But her disapproval of liquor and loose living owed as much, if not more, to her Victorian sensibility and her concern with propriety as it did to religious puritanism. This perhaps explains the startling jump her mind made from the San Francisco earthquake's devastation of Chinatown to her regret that Weyburn does not play tennis, which is "way ahead of Basket Ball." During her years as a social debutante in Bayfield, and while she was in New York, she played a great deal of tennis. Now that she was considering, if she had not already decided, making Weyburn her home, she wished that this more proper and upper-class game were available to her there.

When her mother wrote to her May 10, Margaret was in Montreal and already on her way back to Weyburn. Orm and Margaret were formally engaged shortly after she arrived, and they were married New Year's Day, 1907. The wedding celebration and probably the wedding service (since Knox Presbyterian was not opened until spring 1907) were held at James Mitchell's farm. Will McMurray, Margaret's brother, and Nellie Mitchell, James's eldest daughter, were witnesses to the marriage, and no doubt all of J.T.'s family, Mr. and Mrs. McMurray and Josie, and perhaps some friends were in attendance.

This was the terrible winter of 1906-1907, one of the worst on record, "the longest and coldest . . . that this district has ever had."[13] It was a winter, as Stegner writes in *Wolf Willow*, in which men, cattle, and horses perished, waiting in vain for the chinooks that never came and that turned a romantic young Englishman with dreams of being a cowboy into a realist who learned that "what would pass for heroics in a softer world was only chores around here."[14] It is the winter that Mitchell's Jake in the "Jake and the Kid" stories recalls over and over again: "that terrible winter of Ought-Six an' Ought-Seven" (*AJK* 123). And it was the winter that Alex Mitchell's heroics in getting to the wedding of his brother Orm became the focal point of the wedding itself, a story passed down and firmly imprinted on young Billie.

Orm's brother Alex attempted to travel the thirty-odd miles from Macoun to J.T.'s farm in a cutter drawn by two horses. Perhaps the weather conditions were already bad, for his wife, Mary, did not accompany him. At any rate, he was caught in a blizzard: "He made it with the team to a deserted barn and went inside the barn. He still wouldn't have survived, except that he lay down between the horses and the warmth from the horses' bodies kept him alive. The next morning when it had cleared up he was able to go on to Uncle Jim's."[15] According to Mitchell, "in a family of yappers – which obviously my father was and my Uncle Alex was and I think my Grandpa John was – Uncle Alex was the worst." He was such an "awful talker" that "some of us wished he had perished in the blizzard!"[16]

Orm and Margaret spent part of their honeymoon in Waterdown with Orm's brother-in-law and sister, George and Annie Rohr. As Mitchell remarked, "Annie Rohr was quality and mother liked her."[17] The Rohrs were people of substantial means who had recently moved from Toronto when they bought the Griffin house. This beautiful stone house sits on a high point overlooking Burlington Bay. It has a rich history beginning in 1812 when the original part of the house, now incorporated into additions made in the 1830s and the 1870s, was built by Ebenezer Griffin. According to a story passed down by various owners, the house has a ghost, a former owner who was killed when he drunkenly fell into a half-built cistern. As we discovered, the story, if not the ghost, has some validity – Mitchell's Uncle George Rohr did die in such a fall.

Later, Orm and Margaret and their son Jack spent three or four summer holidays at the Rohrs' house when they visited the Waterdown Mitchells. Margaret was very much taken by the Griffin house, and in later years she often described her visits to it to her sons. In 1949 when she was visiting Mitchell and his wife, Merna, in Toronto, she wanted to see the house again. When Mitchell knocked on the door and asked if it would be possible for his mother to look around the house, he was abruptly refused. The owner of the house, who was wintering in Florida, had turned it into an exclusive dress shop and the sales assistant who answered the door was at that moment in the middle of a private fashion show catering to Toronto's finest. Mitchell went back to his car and explained the situation to his mother. She simply replied, "Nonsense!" got out of the car, and imperiously sailed to the front door:

> MITCHELL: Just like a goddamned battleship in the War of 1812 she went to the door. She knocked at the door and the woman came to the door –
>
> MERNA: She ordered her like a maid. God it was funny.
>
> MITCHELL: And Mother said, "My husband grew up in this house. I came here on my honeymoon in 1907 and I wish to see the house my father-in-law and my husband lived in." She looked up and there was the picture that Annie had painted in the hallway. She said, "Oh yes, Mrs. Rohr painted that. That is the old mill that used to be in the ravine. And in that very mill Ralph Connor wrote some of his famous books. He was a close friend of my father-in-law." Step aside – that was implicit. And the sales assistant just, "Oh yes, yes." She wasn't going to do it for a young punk like me, but she recognized the kind of women who count. And then we went in and walked around.[18]

Margaret's fondness for this house left its mark on Mitchell. But what she told him about it, over the years, underwent some imaginative elaboration. He believed, incorrectly, that it was his grandfather John

Mitchell who owned the house (and fell into its cistern) and that his father was brought up in it.

On another occasion, in 1979, Mitchell happened to be in Waterdown to do a reading and on a Sunday morning found his way to the house. He knocked on the front door and announced, "Hi. I'm Bill Mitchell and I used to live at this house."[19] The owners were quite understanding since they often had people call by "on sentimental journeys with vivid memories of the house." But here was a different kind of memory traveller. The closest Mitchell came to living in this house was in utero in August 1913 when his mother and father and their son Jack were visiting Waterdown. Otherwise, Mitchell lived in this house only in his imagination. It is the kind of house with which anyone would wish to have a close connection and, although Mitchell never visited as a child and his father never lived in it, he imaginatively appropriated it. While Margaret may have redesigned history to fit her elitist ambitions, Mitchell redesigned history to make an entertaining family story, replete with deaths, ghosts, and artists.

For the first year or so of their marriage, Orm and Margaret lived in the apartment above the drugstore. Their first son, John McMurray (Jack), was born in September 1907, and within a year they moved into a small frame house on Fourth Street. Their second son, William Ormond, was born seven years later, 13 March 1914, and her next two sons, Robert James and Richard Skinner, in 1916 and 1918. It is not clear why Margaret waited so long between her first and second child. It appears she had a difficult first pregnancy. Mitchell remembered his mother telling him that she "vomited and vomited" when she was carrying Jack, but when the doctor told her she might have to give up the baby she immediately became better. Mitchell's assessment of this was that his mother was "spoiled."[20] Perhaps she also wanted to make sure that Orm's business ventures were soundly established, and that they had a larger home before having any more children. By the time Billie was born, Orm's various business interests were prospering and he was able to buy a large house, the house in which his wife raised their four boys and lived until her death in 1960.

This house played a significant role in Mitchell's childhood. He drew on this house, its physical as well as emotional presence, for a number of his fictional worlds. It was a particularly impressive house at the time, and its style and amenities reflect the standard of living Orm's income could support and the prestige for which Margaret had always hoped. The house was built in 1903 by Underwood, an English remittance man, who made and then lost a fortune in hotels in Moose Jaw, Medicine Hat, and Weyburn.[21] When he built this house, it was by far the most grandiose Weyburn had seen. In a picture taken just after it was built, the house looks like a beached whale surrounded by flat, empty prairie. If it looked strangely out of place from the outside, its interior must have been even more unusual in this small frontier prairie town.

In 1962 Mitchell wrote a reminiscence, "Of Tar Paper, Shiplap, and Shingles Made," about the importance of one's childhood home, in which he describes the Weyburn house: "Ours was a three-storeyed house on Sixth Street. . . . The façade it presented to the street was very, very high and uncompromising, like my octogenarian grandmother, who lived with us" (*Eve* 87). It was a beige frame house with an impressive front verandah supported by eight square-boxed pillars. Extending from the third storey was a false, small verandah-like structure also supported by pillars. Great attention was paid to detail, with scalloped siding on the third storey and decorated pillars and soffits.

The main floor consisted of a small library, a dining room with a bay window, a sitting room with a fireplace, a music room with built-in shelves and a piano, and a breakfast room. The sitting and dining rooms were separated by a large archway with a heavy brown velvet curtain and had chandeliers and leaded-glass windows, also hung with velvet curtains. These rooms, as well as the library with its glassed-in bookcases, were finished in dark oak woodwork, wainscotting, and beams. The wide stairway to the second and third floors had heavy oak balusters and railings. The living and dining rooms are today much as Mitchell remembered them from his childhood:

> The dining room was magnificent for one thing – a chandelier made up of rows and rows of encircling prisms. In the sideboard drawer were spare prisms, which you could look through and they obligingly broke the light up into violet and raspberry and gold. The built-in sideboard had bevel-edged mirrors along the back and sides so that you could stick your head in and look down a long corridor reflecting thousands upon thousands of heads which had this to recommend them: they were all yours. Just the backs of the heads, that is – whichever side you looked down – just the backs of your heads. (*Eve* 88)

The second floor had four bedrooms, two tiled bathrooms, and a clothes chute to the laundry room in the basement. Billie shared his bedroom with Dickie:

> The bedroom I shared on the second floor with my youngest brother was notable for its wallpaper: boys fishing. Not several but thousands of identical boys with similar rods at precisely the same angle, seated on a fragment of pier and fishing about six inches from each other – over each other – under each other – kitty-corner from each other. I can recall a faint contempt for the person who had painted the wallpaper, for he had done all the boys carelessly; you could see that his hands had skidded slightly so that they were all out of focus. (*Eve* 88)

The third floor was Billie's favourite. A large billiard room with a full-size table occupied one half of the third floor, and across the hall was the play room. Here Billie played with his magic lantern, an activity later humorously elaborated on in *The Vanishing Point* when young Carlyle is discovered by his Aunt Pearl sticking his "pecker" in front of the lantern (*VP* 312). In his reminiscence Mitchell describes the third floor:

> Perhaps the two most important rooms in the house were the billiard room on the third floor and the one across the hall, which was an unused room, or – I suppose – a play room.
>
> This room, furnished only with strewn toys and sporting equipment out of season, had a clothes closet within which the plaster and lathe had been gashed, some mysterious while ago, I suspect now by an electrician called in for wiring changes or repairs. You could climb through the hole as you would into any secret passageway in any castle, and then, crouching, make your way along under the side slope of the house roof. Before you did this you made preparations. First you arranged for your brother to invite a victim, wooing him with the promise of a magic-lantern show. Before they had arrived you took in with you the great morning-glory horn from a deceased gramophone. When your brother had turned off the lights for the magic-lantern show you placed the horn against the wall and moaned through it. This was particularly effective the first time with Keith from the corner, who was a Baptist and had played rummy with you in the hut the afternoon before so that his conscience was bothering him. (*Eve* 88-89)

On the basement level were the kitchen, pantry, coal room, laundry room, boiler room, and a large concrete cistern which collected rainwater for the house's separate hot-and-cold-running soft-water system. The meals cooked by the maid were raised to the main floor in a dumb waiter, another special feature of the house (often used for games by the boys), with a shelf which operated on two pulleys and ropes. There was a call button inside the door of each room, and on the floor by the head of the dining-room table, to signal the maid in the kitchen, where there was a panel of little square flags, designating each room, which dropped when the buttons were pushed. This was a house designed for gracious living, a house Mrs. O.S. Mitchell could be proud of, and a house that could feed the imagination of a young boy.

In September 1913, the population of Weyburn surpassed five thousand, and it was incorporated as a city. The Weyburn Hospital had been built, and there were six churches, four schools, and a movie theatre, the Hi-Art Theatre. Weyburn, the "railroad and industrial pivot of a splendid territory of rich farm land," was thriving.[22] The Mitchell house now towered above some neighbouring homes on Sixth Street, and a few young Russian poplars appeared on this and other residential streets. Mitchell remembered carrying "pail after pail of water" to a poplar tree planted on the Mitchell boulevard, "the lone survivor of eight" (*Eve* 91). Virginia creeper covered the verandah and honeysuckle and spirea grew on both sides of the verandah steps. A hedge of carigana was planted along each side of the property.

The two drugstores Orm started in 1904 in Weyburn and Macoun were the first in a chain of stores that he established in south Saskatchewan communities such as Pangman, Shaunavon, and Radville. O.S., as he was known in the community, put in long hours at the Weyburn drugstore, often arriving home late for dinner. A few years after his death, a front-page newspaper item described how O.S. had built up the business: "Under his management the business steadily developed till it was the equal of any store in the 'larger' cities, it being equipped with handsome fixtures and every facility being added for the stocking of and dispensing of drugs and supplies."[23] He also built up an extensive wholesale business in medical and other supplies to smaller towns. As well as the dispensary, the drugstore sold a wide range of articles, including fine English bone china. Orm, on special occasions, would order a piece of Royal Crown Derby for Margaret.

The drugstore also had an ice cream parlour and was a popular meeting place for customers of all ages. Orm always knew what was going on in town and enjoyed discussing provincial and federal politics. On Saturday nights Orm would not get home until one or two in the morning because the farmers were in town to get supplies and to visit. Perhaps some of these late-night conversations were lubricated with a drop of "medicinal spirits." On one of these evenings Orm arrived home just as the cuckoo clock struck three. He stood beside the clock and cuckooed nine more times. His ruse did not fool his wife but must have amused her, for she loved to tell this story in later years.[24]

Orm's stores must have done particularly well during the Prohibition years – a nice irony given Margaret's attitude towards alcohol. Saskatchewan was the first province to pass Prohibition legislation, on 1 July 1915. Although bars and government liquor stores were closed, it was "perfectly legal in Saskatchewan for druggists to import large quantities of liquor to sell 'for medicinal purposes.'"[25] The Bronfmans led the way in Saskatchewan in setting up a drugstore in Yorkton which was, in fact, an outlet for wholesale liquor. In 1919, when the soldiers were returning from war, "the bars and saloons were gone, and if a man wanted a drink he had either to arrange to have a 'prescription' filled by a sympathetic druggist or visit a bootlegger's joint."[26] O.S.'s income would have been augmented during these Prohibition years by filling "prescriptions" of alcohol. Mitchell had no doubt that his father often "prescribed" for himself and other community members modest amounts of their favourite spirits. His older brother, Jack, remembered his father going to a great deal of trouble to get a case of champagne for Mary, his brother Alex's wife, whose stomach problems, he thought, would benefit from something bubbly. When Orm asked Mary how she liked the champagne, she replied, to his dismay, that she preferred ginger ale. Aunt Mary came from a wealthy St. Catharines family and had a reputation amongst the Saskatchewan Mitchells as a complainer and hypochondriac. Mitchell, who stayed in Macoun with her twice as a child, remembered her "always leaning on a broom and sighing intransitively."[27]

Later in the 1920s, when Prohibition had ended in Canada but remained in effect in the United States (American Prohibition lasted from 1919 to 1933), the Bronfmans set up "export houses" in numerous small towns along the U.S. border. Some of this trade was legal, but some of the liquor got into the hands of bootleggers who took cases of liquor or gallon jugs across the border in the middle of the night. One night Jack, who was about seventeen, asked his mother if he could use the McLaughlin-Buick for a run over the border. It was a seven-passenger car with an eight-cylinder motor nicknamed "the whisky six in those days."[28] Mitchell said that his mother was scandalized:

> My mother said, "Nothing doing. Forget it." And my brother said, "Well, your husband sure made a lot of money out of the liquor-business." And I think that was probably the closest time Jack ever came to my mother's driving him right in the face. And I can remember mother saying, "Your father *never, ever* did." Of course, mother was half right but she was also half wrong.[29]

Orm's other business interests also did well. He invested heavily in Weyburn real estate and, according to Jack, owned most of a block of property on Third Street, a block on Fourth Street, and a block and a half on Eleventh Street. He also owned two farms on which he raised pedigree stock, including shorthorn cattle. Jack remembered that his father's library had many books on stock breeding and that he would go out to the farms to thrash and drive horses. He had a keen interest in trotting horses and with Glen Powelly, a farmer who raised sulky horses, and a group of prominent businessmen, founded the Weyburn Turf Club (the future Agricultural Society). They also started the fairgrounds and racetrack. Jack said his father and Powelly originally co-owned the fairgrounds, which they sold to the city but which came back to them twice before it finally stayed with the Agricultural Society. The Weyburn skating and curling rinks were built by a construction company in which he owned an interest. Orm was a supporter of various sports activities in the city, particularly its hockey team, the Weyburn Beavers. He is described in *The Night the Cat Froze in the Oven: A History of Weyburn and Its People* as a "very generous, big-hearted man" who "gave freely to any and every cause which he deemed worthy."[30]

Presumably O.S. also continued to perform as an elocutionist at various community functions, but there are no announcements of such events in Mrs. O.S.'s scrapbook. He probably did not do this as regularly as he had done back East. Jack did not recall ever hearing him perform, but his niece Jean McSherry heard him recite "Casey at the Bat." Also, one of his boys' elementary-school teachers remembered a performance in Weyburn: "I can see him on the platform yet with his hand up like this – 'I'll never let the old flag fall.'"[31]

Orm, like his father, was a staunch Conservative, and his interest in politics had begun back in the 1896 election campaign, in which he had been a "hard and persistent worker."[32] His help was solicited for the election of 1900, which the Conservatives again lost. Wilfrid Laurier held power for four consecutive terms, losing to the Conservatives in 1911. One of the stories Mitchell's mother told him was that he had been privileged to have been kissed by the great Sir Wilfrid Laurier on one of Laurier's whistle-stop tours through Weyburn. However, it was made clear that it was a servant named Olga who had taken the two children, Jack about ten and Billie about three, to the train station – and not the Conservative parents.

In provincial politics in Saskatchewan the Liberals had a stronghold, associated as they were with the federal Liberals and their machinery, even though Laurier had lost to Borden in 1911. Conservative candidates for the provincial legislature in 1916 took on the role "of defenders of 'provincial rights' and depicted the local Liberals as dupes of a distant Ottawa Leviathan."[33] O.S.'s campaign poster read

"TIME FOR A CHANGE"

This is the man to represent the constituency
of Weyburn in the next Legislature

Vote for

O.S. MITCHELL

"NO COMPRIMISE [sic] WITH WRONG"

Jack recalled sitting in the library with his father listening to the reports and waiting for the phone to ring. According to Jack, Orm took most of the votes in the city of Weyburn, where he was very popular, but narrowly lost the territory. He was defeated by Dr. R.M. Mitchell (no relation), the Liberal incumbent, who had held the seat since 1908.

Orm belonged to various associations, such as the Masons, the Shriners, and Rotary, and often held administrative positions in them, frequently travelling to their meetings and conventions. Margaret always travelled with Orm on these occasions and enjoyed living in style at luxurious hotels in various cities such as Winnipeg, Toronto, Minneapolis, Chicago, and especially Boston, where they stayed at the Parker House. Back home Margaret led a busy life running her household and looking after her four boys. She generally had hired help. The servant girls, usually farm girls who stayed for short periods, lived in the small brown cottage behind the house. When her parents were living with them and when she was sick a couple of times (and probably when Billie, Bobbie, and Dickie were born) she had a nurse living in and once, when her father and Orm were sick, she had two nurses in.[34]

As the wife of one of Weyburn's leading citizens she had a full social schedule with at-homes, bridge and tea parties, dinner parties, IODE and church-group meetings. When guests arrived they left embossed calling cards on a silver tray placed on a small, round walnut table in the front entry hall. She was not at all pleased when one male caller mistook this for a large ashtray and stubbed out his cigar in it. Perhaps this was J.T. Mitchell, her brother-in-law, who had a running battle with Margaret and her Scots-Presbyterian elitism. Mitchell recounted a story that underlines his mother's pride in her status. When Mrs. McMurray moved in with her daughter, Margaret, she displayed a knack for irritating her daughter at her most vulnerable point. Mitchell described how Grandmother McMurray, in spite of her crippled leg, would get to the ringing telephone before her daughter could pick it up. She would then belt out, with no gentility at all, "Maggie, it's for you!"

And her daughter would insist, with her hand cupped over the receiver, "Mother! it's *Margaret!*"

Mitchell described in detail his mother's elegant bridge parties – at which no one called her anything but Margaret:

> When I was a child, a boy named Archie Tait told me that my mother and Mrs. Martin and Mrs. Hilliar and Mrs. Goetz, all members of my mother's bridge club, were going immediately upon death to Hell for playing cards. The Taits were Baptists. I could instantly see my mother and her bridge friends all down there with ladyfingers and brownies and mocha cakes and cucumber sandwiches made from special sandwich loaves from Snelgrove's Bakery, the crusts cut off in a shocking gesture of waste and elegance. I could hear the crystal surf of their voices with Mrs. Gallagher's laugh thrown high again and again in ribald spume. If Archie Tait was right, it would be Hell with deckle-edged calling cards of flowing script, and during the break for tea in Crown Derby cups and saucers, Mrs. Allan would sing "Tying Apples on the Lilac Tree" – yet again. If they belonged in that genteel, Victorian Hell, it would not be for the sin of card playing but for cutting off and throwing away all those crusts in the early twenties while little children in Armenia ate cakes baked of grass and mud. Or so I was frequently told whenever I left any of my crusts.[35]

Margaret, who sang alto in the church choir, would have sung at some of these occasions. Mitchell was quite moved as a child when she sang some of the dramatic love songs which were currently popular:

> She sang "She's Somebody's Sister" – this was a dramatic song about a woman who entered a bar and a male bar guy made a scurrilous or slighting remark and then this one fellow spoke up. And the idea was, how could you do that? She's somebody's sister. That was a tear-jerker. And "I'm Only a Bird in a Gilded

Cage." And this wasn't done to be camp – this was meant, boy. But "The Last Rose of Summer" was the one and I literally recall that I would be weeping.[36]

One of the Mitchell boys' teachers described Margaret as being a fine and well-liked woman, "but not as outgoing as her husband was. She was more reserved":

> TEACHER: She was very tall, slim. She was a nurse, you know. She wanted to do things – well, in the hoity-toity circles, as you might say. That was in the days before the First World War. The First War kind of wiped that out.
>
> NFB: Wiped what out?
>
> TEACHER: Well, the hoity-toityness of the situation. The society of Weyburn. And certainly after the Second World War there wasn't . . . I think we're all probably the same category now.[37]

She described Margaret as a "strict enough" mother who brought her children up well, and she is certain that Mitchell's use of "cuss words and taking the Lord's name in vain" in his novels, of which she strongly disapproved, did not come from his home. These comments are echoed by a number of Weyburn friends and relatives who, in general, described Mrs. O.S. Mitchell as always "prim and proper," even "aristocratic," adding that W.O. Mitchell's "coarse" language would not have gone over with his mother.[38]

Unlike the rather irreverent character he became, Mitchell, in his own recollection, was a good child: "I was – when Aunt Josie said, 'Now be a good boy, Bill' – I was a good boy."[39] Billie's home environment was one in which a Presbyterian and Victorian sense of propriety generally prevailed. Unlike his brother Bobbie, Billie was not usually disobedient, although the tension between wanting his own way and obeying his parents often, he recalled, led to temper tantrums. Quite early he displayed a sense of humour, an awareness of the comedy in situations, and an aptitude for acting.

On a table in the archway between the living and dining rooms there was a large bronze statue of a prowling lion, its tail switching slightly up and to the side. The Mitchell boys were fascinated by this lion because it was particularly well-endowed: "Tucked high up under its tail, the lion had a cluster of three balls. Not two. Three!" (*VP* 312). Margaret generally positioned the lion so that this offending part of its anatomy was not noticeable. However, one afternoon when Margaret was serving the minister tea in the dining room in a chair right by the archway table she noticed a very puzzled look on his face. It was not until he got up to leave that, horrified, she realized his distracted glances towards the living room had been directed at the rear end of the three-balled lion which now directly faced his chair. According to the rules of Victorian propriety, neither the minister nor Margaret openly acknowledged to one another what was going on. But Margaret's embarrassment and annoyance were certainly made evident to the rest of the family when she asked who had moved the lion and demanded that it not be moved in future.

~ BILLIE AND HIS FATHER: 1918 TO APRIL 5, 1921 ~

The boys were fond of their father. One of Mitchell's childhood chums said that O.S., unlike Mrs. O.S. with her reserve, was "likeable to be around." Another childhood friend and neighbour used to sit on her fence waiting for O.S. to come home for supper because he always "had a candy or two in his pocket" for the young children.[40] Billie had only seven years to establish a relationship with his father, and retained few actual memories of him. But these few indicate that O.S. was very much a presence as a father, and that he was natural with his boys, less austere than their mother. Mitchell recalled standing in the black-and-white tiled bathroom as his father tilted back his chin and squeezed out drops in his eyes to treat a case of pinkeye. Another early memory is of his father standing in front of the living-room fireplace and reading from the Bible on Sundays. He remembered, too, "crossing streams" with his father: "My dad made a great thing of our pissing together."⁴¹ This memory became a scene in *Who Has Seen the Wind*, although his editor thought it too coarse and it was cut from the final copy. Another detail used in *Who Has Seen the Wind* was the nickname O.S. and Uncle Jim used to call Billie – "Spalpeen," a word of Irish origin meaning a scamp or youngster. This is the nickname Mr. O'Connal uses for Brian and it was the original title of *Who Has Seen the Wind*.

But his most vivid memory, the one he most proudly recounted, was when he was about four and his father was bed-ridden for long periods. Billie would lie in bed with him and his father began teaching him how to read, phonetically, the *Regina Morning Leader*. In one of these lessons, his father was reading an article on the exploration for Tutankhamen's tomb: "I sounded out 'Tut–ankh–amen.' He was so proud, and he boasted to businessmen that his little guy could read – and read such difficult words."⁴² By the time he was five, Billie was learning to write.

His father would bring him small gifts from the store, such as balloons or a small Japanese folding paper fan. Once he went through the pockets of his father's big buffalo coat, which was hanging in the front hall, looking for presents and his mother caught him and strapped him. But it was a "token" strapping: "We had to hold up our hand and she used Daddy's red Morocco bedroom slipper." She would say, "All right, you're going to get the slipper"⁴³ and then there was the ritual of ordering the victim to go upstairs into Orm's bedroom closet and bring down one of the slippers so she could carry out the sentence. Billie and his brother Jack were never strapped by their father (although Jack said that he was a strict father). Because of his generous nature, Orm found it difficult to discipline his boys, and it was Margaret who put the brakes on. Mitchell believed that his mother often told her husband that he should take a firmer hand with the children and that her problems with Jack during his teenage years developed because he had been spoiled as a child. Gerald O'Connal, Brian's father in *Who Has Seen the Wind*, is modelled on Orm, and in that novel Mitchell describes the differences in the parental roles, which reflect those of his own mother and father: "With the discernment that children have, Brian and Bobbie had both measured the indulgence of their father. They sensed in their mother an immutability that made the consequences of wrong-doing inevitable" (*WW* 92).

When Billie was five he went to kindergarten in the basement of the Baptist church, which was just a few blocks from the downtown business section. His father walked him most of the way to school in the morning and again after lunch, leaving Billie the last few blocks to continue on his own while he went to the drugstore. Billie would walk home alone and, on one occasion, as he passed the Mertz house, he saw an airplane that the Mertz boys had made out of apple crates, planks, and spoked buggy wheels. Ray Mertz, who was three years older than Billie, told him that they were going to fly it. Billie was entranced with the plane, and when Ray said he could fly in it too if he paid a dime he excitedly ran home to tell his father. After lunch as they walked to school, Billie insisted that his father look at the plane. They continued on their way to school, and when his father refused to give him a dime for a ride in the plane, Billie threw a temper tantrum for the benefit of all the other businessmen and townspeople who were on their way downtown:

> I can remember so vividly thinking, I'm going to get that dime. And I started to cry dramatically and loudly – and scream, "I want a dime! You won't give me a dime! My dad won't give me a dime!" – and I am doing it to humiliate my father. And I bet that's one of the only times my dad never gave in. He just kept right on going. So then I just shut up and went on to the Baptist church.[44]

As a child, Mitchell was aware of the power of acting and, probably with some exaggeration, said he often threw tantrums: "I did it all the time. I would get so frustrated with my mother's dominance that I would throw myself on the floor and I would kick my heels."[45] Judging from this and a few other family stories, Billie was perhaps more than usually sensitive to being crossed or having his desires thwarted. However, in spite of his memories of this frustration with his mother in particular, he was not as difficult to control as Jack, nor was he as deliberately disobedient as Bob. He was not a rebellious child.

In fact, by nature (though not physical appearance) Billie may have been like his father, who, while gentle, did on occasion "let loose." Jack vividly recalled his father losing his temper over an empty salt shaker. He and his family generally ate their meals in the breakfast room unless they had company. The meals, which had been cooked in the kitchen in the basement, would be sent up by the maid in the dumb waiter and then served. On one occasion when Orm tried to salt his breakfast eggs with an empty shaker he threw it across the room, yelling that it was beyond him why a household with a maid and a cook always seemed to have empty salt shakers.

Empty salt shakers occasioned similar outbursts from my father around our kitchen table. As long as I can remember he loudly complained about his porridge not having enough salt in it. My mother would say she put in exactly what the directions called for and he would grab the salt shaker and dump more on his porridge. If the shaker was empty, which happened quite often since he used so much salt on all his meals, he would explode, "Jesus Christ, Merna! Why do you put out decoy salt shakers that have no goddamn salt in them?" My father was always much less capable of controlling his temper tantrums than I imagine my grandfather Orm was. Our neighbours within a one-block radius could easily hear his yelling – and within ten blocks if he happened to be outside. In the beginning of their relationship my mother's response to these outbursts was to go into what he frustratedly referred to as her "Baptist sulks." She soon learned to quietly ignore his tantrums or to yell right back. Our family was known around the town as a "shouty bunch."

Orm began to experience the symptoms of a diseased gall-bladder sometime in 1917 or 1918. Jack remembered how, when he went with his parents to church or to the Hi-Art Theatre to see a movie, his father would soon drop off to sleep and his wife would try to nudge him awake with her elbow. It soon became evident that his falling asleep in the middle of church or dinner parties was not normal tiredness. In early December 1919, Margaret accompanied Orm by train to Rochester, Minnesota, for his first consultation and examination at the Mayo Clinic. This examination established that his symptoms were caused by gall-bladder problems. Seven months later he returned to the Mayo for a hernia operation on 6 June 1920. During this operation Dr. Masson discovered that O.S. did indeed have an infected gall-bladder. However, it appeared to clear up and nothing further was done about it.

Margaret had made arrangements for her four children to stay with various relatives while she was away with Orm. Billie stayed in Macoun with his Uncle Alex and Aunt Mary, the intransitive sigher. It was on the first of these visits to the Mayo Clinic that Orm and Margaret, on arriving in Rochester, found the following handwritten note from Billie in their suitcase:

> mir and miss mitchell bobe [Bobbie] is so sory that you are a way dicke [Dicky] is nice He is the nices af the famliy bobe is nice at worns [the Warrens, where Bobbie was staying] wot are you going to bring me.[46]

By January or February 1921 the symptoms reappeared and Orm wrote to the Mayo Clinic on March 2, briefly recapping the history of his treatment there. Orm's condition deteriorated rapidly over the next few weeks. By then he was also suffering the symptoms of pancreatitis and acute hepatitis, including jaundice, for his pancreas and liver as well as his gall-bladder were infected. It would be at this time that Mitchell vividly remembered going into his father's bedroom and seeing his jaundiced foot against the white bedsheets: "I have a visual thing of a white sheet and my father's foot lying out, and it was canary yellow."[47]

Once again Margaret accompanied Orm to Rochester. They arrived at the Mayo Clinic on March 20. Dr. W.J. Mayo examined him and, although Orm was "in very poor condition for operation," Dr. Mayo felt that surgery was his only chance. He operated on Tuesday, April 5, and Orm died shortly after. Dr. Mayo wrote to Orm's brother Alex about the operation and its results:

> The operation was done as largely as possible under local anes-thesia with a little ether. Mr. Mitchell stood it only fairly well. While his mind was clear his condition following the operation was not good, and became worse until he died. Postmortem showed that all stones were removed, and the common duct free; had your brother been fortunate enough to live, he would have got quite well.
>
> As I look over the case, I do not see just how I could have done better. The risk had to be run. If we had temporized your brother would not have lived long, and halfway measures would not have affected the end results. I am very much grieved; Mr. Mitchell was a fine man, and the fact that he was a friend of Dr. Balfour's added perhaps to my personal interest in the case. I want to assure you that we did our level best.[48]

It was his Auntie Josie who told Billie that his "daddy had died in Rochester last night."[49] Orm's death shocked the Weyburn com-munity. The newspaper announced that the flag would fly at half-mast and that the Military Dance planned for that week was postponed.

Although Billie was barely seven when his father died, his father had instilled in him a love of reading and writing, and throughout his childhood and adolescence Billie read voraciously the books in his father's library. Later, it was O.S.'s talent as an elocutionist which would prompt Billie's mother to enroll him in a school of dance, music, and elocution. What Mitchell actually remembered of his father is very little – lying in bed reading with him, "crossing streams," little gifts which arrived in the pockets of his father's buffalo-hide coat, a temper tantrum, the image of a bright yellow foot. The figure of his father in his memory became a composite of a few first-hand memories, second-hand information from his mother and others, and finally imaginative embellishment. But whatever the source, the memory image of his father became a powerful conscious and unconscious presence in his life as a child and in his later life as a creative writer and performer. Mitchell's father became one of his literary "muses," a ghost that "haunted [him] for love" (*SH* 224) and inspired his drive to write – and not just in the specific and literal sense that he, in part, wrote *Who Has Seen the Wind* "for" his father, but in the much deeper and pervasive sense that his writing and performing were gestures which attempted to deal with loneliness and death. In his note to his father, Billie asked, "wot are you going to bring me." As it turned out, although Billie had his father for only the first seven years of his life, his father brought him a great deal.

4

MOTHER, GRANDMOTHER
McMURRAY, AND UNCLE JIM

1921 to 1927

WHILE AN ABSENT "king of hearts" played a key role in Mitchell's formative years, an ever-present and loving, but imperious, queen of hearts was a more immediate and pervasive influence throughout his childhood and adolescence. Margaret was forty-six years old when her husband died, and her children were three, five, seven, and thirteen. Margaret's solitary reign in the Mitchell household brought about changes which particularly affected her two oldest sons, Jack and Billie.

With advice from her brother-in-law Jim and some of Orm's friends and business associates, Margaret looked after the various business interests left to her in her husband's estate. She kept the drugstore for four more years, had a sizable investment in the arena,[1] and also owned a house on the hill, the building where the bus depot was situated, and a farm. She handled her business affairs quite capably, and being a widowed mother may have helped her in her dealings with her lawyers, the bank manager, various tenants, the manager of her Weyburn drugstore (Joe Warren), and the city. One of her bank managers in later years said she knew what she wanted and got it – "She was very, very tough to deal with."[2]

She was understandably concerned about finances. She wanted to maintain the standard of living she had become used to, and she apparently had no inclination to remarry. In later years in Florida, however, when she on occasion went out for an evening, Billie and his two younger brothers would lie in bed talking about whether or not their mother was planning to remarry and imagining scenarios involving cruel stepfathers along the lines of a G.A. Henty story. But Mitchell described his mother as "almost Queen Victorian"[3] in her love and faithfulness to her husband:

> My mother was an eminent Victorian and she thought there were certain fitting things. Like she wore black, grey, white for about six years after my father died and then she really broke loose. She wore – she compromised – she wore mauve, which was kind of nice. A purplish kind of lavender dress. But that woman, then, felt that it was necessary to keep reminding her four little boys about their daddy that they didn't have.[4]

It was not a morbid household, but Mitchell's remark that his mother "really broke loose" by wearing lavender indicated that much of the levity of the household was gone now that O.S. was dead.

For some years, on the anniversary of his death, Margaret took her boys out to their father's grave. She also, for at least three years, had a notice inserted in "In Memoriam" in the *Weyburn Review*. The 5 April 1922 notice, one year exactly after his death, contained a poem with the lines, "I cannot say, I will not say / That he is dead – he is just away!" It was signed from "wife and family."[5] Brian in *Who Has Seen the Wind*, after his father dies, has "dreams in which he was sure that his father had just gone away and was not really dead" (*WW* 287). Later that year there was a notice in the paper that the old cemetery where O.S. was buried was being moved to Hill Crest as of July 1922.[6] The boys were told of this, and the idea of exhuming the bodies spurred Billie to ask his mother what his father looked like after a year in the grave. No doubt this question arose from an innocent curiosity about the physical facts of death, but also from a sense that his father's image was receding, was becoming less real to him.

Billie formed an idealized version of his father as an important and wealthy citizen and as a near-perfect father and husband. It was with his mother that he came to have those unavoidable adolescent conflicts. Margaret's campaign of reminding her children of their father had some negative implications. Because she felt she had to be much more careful with her finances and perhaps because she felt the boys needed a firmer hand, they were now frequently denied things which before they had taken for granted: "She would keep saying to us (Bob and Dick and me and Jack), 'Your dear daddy,' and, 'No we can't afford that. You haven't a daddy now who is bringing in money,' and all this stuff. She told me later on that she had done it quite deliberately."[7] Mitchell felt that his mother was not a generous person to begin with and that this "niggardliness" in her nature was brought to the fore with the death of his father. He contrasted his mother's parsimony with what he imagined to have been his father's easygoing generosity.

His mother refused to buy him a bicycle when he was eight years old:

> I am ashamed of the anger that I felt with my mother. My mother was not a generous human being. She would give time, she would give attention. But in fact she was extremely, extremely niggardly. My mother wasn't capable of capricious gestures, of loving-hearted generosity. And an example of that was the bicycle. I wanted a bicycle so much I ached. And mother didn't get me a bicycle until I was thirteen, a good five years after every kid in Weyburn who was not in a state of affluence as we were. She did not want to spend the money on a bicycle for me.[8]

Mitchell recalled that he finally (after five years!) wore her down, and added that, "knowing what I must have been like, it must have been hell for her." Now, rather than throw tantrums to get his way, he wheedled and argued with his mother. After he had sufficiently "bombarded" her, she relented and then she "really went [all] out" and bought him a brand-new red CCM bicycle for Christmas. This "ache" for something denied that Mitchell experienced as a child is dramatized in many of his child and adolescent characters (Brian for a pair of skates in *Who Has Seen the Wind*, the Kid for a horse in *Jake and the Kid*, Jacob for a mouth organ in *The Devil's Instrument*, Hugh for a pair of long pants, instead of a middy suit, in *How I Spent My Summer Holidays*).

Mitchell was twelve or younger when he finally got his bike. In retelling this memory he exaggerated his age to emphasize how unjust he felt his mother had been. He also recalled "thinking that she didn't love me enough to give me a bicycle." When discussing this incident he admitted that he carried for years a guilt that he did not love his mother because of her niggardliness, and yet he added, "Come on, what else is different – the way a child feels against a disciplining parent?"⁹ Billie's need to feel loved and his mother's inability to be generous with her love created difficult emotional moments.

There is some uncomfortable self-recognition here. Mitchell described himself as "pretty damn niggardly"¹⁰ when, as a thirteen- or fourteen-year-old, he began hoarding his money to buy a glider kit. While it is not unusual for a boy to save his money for a special project, his later life showed that he had that Scots thriftiness implanted firmly in his nature. The caption under his photo in the University of Manitoba yearbook reads, "Does he ever pay?" However, his niggardliness, unlike his mother's, was limited to money matters, for he had that capriciousness and loving-heartedness that he felt his mother lacked – and which his father had in great measure.

Billie was attracted to his Aunt Josie, Margaret's younger sister, because of what he saw as her generous-heartedness. He later came to see that the sisters' relationship was close but complicated:

My mother and my aunt were not very friendly at all but they were caught in that dreadful Victorian relationship of because you were sisters, even though you hated each other's guts, you had to hypocritically pretend that it didn't exist. My mother was better at that pretense than my aunt was. Our families were very close, actually. My Auntie Josie was rather gutless, in that she took hidden shots at my mother at all times, or other people, laughingly. Because she wanted to be respected and loved very much, she would do anything in order to be this. The result was that it made her a very charming woman. I loved her very, very much. And she was very kind to me.

While Margaret rarely gave her boys money, Aunt Josie often slipped Billie fifty cents:

She would say, "Here, Billie, take this. But don't let Auntie Margaret know I gave it to you." She was always undermining my mother. But my mother never, ever gave money. Except at Christmas and birthdays she could be quite generous. Quite unlike my father, I am quite sure. Auntie Josie sensed this and knew that she could win Bob's and my and Dick's and Jack's affection from my mother by slipping us money, and she was always giving us money.[11]

Margaret, in an almost ritualistic way, divided up the brothers' filial responsibilities. She urged her two oldest boys to take on fatherly roles and look after their younger brothers: "Mother would always say, 'Now, Billie, Dickie's your boy and Bobbie's Jack's boy.' So before Jack would go away to St. John's, Dickie and I shared a bedroom and Bob and Jack had their bedroom."[12] As a result, while Billie developed a close relationship with Bobbie, he became particularly fond of Dickie. He shared a room with Dickie until he went away to university.

However, right after his father died Billie often slept with his mother. He must have found a great deal of comfort in her company and she in his. In *Who Has Seen the Wind*, young Brian, who has had a frightening experience at school and begins having nightmares, is for a number of nights taken into bed with his mother and father (*WW* 115). In writing this scene, Mitchell evoked that emotion of comfort that his mother had given him at a vulnerable time. But, although Billie, like most young children, was happy to sleep with his mother, the arrangement did have some drawbacks, particularly as he got older:

> For a number of years afterwards my mother wanted me to sleep with her. So I probably slept in with my mother at least until I was ten – and maybe eleven. And my mother always read the *Regina Leader-Post* at night and I hated it. And I would lie there curled up and facing away from her. The goddamned rattle of that paper! The other dreadful thing which I trace back – we would have a barrel of McIntosh apples in the pantry down in the basement. And mother – there was the same ritual – the *Regina Leader-Post* and an apple. And the rending crush and sound of that apple – I just – I would lie there seething, seething with rage.[13]

In telling this anecdote the import for Mitchell was the anger he felt towards his mother for keeping him awake. "Seething with rage" is a strong expression. Perhaps Mitchell's recall of this scene reflects not simply anger over what he perceived to be his mother's self-centred lack of concern for her son's tiredness, but a sense of being overwhelmed by his mother's demands in a general way.

Jack, being the oldest, took the brunt of the pressure to do well and emulate his father. He was expected to live up to his father's role in terms of duties around the house, which included acting as father to his younger brothers. Orm had been an indulgent father and had never really taken a firm hand with Jack when he was a child. Jack recalled that the only time he was "whipped" by his father was when he disobeyed his mother and went down to the skating rink to watch a hockey game on a school night. When he got home his mother said, "Orm, you look after Jack now." His father took him into the bathroom and closed the door. Then, taking his razor strap down, he told Jack to yell as he whacked the edge of the bathtub with the strap.[14] In the year and a half following his father's death, Jack did poorly at school and finally proved to be too difficult for his mother to handle. In September 1923, after failing to complete his grade nine, she enrolled him in St. John's College, a boarding school in Winnipeg which had a reputation for dealing with problem boys.[15]

So from September 1923 for most of the school year Billie was the oldest male in the family, and he in turn was faced with extra demands from his mother: "I used to think as a child that it was unfair – she let Bob get away with murder, and that is accurate. Bob never, never was forced to stay in on a Saturday and dust and mop floors or beat carpets or do any of those things."[16] Mitchell felt that even though his mother tried to be justly careful about treating her boys the same, Bobbie had a special status: "Everybody would say, 'Oh my, how much he looks like O.S.' He was blocky, masculine, had very, very blond hair, had much lighter eyes than I have, more like my father's green-blue eyes. I think every time my mother looked at Bobbie, she looked at Daddy."[17] Bob also had O.S.'s charisma and, as Mitchell recalled, "Everybody loved Bob. And he used that charm."[18] Mitchell's sense that Bobbie was everybody's favourite is supported by one of Dickie's elementary grade-school teachers who, when asked in the NFB interview what Billie was like as a child, said, "He was quite a nice youngster but as I said before it was always Bobbie that we all took for."[19]

Mitchell recalled a number of episodes in which he resented both his mother's denying him and her different treatment of Bobbie:

But again that use of ascendancy and power to direct somebody to do something. There's so many things – like wanting rubber boots and not being given high rubber boots simply because I might go over them and fill them up. And then my bloody brother Bobbie went down to McKinnon's store – he's two years younger than I am, for Christ's sakes! – and he orders a pair of bloody rubber boots and puts it on the bill and comes home and now he's got rubber boots. *Then* I got rubber boots.[20]

When he was about nine, Billie had a major clash with his mother over a haircut. In the spring all of the Weyburn boys got what was called a "pig-shave." The barber "just mowed your hair" so you had no hair until it grew back in by fall. But Billie's mother insisted that her boys continue through the summer with their long Buster Brown haircuts. Jack Andrews, who went to school with Billie from grade one through grade eight, said that the Mitchell boys were the only kids in Weyburn with Buster Brown haircuts and that one spring Billie rebelled and went downtown to the barber and got a pig-shave. According to Mitchell, he was following Bobbie's initiative:

> Bob goes down to Leon's barber shop and he gets himself, not a pig-shave, he got his hair cut like a boy should have his hair cut. *This* time, unlike the rubber boots, I went down and I got a pig-shave. Jesus, was my mother angry. I don't think she belted me that time. She was so furious! And you know, it was a mistake. I was mortified by it myself. I got a look in the mirror and, you see, I had the funniest-shaped skull. It's divided into three parts – there's a goddamn gully runs right down here, goes up like this, and then it divides at the back, and there are two bulbs on here, and this is what I end up with.[21]

Jack Mitchell said his mother cried when she saw Billie's shaved head. Billie must have been particularly galled by this incident, for he had asserted his independence against his mother's control only to have it backfire and to end up looking, in his words, "like a goddam rhesus monkey."

I remember when I was about twelve years old sitting on a stool in the middle of the kitchen, a towel draped around my shoulders, and my father cutting my hair. I was in tears, caused by both pain and mortification. He was using the hair clippers he had bought to trim Demi Tasse, our miniature French poodle, and they kept snarling and pulling my hair – which is curly and difficult to cut. And I knew, being the first human my father had ever given a haircut to (my brother Hugh was anxiously watching and waiting to be the second), that the haircut I was getting was not going to enhance my looks. Now this had all started as a result of my father's inherited Scots "niggardliness" and I was the third domino in a chain reaction of "savings." Soon after we got Demi Tasse my father discovered that he would have to be regularly clipped at the vets in order to keep his coat in good condition. He felt the vet's price for a clipping was too much and decided to buy some clippers and look after trimming Demi Tasse himself. But the clippers were quite expensive, and he hit on the idea of making extra savings by cutting Hugh's and my hair. When my mother saw the haircut he had given me she refused to let him do Hugh's hair – which was redundant, since Hugh had disappeared. My mother ordered my father to take me down to the barber, explain what had happened, and have him repair as much of the damage as possible. My father drove me down and dropped me off, leaving me to do the explaining. It was two months before the ravages of my father's barbering grew out.

Mitchell rarely openly rebelled against his mother's control. Perhaps he sensed how vulnerable she was. On one occasion, a year or so after her husband's death, Billie misbehaved and she ordered him to go upstairs and get the slipper: "And the poor woman didn't think. And here's little Billie standing there, ready for it. I remember, vaguely, that she just burst into tears, put her arms around me when she saw my father's red Moroccan slipper."[22] Seeing his mother break down was as much a deterrent to misbehaviour as being smacked. In any case, Mitchell felt he paid a price for not venting his anger: "When Aunt Josie said, 'Now be a good boy, Billie,' I was a good boy. But at the awfullest cost in bottled-up frustration." During or after "these moments of incandescent anger" Billie would retreat into self-indulgent fantasies of running away and death:

I would go upstairs into the third floor or into the root house under the basement and sit there and perform scripts including – which I've run across again in these psychiatrist books – of what would happen if I died. And discovering in this thing that almost unrelievably the reason people commit suicide is to punish others. And of course it's very interesting that Mark Twain has Tom Sawyer do this.[23]

Mitchell later ascribed such feelings and fantasies to Brian in *Who Has Seen the Wind* when he runs away from his uncle's farm after being scolded by Ab and Annie:

He wasn't staying around them any more. He'd go home [to his house in town].

Delicious self-pity flooded his whole being as he walked down the road stretching and thinning ahead of him, the spidering telephone wires reaching to the far horizon. He'd go home and leave them; pretty soon they'd be running all over the farm, trying to find out what had happened to him. They'd look in the irrigation dug-out for his body. They would be very sorry for the way they had treated him. (*WW* 268)

Margaret Mitchell was "erect" in attitude and mind as well as physical bearing and, as Billie grew older, he came to admire his mother's sense of fair play: "I think she was probably the most just human I have ever known or ever will know."[24] Even though he believed as a child that she treated Bobbie differently at times, he feels that she tried to be careful about treating her boys equally. She was sensitive about rewarding Billie when she called on him to do extra chores for her:

My mother knew she was being unfair. And I knew that she knew that, maybe not at the time. But what she would do was I would have fucked up my whole Saturday doing women's work – mopping and dusting and waxing. And Bob, where the hell is he? Off somewhere. And it didn't do any good to say he was younger and I was older, which is the thing Mother would use. What happened would be that Mother, late on in the afternoon when I'd just about had it and she knew it, would say, "Billie, there's a marvellous film on at the Hi-Art." It was at a time when you were allowed to go to the matinee on Saturdays – but to go to a film at night! No way. And they didn't show the same things at the matinees that they showed at night. It worked for her every time, to now do something nice for me for the unfair way she had treated me through that Saturday. She didn't tell me before, blackmail me, ever. She didn't say, "If you do this house-work, *The Cat and the Canary* with Lon Chaney is on at the Hi-Art Theatre."[25]

Margaret probably felt that going to a film at night was an appro-priately adult reward for his work. Also, it is likely that Margaret wanted her older son's company. Being a widow was awkward, par-ticularly in small-town Weyburn, for someone like Margaret, who enjoyed going out.

Billie Mitchell inherited a contradictory combination of his father's generosity and his mother's Scots canniness. Although he was very close to his mother and loved her dearly throughout her life, some of his most vivid memories of her from his childhood have to do with her dominance and sense of justice, with her denying, disciplining, and controlling him. He admitted, "I probably needed what she was giving me when I was younger."[26] But he felt that those bottled-up frustrations from his childhood had a lot to do with shaping one aspect of his personality which he always had some difficulty in controlling: "I am probably the most easily impatient and annoyed person at anybody coming into neutral or my own ter-ritory."[27] The invasion of the individual's various territories (social, cultural, emotional, psychological, imaginative) by an ascendant guardian or authority figure became a central concern in Mitchell's fiction and drama.

∽ "GOD, HOW I WANTED TO BE AN ACROBAT!"[28] ∽

Billie and Bobbie, more than the other two boys, had inherited their father's ham genes and were encouraged to perform. At least as early as 1919 Billie began to respond positively to the look-at-what-my-child-can-do pressure most parents are prone to bring to bear on their children. For various reasons he felt more than the usual amount of this pressure. His father had proudly shown off his five-year-old son's ability to read difficult words and, judging from one of the stories his Aunt Josie enjoyed telling, Billie as a youngster liked to be centre-stage:

> One of the things Aunt Josie would bring up, to my mother's annoyance, would be to say, "Oh, Billie's a lot like Uncle Orm, he likes to show off, he likes to be up on stage. One time he [Billie] suddenly shouted, 'Listen to me! I'm talking! Listen to me!' And when nobody paid attention to him, he just lay down on the floor and he just drummed and kicked the floor in a rage."
>
> At which point my mother's face, which could be extremely forbidding with those McMurray eagle eyes, would freeze, and she'd say, "None of my four boys ever, *ever* lay on the floor and kicked their feet." Unfortunately, I can remember doing it.[29]

Margaret Mitchell had always been proud of her husband's ability and reputation as an elocutionist, and she hoped that at least one of her boys had inherited his talent. At her promptings Billie took part in Sunday School concerts and a nativity play at Knox Presbyterian Church, a style show at McKinnon's department store (he was a flower boy and a ring bearer), and a play called *Ten Little Indians*. When he was about nine his mother made him an elaborate costume for his part in a health play that was staged in the Hi-Art Theatre:

> All the children played the part of foods. There were little vegetables. Then there were villainous roles – coffee, tea, and candy.

I was candy, for which purpose my mother made me a red-and-white clown suit with a pointed cap. On my fingers I wore peppermint sticks. Now the idea was all of us foods were trying to win Eleanor McKinnon, a dear little girl, who didn't know what foods were good for her. One little girl – I have a vivid picture of her in my mind – was a tomato. Her head was nested in a great puffed-up tomato body. It didn't change her appearance all that much because she was an extremely chunky girl to begin with and did have a high flush on her cheeks. In the end the little girl makes the right choice and she didn't go for me, who was candy – or coffee or tea or any of the other dreadful things.

That winter at the ice carnival Billie wore the clown suit with the peppermint sticks taped to his fingers and, to his "utter astonishment," he won first for the comic section for kids. But his mother was one of the judges, which "somewhat spoiled the victory for me."[30]

When Billie was about nine, he found a large Gilbert's Magic Set in one of the pool-room cupboards. Given to his brother Jack as a Christmas present some years before, it had an instruction booklet and little mechanical devices for accomplishing feats of magic. One of these was a small bullet-shaped tube attached to a woven black elastic which was tied to the magician's belt and was used to make a large silk scarf appear to materialize out of the palm of his hand. He practised for hours in front of a mirror and learned how to palm coins and to make the four nesting red cherries that came with the set appear one by one between his fingers and then disappear again.

He was an avid reader of *Boy's Own Annual* and *Chums*, which often had items describing how to do magic tricks. From *A Thousand Things a Boy Can Do* he learned, with Bobbie or Dickie as his assistants, how to perform a number of illusions, including a levitation act. One of their favourites was "The Dwarf," in which, using a large, loose sweater, a pair of Dickie's boots, and long black stockings, a card table in the living-room archway, and the velvet drapes, the two boys appeared to be a two-and-a-half-foot dwarf. The boys put on the loose sweater and then Billie, in front, put

Dickie's stockings and boots on his arms and rested them on the card table so they looked like the dwarf's legs hanging just below the sweater. Bobbie from behind put his arms through the sleeves of the sweater and appeared to be the dwarf's arms and hands. Billie liked to develop and perform magic acts for the family but, often to his chagrin, his mother began arranging to show him off to whatever larger audiences were handy:

> My mother generally spoiled things by getting me to perform in front of her Knox Presbyterian Church choir, or the Admiral Sturdy Chapter of the IODE by either getting me to do a magic act or recite "The Flag" or, in this instance, it was "The Dwarf" with Bobbie helping. Now, my brother Bob was a charmer. And utterly irresponsible. So, we set it up and the ladies were very amazed because I remember we opened the curtain and Bobbie had a cookie in his hand. He lifted it up in the general direction of my mouth and I saw it and put my head forward and took it in my mouth and the little dwarf ate a cookie. And then did a little dance. But what was not prepared for at the very last was Bob lifted up his bloody hand, extended his fingers, stuck out his thumb, caught my nose, and wiggled his fingers at all the members of the Admiral Sturdy Chapter of the IODE. They thought it was funny, actually. But I got credit for doing that — my mother couldn't quite keep clear in her mind that it wasn't Billie who had done it.[31]

One of Billie's acts did not please his mother. He was involved in a children's circus that was put on at the Weyburn Mental Hospital. His mother's bridge club often had bridge parties at some of the hospital's administration homes and the ladies, probably at Margaret's suggestion, took time out to watch the children's circus:

> I was a snake charmer and I had a lot of garter snakes and my act was to take the snake's head and put it inside the collar of my shirt and wiggle the snake down and then out of my short

pants. Mother was humiliated and disgusted. Mother didn't rage
at me but she sure showed her distaste. What she didn't know
was that I was wearing two sets of clothes and I made damn sure
that snake was going between the outer and inner set.[32]

About this time Billie became passionately interested in acrobatics. This probably had something to do with his slight build,
which put him at a disadvantage in team sports but was ideally
suited for tumbling. He had a supple back and quite early he had
taught himself how to do a back-bend. George Agnew, who had just
moved into the house next door, coached Billie. He had been an
American pilot and was now in the lumber business in Weyburn.
George was one of a few father figures who were significant in Billie's
childhood: "God, I liked that man. Indeed, he must be one of
several who made up the composite of [King Motherwell in *How
I Spent My Summer Holidays*], that hero in the eyes of the young. I
really liked him. He had a lovely impromptu affection for young
people."[33] Billie spent hours practising tumbling tricks on an old
mattress he laid out on the front lawn (where he was more likely to
have an audience and catch George Agnew's coaching attention):

> I guess I was an extremely stubborn person when I wanted to
> do something, especially if it involved a rehearsal or a practice
> alone, that I might later show somebody whether young or old
> – to show them something I could do. Very quickly I could do
> a handspring and a snap-up. I could walk to beat hell on my
> hands and do a handstand. Because of the very lissome back I
> had been born with, my favourite position was to let my back
> arch over and my knees go loose so they kinked and literally rest
> my feet on the back of my head or my toes tapping the back of
> my head as I walked.[34]

Billie's agility and balance impressed his friends and brothers. Jack
Andrews said Billie used to "hop" down the verandah stairs on his
hands.

With Bobbie and Dickie, Billie created an acrobatic act. Even though Bobbie was two years younger than Billie, he was now bigger and much more solidly built. So he became the anchor-man for the double and triple routines the three brothers developed. He also was the clown, whose attempts to imitate Billie's graceful handsprings or handstands resulted in awkward pratfalls. The boys built a small set of portable steps and for the climax of their act Billie would go up into a handstand on the top step and then walk down them on his hands. Grandmother McMurray made the boys a matching set of clown costumes with pointed caps and the boys performed their act at various venues, including Sunday School concerts, the IODE, the Oddfellows, and a Rotary father-and-son banquet.

Paradoxically, while Billie became "hooked on the idea of performance" and "the approving partnership"[35] with an audience, his childhood friends recalled him as a shy and retiring boy. Billie was embarrassed about his small size and his appearance. He perceived himself as "funny-looking" – a perception partly explained by an eye condition he developed when he was about nine. Billie's mother first noticed that his eyes looked strange when Jack casually observed, "The kid's cross-eyed." He was diagnosed as having a lazy left eye and was fitted with horn-rimmed glasses, which he wore until he was about seventeen. He hated these glasses for, like Hugh in *How I Spent My Summer Holidays*, he thought they made him look "like a ground owl in a middy suit" (*SH* 112). In fact, Billie looked a lot like Harold Lloyd would have looked as a child. And maybe it was their similarity in looks and Lloyd's uncanny ability, in spite of his innocently daft appearance and seeming ineffectiveness, to be victorious in the end which so attracted Billie to the Harold Lloyd movies his mother took him to on Saturday nights: "I'd kill for Harold Lloyd. He was a boob, but he always won."[36] However, Billie certainly did not want to be seen as a "boob":

I have always been a stylist. When I was tumbling, when I was springboard diving. I don't like boobs, I don't like awkwardness. . . . You shouldn't inflict vulgarity. . . . I suppose I have always

been concerned about what others might think of me. I don't
have that reputation, I know. I'm supposed to be a blunt, candid
person who doesn't care. But I don't want to look like a boob in
front of anybody. I think as a child that bothered me.[37]

Mitchell also believed that his drive to perform as a child had a
great deal to do with his small size: "Very, very early I was a performing elephant, a smartass. And that in turn must be because I
was small. If you're fat when you were little or you're small when you
were little, one of the most effective defences against getting
punched out by a bigger kid is to make him laugh, or be funny. You
can't hit someone who is funny – as easily."[38]

There were, then, a number of forces, some conflicting, that
contrived to develop Mitchell's budding creative sensibility and performing talent. His mother's encouragement, which he both welcomed and resented, was perhaps the largest factor. His own desire
to perform with style was a challenge to which he naturally rose. He
seemed, at once, to have a natural instinct to be the centre of attention and to have an introverted shyness because of his small stature.
He had a fear of appearing to be a "boob" and yet he cultivated that
effect by playing the clown. Perhaps underlying all of these was an
acute yet unconscious sense of his own mortality. That is, his
mother's pressure on him to be a performer like his father was com-
plemented by a deep-seated compulsion to engage an audience with
tricks and illusions *for* his father and himself as a "defence" against
the biggest bully of them all, death. Making things appear which
had disappeared, creating silk scarves out of thin air, presences from
absences, had a special appeal for Billie. The ultimate magic trick
humans aspire to is to "fool" death, to pull the rabbit-self out of
death's black top hat.

~ UNCLE JIM ~

Like most children, Billie had a favourite uncle – Uncle Jim, O.S.'s
older brother. Because of the early death of Billie's father, Uncle

Jim, and a few other adults like George Agnew, took on an added importance in his life. Jim had been particularly fond and proud of his younger brother and he "kind of stepped in" after O.S. died. He often came into town to visit with his sister-in-law and to do various things for her such as repairs around the house. Margaret disapproved of her brother-in-law's language and smoking, but she liked him. She got vegetables from his farm during the summer and in the fall would load up the McLaughlin with a winter's supply for storage in the root cellar. Although he charged Margaret for this (he was quite aware of how well off-she was), he was generous with his time and concern for her and her children. Mitchell remembered his visits:

> When I was sick, or pretending to be, Uncle Jim would come in and sit by my bed or by me on that couch in the living room. And I can see that old Model T out there with no top and the bathtub bottom. Oh God, I loved it when Uncle Jim visited. Because he would get going – he was a talker too. But he was interesting whereas Uncle Alex would bore the ass off you.[39]

Jim, or J.T. as he was known, was a successful farmer but, in the opinion of his neighbours, an unorthodox one. Jack Mitchell claimed that Uncle Jim was the only farmer in the area to drain sloughs with pumps, to surface-irrigate, to raise pigs, and to grow a large crop of vegetables, which he sold every Saturday to Weyburn stores and cafes. His vegetables and Yorkshire boars often won prizes at agricultural fairs, including the CNE in Toronto. About 1912 Jim and another farmer bought a calf that they raised to become the largest steer in Canada – Jumbo weighed thirty-six hundred pounds.

The boys and their mother regularly went out to Uncle Jim's farm six miles south of town to visit and play on weekends. He once offered Billie a cent for any potato bugs he collected. Billie was disappointed when he brought a Mason jar full of potato bugs to his uncle but only got a penny for the whole jar, not for each one. Although Uncle Jim was "tight" in some ways (he never brought little presents to his children or nephews as Orm had done), "his house was always open" and a "great groaning table" was laid out for the Sunday meals.[40]

Uncle Jim must have been particularly fascinating to Billie and his brothers, given their polished and civilized home environment. Billie always associated the strong smell of pipe or cigar smoke with his Uncle Jim. When he smoked a cigar and got down to the stub, he jammed it into his pipe and smoked it and then knocked out the "tarry mess of dottle" on whatever was handy. Because Jim had stayed on the East Flamborough farm with his father, his speech retained a pronounced County Down edge which high school and university had refined out of the speech of his younger brothers. But even more fascinating for Billie than his uncle's accent was the content of his language. On six days of the week it was riddled with the characteristic curse and colour of the Western prairie. He delighted Billie and his brothers with his "black language" (*WW* 134) and expressions such as: "It's enough to give a gopher's ass the heart burn"; "Hailstones the size a both yer balls that'll knock her [wheat] down flatter'n a saucer a sour cat [piss]" (*WW* 135-36); "He's so tight he wouldn't pay a dime to see a piss ant eat a bale of hay." But when his sister-in-law was around, he suppressed his swearing: "Uncle Jim and Duff Spafford were considered the most foul-mouthed men in southern Saskatchewan. But he never swore on those Sunday weekends when we were out."[41]

Mitchell used Uncle Jim as his life model for Uncle Sean in *Who Has Seen the Wind*, the true "keeper of the Lord's Vineyard" (*WW* 21) in drought-ridden southern Saskatchewan during the Depression. Uncle Sean's energetic and prophetic language of curse and his visionary farming methods are contrasted to those of Bent Candy, a clean-mouthed Baptist elder whose farming practices, while giving a quick financial return, intensify the effects of the drought and destroy the land. Like Brian and Bobbie in *Who Has Seen the Wind*, Billie and his younger brothers were "held speechless by him. His language hypnotized, but not with the monotony that is in most men's swearing; Sean's flow was agile and expressive, particularly when he was angry" (*WW* 134).

‑ "AHH, GRANDMA WAS NEAT"[42] ‑

Because Grandmother McMurray's husband, John, died five months after O.S., she came to spend considerable time with her daughter and the four boys. In fact, Jack Mitchell remembered his grandparents often staying with them when O.S. was still alive. When Grandmother McMurray was not living with Margaret and her boys, she lived with her other daughter, Josie McSherry, and her family just one block behind the Mitchells. So from the time Billie was about five years old until he was fourteen, his Grandmother McMurray was a member of the Mitchell household for long periods. She too proved to be a presence in Billie's life.

By this time Maggie McMurray was badly crippled with rheumatism. She wore a leg brace with three hoops which fastened around her hip, knee, and shin, and she had to use a cane or, frequently, one crutch. She endured her crippled condition stoically. Having to contend for years with continual rheumatic pain may partially explain what appeared to many as her forbidding demeanour. She was a stern woman who did not suffer fools gladly and she used to warn Billie not to be a "gowk" (Scots for fool or cuckoo). One of Mitchell's childhood friends, the son of the minister of Knox Presbyterian Church, remembered calling to play with Billie and being rather frightened when this brusque, formidable woman, who always dressed in black, met him at the door.[43] She reminded her grandson of the soapstone plaque of John Knox which hung along with one of Mary Queen of Scots over her bed:

> She looked a great deal like a more finely drawn John Knox, if he had worn a black velvet ribbon high around his neck. Under the attached throat-piece of lace my grandmother kept a goitre. It was an *outside* goitre as opposed to an *inside* goitre. Had it

been an inside goitre she would still have worn a black velvet
band with a lace throat-piece. (*Eve* 81)

Mitchell described her as a strict woman who took her
Presbyterianism seriously but not ostentatiously: "She was not an
evidently religious woman: grace before meals, church and Sunday
School attendance, christening, marriage, funeral ritual."
Although she was a passionate card player and often played with
Billie, on Saturday nights "she played with one eye on the clock,
for at midnight the cards must be put away and not brought out
again until Monday. The Sabbath and cards simply did not go
together."[44] But she refused to have anything to do with such obei-
sances as "God be with you" or "The Lord be praised" and scorned
the public confession of Methodists, whom she considered to be
self-righteous and straitlaced:

> She disapproved of people baring their ass in front of other
> people (that wasn't her phrase) – but making a spectacle of
> themselves in front of other people. See, Methodist was very,
> very evangelical. And people getting up and confessing all of
> the dreadful things they had done in front of everybody else.
> And I often thought as far as my grandmother was concerned,
> or my mother, it was between her, the Trinity, her minister,
> and God, and nobody else. And she wasn't too sure about the
> minister either.[45]

Both Maggie McMurray and her daughter Margaret strongly
opposed church union, which came about in 1925. Mitchell recalled
hearing them saying, " 'If we lose our church we're not going to join
the Methodists.' And mother meant it. We would shift to Anglican,
which mother in her Victorian cast of mind considered closer to the
church she knew."[46] The anti-unionists won the day, and their
church did not join.

Every Sunday, Billie and his brothers, mother, and grandmother attended Weyburn's Knox Presbyterian Church, a stout grey

sandstone building with beautiful stained-glass windows, one of which depicts Christ "all grapes and bloody" carrying "a lamb with its legs dangling down" (*WW* 6). His mother sang alto in the choir and the boys sat with their Grandmother McMurray, always in the same pew, four rows from the back on the right-hand side. After the first part of the service the boys would go down to the church basement for Sunday School. It was here when Billie was eleven that he gave one of his first dramatic performances, which Mitchell later recalled in 1960:

> In the basement of Knox Presbyterian Church, Margaret Finlay had played Mother Mary again in our Sunday School concert. Sheeted, Fat and Ike and I had sat before a red tissue-paper fire glowing from the bulb in a plumber's extension light supplied by Mr. Kalman, our broomstick camels grazing nearby. Then Ike said, "Lo."
>
> Fat said, "It is a star."
>
> I said, "It is the star of the East."
>
> We mounted and we galloped across the stage to the stable furnished with hay from Stinchcombe's Livery Barn and my gift for the baby in the manger was "frank-in-cents-and-meer," whatever that was. Jack Andrews played "The Robin's Return"; Bill Stinchcombe recited "'Twas the Night Before . . ." as also did Jack Graham and Willis Ballantyne and Russel Sales and Clara Gatenby. The week before Christmas our town generally had a surfeit of "'Twas the Night Before"'s, since it was not a predominantly Presbyterian piece and was being done in the Anglican, Baptist, Methodist, and Catholic basements as well, or rather also. (*Eve* 82)

Billie did not look forward to Sundays: "When I was a kid Sunday was the worst day of the week because adults really had wrecked it for us."[47] But he was a regular churchgoer and, when he was ten, he, like Hugh in *How I Spent My Summer Holidays*, was awarded a Cross and Crown certificate of attendance and a Bible:

> For over one and a half years I had not missed Sunday school a
> single time. I belonged to the Cross and Crown. A year and a half
> before, I had won a Bible for unflawed attendance and also a
> Cross and Crown badge I could wear on the lapel of my Sunday
> suit. This was a slippery enamel lozenge, white with a scarlet
> cross encircled at the top by a gold crown. It looked very valu-
> able. The only absences excusable were those caused by truly
> serious disease: infantile paralysis, typhoid, terminal consump-
> tion. This year I was trying for the gold wreath that would snap
> around my first-year badge. For each succeeding perfect year I
> intended to win the narrow gold banner that would hook and
> hang from the gold wreath; only adult maturity would stop me
> from having them chaining down to my belly button. (*SH* 58)

The Scots-Presbyterian background of Mitchell's childhood stayed
with him, and indeed may have "chained" him in some very subtle
and complex ways. But by the time he was twelve Billie quit going
to church regularly because it was "boring and unchallenging."[48]
His brother Dick's attitude was much the same: "I figure that by
the time you're twelve you get enough church to last you the rest
of your life."[49] Their mother was not as deeply religious as
Grandmother McMurray – indeed, church was more a social event
for her – and she did not make an issue of her boys' loss of interest in going to church.

Maggie McMurray's character was as surprisingly contradictory
as her soapstone plaques of Mary Queen of Scots and John Knox.
She taught Billie "an appreciation of both the Puritanical and the
Rabelaisian elements in life" (*Eve* 81). She had an uninhibited attitude towards the body and "a very, very earthy streak," which often
mortified her daughter:

> I remember, my Grandmother was like me – she didn't give a
> shit. I saw my Grandma's tits again and again – they were dugs
> hanging down – because she would undress and she didn't care.
> I never saw her crotch, but it didn't bother her that she took off

her corsets or anything and I saw these deflated Goodrich tires down there. But it bothered my mother. And she would say, "Mother! Pull down the shades!" My Grandma didn't give a damn. She really didn't.[50]

Perhaps it was Maggie McMurray who had carelessly, or deliberately, repositioned the bronze lion on the dining-room archway table. Grandma McMurray taught Billie a few Gaelic expressions, including "*pogue mahone*, which means kiss my ass."[51] She had a quick wit and often got into "very friendly differences of opinion" with Billie's Uncle Jim, in which they traded insults about "shanty Irish" and "tight-assed Scots."[52]

Maggie McMurray was the main model for Mrs. MacMurray, Brian's grandmother in *Who Has Seen the Wind* (however, the more proper Victorian aspects of this character, such as her running feud with Uncle Sean over his swearing and earthy language, are borrowed from Mitchell's mother). Just as Brian's grandmother "had come to meet him spiritually in her declining years" (*WW* 287), Maggie McMurray began to develop a very close relationship with Billie soon after Orm's death. Probably she, more than anyone else in the family, knew how Billie felt when his father died, for she had lost her father when she was only about ten. Billie loved to hear her stories about her mother's Atlantic crossing and the McMurray family's homesteading adventures, and she, along with his Uncle Jim, introduced him to prairie tall tales. Some of her stories were frustratingly pointless:

> She would always tell me this pointless story about Uncle Will and the bobcat. As he came to this fence post, there was this bobcat sitting on the fence rail. And it looked at him and he looked at it. And as he walked to the house, the bobcat walked down the fence line. And then he went into the house. There was no goddamned ending to this story. You didn't know whether he shot it or whatever the hell he did or whether it had showed up again. There was no *point* to Grandma's story.[53]

Nevertheless, her stories stayed with Mitchell, and even the pointless story about Will and the bobcat, embellished into a tall tale with an ending, is told to Brian by his Grandmother MacMurray in *Who Has Seen the Wind.*

Because of her rheumatism, Grandmother McMurray found it very difficult to move around, and she came to rely more and more on Billie to do things for her. Their relationship developed a "teasing" element. She was quick with witty comments and retorts and Billie began to try to match her:

> I had a very close rapport with my grandmother. I guess I loved to tease her. And she would generally be sitting in a chair and her crutch always resting up against one arm. One of my most continuing flashes – visuals – is the sight of one of those rubber mushroom caps, the rubber tip on the end of her crutch, missing my nose by about four to six inches. I had firmly fixed in my mind the gestalt relationship involving my grandmother's reach, the length of the crutch holding the hand clasp part of it, the length to the end of that rubber cap on the end of the crutch, and where my head was. So I could judge the arc pretty good and would tease her – lovingly, I thought. All of a sudden she would swoop that crutch out and make a swipe at me with the end of the crutch and I would jump back, instant reflex, and she would miss me.
>
> One morning before I had gone to school I had teased her and she had missed me with the end of her crutch. When I got to school I found out from some of the others that Coca-Cola, in a promotion thing, were giving away a free circus. It was a beautiful gaudy cut-out thing. It was really impressive – the big tent that opened up, then the tabs fitted in, and there were circus wheeled cages for the parade with all the gold and curlicues, and lions to go in, clowns, the whole works. I rushed home (and my grandmother loved Coca-Cola) and said, "Hey, Grandma, give me a nickel so I can buy a bottle of Coke and I don't want any of it, you can have the whole works." I explained

Ormond Skinner Mitchell, Waterdown, 1898, and Margaret Lutecia McMurray, Clinton, around 1900.

Margaret (*left*) and Josie (*right*) in front of the McMurray sod house, south of Weyburn, around 1904.

Ormond and Margaret Mitchell with Jack, seven,
and Bill, three months, Weyburn 1914.

Weyburn and the Little Souris River in the 1930s.

Left: the Weyburn house around 1922. *Right*: Mrs. O.S. Mitchell and Josie (*left*) around 1955 in the Weyburn house living room. The room as shown was little changed from the way it appeared during Mitchell's childhood.

Above left, at Uncle Jim's farm (*left to right*): Bobbie, Mrs. O.S. Mitchell, Dickie, Uncle Jim, and Billie; and *above right* (*left to right*): Dickie, Bobbie, Grandmother McMurray, and Billie. *Left*, the boys in acrobatic costume (*from the top*): Dickie, Billie, and Bobbie. Below, Carlyle Lake, summer 1928 (*left to right*): Bobbie, Mrs. O.S. Mitchell, Dickie, and Billie.

Billie, Long Beach, California, 1927; Bill and glider parts in the back yard of the Friselle Apartments, St. Petersburg, 1931.

Billie and Dickie, Long Beach, California, 1927; Bill and his mother in St. Petersburg, Florida, around 1929.

St. Petersburg High School as pictured in the yearbook, 1931; and (*inset*) Miss Emily Murray, Bill's English and drama teacher.

Top: Bill (*centre*) tap-dancing, St. Petersburg, around 1928. *Above*: The cast of *Skidding*, with Bill in the front row, 1931.

Bill's St. Petersburg high-school graduation picture, 1931.

about the circus and everything, and she looked at me and she said, "No." She would not give me a nickel to get a bottle of Coke so I could get the circus fold-out. And she said, "I would not pee in your ear if your brain was on fire."[54]

I can remember as a child laughing until the tears came when my father told my brother Hugh and me this story. I also recall his description of Grandmother McMurray's oatmeal porridge, for which he developed an almost fetishistic love in later life in spite of his hatred of it as a child. When Hugh and I complained about having to eat porridge with him every morning, he said we were lucky we didn't have to have it for lunch too. He described how Grandmother McMurray cooked a large batch of it every morning ("enough to feed the North and South armies of the bloody Civil War") and fried what was left over for lunch. He said he especially hated fried porridge with its crusty surface and inner gluey texture, which looked and tasted like "fried snot," and he would sit stirring it around, trying to persuade his grandmother that he wasn't hungry. When he had run out of excuses and she imperiously ordered, "Ye eat it now, Wull," he was faced with having to bolt it cold while she watched. And thirty years later, Hugh and I were drowning our porridge in milk and brown sugar and spooning it down as quickly as possible (because warm snot was preferable to cold) while our father ate his, telling us how good porridge was for you and asking, when we finished, "That wasn't so bad, was it?"[55]

In the fall of 1960, shortly after his mother died, Mitchell wrote "Take One Giant Step," a short reminiscence in which he describes how, with Grandmother McMurray's help, he took a giant step on his eleventh Christmas. The boys associated both Christmas and their birthdays with middy suits. Their grandmother was a "consummate craftswoman with needle and thread," and she collected cast-off clothes from all of her Weyburn relatives, "ostensibly for hooking rugs or making log-cabin quilts." But half of these salvaged articles went into middy suits for her grandsons:

> I hated these suits, which came in three parts: the broad-collared middy itself, the stovepipe pants, and a waist. The waist was a foundation garment quilted rather like a lifejacket that had been on a severe diet; it buttoned up the back with thirteen small buttons so that you pretty nearly had to share a bedroom with a brother in order to undress at night and dress in the morning. The pants buttoned to this waist; long snap garters dangled from the front of it to hold up stockings. After swimming had opened officially in the Little Souris on the twenty-fourth of May, my brother Bob and I would walk over the prairie west of town, undress a quarter of a mile before we had reached the swimming hole, hide our clothes under a clump of brush and continue the rest of the way naked through prairie wool and spear grass, hoping thereby to avoid mortification. We were quite unsuccessful; it was known throughout the district as far as Brokenshell, Trossachs, Estevan, and perhaps even around Oxbow, that the Mitchell boys wore corsets. (*Eve* 84)

On Christmas morning of 1925, Billie and his brothers came downstairs to open their presents. Billie knew that his grandmother's gift would be yet another "detestable middy suit." He recognized it immediately under the tree by its "fat and shapeless bulk and by the spidery, angular handwriting which said, 'For Will,'" and he left opening it until last:

> Some time after the first intoxication of Christmas morning had left me, after Bob and Dick had each stoically and dutifully unwrapped a middy suit (Bob's, blue serge via Uncle Frank; Dick's, pepper-and-salt tweed courtesy of Grandfather McMurray) I turned to mine.
>
> It was wearing apparel, of grey flannel, but without the usual bitterness of mothballs – quite unfamiliar material. As I lifted it up and shook it out I was surprised that no white waist either dropped to or remained on the opened paper. Then I realized what my grandmother had made for me. Time can never

dissolve those stunning moments that I held up my first pair of long pants.

I pulled them on over my pyjama bottoms and looked down at my no-legs. A balloon was inflating inside me and I had grown one foot. I was taller; I was male-er as I stared down the long unbroken creases "with a wild surmise . . . silent on a peak in Darien."

Ah – there was a Christmas! There was a grandmother! There was the ritualistic birth of a man! (*Eve* 84-85)

The Maggie McMurray elements in Billie Mitchell's childhood litmus bath were substantial. Her sense of how to be in life – "not to: whine, squeal, cheat at casino, tell tales, conform, settle for less, or grow up into anything but a Liberal" (*Eve* 81) – was taken to heart by Billie. He avoided being a "gowk" and did, unlike his father, grow up into a Liberal. She was partly responsible for the Scots-Presbyterian imprinting which marked Billie as a child and continued to influence him throughout his life. Mitchell kept the Cross and Crown certificate[56] he won for his unflawed attendance at Weyburn's Knox Presbyterian Church, and the soapstone plaques of Mary Queen of Scots and John Knox which used to hang over the head of his grandmother's bed hung in the hallway of his Calgary home until his death. Mitchell hated porridge as a child and wondered how he ended up "doing exactly what my grandmother and mother did" by forcing it on his own children and grandchildren: "I eat it myself. I don't understand what happened. I guess if you get programmed badly enough when you are a kid, you will eat anything, even porridge."[57]

Perhaps the Rabelaisian, story-telling side of Maggie McMurray made up, in some small way, for the missing father with his warm and humorous wit. Certainly his grandmother was partly responsible for Mitchell's early interest in stories, and for his own rich Rabelaisian streak. The poignancy of "Take One Giant Step" and his repeated use and performances of this piece are indicative of the importance of Grandmother McMurray in Billie's rites of passage from childhood to adolescence.

5

BILLIE'S CHILD SOCIETY

— 1920 to 1927 —

ACHILD'S LIFE in Weyburn in the 1920s was much as Mitchell describes it in *Who Has Seen the Wind* and *How I Spent My Summer Holidays*. Although officially a city, Weyburn was a small community which afforded children an inordinate degree of freedom. While Billie's home and school life were quite disciplined and ordered, he spent many hours after school and on weekends out on the prairie, sometimes with friends and brothers, sometimes alone. His experience of both the "wild and the tame," that is, prairie and town, clearly marked Mitchell's personality and figures prominently in his fiction.

As youngsters, both Billie and his younger brother Bobbie were active explorers of the town. In *Who Has Seen the Wind*, the fictional Bobbie's "daily Odyssey" to the pool hall, post office, fire hall, and blacksmith shop is based on Mitchell's memories of his own travels around Weyburn, often with his brother Bobbie: "He travelled by red wagon, one knee up, one leg propelling him along as he steered with the tongue in his fat fist" (*WW* 93). Billie and Bobbie had established a milk-and-cookie trapline. One of their stops was the Hanton brothers' Dickson Hotel:

88

Bobbie and I would be going in there as little farts and [Hanton] would give us a bottle of Orange Crush and we would have got a little package of candies we loved – imitating Chesterfields – they had a camel on them. And we would suck on them and spit the chocolate into the spittoon and drink our lime or Orange Crush.[1]

Another of their stops was Jess Hart's three little cottages on the edge of town by the fairgrounds. She had been a nurse in the First World War but was now known in Weyburn as a milliner and had a number of young women working for her. Mitchell recalls her as "a most engaging person who liked children – you could tell she liked children because she paid attention to them – she listened and she was interested and she laughed a great deal."[2] Apparently Jess Hart could not resist Bobbie's charm: "Bob discovered that place before I did. And Bob and I, when we would come from the sand-pit hole, would drop in and she'd give us ginger snaps."[3] Mitchell remembered seeing her at the fairgrounds where a pilot, for a penny a pound, took people up for a ride:

Mother wouldn't let me go up. One of my big images is of a plane landing and Jess Hart getting out, her eyes just alight and saying how great it was. And she was wearing all khaki – she had a kind of khaki tam on. And she was wearing breeks – the kind that were very in in the twenties for women for camping and roughing it. And she was nice to us.[4]

Margaret Mitchell was for the most part oblivious to what her boys were up to in town or out on the prairie, or, later in California and Florida, down at the municipal pier or bay.[5] In *How I Spent My Summer Holidays* the narrator, Hugh, comments on the child and adult worlds of his town: "The village of my prairie boyhood was not really one unified community; it contained several societies distinct within the larger constellation. The largest and most dominant was adult of course, but our child society was real and separate, and we tried to keep it for our own" (*SH* 5). Margaret would not have approved if she had known that Jess Hart was on Bobbie and Billie's milk-and-cookie run. She would have been aware of what Mitchell learned during a 1939 visit to Weyburn – that Jess Hart and her girls may have been milliners during the day but they carried on a more lucrative business at night.[6]

From the fall of 1920 to June 1926 Billie attended Haig Elementary School. Haig School, a one-storey brick structure, had been opened that September when Billie started grade one. One of its special features was a large central auditorium which Mitchell can recall trooping into with all the elementary-grade children to hear William Lyon Mackenzie King give a speech in the election year of 1921: "I was quite impressed because he wore a vest that had a white piping around it." Later that day Billie was even more impressed when he went downtown to Stinchcombe's livery barn and saw a two-headed calf. He ran home and excitedly announced to his mother and Auntie Josie, "I've seen everything today! I saw William Lyon Mackenzie King and a two-headed calf!"[7]

Billie was very fond of his grade-two and -three teacher, Mildred Mitchell, who was his Uncle Jim's oldest daughter and who had been particularly kind to him when his father died. Mildred is one of the four mentors Mitchell listed under "IOU's" on the dedication page of *Since Daisy Creek*. Mildred, like Miss Thompson in *Who Has Seen the Wind*, was a teacher who had taken a course in "Child Mediumship" and could achieve with her students that "delicate meshing of minds that was so necessary" (*WW* 90).

Jack Andrews, who was in Billie's class throughout this period, recalled him as a "quiet and serious kid" who did not show off or joke around but who took an active part in school projects. While he was involved in many after-school and weekend activities in Weyburn's child society, according to Andrews, Billie did not participate in team sports such as baseball, hockey, and soccer very much. He preferred acrobatics and tumbling and was "all by himself in that, self-taught."[8] Billie regularly played with half a dozen boys, many of whom appear in his stories: "My friends were Ike and Fat, Hodder, Peanuts, Mate, Fin. . . ." (*Eve* 30). These were the actual nicknames for Billie Parsons, Jack Stewart, William McConachie, Maitland McConachie, and Harold Parsons. Peanuts is a wholly fictional character.

Billie was especially fond of going with his friends to the Hi-Art Theatre for Saturday-afternoon matinees to see the films of cowboy stars William S. Hart ("He had neither name nor friends, knew no law but his big black guns, so he always kept traveling on"[9]) and Tom Mix. This was also the heyday of slapstick comedy and Billie's favourites were Harold Lloyd, Charlie Chaplin, and Fatty Arbuckle.

Another favourite activity was playing at the Mitchell house, largely because of the third-floor billiard room and the dumb waiter. Billie and his friends would take turns crouching in the lower compartment of the dumb waiter to be hauled up and down from the basement kitchen to the first floor. When their mother was not around they slid down the curved oak banisters from the third to the first floor. On the pool table they did everything except play billiards. One of the favourite games was for one boy to take off his shoes and socks and stand on one end of the table while the other boys whipped billiard balls along the felt and tried to hit his feet.

For prairie boys the main activity in the spring was hunting gophers and drowning them out. The City of Weyburn offered two cents a tail, and one report in the newspaper in 1922 indicated that twenty-five hundred tails were brought in during one week in April.[10] Every spring there were gopher contests:

Look, boys and girls!
Here are just a few of the prizes

SIX SHETLAND PONIES, pair of ewes with their lambs, 24 registered purebred young pigs, phonographs, hot lunch outfits,
tennis outfits, baseball gloves, footballs, croquet sets, 12 Steven's

Marksman's rifles, 35 fountain pens, etc. See your teacher about
entering the competition.

Department of Agriculture.[11]

Although Billie never won any of these prizes he certainly joined in
with the other boys, and his first-hand experiences are the basis for
episodes in his "Jake and the Kid" stories and for the memorable
scene in *Who Has Seen the Wind* in which the Young Ben mercifully
kills the gopher whose tail has been ripped off by the young sadist,
Art (*WW* 148).

The combination of Billie's love for contests and his entrepre-
neurial skills led to another adventure that formed the genesis for
one of Mitchell's favourite memoir performance pieces, "The Day I
Sold Lingerie in a Prairie Whorehouse."[12] Billie discovered the Ten
Thousand Dollar Contest in the back of their housekeeper's *Ranch
Romances* magazine:

> The contest was illustrated with the picture of a lovely woman
> who had just been splashed with mud from a passing Stutz
> Bearcat; the balloon issuing from her mouth contained a lot
> of jumbled up numbers. By the substitution of "a" for 1, "b"
> for 2, and so on, you were to decipher what she said. The result
> was enigmatic to me: "Oh my, now you will have to buy me
> new hose. The best is none too good for me. It will have to be
> Tite-Wove Lingerie for real value, style, and freedom of
> action!" (*Eve* 29-30)

Billie mailed away his solution and some weeks later received a large
carton of "Wear-Rite Beauty Garments and Tite-Wove Lingerie"
with a letter, addressed to "Miss Mitchell," congratulating him on
winning a place in the semi-finals of the contest. He had tied with
nineteen other contestants. All he had to do to stay in the contest
was sell the consignment of goods. He had no trouble selling the
stockings to his mother and Aunt Josie. But the "contest-breaking
chemises and slips and nightgowns" (*Eve* 33) were another matter:

> Now, pulling the carton behind me in my brother's wagon, I
> had the distasteful task of selling the other stuff from door to
> door and to ladies I didn't know. It was like trying to commit
> an inept crime over and over again. I had to twist door bells and
> interrupt ladies at their baking or ironing or napping; it was a
> sort of wrongful and mortifying assault – to enter strange homes
> uninvited. (*Eve* 31)

When it was obvious that this merchandise did not suit the women
of his neighbourhood, he remembered Jess Hart and the ladies who
worked for her in the cottages by the fairgrounds. After cookies and
a glass of milk, Billie sold most of the lingerie.[13] His mother never
knew, or at least never said anything, about this. He sent the money
and remaining goods back and three weeks later received another
carton, this time a gross of bottles of perfume "with an enclosed note
telling him that the deadlocked contestants had been thinned down
to nine" (*Eve* 34). At this stage his mother stepped in and insisted
that he send the perfume back in spite of Billie's protestation that he
could easily sell most of them out at Jess Hart's.

 When gopher-hunting season was over there was always the long
and involved process of building underground forts or caves in the
sides of the higher banks of the Souris. Swimming in the Souris was
the boys' favourite pastime in late spring and early summer. After
school and on weekends, Billie and Bobbie walked a couple of miles
from the town across open prairie, helped each other out of their
middy suits, and joined their friends at the train-bridge swimming
hole or the sand pit, which was a hundred yards off the river further
upstream. Jack Andrews said that they never wore bathing suits and
that once he had to go to the doctor to have a bloodsucker removed
from his "pecker." Mitchell remembered how they would climb up on
the train bridge and cannonball or dive into the river when the Sioux
Line train was crossing. The engineer would send out a jet of steam as
the engine went by to hide the boys' nakedness from the passengers.[14]

 In the summer the Souris was a slow-moving prairie river, its
mudbanks speared with cattails and the odd bunch of silver willow,

wild-rose bushes, sage, and mint. The water turned brown from the swimmers' churning the mud up from the bottom and climbing up the slippery clay banks of the swimming hole. In the early part of the swimming season the boys kept a fire burning on the riverbank, which the naked swimmers huddled around between forays into the cold water. The Souris looks quiet and innocent these days, but in Mitchell's childhood it was wider and stronger – strong enough in the spring of 1924 to claim a young boy's life.[15]

It was at the swimming hole that Billie met one of his childhood heroes, Roy Murray. He had been a sniper in the First World War and had been "highly decorated."[16] Murray was in and out of work, originally setting up a financial business which dealt with insurance, loans, and income tax, but this did not last long.[17] He also worked as an attendant at the Weyburn Mental Hospital for a short period. He played goalie for the Weyburn Beavers hockey team, was an excellent swimmer, and hung around the Royal Pool Hall, Dickson's Barber Shop, and out at Carlyle Lake with a group of young men who also had been in the war. He was one of those mid-twenty-year-old males who frequently attract older children and young teenagers because, although they have the freedoms and privileges of the adult world, they are still "playing" in the child's world. Roy Murray was, along with George Agnew, one of the inspirations for the character King Motherwell in *How I Spent My Summer Holidays*.

When Billie was about ten years old, every male child in Weyburn idolized Roy Murray. Billie and Bobbie were particularly attracted to him: "I loved him. He would throw Bobbie and me into the Little Souris. He gave Bob and me and Jack his green Peterborough canoe. Just gave it to us." He gave them "that warm gut feeling that this adult is different from all other adults."[18] Hugh's memories in *How I Spent My Summer Holidays* of King Motherwell are exactly Mitchell's recall of Roy Murray at the Souris swimming hole:

I can feel his hands making a steady stirrup under my right foot. I am facing him, my own hands on his shoulders, in towards the column of his neck. The cords tighten; his hands lift me up with a powerful upward thrust and I am arching into a back dive or balling up in a backward somersault into the muddy Little Souris. Then there comes to me the escargot taste and smell of the river in the back of my throat and nostrils. (*SH* 18-19)

King Motherwell is an ambiguous character, for, although a hero in many ways, he entices the boys into dangerous games. Roy Murray was similarly complex, for hero though he was to the young Billie, Mitchell later learned that he was a "loser" involved in gambling, heavy drinking, and rum-running. One of Billie's chums said that Roy Murray did not instruct him in swimming, as he did the Mitchell boys; rather, he taught him how to drink.[19]

Billie associated the Souris swimming holes with the Weyburn Provincial Mental Hospital. On occasion, when he and his friends were swimming, some of the patients from the hospital, which was not far from the sand pit, would walk down to the river to watch them:

There was Blind Jesus, who always stared up into the sun. And there was a Buffalo Billy, who wore a cowboy suit with fringes and had holsters and pistols. And these two were together. Blind Jesus couldn't have survived without Buffalo Billy. I wondered about, not then but subsequently, how those attendants let that almost hebephrenic patient out loose. There was one guy I can recall with an anguished face covered with sores like abrasions who never said anything, who always stood off a little and watched our naked little bodies as we went on the springboard, whom we called Horny Harold.[20]

The mental hospital was both a treatment and a training hospital. During Mitchell's elementary-school years it had a population of about eight hundred patients and staff and had established itself as a major psychiatric hospital in Western Canada. Its concept of "therapy through work" meant that it was largely a self-contained community which raised farm animals and produce and had its own power plant and maintenance crews.[21] There was a considerable interaction between it and the town. The hospital had an orchestra and frequently hosted dances and other events that the townspeople attended. The doctors and administrative staff were a part of that professional or elite class that Margaret Mitchell enjoyed associating with, and Jack Mitchell recalled going out to some of these dances with his mother where he danced with some of the patients. Afternoon teas were often held and Mrs. O.S. Mitchell was one of the ladies who poured at them.[22]

Mitchell described one of the hospital inmates, Bill the Barber, as "the most glamorous human to us in Weyburn." He was "a magnificent escape artist."[23] Every spring he escaped and then, after spending the summer and fall in Winnipeg, would allow himself to be captured again so he could spend the winter back in the hospital. In May 1924, when Billie was ten, the *Weyburn Review* reported that Bill the Barber had escaped for the second time that month and the fourth time since being held in custody. Judging from a similar report the following year, which described yet another of Bill the Barber's escapes and recaptures, there was a mixture of amusement and sympathy for the man who desired "an annual excursion into the free air of the great outdoors contrary to the regulations of the institution in which he was housed." Apparently Bill was always "a willing captive" and greeted the police with a friendly smile and a resigned, "Well, got me again, Ed?"[24] Obviously Bill the Barber captivated the imaginations of the young people. He was brought even closer to Billie's world when one of his friends, Jim Frederickson, discovered, perhaps during the 1924 or 1925 escape, the shackles that Bill the Barber wore. Mitchell recalled hearing his mother and Aunt Josie marvelling at the ingenuity of one of Bill the Barber's escapes from an "escape-proof" basement cell which had only one small barred window in the high ceiling. This man was obviously clever and claimed to have been at one time "a professor in Prague University."[25] Bill the Barber became one of the models for the character Bill the Sheepherder in *How I Spent My Summer Holidays*, although the character is greatly expanded from the original and is more dangerous.

Billie often saw the "crocodiles," lines of inmates with attendants at the front and rear, winding their way along the roads and gardens at the hospital and on their visits to town. On occasion he went into the hospital with one of his friends whose father was head of engineering there:

> That's when I saw something I would never forget. It was a hebephrenic, where the flight within has become so complete that if a person lifted a hand up on a patient it would stay up there. And I remember watching two attendants and a hebephrenic patient. They had one of those big heavy weights on a handle and they were waxing the floor. And the guy would just take this patient and point him at the other guy at the end and give him a shove and he would just go right down like an automatic wound-up toy. The other guy would catch him, turn him around and put him over and give him a shove and send him back.[26]

Billie's curiosity about the mental-hospital inmates, along with his father's anatomy texts and his mother's high regard for doctors, was a significant factor in kindling his interest in a medical career in psychiatry: "I was fascinated with the nervous system. I used to read two large anatomy books of my father's by the fireplace behind the couch. From an early age I intended to be a doctor."[27] This early interest in psychiatry stayed with Mitchell throughout his writing career and his creative imagination was often drawn to eccentrics and the mentally unbalanced, such as the crazed prairie hermit Saint Sammy in *Who Has Seen the Wind*, the three mad women in *Back to Beulah*, the mental patients in *How I Spent My Summer Holidays*, and the psychopath Charles Slaughter in *Ladybug, Ladybug*. . . .

There are two Weyburns that play a role in the development
of Mitchell's creative identity and in his fictional worlds. There's
the Weyburn he knew as a child and the Weyburn he learned about
as a young man when he went back to visit with his mother in 1939
and 1944. It was in part the shocking disjunction between these
two communities – one comparatively innocent, the other dark
and more complex – which lies behind the genesis of *How I Spent
My Summer Holidays*. Billie was completely unaware that as he and
Bobbie were drinking their Orange Crush at the Dickson Hotel,
the men standing with one foot on the brass rail at the bar were
being served bootleg liquor from a trapdoor behind the bar, nor
was he aware that Jess Hart and her girls were prostitutes. What
Billie innocently experienced and collected in his "subconscious
notebook" as he moved through the various levels of Weyburn
society later took on more meaning in Mitchell's memory loops
and adult imagination.

⁓ CARLYLE LAKE AND OLD SHEEPSKIN ⁓

The "Social and Personal" column of the 5 July 1922 issue of the
Weyburn Review announced that "Mrs. O.S. Mitchell and children
are holidaying at Carlyle Lake."[28] Billie spent most of his summers
at White Bear Lake, at that time called Carlyle Lake. It was five miles
long and had four beach areas. By 1922 it had become a favourite
summer holiday spot for many Weyburn people and had about 130
cottages. When Billie's father was alive the family had rented a
cottage, but Margaret soon bought one. Their cottage was on Hotel
Beach, half a mile from the hotel and dance hall, which were "very
primitive."[29] In his memoir "Hang Your Mink on a Hickory Limb,"
Mitchell contrasts the "sybaritic comfort" of contemporary cottages
with those of his childhood: "These cottages twinkled with not one
single pane of glass, just screens and their shutters. During a sudden
rain or wind storm, the shutters could be lowered by ropes, though
sometimes they clattered down automatically." Their cottage had
"no ceiling at all, displaying its stud and rafter ribs to all within," no

electricity and no water – you had to walk "half a mile for it at the hotel pump" (*Eve* 118).

As soon as school was out in late June, Margaret packed up the McLaughlin and the Mitchell family, including Grandma McMurray, and migrated eighty miles east over rough prairie roads to spend July and August living at the cottage. It was about a ten-hour drive, including a stopover at the town of Carlyle to load up with groceries at Stockton's store. Margaret drove until Jack was old enough to take over. The Mitchell boys knew that their hot and dusty drive was almost over when the McLaughlin headed north from Carlyle for the last nine miles and drove off flat, bare prairie onto a winding road skirting marshes and then into the Moose Mountain area with its trees and soft, swelling hills. Mitchell recalled the sudden and dramatic change from "the dry desert emptiness of prairie to leaf and glade and leaf mould" as they drove the last few miles through the Indian reserve to their cottage:

> It must have been as early as five that the real presence of Indians came to me. I think that the most exciting thing we looked forward to, besides the appearance of trees as we moved, was the first pale flash of the teepee. And this would be very soon when we entered the boundary of the Carlyle Lake Reserve. This sudden sight of the white teepee told us, yes, Virginia, there are Indians. This was quickly forgotten as we undressed in the back of the McLaughlin piled high and we were sitting on top of this seven-passenger touring car when we hit the road to Sandy Beach going to our cottage and my brothers and I had already undressed, put on our bathing suits, and we hit the ground running and ran down past the hotel and dived into the water which, the first day of July or last day of June, was as cold as ice.[30]

The brothers lived in their bathing suits for most of July and August and, as one of Mitchell's sisters-in-law put it, the Mitchell boys "owned" that lake in the summers. Here, often under Roy Murray's coaching, they learned to swim, canoe, and sail with a lateen and leeboards on the canoe. One of Mitchell's "vivid" images was of Grandma McMurray in the lake:

> And she went down to the beach each Sunday afternoon to bathe, making it with my arm and her cane to the water's edge. She sat then in the lake, to her navel, and she bathed – literally with soap foam lapping about her middle as she went over her neck and face and arms and legs with a washcloth. Children splashed and dog paddled around her. Several hundred people on the beach watched her. They were compelled to, for as well as her skirted cotton bathing suit, she wore her velvet neckband and the attached lace that hid her goitre. She was the only bather on the beach, wearing a black velvet neckband and a Queen Mary hat, a high black turbanish affair with a polished jet gadget like a miniature coach lamp fixed to the top rim. (*Eve* 119)

In the cool evenings, "in the luke light of a lamp with its body-odour smell of coal oil" (*Eve* 118), Billie and his grandmother would sit in front of the Quebec heater and play 500 or pinochle together: "And I would accuse her of cheating, which she 'did na doo.'"[31]

Billie and Bobbie, apart from the usual fraternal friction, were close as brothers and worked together on joint projects at the lake, such as refinishing the canoe, sailing around the lake and exploring its shores, and catching frogs to sell to fishermen for a cent apiece. They scoured the marshy areas along the lakeshore and collected pails of frogs, which were then transferred to a large master barrel holding as many as three hundred frogs. Each day they would carry their barrel down to the hotel dock and scoop out frogs for their customers with a little lard tin with holes in the bottom. One day, however, Bobbie took the master pail into the hotel lobby, which also served as the post office and grocery store:

> Between the grocery counter and the lattice covered with life-size pictures of bather girls with rubber roses and rubber

butterflies on their rubber bathing caps, my brother stubbed his toe, or was tripped, and went flat on his face. The lard pail flew, and on impact with the floor, sprung its lid off, emptying four gallons of water and two hundred frogs amongst the bare feet and legs of seventy-odd mail-expectant girls. (*Eve* 119-20)

The owner of the hotel banned the boys from the premises for the rest of the summer.

During the summers at the lake the three boys saw much more of their older brother, Jack, who came home from St. John's in Winnipeg only during school holidays and the summer break. Billie and his brothers looked up to Jack. He was "bloody witty" and had grown into a very tall, good-looking young man who was "a charmer with girls." Mitchell recalled how one year when Jack came home he was no longer a teenager: "I remember looking at him. He was a hero of mine. He had a blue suit on and it had a vest and it had a coat and everything. And he was smoking Millbanks."[32] Jack put up a peeled birch bar between two cottonwoods by the cottage so Billie and his brothers could practise gymnastic routines on it. He was amused by Billie's and Bobbie's various projects. Jack was particularly impressed one day when Billie came back from an exploratory trip to one of the uninhabited sides of the lake. He had sailed over in the canoe in search of new frog-hunting territory and found a slough which had hundreds of giant bullfrogs the size of a "bread-and-butter plate." Billie was actually disappointed because they were much too big for bait, but he brought one home to show his brothers:

Jack's eyes bugged out. He'd been into Winnipeg you see and he was sophisticated and he had eaten frog's legs. He said, "My God!" And I said, "What do you mean?" And then he demonstrated – killed the frog and cut off the legs. He peeled the skin right back and here was this lovely white frog's legs and he rolled it in flour and he put butter in the frying pan. He said, "Just taste this, kid," and my stomach is coming up to here, and then I tasted it and oh Jesus! They were lovely.[33]

For the rest of that summer Margaret and her family often enjoyed frog's-leg feasts. These gourmet dinners may not have had the posh surroundings of a big-city restaurant, but the price of the main course, and the saskatoon-pie desserts, were hard to beat.

There were evening dances in a large dance hall behind the hotel where Mart Kenney's orchestra played for several years before it became one of Canada's best-known dance bands. In his last four summers at the lake, Billie worked for the hotel owner cleaning out the dance hall and handling the tickets. The front and sides of the dance hall had large screened windows with shutters which were pulled up for the dances: "Under the trees parents, older relatives, onlookers would stand and listen to the music and watch the dancers. You were given tickets like little theatre tickets for which you paid ten cents and in the middle of a dance the orchestra stopped and my job was to leave the booth and go along collecting from the guy or girl each one of these tickets."[34] One of the Weyburnites who also loved the dances at Carlyle Lake remembered that Bill helped her and her sister, who, because they were Baptists, were not allowed to go to the dances. They would sneak out and take part knowing that Bill would whistle if he saw their parents arriving at the hotel.[35]

It was during these summers at Carlyle Lake that Billie had his first close contact with the Plains native people. He and Bob formed a close, if taciturn, relationship with Sheepskin, an old Assiniboine chief of the Carlyle Lake band who, in the summers, often sat under a birch tree just down and across the road from the Mitchell cottage:

He sat there and he liked me and I liked him. He always had moccasins, bows and arrows – I think the bows were generally made of Saskatoon. And the arrows were flecked with a grey goose-like feather. Sheepskin spoke only in single words. He gestured a great deal and pointed and used his hands but we understood each other perfectly. I had a cousin Jean McSherry who came out and stayed with us and Jean and I generally had an unsteady truce going between us. She was a year younger

than I was and a very strong character. Not a particularly handsome child with a Buster Brown haircut and very full cheeks.
And that old guy knew. He liked Jean too. He knew damn well
the way to tease me. He'd be sitting there and Jean would be
with me – he would just look, he'd point to Jean and nod his
head and then say, "You squaw." And this was a great joke.[36]

Sheepskin's bows and arrows were not the kind of Indian craft toys
sold in tourist shops. The sharpened tips of the arrows were stained
with pincherry juice that looked like bloodstains and one day Billie
accused Sheepskin of duplicity. Sheepskin quietly nodded towards a
grey squirrel sitting about fifteen paces away, took an arrow in "his
long thin fingers," notched it to the deer-sinew bowstring, "pulled it
back and then just impaled that squirrel."[37]

Through Sheepskin, Billie learned the art of bartering. During
his first summers at Carlyle he discovered that old shoes and boots
were quite valuable to the Indians. So over the winter and spring
he and Bobbie would collect cast-off boots and shoes from the
Mitchell clan and the garbage dump so that when they arrived at
Carlyle Lake in the summer they had a good supply of "cash" to do
deals with Sheepskin:

> And one pair of boots would buy me one bow and arrow. One
> pair of boots would let me use a horse with just a bridle on it
> for half a day. I think it was Sheepskin who taught me to wheel
> and deal because as I recall there used to be a proposition and
> counter-proposition as to how much he would let me have. Also
> he would have with him Rogers Golden Syrup or Maple Leaf
> Lard tins filled with saskatoons or with wild strawberries or wild
> raspberries. And they were expensive too. I think it was a buck
> or maybe fifty cents for a can of wild raspberries.[38]

Mitchell recalled Sheepskin as seeming continually amused and suspected that the "amusement was at us whites who went into the lake
and got wet and came out for no reason at all . . . and who couldn't

dance as well as they danced when they did the snake dance or the hoop dance or the grass dance." One day, Sheepskin brought a tin of saskatoons around to the cottage to do a trade with Billie and he met another "elderly cynic," Grandma McMurray. Mitchell described this encounter in a short article, "Debts of Innocence":

> During one of these deals, in the summer I was ten, my grand-mother's and Sheepskin's friendship began. He came to the back door of the cottage; my grandmother was putting on the kettle for some tea. She offered him a cup. He could have drunk it on the back door step if she had not invited him inside. They drank their tea together in the kitchen.
>
> I think on his next visit he brought her a pail of berries to buy. She couldn't buy them, because she had no old boots to trade him and it would have been quite immoral to pay *money* for berries that grew naturally on bushes to be picked. She had her second cup of tea with him. Their friendship properly primed, Sheepskin's tea visits came at least three times a week. As a child I discovered a startling similarity between the two as they sat opposite each other and silently drank their tea: the same hawk-clarity of feature; both mouths had a downward droop at the corners, were combed with creases of age. And it seemed to me that for once Sheepskin's dark and pupilless eyes had lost some of their inner and secretive amusement – at us whites.[39]

Mitchell recalled that there was little if any exchange between the Indian community and the white cottagers on Carlyle Lake:

> They watched us whites. I suppose the intercourse between Sheepskin and me and my brother Bob was about as complete a bridging that was ever done between the red and white seg-ments of that lake society in the summers. They stood and watched during the daytime period under the trees and looked out at the beach at these white people in bathing suits going

into the water and coming out. I never saw an Indian swim. They wore black hats. They were like great black gumdrops, uncreased, perfectly round, but always underneath a bandana or kerchief of red or blue which curtained down the sides of the face and down in to the collar of the coat.[40]

Mitchell may have inherited his natural ability to cut easily across barriers of class, race, age, social, or economic status from his Grandmother McMurray. Or perhaps their friendships with Sheepskin were examples of the very young and the very old being "uncluttered" by the baggage of society's conventions and attitudes – the young because they have not yet been fully programmed by them, the old because imminent death as well as experience has exposed the meaninglessness of them. This uncluttered view of people stayed with Mitchell throughout his life and he certainly did not inherit it from his mother, who would never have dreamed of offering a cup of tea to an Indian, let alone inviting him into the kitchen to drink it with her.

‑ OLD KACKY ‑

One of the "most operative emotions" in Mitchell's childhood was fear, fear of "bigger guys, somebody's Holstein bull, and adults."[41] And one of the most frightening adults Billie encountered during this period was his grades-six-to-eight teacher, Mr. MacKay, who was also the Haig Junior School principal. Behind his back his students called him "Kacky" a pun on "cacky," slang for human excrement. Mr. MacKay was a Presbyterian Scot who had a reputation as a strict disciplinarian. He had been a friend of Orm's from Waterdown days, and as a teacher in Waterdown he had taught Tolbert, one of Uncle Jim's boys. Jack Mitchell said that Tolbert "hated his guts." And Jack, who also had him as a teacher, recalled with bitterness even after seventy years how Mr. MacKay accused him of lying and strapped him: "He had a leather strap with slits in the end – both my wrists were bleeding when he was through with me."[42] However, Mr. MacKay was "pretty high" on Billie because, "MacKay, I think, figured I was like my dad."[43]

Billie enjoyed learning and was competitive enough to want to lead his class. His mother was eager for her boys to excel and, since students' results on the Christmas and the Easter exams were recorded in the *Weyburn Review*, she may very well have put pressure on her boys to achieve top marks. Mitchell recalled that he "could never beat a girl called Betty Tree." Mitchell remembered correctly. From grade four on, as announced in the newspaper, Billie Mitchell was nearly always second, behind Betty Tree.

He had a natural curiosity about books. Jack Andrews said Billie read a great deal and he envied Billie's large collection of books and magazines, such as the Horatio Alger books, the G.A. Henty books, George Wilbur Peck's *Peck's Bad Boy and His Pa*, *The Boy's Own Annual*, and *Chums*. Billie also read widely during this time in his father's library, which included Dickens, the Brontë sisters, Shakespeare, and most of Mark Twain's work. Mitchell recounted many times the delight he took, at an early age, in looking at his father's anatomy texts, and in *The Vanishing Point* he ascribes to Carlyle and his friend, Mel, the fascination these books had for him:

> When they were ten, Carlyle had showed him his father's medical books with the marbled covers that had maroon corners and raised welts on their spines. There was a set of four, and, in the front, the first one had the man with his arms straight down at his sides and the opened palms held outwards. "See, I have nothing on – not even my skin." It was rather sad-looking, and you could peel back the pages like onion layers so you could see the pleated muscles criss-crossing like cartridge belts and the balled eyes staring out blue. (*VP* 328-29)

Like Mel, Billie enjoyed looking at the "page with all the female parts – rows of them – sort of like a graduation picture or a stamp-album page" and was fascinated by the descriptions of sexual diseases.

Even though Billie was a quiet, diligent, and bright student, he, too, ran afoul of Mr. MacKay:

In the schoolyard before school this one morning in the fall, Jack [Andrews] had a little tube. He said, "You want to see a hoochie-koochie girl?" Well, I wasn't turned on about it all that much but I was interested, but not pruriently so the way Jack was. He was the horniest kid I ever knew. It had a black felt eyepiece on it. He said, "Put it to your eye, close your eye, and hold it up to the light." I did and I couldn't see anything. "Now," he said, "turn it, turn it, and as you keep turning it she'll do a shimmy." And I did it and I did it and didn't see anything. Then the bell rang and we went in. We were in Mr. MacKay's room. And I just got in and sat down and Mr. MacKay just pointed me out and said, "My office." And I went into the office and he said, "All right, why did you do that?" "What?" "Your eye." And the other kids had giggled at me but I never got wise to it. And he had a mirror and he showed me and here I had a great big black ring around my eye. And this was the trick, and what they did was fill it with soot or coal dust and then tell you to see the shimmy and you don't know you've got a black eye. And without meaning to I said, "Well, gee, I just looked through this thing Jack had." And he goes and he gets Jack and he strapped us both. That man was sick.[44]

Mr. MacKay "welcomed" hysterias or fads, which often swept the school, such as gambling for hockey and cigarette cards the boys collected. The cards could be used to win hockey sticks and pucks or, in the case of cigarette cards, even larger prizes. When Mr. MacKay discovered that some boys were shooting craps and using a small homemade pinball machine to gamble for cards, he lined up all the males in the school, told them to empty their pockets, and confiscated all of the cards – "We figured Mr. MacKay had a hell of a lot of hockey sticks and pucks." Another of these schoolboy fads resulted in a mass strapping:

You couldn't have a slingshot. That was an automatic strapping if you showed up at school with a slingshot in your hip pocket. But we would make ingenious little wire slingshots out of heavy hairpins, and bend them up and out and around and then put little elastics on them and then you could do spitballs with them. And sure enough he always had a reason very early in the fall to line up all the males from about grade three through grade eight and then you would unload your pockets and toss them out. You never saw so goddamn many slingshots. Then he strapped everybody. He just went down the line, whango, whango, whango, and then that kid left. And the next one, whango, whango, whango, and that kid left.[45]

Many of Mitchell's childhood friends remembered MacKay as a mean, quick-tempered, and tough teacher. Even the girls were not spared – Eleanor McKinnon said that she and two of her girl friends were strapped for singing "Yes We Have No Bananas" in the girl's line-up after recess.[46]

As a child in grade six, Billie did not question Mr. MacKay's authority and discipline and did not at the time feel the same kind of frustration with MacKay's control over him as he felt with his mother's. But as an adult looking back, his view of this experience with Mr. MacKay was as emotionally charged as his brother Jack's: "He was so supreme and so powerful. And in later years, that's one of the dreadful, horrifying things I think of – that I never realized what a vicious, horrible shit that sadistic son of a bitch, that man, was."[47] Mr. MacKay was partially responsible for what later became one of Mitchell's perennial concerns as a parent, as a teacher, and as a writer – the impact adult guardians have on the lives of children. Mitchell's memories of Mr. MacKay were part of the "life lumber" of a number of characters in his fictional worlds, including Miss MacDonald in *Who Has Seen the Wind*, Old Kacky in *The Vanishing Point*, and Mr. Mackey in *How I Spent My Summer Holidays*.

During the 1926-27 school year, along with a number of other students, Billie skipped grade seven and entered grade eight at the

Weyburn Collegiate Institute. Academically the transition to grade eight at the collegiate went relatively well, but in the spring he was withdrawn from school for the remainder of the term. Earlier in the fall Billie had discovered the horizontal bar in the collegiate school's gymnasium and began going there regularly to practise acrobatic routines on it. During one of these sessions, he fell off a gym ladder and injured his right wrist. At first he did not think anything about the injury, but over a few weeks it grew more swollen, inflamed, and painful. When he showed his mother how his wrist made a funny squishing noise when he squeezed it, she took him to see the family doctor, Dr. Eaglesham. His mother told him that Dr. Eaglesham diagnosed a ruptured bursis sac in his wrist and said that the condition was called synovitis. Billie learned by rote his mother's version of his condition so that whenever he was asked what was wrong with his wrist, which was quite often, he responded like "a mad scientist child, 'Oh, it's synovitis. It's the inflammation of the synovial sac which lubricates all joints.'"[48]

At first he had to wear a plaster cast on it which was replaced every six weeks, and then he was referred to Dr. MacKinnon at the Galloway–MacKinnon Clinic in Winnipeg, which specialized in orthopaedics. His wrist was X-rayed and fitted with an aluminum brace to immobilize the joint. He then had to wear it night and day for the next four years: "God it stank. You know, it was padded leather and strapped around."[49] During the first year he had to go back to the clinic in Winnipeg a number of times to have the splint readjusted.[50] Billie went alone on the last two trips and, as he was getting on the train at the Weyburn station, his Aunt Josie slipped him some money. He stayed at the Marlborough Hotel and went to see *The Mikado* and some vaudeville shows at the Orpheum Theatre.

The fall of 1926 through the summer of 1927 was a frustrating but crucial period in Mitchell's life. He was in grade eight (turning thirteen in March), a watershed year for most children, when their school society plays a central role in their metamorphosis into adolescence. Billie missed a great deal of school and was cut off from many of the normal sports and social activities in which his friends were involved. He had to have afternoon naps, take daily doses of cod-liver oil, learn to write lefthanded, and do a number of other daily tasks with his left hand, such as tying his shoes or doing up his fly.⁵¹ Billie was under strict orders to be extremely careful with his wrist. Although he was not aware of it at the time, his mother was very concerned about his condition, for there was a good chance that it could worsen if the joint was not protected from further injury and given complete rest. So most of Billie's physical activities such as gymnastics and tumbling, canoeing, sailing, and swimming were severely hampered or completely eliminated. However, in the spring he saw a wire act at the Johnny J. Jones Circus, which annually came to town and set up in the fairgrounds, and he was inspired to try tightrope walking. He stretched a rope between the two clothesline poles in the back yard and spent hours stepping off a chair onto the rope and trying to balance. He never succeeded in getting more than two or three steps because he could not get the rope taut enough.

Billie's tightrope-walking attempts led to what he refers to as an "interesting confusion." His brother Jack had just come home from St. John's for the holidays and one evening came into Billie's and Dickie's room to have a chat with Billie. Apparently their mother was concerned that Billie was reaching the age where he needed some guidance about the "facts of life" and she felt that since "the boys had no daddy, the older Jack should do the sort of manly things that a father would do":

> He sat down on the bed and with the most remarkable subtlety and care he looked down at me – I guess I'd be about twelve. And he said, "Are you pulling your wire?" And I said, "Huh?" And he said, "Are you pulling your wire?" "Oh," I said, "that. Do you know, I stretched it and stretched it between the two back clothesline poles and you know I couldn't –" and he looked stunned. And I said, "I couldn't get anywhere with it. I managed to take only about two steps and then I'd fall off to one side or the other." And he said, "What the hell are you talking about?" I said,

"Well, when I saw the wire act, you asked me if I – what did you ask me?" And he said, "Forget it, forget it."[52]

Billie did not know what his brother meant until a few years later: "I was an extremely innocent boy, I think. Of course, I think we were all innocent, though many of us pretended not to be."[53]

The ramifications of Billie's injured wrist went far beyond creating immediate frustrations for him by limiting his athletic ambitions (and increasing his mother's protective vigilance over him). His relationship with Grandmother McMurray grew even closer since they now shared a similar physical handicap, and he spent more time visiting with her. As a result of his injury he was taken out of circulation in the mainstream of Weyburn's childhood society. He became more an observer than a participant. Although he was not actively ostracized by others, he felt at "the edge" of things and at times was very lonely. His solitary excursions onto the prairie during this year sharpened his awareness of the external world, but also drove him inwards. Mitchell, in fact, believed his injury played a key role in his becoming an artist: "That wrist injury and going out onto the prairie, which forced me to pay more attention to the inner conversations and to examine what my senses presented me with – probably had that sort of thing not happened I wouldn't have gone on to be an artist."[54]

Finally, Billie's injury was a major factor in his mother's decision to move. The doctors had told her that Saskatchewan winters might exacerbate Billie's wrist condition and they advised her to spend the winter months in a warmer climate where it would heal more quickly. She rented her Weyburn house to a judge and for the next four years she and her family spent the school year living in rented apartments, the first year in Long Beach, California, and the next three years in St. Petersburg, Florida. Margaret also viewed the move as an opportunity to expose her boys to the more cosmopolitan life of the city and be afforded the advantages of larger schools with high academic standards and reputations. Mitchell often commented on the dichotomy of worlds he experienced as a child in Weyburn: "I was printed with wild and tame."[55] On the one hand he lived in a house which had all of the amenities and luxuries of the average well-to-do upper-class houses in the larger North American cities. But he could step outside his front door and within three blocks the boardwalk stopped and he was on wild open prairie. And even life in the town of Weyburn was relatively "wild." The town was a comparatively soundless world relieved by the sounds of pervasive prairie wind rather than the ever-present background noises of city traffic and life. The next four years of Billie's life were strikingly different from anything he had experienced in Weyburn.

6

HIGH-SCHOOL YEARS

— 1927 to 1931 —

O N A BITTERLY cold November day in 1927, Margaret Mitchell shepherded her three boys and Grandmother McMurray (now seventy-eight years old) along the Weyburn station platform and onto the Sioux Line train. Billie was helping his grandmother and whining about the cold. The black porter helped them on the train and then loaded all of their luggage. When Margaret asked if he was sure that he had gotten everything he grinned and said, "Everythin', lady, but the birdcage and the coal scuttle." It was a good thing that their porter had a sense of humour and an easygoing nature: "He was a dear guy, and he had to be because the three of us little boys – we travelled the length back and forward of that train all the time." The three boys slept together in the upper berth and their mother and grandmother slept in the lower berth.[1]

One of Margaret Mitchell's daughters-in-law observed that Margaret, in the years following her husband's death, relied a great deal on her oldest son, Jack, to help her look after "these brats that were getting into all the mischief."[2] She must have been made of particularly strong stuff to have survived the trip to California with her three boys and her mother without his help. Billie and Bobbie found ingenious ways to keep from being bored on this trip. Mitchell said that while he was good at "sales-pitching," Bobbie was good at "getting an idea and doing it."[3] Between Calgary and Banff, Bobbie discovered that by feeding the first few feet of a roll of toilet paper down the bowl, sticking his fingers in the ends of the roll, and then standing on the toilet flusher, the suction would spin the whole roll of paper out in less than a minute. As the train approached Banff, the wicker chairs in the observation car began to fill up with people, many of whom were about to see the Rockies for the first time. Billie immediately realized he and Bobbie now had an audience and prepared for a performance which would upstage the grandeur of the Rockies. The boys raided the toilets along the length of the train for rolls of paper. Bobbie used the washroom in the car just ahead of the observation coach. Billie preferred to innocently wait with Dickie in the observation car to see the effect of their stunt, the looks of amazement and "the oohs and aahs as this great quarter-mile-long of toilet paper came just serpentining out the whole length of the track."[4] The porter put a stop to their game.

More excitement was soon provided by Grandma McMurray when the train came to a sudden halt near Golden:

It happened after mother and I had helped my grandmother the whole goddamn length of the train, and she had then sat down in the observation coach in one of these great wide-armed wicker chairs. When the train stopped my grandmother went ass over tea-kettle. I remember my mother saying to her, "Mother, why do you always – it was absolutely unnecessary for you to go over like that. Why do you have to throw up your arms and kick up your legs and improve it?" And this was true of my grandmother. I think she had a sense of effect too. Well, there was a hell of a fuss and the next thing we knew we had been shifted from our upper and lower berths and we had been given the royal bloody compartment.[5]

The CPR was very concerned about Mrs. McMurray's fall and at Kamloops two CPR claims adjusters and a doctor came on the train. After some bargaining between the adjusters and Margaret Mitchell, during which Grandma McMurray repeated in a querulous voice, "I cannot see – my vision is extremely blurred, I cannot see," they arrived at a settlement:

> The guys got out the papers, everything was ready to go. Grandma got ready with the pen and a slight tremble in her hand and she said, "I cannot see. Where is it, Maggie?" Mother's pointing out to her where to sign it and to my mother's horror Grandma said, "Oh – no wonder I cannot see." And mother could have pounded her through the floor. "I've not got my glasses on." They had come off during her fall. I think Mother said, "Sign it, Mother, sign it, for heaven's sake." And grandma signed it and I can recall these three guys were smiling and as they folded it up the guy said, "Mrs. Mitchell, you know just as well as I do that your mother is in just as great shape as she ever was before that wicker chair went over."[6]

Mitchell recalled the settlement as being something like eight hundred dollars, which more than covered the expenses for her trip and visit to California.

When they arrived in Vancouver they took the boat to Victoria, where they had a two-day stopover. Margaret left her mother on the boat while she took her boys to swim in the Empress Hotel's indoor swimming pool and to see the Butchart Gardens. While Margaret and her boys were taking in the sights of Victoria, two "nice young men" struck up a conversation with Grandmother McMurray as she was sitting on the deck of the boat. She quite happily told them her life story, beginning with her parents' stormy crossing of the Atlantic back in 1832, on to her husband's homesteading years (his terrible bouts with rust, grasshoppers, sawfly, and drought), ending with his and her son-in-law's deaths in 1921. It turned out that she was talking to two plainclothes American immigration authorities, and her story of hard times convinced them that she was destitute and totally dependent on her daughter, who was a widow with three small children to support. They suspected that her daughter was going to dump her in California and then come back to Canada and they ordered her and all of their luggage off the boat. Later that afternoon when Margaret and the boys arrived back at the dock, they found Grandma sitting on the dock with all of their luggage surrounding her. Margaret was furious with her mother. They stayed over in the Empress Hotel while they waited for statements to be wired back from Grandma McMurray's banker in Weyburn proving that she was, in fact, quite well off and that her daughter was not going to leave her on welfare in California.[7]

The next morning, Billie and Bobbie got into a water fight, filling their mouths with water and squirting it at each other, which ended with Billie dropping Bobbie's red-and-white striped pyjama bottoms out of their fifth-floor hotel-room window. Later when they left the hotel one of the boys looked back and exclaimed, "There they are!" Bobbie's pyjama bottoms had caught on something on the way down. And printed indelibly in Mitchell's memory was the punchline to this story, which his mother repeated over and over again in later years: "The boys and I looked up and there were Bobbie's pyjama bottoms waving in the breeze, just like the Stars and Stripes at half-mast!"[8]

While Margaret Mitchell hoped that her boys would benefit as she had from travelling, she was also concerned about the perils of city life. During their trip, Margaret repeatedly warned her sons about the danger of picking up disease in public toilets and she instructed them always to put toilet paper on the seat when using them (perhaps this is what sparked off the toilet-paper caper on the train). In San Francisco, she was particularly watchful over her boys. As they went through Chinatown, their mother warned, "Stick close to me, boys – this is the wickedest part of any city in the world." Billie looked around and thought, "Geez, it's interesting – it sure doesn't look wicked to me."[9]

When they arrived at Long Beach, Margaret settled her family into the Torrey Pines Apartments on Ocean Boulevard. Right out their front door was the ocean and sub-tropical flowers and palm trees. Across the street was a boulevard park with a steep escarpment down to the beach where Billie, his brothers, and some other boys who lived in the apartments played after school. Long Beach "was a very exciting time of our lives," recalled Mitchell.

On November 22 Billie enrolled in grade nine at Franklin Junior High School. Noted on his Franklin School transcript was his physical disability, "synovitis." He did quite well in his classes, particularly grammar. On one occasion he was complimented by his teacher in front of the rest of the class, but her praise also irked him:

> There I did very well in grammar, as opposed to my American colleagues, because I had taken grammar ever since grade three. They gave tests and I remember my teacher saying, "Here is a perfect paper, and it is the third in a row from Billie Mitchell. And the reason for it is, I think, that he learned his grammar in Canada and Canadian schools are sticklers for grammar because they're like the English schools." And my delight in being singled out as being good in grammar was completely erased. I was quite offended, and contradicted her. "No. Canadian, not English. I'm a Canadian and it's a Canadian school system."[10]

This was one of the first of many instances during the six years that Mitchell lived in the States that his sense of what it was to be Canadian was sharpened.

Billie may not have learned anything new about English grammar at Franklin High, but his five months in Long Beach educated him in other areas. At school and on the Pike, the carnival area of the beach, he became more aware of an extravagant quality of life in his new community. What might have been the ordinary tittering stories about sex of a young adolescent boy took on a darker, more sordid side. When they first moved into the apartment, "one of the exciting things" was that he could see Fatty Arbuckle's mansion. Roscoe "Fatty" Arbuckle had been an immensely popular silent-film comedian, "second in popularity only to Charlie Chaplin."[11] But in September 1921 his career came to an abrupt end when he was involved in the death of a woman during a wild party in a hotel. Billie heard about this incident a few years before they arrived in Long Beach:

> I was not clear at that age what had happened to Fatty Arbuckle. I remember overhearing my mother and Aunt Josie speaking and I jumped into the skipping rope and said, "What happened, what did Fatty Arbuckle do?" And Auntie Josie looked at me and said, "Well, he was unkind to a woman." And I said, "What did he do to her?" And she said, "He kicked her in the stomach." And I figured that was pretty unkind to a woman.[12]

But here at Franklin High, Billie learned the lurid details of Fatty Arbuckle's fall from movie stardom: "I found out from kids at school that in a bacchanalian party he had shoved a Coke bottle up one of the girls and she died and that was the end of his career."[13]

At thirteen Billie was at least a year younger than most of the grade-nine students at Franklin High. He had begun to take notice of the girls in his class, but soon discovered they were too old, in many ways, for him. In his homeroom he sat beside a fifteen- or sixteen-year-old blonde:

> She had the most impossible straw-coloured electric hair, fly-away bleached blonde like one of the clown wigs, and used heavy make-up. I remember her whispering to a really good-looking dark-eyed girl who was ahead of me and catching the phrase, "Does it tickle up inside – did you get that funny feeling inside?" I sensed that they were talking about sexual intercourse, comparing notes about how it felt.[14]

Billie was surprised how often he saw her down at the Pike, each time on the arm of a different sailor. He subsequently guessed that she was getting tickled for a price.

The Pike was a "sort of permanent carnival." It had sideshows and barkers, games, a house of mirrors, and rides, including a roller-coaster. It was in a very tough part of town, a red-light district popular with sailors on leave from across the bay at San Pedro, which was a major American navy port. Billie, Bobbie, and their friends would go out in the winter evenings to play in the park and make their way down the beach to the Pike at Horseshoe Pier:

> There were games of skill and chance, shooting galleries with the smell of the .22 rifle smoke on the air, the smack, crack, and whap as sailors and revellers were knocking over ducks and rabbits. Out in front of every one of the sideshows would be a barker, and that was entertainment in itself. One of the interesting shows had a short dwarfed young man – they said he was Inca the Pinhead Boy – and his head had that shape as though it had been pressed between boards as his skull developed and had grown. He never said anything when he was out. He was a performer – he knew he was out in public and shining and stood there – and the barker would make wisecracks about him. He would then offer to play "The Arkansas Traveller" on his fiddle *backwards* – he simply put the violin behind his back and ran the bow up and down and played a few bars.[15]

Billie also saw "the Wild Man from Borneo who bit the head off a live chicken" and the "Rubber Skin Man, the guy who shoved knitting needles and nails through his skin." Although he was drawn to this place, it was not with the gawking excitement of seeing deformed humans, but with horror at the "display of such people for money" and with disgust for the people who got "a kick out of looking." He said, recalling "Montaigne's expression," that the "ultimate horror" was that these people "did not recognize the horror," making it possible for them to do "unforgivable things to other human beings."[16] Some of the details of the Pike experience surfaced later in Mitchell's con man, the evangelist Heally Richards in *The Vanishing Point*, and the emotional repugnance Billie experienced here is a part of the nightmare horror of *How I Spent My Summer Holidays.*

At Long Beach, Billie was also introduced for the first time to two other kinds of carnival barkers, real-estate salesmen and evangelists. Almost every Long Beach street corner had a parasol stand with a real-estate agent handing out folders on new developments. One of these developments was at San Clemente, down the coast from Long Beach, and the real-estate people offered potential customers a free trip in a touring car, with a free box lunch. Margaret, "who was very close with money and anything free was great," decided to take up the offer, and the whole family, including Grandmother McMurray, went to listen to the spiel in a big chautauqua tent. Mitchell recalled how the con, to make his point that people should seize an opportunity when it comes their way, held up a five-dollar bill:

> "Now," he says, "this is a five-dollar bill, you can see that. What'll you give me for it?" There's a pause. He said, "Come on, it's a five-dollar bill, what will you give me for this five-dollar bill?" I said, "A dime." And I end up with this five-dollar bill. Well, that tickled my mother so much! She knew she had a goddamn financial genius on her hands here, you see. And with those horn-rimmed glasses, Christ, I would go up, I'd be head of the Bank of Canada before I knew it. Or the Bank of England.[17]

Cults and new religions were starting up with abandon in California at this time, and the leaders of these groups became as popular as movie stars. A day or two after hearing the real-estate spiel, Billie and a friend, Jack Edmison, wandered into a chautauqua tent and heard Gypsy Smith's plea to "Come to Jesus." Mitchell described the story Gypsy told of being urged by his dying mother to turn from his infidel religion to Christianity:

> And [the mother's] last words were, "Gypsy, Gypsy, go the goyim way, take Christ into your life." I had never to that point in public ever been as emotionally moved – ever. And the goddamn tears were streaming down my cheeks and the guy next to me and the woman next to him and I didn't dare look the other way because I knew that Edmison wasn't crying. And then the collection plate. As we left the tent, Jack said, "What did you put on that collection plate?" I said, "I put some on." He said, "It was five bucks!" It was my five bucks [from the real-estate con].[18]

Although Billie was more moved by Gypsy Smith, Aimee Semple McPherson was the most famous evangelist that he heard. McPherson had, in fact, been born and brought up in Ontario, and in 1926, the year before the Mitchells arrived in California, she made headlines all over the world with news of her mysterious kidnapping. Eventually she and her mother were charged by the Superior Court with obstructing justice by perpetrating a hoax. These charges were dismissed, but Aimee and her mother were still headline news in 1927 because of a major quarrel and an estrangement.[19] Mrs. Mitchell would have been very aware of all the headline news, and, no doubt out of curiosity, wanted to hear Aimee. On this occasion, in the famous Angelus Temple, and "dressed all in white" and "with a choir and everything," Aimee Semple McPherson urged Billie and thousands of others to make a donation for a bicycle for a poor little crippled boy and his widowed mother so they could make an income from a paper route: "And her first words were just like that real-estate man: 'Who will give me a bicycle? Who will give me a bicycle?'"[20]

Billie's transition from child to adolescent was abrupt. The child who, five months earlier, had delighted in unrolling toilet paper from the train had been exposed to a dramatically darker and seamier side of life. Obviously, his memories of these con events were filtered through his adult imagination, but they indicated that he, as a thirteen-year-old, was aware of more than the circus going on in front of him. Although he readily admitted that he was taken in by some of the cons, there was planted in his sensibility an ambiguous response to these unfortunate people, a fascination, a sympathy, and a horror.

During the Easter holidays the Mitchell family left Long Beach and headed for Vancouver where Billie was enrolled in King George High School for the last two months of his grade nine. At the end of June they "proceeded direct to their cottage"[21] at Carlyle Lake for the summer. Margaret's hypersensitivity about public toilets on the trip down to California and the posters Billie had seen in the CPR washrooms saying "BEWARE OF STRANGE WOMEN" led to an amusing episode that summer. During the annual epidemic of "Riel's Revenge" Billie had been "caught short" and had run up from the beach to use one of the hotel backhouses, but he had failed to put the precautionary toilet paper on the wooden seats. Soon after, he developed itchy sores on his buttocks and groin. Because he had read his father's anatomy texts "with special interest for the urogenital system of the opposite sex and especially the venereal diseases," he became increasingly alarmed. His sores developed into what looked "just like the picture of the strawberry-red chancre" in his father's anatomy text: "I knew the incubation period for syphilis. And right on time . . . I developed the most loathsome primary lesions for syphilis all over my crotch." He could not bring himself to tell his mother or anyone else and for two weeks he suffered great emotional anguish in silence: "I actually went up to Pringle's Point between Sandy Beach and Hotel Beach and went to the edge of it and thought of throwing myself off."[22]

One day Jack came into the tent while Billie was changing and when he clapped his hands over his crotch Jack demanded, "What the hell's wrong with you?" Billie showed him his sores and, with some relief, confessed: " 'I got syphilis.' And to this day I don't know whether it was an insult or a compliment. Jack said, 'Who'd you get it off?' I said, 'The chambermaids – they used the hotel toilets and I didn't put paper on the seat.'"[23] Jack took Billie down the lake to the Edmison's cottage. The Edmisons were old family friends of the Mitchells from Brandon, and their son Max was interning in medicine at the University of Manitoba. Jack asked, "Max, what are we going to do? This little guy's picked up a dose of syphilis." Max Edmison examined Billie and, much to Billie's relief, announced that it was scabies:

> That's what it was. It was not syphilis; it had been a wrong diagnosis on my part. But by Jesus! Jean McSherry got it. Auntie Josie got it. I got it. Mother wouldn't let me know if she got it. Bob and Dick and Jack got it. Even though she boiled all the sheets. You see, it's highly infectious. It's a little mite that burrows under the skin and then it festers and then it blisters and then they suppurate and then they scab.[24]

Margaret had to boil all of the bedsheets, towels, and Billie's clothes, and Swedish ointment from the Carlyle pharmacy cleared up Billie's blisters.

— ST. PETERSBURG, FLORIDA —

In the second week of September 1928, Margaret and the three boys again headed south, this time to St. Petersburg, Florida. While Margaret looked for a permanent apartment and got her boys registered in school, they lived in downtown St. Petersburg at the Binnie Hotel, in a "chintzy little box of a room."[25] During their first week in St. Petersburg there was a major hurricane warning. Margaret became alarmed when she heard all the radio bulletins and saw the downtown stores preparing for the storm by bracing and boarding up their large plate windows. Mitchell recalled being wakened by his mother as she tied a baggage tag around his neck: "She had printed out our names and our address in Weyburn, Saskatchewan, and was putting them around our necks in case she was killed in the hurricane and people might find these little boys' bodies and they would go back to be buried, properly interred, in the Weyburn cemetery alongside my father."[26] St. Petersburg escaped the full brunt of the hurricane, but, as the reports of casualties and damage were announced in the *St. Petersburg Times*, Margaret must have wondered whether she had made a wise decision in moving her family to Florida for the winter. She got her family settled into the Friselle Apartments by the end of September. It was a small apartment with only one bedroom for her and two Murphy beds in the living room for the boys, but Margaret was satisfied enough that she kept it for the three years they wintered in St. Petersburg. According to Jack, who was now working at a bank in Saskatchewan and came down for occasional visits, the rent she received from the Weyburn house covered most of her living expenses in St. Petersburg.

Margaret led a busy social life, playing bridge and shuffleboard, going occasionally to the greyhound races, attending Canadian Club and Shrine Club socials, dances, and events, and moving in a well-to-do circle, which included a number of Canadians who wintered in St. Petersburg. She is mentioned a number of times in the *St. Petersburg Times*: "Mrs. O.S. Mitchell of Weyburn, Saskatchewan, Canada had as her guests at the St. Petersburg Shuffleboard Club yesterday W.M. Martin, the honourable chief justice of the supreme court of Saskatchewan [Martin was also premier of Saskatchewan for six years], and Mrs. Martin, and Mr. W.M. Martin, Sr. The party played a game of shuffleboard and pronounced it a very interesting game."[27] She also spent a lot of time with her close friends from New York nursing days, who became extended-family "aunts" to her boys: Aunt Emma (Rose), and Aunt Nell (Bell).

There were daily band concerts in Williams Park (the Moses and Sousa bands played there during these years) and performances by famous artists of the day such as Galli-Curci and Madame Schumann-Heink. On one occasion Madame Schumann-Heink sang at the Congregational Hall Church which was adjacent to the Friselle Apartments. Because of the heat the back windows of the church were wide open and Bobbie, quick to see a good money-making opportunity, borrowed some sawhorses and planks from next door, lined them up against the back of the church, and charged twenty-five cents admission.

Mitchell recalled that St. Petersburg's downtown sidewalks were paved with large octagonal concrete blocks of blue, red, yellow, and orange and were lined with its famous green benches. Billie was particularly impressed by the tropical trees and plants – the large labyrinthine banyan tree at Mirror Lake, the Spanish moss in the trees at Williams Park, the "torching poinsettias" and bougainvillaea which lined the streets, the mango trees at the front of their apartment. Florida had a different smell from the arid Saskatchewan prairie, "much more alive and fruity" (*LL* 67). Billie could pick oranges or grapefruit from the trees that lined the boulevards, and he and his brothers played a kind of bowling game, rolling grapefruit onto the road at the wheels of oncoming cars to see if they could make a "strike" and see it squish. Killing cockroaches was another game they played. They would turn off the lights, leave the kitchen for a while, then turn the lights on and start slashing at scurrying cockroaches with the mop and broom: "We had a competition going to see who could get more cockroaches. We marked notches on handles for kills."[28] There were also moments of reflectiveness like those he had experienced as a child on the prairie (or in the root cellar of the Weyburn house). In particular he recalled on a visit to St. Petersburg in 1985 how he used to be fascinated with the chameleons:

> One of my first lovely things was lying out here where the chameleons were. And they were not nervous. And I can recall, in a moment of sadness or isolation, watching a dear little chameleon whom I would move from leaf to leaf. And you could – they didn't scurry away, or at least this one did not – watch its colour slowly tint and change on given leaves.[29]

Bobbie was more interested in a pet alligator (about a foot and a half long) he had picked up and which he kept tied up on a leash to the back stairs of the apartment block. The Friselle sisters, who owned the apartment and lived upstairs, were not pleased and told Margaret that the alligator had to go. Bobbie, who was in constant warfare with the Friselle sisters, decided to get his revenge by laying around the back yard and up into the apartment a faint trail of sugar: "Now this is the tropics and you would not believe how populated that sugar trail became – with ants, marching up and in and through to the Friselle ladies' apartments."[30]

The boys spent most of their free time down at Boca Ciega Bay municipal pier (also called million-dollar pier) on Tampa Bay. They wore their bathing suits under their school clothes and on the way back from school left their clothes under a palm on the cochina-shell beach while they swam. One day a tide brought thousands of faintly green-tinted jellyfish into the bay and immediately the air was filled with flying jellyfish as children and adults engaged in a free-for-all jellyfish war. Billie often fished off the pier for "grunts," small, muddy-tasting fish which when landed made a grunting noise. Sometimes he would catch a blowfish and once he caught a stingray. The boys were introduced to some new dangers here. Once, while standing on million-dollar pier, Billie watched dolphins form a ring around a large shark and bunt it. He and his brothers were repeatedly warned never to swim out at the end of the pier because a girl, a champion swimmer from St. Petersburg High School, had been attacked there by barracuda and had died. One day, a Portuguese man-of-war jellyfish tentacle slipped down the front of Billie's bathing suit: "Suddenly I felt this firebrand right down my chest and stomach. I came rushing in and straight for the lifeguard, who had a bottle of ammonia to sop on it and counteract the acid."[31]

Million-dollar pier harboured human dangers as well. Mitchell remembers one afternoon in particular when Bobbie was swimming by the pier and was accosted by a pedophile:

> I saw a guy, and then I saw Bob dive under, swim underneath the water, come up behind a pier, swim under, and come up again and circle around into shore. Bob came to me, and he

was a little bit upset, and he said, "That guy came up to me and he pinched me and he said, 'Oh, you got nice titty on you, boy.'" This was a new sort of thing to us.[32]

Another dark note in St. Petersburg was its racism. In Weyburn there had been one black family, the Johnsons, whom Billie had known quite well. He recalled that the Johnsons and the Chinese families in Weyburn were accepted as a normal part of its society, and that only one boy he knew had indulged in racial name-calling. When he first arrived in St. Petersburg, however, "it was a shocker" to notice the segregation. Often in the early morning on his way to school, looking down from the streetcar window, he saw prisoners, mostly black, in leg irons being taken out in trucks to work in the phosphate mines. The city was clearly demarcated in terms of neighbourhoods, as were the public areas, including the piers:

> South was black, north was white. And there was absolutely no intercourse whatever except on a servant relationship in our part of town. If anyone saw a black person, they would say, "What are you doin' here, boy?" Very early I was interested in fishing and went down to Boca Ciega Bay with a bamboo rod and a bobber using shrimp for bait. And I moved over and south to an old wooden pier, commonly known as "nigger pier." I didn't know that at the time. And it was there I found myself sitting several days beside a Negro who had a melanesian body thing so that patches of his skin were almost fluorescent pink, white. And he was known as the pinto nigger. I was a chatty kid, but he didn't answer much. And finally, about the second time, he just said, "You better get yo' ass off nigga' pier, white boy."[33]

The Mitchells arrived in St. Petersburg in the middle of a presidential election fight between the Republicans' Herbert Hoover and the Democrats' Alfred E. Smith, Governor of New York. In Florida, racism was a particularly hot issue with white supremacists backing Smith (with Joe T. Robinson, Senator from Little Rock,

Arkansas, for vice-president) against Hoover. On November 1, five days before the election, the Smith–Robinson Democratic Club ran a full-page political advertisement in the *St. Petersburg Times* denouncing Hoover and the Republicans under the following headlines: "WHITE SUPREMACY, NOW AND FOREVER THE ONLY ISSUE IN FLORIDA AND THE SOUTH"; "'Government by Men With Straight Hair' Is Menaced by the Republican Platform and by the Attitude of the Republican Presidential Nominees – Read the Proof, and Vote to Preserve Southern Homes and Governments Against Indignities and Insults." Even though Billie was a visitor, and by nature as well as age apolitical, he could not have been completely immune from the added excitement in the air of this racial debate between the supporters of Smith and Hoover. Hoover and the Republicans went on to win a landslide victory on November 6 and succeeded in breaking a "solid South" as well as routing Smith in his home state of New York.

– MRS. WILKINSON'S SCHOOL OF MUSIC –

Within a month or so of getting settled in St. Petersburg, Margaret Mitchell enrolled her three boys in various performing activities. For a brief time they took tap-dancing lessons. Mitchell can remember dancing to "Shuffle Off to Buffalo," but he thought this was "silly" and quit in less than a month.[34] Next he was enrolled in Mrs. Leonora Wilkinson's School of Music, which gave lessons in art, music, and "expression and dramatics." His mother believed that, like his father, Billie had an innate talent for elocution. Billie, however, argued – to no avail – that at thirteen he was a "horn-rimmed-spectacled wishbone of a child with the stage presence of an introverted chameleon" (*Eve* 3).

In "The Day I Spoke for Mr. Lincoln," written in 1962, Mitchell recalled these lessons.[35] On Saturday mornings, when he would rather have been swimming with Bobbie, he roller-skated to Mrs. Wilkinson's, "fifteen blocks of cathartic grind and crack-clicks under the shrill lace of pepper trees, past the stubbed trunks of palms with funeral-wreath fronds, the arterial red of poinsettias, shoving on the skates with anger and indignation and rage" (*Eve* 4). Here he spent an hour with his elocution teacher, Gertrude Nay, who was well known in the city for performing "readings in her usual charming manner."[36] Miss Nay gave him "gestures and facial expressions and postures to go with such pieces as "The Fool":

> ". . . look from the window . . . all you see was to be his one day – forest and furrow – lawn and lea. And he goes and chucks them away . . . chucks them away to die in the dark . . . somebody saw him fall . . . part of him mud . . . part of him blood . . . the rest of him . . ." (LONG LONG PAUSE – PUT OUT LEFT HAND IN THE SPURNING GESTURE AND CLOSE THE EYES IN THE-PAIN-TOO-GREAT-TO-BEAR EXPRESSION – LOWER THE VOICE BUT DON'T FORGET THE CHEST CHAMBERS) ". . . not at all!" (*Eve* 4-5)

She also had Billie learn dialect pieces such as "A Negro's Prayer" and "Giuseppe Goes to the Baseball Game." Following each lesson Mrs. Wilkinson would be waiting at the door to collect the two-dollar lesson fee from him as he left.

In September Billie and Bobbie joined the St. Petersburg Good Citizenship Club, which had been formed by Captain E.B. Holly. According to an article in the *St. Petersburg Times* "hundreds of boys have been helped mentally, morally, physically, and spiritually almost entirely at Capt. Holly's expense." Holly acted as a truant officer, urging boys to attend school, and, on weekends, he provided recreation which kept them out of trouble and protected them from "danger on the water front."[37] Mitchell recalled Captain Holly as "an old bastard who had no teeth and wore a little captain's cap and over in the yacht basin he had a scow-type hull and a shack top on it, 'Captain Holly's house boat' – that was a euphemism for what it was."[38] The club was free and the boys liked Captain Holly and appreciated the various projects he organized. He took the club members regularly to free shows at the Pheil and Alcazar theatres and organized weekly archery contests with prizes. One Saturday he took the boys out in his boat and they caught fiddler crabs off one of the keys and then went out fishing in the bay. At a sports event, organized by Captain Read and Captain Holly, held on Saturday, October 6, Billie won first prize for "novel stunts."[39]

The Good Citizenship Club arranged a benefit to raise money to buy canvas and barrel hoops for the boys to make canoes. Billie volunteered to recite at this event, which was held November 12 as part of the Armistice observances at the yacht-club pier on Boca Ciega Bay. The star attraction was Palm Tippy, "a six-year-old aquatic marvel."[40] Billie felt unfairly outclassed:

> I recited "The Bald-Headed Man, the Boy, and the Fly" in my elocution suit. But I came after Palm Beach Tippy, who was supposed to be only five or six years old, who dived from a special tower they had put up into Boca Ciega Bay where his father had spread gasoline and ignited it. He was wearing a dutch cut and very blond hair – I remember I felt so sorry for him because I could see the little bugger was scared shitless and his tough old father was shoving him up that thing.[41]

The next day the *St. Petersburg Times* reported that Palm Tippy did his ninety-foot platform dive twice. No mention was made of Billie's recitation, but it was reported that he had won the grease-pole climb with Norman Perouche.

Captain Holly's interest in his boys had an ugly side to it. Billie noticed that Captain Holly was interested in one young boy in particular who, frequently, would sit on Holly's lap:

> Captain Holly told the story of how he had thrown himself under the wheels of a truck to save a little baby girl who had toddled out in front of it and the wheel ran right over his stomach. And this is why this handsome, young, lithe junior-high-school boy very frequently sat on his lap. Holly said that

he was experiencing great pain, and he would keep pressing the boy up against where the truck had ridden over him. It was always the same boy.

Fifteen-year-old Billie was not really aware of what was going on: "I believed that he had saved a baby girl. But I knew there was something wrong the way he squeezed this boy up against his stomach."[42] Dr. Miller, who lived across from the Mitchells, warned the boys' mother about Captain Holly, and she discreetly but firmly put an end to their association with him.

After a few months of lessons, Billie qualified for the recitals Mrs. Wilkinson held monthly on a Sunday afternoon, "incestuous affairs attended only by parents and close relatives of the students" (*Eve* 5). At the end of the season Mrs. Wilkinson held formal recitals at the Art Club, and these were announced in the *St. Petersburg Times*. Billie was one of four readers at the April 11 "Boys Recital" and again in the junior program of the school's end-of-year class recital on May 15.

But Billie's mother was not satisfied with these recitals: "In her opinion I had been expensively loaded, and it was time to truly discharge me publicly" (*Eve* 6). She arranged for him to perform at other venues. For these events his mother had bought him an elocution suit, "a double-breasted blue serge coat and cream flannel pants" (*Eve* 6). On March 25, 1930, "little Billie Mitchell, of Saskatchewan"[43] recited "Giuseppe Goes to the Baseball Game" at the Canadian Club. Although he was called for an encore, his mother was not pleased: "She was just mortified. I had my elocution pants on and they didn't quite come down, and I had no socks on and my ankles were dirty. And Mother was looking at my bare dirty ankles and was just humiliated."[44]

In his third year in St. Petersburg, Billie was selected to take part in the Decoration (Memorial) Day program at the Williams Park bandshell on 30 May 1931. He was to recite Lincoln's Gettysburg Address. The memory of this event is shaped into his piece "The Day I Spoke for Mr. Lincoln." At first he was proud, as was his mother, to have been chosen to deliver the address, but as he worked on memorizing it, his "patriotic conscience" began to give him second thoughts:

> Before accepting the honour I should have remembered that I was a Canadian, owing allegiance to the King, the Beaver, and the Maple Leaf. How I had overlooked it, I do not know, for every time I turned around I knew I was amid alien corn. These people said "zee" for "zed," divan for chesterfield, napkin for serviette. They accused Canadians of saying "hoose, moose, and loose" for "house, mouse, and louse," denied our smashing victory in the War of 1812, insisted they had won the First World War. They celebrated Thanksgiving on the wrong day and in the wrong month. Their picture shows stayed open on Sundays, and the backs of their church pews were stocked with fans for fanning themselves sacrilegiously during the Scripture reading and the sermon. (*Eve* 6-7)

Billie hit on a solution to his dilemma by memorizing Lincoln's Gettysburg Address with some very slight changes: "Wherever Mr. Lincoln had said 'we' or 'us' or 'our,' I changed it to 'you' or 'your,' so that the opening sentence started out: 'Four score and seven years ago *your* forefathers brought forth. . . .'" His adapted ending became, "'With malice towards none, with charity for all, it is for *you* to resolve that this nation, under God . . .'" (*Eve* 7). Billie thought that he had everything under control, but when he was called on to perform he found he had caught nervous "palsy" from the old Civil War veteran he was sitting beside on the stage and he forgot his lines: "I managed the opening paragraph but from there on I left Mr. Lincoln, or he left me. I kept right on by myself, however, ad-libbing in a Lincolnesque way, then caught up to him and solid land for the last paragraph: '. . . shall have a new birth of freedom; and that government of the people, by the people, for the people, shall not perish from the earth'" (*Eve* 9).

Fifty-four years later, on a visit to Williams Park, Mitchell recalled some of the details of the day he spoke for Mr. Lincoln and assured us that most of what he had written was true:

> Is this Williams Park? If it is, it's been shrunk. In fact, it's mangoes [not banyan]. There was a hell of a lot more Spanish moss then. Everybody had fans. In my recall they were fanning the fans so hard that the Spanish moss was all waving too. That was Decoration Day, in May. There was generally a big parade for Decoration Day and the windup was here. Babe Ruth was up on the platform. Master of ceremonies was in fact a senator from Tallahassee, a state senator. Madame Schumann-Heink *did* sing with John Philip Sousa and his band, which played here every Sunday. And I *did* recite, and I *did* forget and get lost, and I *did* ad-lib. And I *did not* step into the spittoon.[45]

As he stood in Williams Park recalling these events, he mused about his mother's role in his developing interest in stage performance:

> My mother really, in a sense, was a stage mother in a funny way – because my father did perform and mother wanted me to. But I was not aware of it at the time. All I knew was when she had bridge club or something, or one time at the lake at a bonfire at Sandy Beach, she would say, "Oh Billie, go and do for them 'Giuseppe Goes to the Baseball Game.'" And I hated it. I hated it. And yet, except for that momentary impatience, I was not aware that she was putting me forward.[46]

Although Billie felt this "momentary impatience," he did enjoy the audience response to his recitations. This is obvious in Mitchell's description of the response to his recital of the Gettysburg Address: "The fans stopped; leaves and Spanish moss were stilled; then every Northerner in Williams Park, in or out of a wheelchair, cut loose with applause that would have made Palm Beach Tippy and his death-defying dive into flaming gasoline look like a piker" (*Eve* 9).

~ SPRINGBOARD DIVING ~

In fact, Palm Tippy's diving act may have helped spark Billie's interest in a new sport. During the winters Billie and his brothers often went swimming at the St. Petersburg Spa by the yacht basin on Boca Ciega Bay, where a group of young divers were regularly coached by Pep Smith, a former springboard diver from Miami. Billie watched the divers and began to try some of the dives on his own. He was still wearing his wrist brace at this time but would take it off when he went swimming. When diving, he perfected a one-armed entry to protect his wrist: "rather than chance a sudden outrage to my hand and wrist, when I completed the dives I simply slapped my right hand against my thigh and held one up and went in."[47] Pep Smith noticed Billie's attempts and allowed him to take part in his formal coaching sessions:

> I was not permitted to be part of the spa diving team because obviously a guy that could only go in with one arm stuck out ahead would lose points and couldn't compete. That didn't stop me from going in where there would be half a dozen divers. In time I was able to do a two and a half, a one and a half gainer, and a back one and a half. I must have been an eager little son of a bitch, and I just came and he let me take my turns with the others. And we would comment on each other's dives, how high we'd dive and whether we were too far out from the board, how good the entry was, how good the form was in the air.[48]

Billie was a fast learner. In November, in a swimming tournament at the spa sponsored by Captain Holly's Good Citizenship Club, Billie won first prize, and was made captain of the team.[49] He attacked springboard diving with the same obsessive persistence and desire for perfection with which he had attacked his tumbling. During the coaching sessions Pep Smith would sit by the edge of the pool and give the boys critiques on each dive. After a dive Billie would surface and eagerly look to Pep Smith's hand signals to see what score he had achieved: two thumbs down – "stinks"; one up and one down – "O.K., keep working on it"; and two thumbs up – "bingo, keep doing it."

At Carlyle Lake in the summer of 1929 Billie helped design a diving tower that he had persuaded Mr. Wellwood, the park warden, to build. It had one-metre and three-metre boards plus a six-metre platform at the top, and was designed so it could be taken up on the beach in the fall for the winter. So when the Mitchells left St. Petersburg to spend their summers at Carlyle, Billie practised his diving. One of Billie's Weyburn friends remembered Billie diving off the Carlyle Lake tower: "He was the most graceful person in the air I think I ever saw. Brilliant. Bill tried to teach us but I didn't have the guts to do it."[50]

~ ST. PETERSBURG HIGH SCHOOL ~

St. Petersburg High School was a very competitive and progressive school which attracted and nourished scholarly as well as athletic "achievers." Under its first principal, Captain W.W. Little, the school had quickly established a reputation for high academic standards. He appears to have instilled and fostered, in both his faculty and students, a school pride and desire to perform well. Harriette (Smith) Blackmar, one of Billie's former classmates, said St. Pete's was an academic school with an excellent reputation: it was "lots of fun, but no nonsense when it came to studies. You either made it or it was out. No hangers-on."[51] Another of Billie's former classmates, Emma Lee (Burke) Chilton, described the school as having a "campus atmosphere":

> Most teachers were excellent. Among the faculty only one had a doctorate but many had master's degrees and about a dozen had done graduate work at Columbia or University of Chicago. Among the women there were Smith, Wellesley, and Vassar graduates. Nearly all of us students expected to go to college and I imagine most did.[52]

St. Pete's was a "state-of-the-art" high school, "one of the most modern and completely equipped educational institutions in Florida."[53] It was, and still is, a very impressive white two-storey structure in Spanish–American style. The main building, in the form of a huge letter B, encloses two open quadrangles surrounded by cloister walkways. The large front portico has high arched entrance doorways and windows flanked with decorated pillars. St. Pete's had excellent sports facilities and a huge auditorium, with a balcony, which could seat up to 1,500 people. The first year Billie attended the school it had 960 sophomore, junior, and senior students who came from all over the United States. Many of these were visiting students, including a number of Canadians, whose parents wintered in St. Petersburg.

At eleven o'clock every morning all of the students were assembled in the auditorium for chapel. Chapel opened with one of the students reading a lengthy passage from the Bible and then leading the school in the Lord's Prayer. Billie was very proud when he was invited by Captain Little to do one of these readings. Then followed a talk or performance by a visiting dignitary or by St. Pete's students. Tuesday assemblies throughout the year centred on presentations from the fifty or so clubs which were annually formed at the high school. Billie's reputation for doing dialect recitations must have spread, for the sophomore representative, Ely Katz, asked him to perform at chapel on sophomores' day: "Ely confronted me in the cafeteria and he said, 'All right. You do it. But you're not going to do any comic Jew ones!'"[54] At the conclusion of chapel, "Captain Little would stand up and they would all sing 'My Country 'Tis of Thee' – except for Billie Mitchell. And I would be belting out, all three years I was here, 'God Save Our Gracious King.' It made you more Canadian to be here."[55]

Billie made quite a few high-school friends during these years, many of whom (Tom McNulty, Paul Hanna, Bill Cass, and Harriette Smith) ended up working together in the senior drama production of *Skidding*. Tom McNulty, whose father was the fire chief of St. Petersburg, was the closest of these friends. They were an unlikely looking pair:

> What would I weigh about this time? Ninety pounds maybe? Tom McNulty, a hundred and sixty-five, Irish bruiser, played fullback on the Devils football team. Tom became a Franciscan brother. Had you looked at the two of us in those days you'd say this little mosquito with the horn-rimmed glasses and the brace on his right arm will probably end up being a follower of St. Francis of Assisi. This bruiser here will probably have a tough time staying out of the police court news.[56]

They spent a great deal of time together and often collaborated on school projects. McNulty described how they built a puppet stage and puppets and put on the ghost scene from *Hamlet* in the school's little theatre for Miss Murray's drama class:

> We were up behind the stage and as we began the play we noticed that people were tittering. We couldn't discover why. We had three controls each, one for each hand, and the third one we put in our mouths, and when we would raise our heads slightly so we could read the text, the puppet on the stage would rise up about an inch or two and so Hamlet and the ghost would do a sort of dance as we were going through it.[57]

Following graduation, they wrote to one another every day during the summer of 1931 and then two or three times a week during the next year. When Mitchell and McNulty were interviewed together for the NFB film, Mitchell recalled, with some amusement, their rather sanctimonious disapproval of swearing:

> Tom and I were actually rather righteous, as I remember it. I remember when you and I, and this is the first time I have ever confessed it to anyone, when we expressed quite seriously to each

other . . . that we were a little distressed that people were saying gosh and darn. So we made a kind of deal that we wouldn't say heck, or gosh or darn, let alone what they stand for.[58]

During his 1985 visit to St. Petersburg, Mitchell, now not so sensitive about rough language, recalled another telling example of his puritan imprinting, the "obscene ducks" at Mirror Lake Park which also distressed him: "And again we get into the puritan thing. These ducks, when I was here, they swam a great deal, and they ate a great deal. But these ducks fucked more than the senior citizens over here played shuffleboard."[59]

Although Billie had long ago stopped attending church regularly, he was still very much a product of his early Presbyterian upbringing. He voluntarily attended, with Tom McNulty and Paul Hanna, the Stories from the Bible Club led by Captain Little after school, but only because he respected Captain Little. Paul was from Paisley, Ontario, and spent the winters in St. Petersburg with his widowed mother, a devout Presbyterian. Billie found out from Bill Cass that Paul's mother would not allow him to read O. Henry's short stories because O. Henry had been jailed for embezzlement.[60] Paul was also a little suspicious of the Stories from the Bible Club because Captain Little was not Presbyterian.

Billie met Bill Cass in his sophomore Latin class. His parents were also Florida winterers from Canada and Mrs. O.S. often socialized with them at Canadian Club events. On one occasion Bill Cass, Tom McNulty, and Billie went to a fair in Largo, a small town about ten miles north of St. Petersburg. It was a "really low-thought-of-district" and the fair consisted of sideshows, freak shows, and strip shows. Here there were no black-white barriers. The boys, especially Billie, were too young-looking to get into the strip shows, but one freak show, the alligator lady, left a lasting impression on Billie: "Her lids, her skin was corrugated like an alligator's skin. When those eyelids closed they were like the bump eyes on an alligator."[61] This Largo experience made enough of an imprint on him that years later,

in the early 1970s, he ascribed it to his character Heally Richards in
The Vanishing Point.

⁓ MISS EMILY MURRAY ⁓

Billie met Miss Murray, an English and drama teacher, in the fall of
1929 when he walked into his first junior English class. He was
utterly captivated by her: "I suppose that within two months I
had fallen in love with her without knowing it."[62] Miss Murray had
graduated with an M.A. from Columbia University, and had acted
at the Pasadena Playhouse for a while[63] but came back to St.
Petersburg to be with her mother when her father died. Her father
had been the first mayor of St. Petersburg, and she had grown up
there. She was an attractive woman, about thirty at the time, who
devoted herself to her teaching and to her widowed mother. She
often volunteered her after-school and weekend time to helping students with school projects, and had students over to her house for
play rehearsals and debating practices. Miss Murray's public-
speaking class and the various drama projects which grew out of it
had gained a high reputation among St. Pete's students and the St.
Petersburg community.

It was while studying some of the Romantic poets in her
English class that Billie became particularly intrigued by Miss
Murray's discussion of the concept of "grace":

> One day in English class, and I don't know whom we were taking
> up – it could have been Keats, certainly wasn't Wordsworth – and
> Miss Murray used the term "grace." I remember, before I went
> out, going up to her desk and saying, "What is grace?" And she
> said, "Well, you dive." And I said, "Yeah." And she said, "It
> looks easy." And I said, "No, it isn't," and went on to explain
> that I whipped the board probably two hours a day down at the
> spa and went all through six, seven, eight times a day each of my
> optionals and then my compulsories. And she said, "Well, it is

a graceful thing, a dive." I said, "I guess so." "Well," she said, "perhaps that's it. Doing something so that it looks as though it were easy, but in order to achieve that effect it took a lot of work."[64]

Mitchell later referred to "grace" as the art which conceals art, and it became a central tenet in his aesthetic credo and his life. Mitchell pointed out that it is not often that you can clearly pinpoint when you learn something that influences you forever. But he knew that Miss Murray "marked" him: "It [grace] stood for a lot of things for me in the course of living. And I think I value that quality of grace as much as any quality in any art or in any human relationship."[65] In this discussion were the seeds for Mitchell's essay, "Grace and Illusion: The Writer's Task" (1963), and his long-standing disapproval of the "Ain't-I-clever, ain't-I-smart" exhibitionist style of writing and performing. It was also in one of Miss Murray's English classes that he first read Wordsworth's "Ode: Intimations of Immortality from Recollections of Early Childhood." In spite of his later dismissal of Wordsworth, he remembers that his first reading of this poem "hit me a hell of a wallop."[66]

Miss Murray's public-speaking class, which he took in 1930-31, inspired in him a love of serious drama and a respect for performance that had been missing from his elocution performances. There were about thirty students in the class, including some of Billie's best friends. Mitchell described this class as "English in the oral tradition," and its main business consisted of practical experience in debating, giving speeches, and performing skits. Miss Murray valued humour and wit (Mitchell recalled that she introduced her students to Stephen Leacock's work), and she was adept at creating a rapport with her students and encouraging them in their attempts to perform in front of their classmates. Harriette Blackmar described Miss Murray as a marvellous teacher: "Sometimes we would get in the longest discussions and all of a sudden the bell would ring and we didn't think we had been there fifteen minutes!" However, Miss Murray was always in control, and "when it was time for the curtain, as she would call it, why that was it."[67] Mitchell recalled in some detail his experience of the kind of exercises Miss Murray had her students do:

> You were given assignments, topics, or you selected your own, and you had to deliver a speech to the class. She told us that we must not memorize the speech. Even now as I look back I can remember how dreadful I felt when I knew it was my turn to get up in front of the class and deliver a speech. Near nausea. I turned out to be pretty bloody good at it very quickly. She encouraged you to be funny and I did silly speeches. I did witty speeches. I did end-to-end funny speeches. I did one on taxation imagining what the first taxes by Neanderthal man would be. I did ironic speeches. I did sarcastic speeches. And by God, I made them laugh.[68]

If Miss Murray had not noticed Billie the year before in her English class, she certainly did this year in her public-speaking class. Harriette Blackmar commented that Miss Murray was particularly attentive to Billie: "She thought the world of him because he was such an apt pupil and such a good scholar and such a quick study."[69] Billie also made the debating team, which was coached by Miss Murray.

Pantomimes and skits which were worked on in Miss Murray's class were occasionally performed at chapel. Billie did a mime in which he sewed his fingers together and also a scene from "Station YYYY" by Booth Tarkington, in which two adolescents fool their parents by getting behind a chesterfield and faking a radio program. But the main project of the class and the most important annual event of the school was the senior play. For the 1931 play Miss Murray chose *Skidding*, the first of the Andy Hardy series of plays by Aurania Rouveral. It had been a broadway hit a few years before with Mickey Rooney playing the lead role of Andy Hardy. Billie acted the scene from "Station YYYY" for the tryouts and won the role of the adolescent Andy Hardy. Harriette Smith won the role of

Andy's sister, Marion; Paul Hanna, the part of Grandpa; and Bill Cass, the lover. Tom McNulty was the business manager for the production. Harriette said that she had been paired off with Billie "in all sorts of different things" in Miss Murray's class and that "he was fun to act with." They worked hard on the play, rehearsing five nights a week and on Saturdays and Sundays going down to Miss Murray's house to read their lines.[70]

Skidding was an "outstanding success" and cleared a profit of a thousand dollars.[71] The 1,500-seat auditorium drew a standing-room-only crowd of 1,800, which marked the first time the auditorium had been completely filled. Billie had never before had an audience like this and, according to the *St. Petersburg Times*, he rose to the occasion: "From the opening of the curtain, Bill Mitchell captivated the audience with his portrayal of Andy, the typical adolescent. His enjoyment of the part made it a triumph and many said he stole the show."[72]

Forty-two years later, in January 1973, Mitchell's wife, Merna, engineered a reunion between Mitchell and Miss Murray. Through a long process they found Miss Murray's phone number in Hanford, California, where she had moved in the mid-1930s. During the telephone conversation Miss Murray told Merna what happened at the end of the last full-dress rehearsal for *Skidding*: "I took Billie aside and said, 'It's customary for the leading man, after the curtain calls, to give the leading lady a bouquet of flowers. I would suggest you present Harriette with a dozen long-stemmed red roses. This is customary, Billie, and you must arrange to have them ready.' And he said, 'Who pays for them?' And I said, 'Well, of course you do, Billie.' And you should have seen his face!" Merna responded, "Oh, Miss Murray, he hasn't changed a bit!"[73] On that night in 1931, after the curtain call, Billie magnanimously presented Harriette with a bouquet of red roses.

A month later Billie was on the auditorium stage in front of the whole student body and again he stole the show:

Harriette Smith and I and Paul Hanna did a scene for chapel. Harriette Smith did Portia; I did Shylock. Now there was a thing here called the zits game. You would stick out your second finger and hit a person in the upper arm just between the shoulder and the elbow, sharply, and it would instantly come up in a gumdrop boil or a hickey. The rule of the game was the first guy to see someone with a beard and yell "Zits" could hit the other guy with impunity and raise a hickey. When I appeared on the stage in a Malabar beard the whole goddamn football team, the seniors, and everybody else, the whole auditorium became filled with "Zits! Zits! Zits! Zits!" – people hitting the next person.[74]

Harriette Blackmar said that, in spite of the "zits," Billie was wonderful in this role: "He played that beautifully. You just would have sworn that he was the age of that man. [He] had that brace on his arm, but he wasn't slumped or anything. But believe you me he was slumped on stage. He was marvellous."[75]

Everyone became aware of him after his performance in *Skidding*. "*Inimitable Andy!*" is the tag under his yearbook photo, and he is referred to as "Bill (Andy) Mitchell" in the "Hall of Fame."[76] Billie also made it into the "Rogue's Gallery" (with nine other rogues). His aliases were "Willie the Weasel" and "Andy the Ape" and his crime was "Springing his scurrilous ipecac joke in polite society."[77] Just like Grandmother McMurray, Billie may have been distressed by "gosh or darn," but he was not averse to jokes about purgatives.

Billie was recognized for his scholarly ability as well as for his clowning. Harriette Blackmar recalled that "he was a good student, always. I knew that. And he was sharp. He had a good mind."[78] Emma Lee Chilton, who took psychology with Billie in grade eleven from Captain Little, "thought of Bill as serious and studious."[79] The three years Billie spent at St. Petersburg High School played a crucial role in nourishing his intellectual curiosity and his

sense of identity. Here he did not feel isolated from student activities, barred from participating in them because of his arm brace. He
could dive, act, and score as a scholar among his peers. When
he graduated in 1931 he was one of the 272 graduating students to
be singled out in a select group for his senior-year activities, which
included the swimming team, the Junior Chamber of Commerce,
the senior play, the *Palmetto and Pine* (the school newspaper), the
Annual (yearbook), and the debating team: "You became an
achiever in this school with such a large population – if you wanted
them to take you importantly."[80] Although he could portray himself
in all seriousness as "an introverted chameleon," he also knew full
well that he wanted to be important:

> And that's why I was called Inimitable Andy, because I was a
> charming clown. And I was important. The thing to do was to
> become important within that high-school society. Otherwise
> there were a hell of a lot of anonymous people. It was a very
> interesting society. And I suppose it's true of all high schools and
> people at that age that you want to be important, you want to be
> noticed, you want to make people laugh, you want to score. And
> of course, sports was the big way, so you had the football team
> and the baseball team and the swim team. But in St. Petersburg
> Senior High scholarly ability was an important thing.[81]

One day towards the end of the school year Miss Murray took
him aside after class to talk with him about his plans after graduation. She told him that he had potential as an actor and suggested
that he consider taking up acting as a career. Billie was surprised:
"Oh no. I am going to be a doctor. I'm going to take medicine at
Manitoba University."[82] But Miss Murray's instinct for what Billie
would become was prescient. Fifty-three years after his senior
year with Miss Murray, she was listed on the dedication page of
Since Daisy Creek (1984) among four of the mentors to whom
Mitchell owed a debt in his development as an individual, a writer,
and a performer.

— THE HYDROPLANE GLIDER —

In the summer of 1928, when Billie was in Weyburn, he struck up a close friendship with Bill Cameron, the son of the new Presbyterian minister who had just moved to Weyburn. They would go swimming in the sand pit or out on the prairie to hunt gophers with Bill Cameron's .22. Cameron was intrigued with "this man from Mars – from Florida" who wore a leather-covered brace on one arm and was an accomplished springboard diver (he saw him diving at the Weyburn swimming pool). He did not see the "clown" side to Billie; in fact, he commented that Billie "had no side to him." He was "relaxed" and "natural," showing nothing "of that flair" that he later developed.[83]

What really brought them together was their passion for building model airplanes and flying them. Cameron said that no one else in Weyburn was flying model planes at this time and described Billie as being "very sophisticated technologically." For the next three summers the boys would get together when Billie was not at Carlyle Lake, and they would fly their planes in the gymnasium at the Weyburn Collegiate School.

Billie had picked up this interest in Long Beach and St. Petersburg, where building ROGs ("rise off ground") had become a very popular hobby. The ultra-light planes were made from balsa wood and rice paper and their propellers were attached to bent pieces of piano wire which hooked onto heavy elastic bands. In St. Petersburg Billie's interest and expertise in this hobby flourished under the guidance of two American friends who had won the U.S. Eastern competition for ROGs. ROG enthusiasts spent their afternoons down at the ballroom of St. Petersburg Coliseum flying their model airplanes and competing for the longest flights.

During his last year at St. Petersburg, Billie had become bored with the small balsa-wood planes that he and Bill Cameron had flown in the high-school gymnasium, and he began building larger lifelike models of planes. In the winter of 1929-30 he built a model Savoya-Marchete, "a big amphibian plane with pusher propellers

that was supposed to take off from the water and fly and land."
After two months of painstaking work he took it down to the St.
Petersburg Spa to fly: "That was one of my great disappointments.
That's when I learned you couldn't trust a *How to Build It* maga-
zine. There was no way that thing was engineered to take that great
big body."[84]

But this disappointment did not dampen Billie's enthusiasm.
He had an even more ambitious plan – to build and then fly a one-
man glider at Carlyle Lake in the summer of 1931. Again he found
plans in a magazine:

> You sent away a dollar, and they sent you the prints for a
> hydroplane, and this was a great bloody biplane with one main
> large pontoon. Under the wings were the two little [wings] and
> then it had a structure like a primary glider with outrigger struts
> and then the stabilizer, the rudder, and a bucket seat on top of
> this thing which was like a sea sled.[85]

The advertisement for the blueprints recommended using a large
powerboat to get the glider airborne. In the summer of 1930 Billie
struck a deal with Connie Benson, a friend of his at Carlyle Lake.
Billie would build the glider that winter in St. Petersburg and have
it shipped to Carlyle Lake in the late spring and Connie (actually
Connie's father) would supply the large powerboat to get it in
flight. Years later Mitchell excitedly recalled this project, "I'd
build the bloody hydroplane and, Jesus, we would fly all over that
lake together!"[86]

During the previous year and the summer of 1930, Billie saved
money from various enterprises to pay for the blueprints and
materials: "I had used my own money for this, money I had made
from selling frogs at the lake for bait, money I made during the year,
and I put it in the bank; I was very tight-assed and I couldn't tell you
the amount of money I had saved up."[87] He spent most of his spare
time from the fall of 1930 through the spring building the glider out

behind their apartment. The Friselle sisters were not pleased with the clutter of tools, materials, and the growing pile of assembled plane parts, especially the thirty-foot wing, which slowly took over their back yard. He recalled in detail the jig from which he made the ribs and body, cutting out the rib pieces in the school shop, and the glue he used: "Casein glue that was as strong as iron and smelled like sour milk and it was a tan powder you mixed up."

By the late spring of 1931, Billie had completed most of the skeletal structures of his glider's wings, body, and rudder and had crated and shipped them to Carlyle. All that remained to be done was the pontoon, the stabilizer, and the fabric covering – "the equivalent of sailcloth" – which would be stretched tight using acetone. His mother's view of this project was mixed. She was pleased to see her son's enterprising initiative and his dedication to this project, but she was appalled at the prospect of his actually flying.

They arrived at the lake as usual in mid-June and Billie immediately began building the pontoon while anxiously waiting for his crated glider parts to arrive at the CPR freight yards in Carlyle. Connie Benson arrived at the lake with the new big motor for the boat which would power the glider into the air. Every day Billie got a ride into town in the back of the hotel truck. "What I went through for that damned thing," he said, as he recalled the time the driver "spit a big wad of tobacco juice and it just came right back and I got it in my face. And God does that sting." He kept working on it but the sad truth became apparent: "I built the pontoon, but I didn't get to put the seat on it or anything else because I knew we weren't going to get [the glider]. It was lost."[88] The nearest they came to flying was to mount the motor on the completed pontoon and use it as a makeshift power surfboard.

The summer was spoiled by another project. He had to study. He had been granted entrance to the University of Manitoba on the condition that he complete high-school matriculation courses in British and Canadian history, two subjects he had obviously missed in the American high-school curriculum. He studied the material on these courses out at the lake and wrote the exams in Winnipeg in mid-August. The results were disappointing.[89] However, on the condition that he pass a Canadian-history course in order to graduate, he was granted admission and in September 1931 he enrolled at St. John's College, University of Manitoba.

7

UNIVERSITY OF MANITOBA

– 1931 to 1934 –

I N THE THIRD week of September 1931 Bill caught the train for Winnipeg. He was, like his character Carlyle in "The Alien," excited and nervous about leaving home for university. He felt "the breathlessness of anticipation," but it was "tinged with apprehensiveness – a mild understir of panic as though he had been tipped without warning and was not too sure of regaining security" (*A* 12-13). At seventeen, Bill was a year younger than most of his fellow students, who recalled him as young-looking and naive.[1] Mitchell himself said he "looked fifteen" and was "an innocent among sophisticates."[2] While he looked young and vulnerable (and, as a result, quite unconsciously exacted a protectiveness from his friends, a phenomenon which stayed with him throughout his life), he was not shy about getting involved in all sorts of activities on and off campus. His innocence was a kind of wide-eyed boyishness that led him into new experiences rather than away from them.

The University of Manitoba, the third-largest in Canada at the time, had an excellent reputation. During the years that Bill attended, it was a thriving, energetic campus whose student leaders included many who were later to become well-known critics, actors, historians, and politicians: Marshall McLuhan, Tommy Tweed,

W.L. Morton, Frank Pickersgill, Jack Pickersgill, Stanley Knowles, and Mitchell Sharp. Bill enrolled in the Faculty of Arts and Science, intending to study medicine as a preliminary to a career in psychiatry. From an early age he had been deeply curious about human personality and its inner workings, a curiosity influenced by his awareness of the patients from the Weyburn Mental Hospital.

Bill registered in Chemistry, Botany, Zoology, Physics, and two Arts courses, English and French. He did not particularly shine in English II (the only English course he took in his three years at Manitoba), and his other grades were somewhat erratic, but averaged around 70 per cent, except for Chemistry, in which he failed his labs. Apparently Bill, like Carlyle in "The Alien," did not enjoy his course of study this year:

> . . . with the possible exception of Zoology he was not finding his pre-medical science course engrossing, discovering in himself an impatience with the detail of laboratory work, which quickly became boredom and then distaste. He had come to dislike the very atmosphere of the Science building pervaded with the faint rottenness of hydrogen sulphide, the perfume of esters laced with the decay of formaldehyde and the citric smell of acid. (A 87-88)

During his first week Bill was rushed by Delta Kappa Epsilon (DKE) and became a "pledge." This was flattering and, given his mother's ambitions for him, particularly welcome. At the beginning of October Bill moved into the fraternity house on Maryland Street, and shortly after that the initiation period called Hell Week began. During Hell Week the fraternity brothers put the pledges through a series of tests. Some, said Mitchell, were "dreadfully silly things" like having to swallow simulated goat's entrails. Other tests went beyond "silly" and gave sadists ample opportunity to indulge themselves. Bill had to wear humiliating headgear, he was paddled and sleep-deprived. The branding ritual was particularly frightening for Bill because he vividly remembered from his childhood the raised scar triangle with the letters DKE branded on George Agnew's arm:

> One of the last final dreadful tests was that you were told that all Dekes were branded with the letters DKE. You were shown a great glowing branding iron and then, after you had been blind-folded, you were held down and in the small of your back, where you were about to be branded, a great chunk of ice was placed. And that was that.[3]

Although Bill was disgusted by these demeaning power games, he was willing to put up with them for the sake of belonging to the group.

It was later, in two unpublished novels, "The Alien" (1954) and "Brotherhood: True or False" (1990s), that Mitchell explored the emotional and psychological ramifications of the practice of hazing, how it undermined one's already vulnerable sense of identity and self-esteem. In "The Alien" Mitchell dramatizes a ritual in which the initiate, Carlyle, is told that "from now on you will have no name – you will be a number – number one. You will refer to yourself as it. You will not use the personal pronoun" (*A* 56). When his fraternity brother asks him if he understands the initiation requirements Carlyle is trapped into committing his first infringement:

> "Do you understand?"
>   "Yes. . . . "
>   "Say it – I understand!"
>   "I understand, sir."
>   "One sixty-fourth of a black mark. It has just received its first black mark for forgetting to refer to itself as it! It – it – it for Christ's sakes can't it get it through its thick head that it is an it! It had better get the hell to its room and read over the rule – if it can read!" (*A* 61)

Although these fictional accounts of Hell Week are autobiographical in these novels, Bill was never as scarred as were his characters. But he carried away from this experience ambivalent feelings which fed into his overall repugnance for authority and institutions that use ritual, "tests," or behaviouristic methods to program and control individuals.[4]

However, the fraternity experience had an attractive side as well. Jim Duncan, another pledge, said that he and Bill became friends *because* of Hell Week, because they were joined together against a common enemy.[5] The frat house provided residence for between eight and ten men. Besides Jim, Bill became friends with Blair Ferguson and Peter Lehmann, although Lehmann did not live at the house. The friendship, enjoyment, and self-importance that Bill felt among his fraternity friends is captured by Blair's first memory of meeting him: "It was rushing time and Bill was sitting on the couch surrounded by other young men telling them of his adventures in Florida, which at that time was almost like a foreign land to us in Winnipeg."[6] Fraternity life brought ready-made friendships.

Bill never liked the exclusiveness of the fraternity. From the beginning he developed friendships and activities outside it. Peter Lehmann commented that Bill "certainly had no concern about being different. The rest of us were trying to conform. He was himself."[7] The DKE fraternity was the closest experience Mitchell ever had of joining an organization and in many ways it made him wary of group associations.

Bill continued with springboard diving during his first year in Winnipeg. The prestigious Winnipeg Winter Club was the only facility that offered diving, and a friend of his mother's had arranged for him to dive there and receive some coaching. It was not long before he noticed Judith Moss, who had just started diving and had a natural talent. A year younger than Bill, she was attending Rupert's Land Ladies College. Practices were held five days a week every afternoon after school, so he saw a lot of her and they soon started going on the occasional date.

Bill had not dated much before. In his last year at St. Petersburg High he had fallen for Margaret Campbell and had finally got up enough nerve to ask her to the Cotton Club Ball. But, as he recounted, because she could not dance, it had not been a very successful evening. Judy recalled that she and Bill went to a few movies, and that Bill "was fun" to be with. As he walked her home, "he would wander down the street waving his hands and telling these impossible stories."[8] However, it was not a steady romance. They did not go out "constantly," and there were "lots of upsurges and depressions,"[9] suggesting that Bill was kept somewhat off balance. However, he took Judy to the big event of the year, the spring fraternity formal, and decked out in black tie and formal gown, they had a wonderful time – and danced!

The major diving event of the year was the Provincial Championship Diving and Swimming Meet held 27 February 1932. This was a big night for Bill but, although he felt that he put in his best diving performance ever, he was disappointed: "What happened was I had my usual bronchial sneezing, and when I got up to do my final-degree-of-difficulty dive – which we called a cut-away one and a half against the board – as I got up I sneezed. And as I sneezed my foot slipped and I fell in the water." Bill got up on the board again and performed the dive – "it was a nine" – but the judges would not count it.[10] He placed second, behind William Munro. Judy won the women's diving championship.

If it had not been for that sneeze he felt he would have won the provincial championship. His aspiration was to compete in the Canadian championships and at the Olympics to be held that summer in Los Angeles. He knew that the diver he had to beat was not Munroe, but Alfie Phillips, who was the Canadian diving champion from 1926 to 1934. Mitchell said that Phillips could perform higher-difficulty dives than he could and was much more consistent.[11] Over the summer of 1932, when Mitchell had the opportunity to test himself against the Saskatchewan and Alberta champions, he outperformed them and thought he might have been able to place second to Alfie Phillips in the Canadian tryouts. Judy confirmed that Bill was "very good" at diving, that he "had very little fear," and was willing to take risks with his dives.[12] In spite of his second-place finish, Bill claimed that he was selected to go to the Canadian team tryouts in July in Vancouver. Judy, who had not taken her diving seriously that year, decided not to go to the tryouts. However, two years later, it was a different story. She won the Canadian springboard-diving championship and then went on to win the gold medal in springboard diving at the British Empire Games in London, England, in August 1934.

Bill also became involved in drama in his first year. Every fall the University of Manitoba Dramatic Society put on two evenings of one-act plays performed by six different groups within the university. It was through the Science Society, headed by Tommy Tweed (who, some years later, played the role of Daddy Johnson on the CBC *Jake and the Kid* radio series), that Bill was given a role in "The Grand Cham's Diamond." Playing the husband of a cockney woman who has acquired a stolen jewel, Bill gave a "lively" performance in this comedy.[13]

— SHEET WRITING: SUMMER 1932 —

Around the end of April 1932 Mitchell began to think about summer work. His mother had supported him during his first year at university, but Bill decided that he should make an attempt to help out with the next year's expenses. From one of his fraternity brothers he heard about a job selling magazine subscriptions. Bill joined in with others who were taking a short course from a Texan who had come up to teach them the fine art of "the track" (the sales pitch used to sell subscriptions): "You announced that you were a student from university and this was your summer break and it was hard times and you wanted to get back to university through the generosity of the *Farm and Ranch Review* or the *National Monthly* or *Maclean's*. So if I could just have your name I'm given five points and if I get the points, by gee, I'm going to make it."[14]

Bill intended to sell magazines until it was time to go to Los Angeles for the Olympics in August, and by the first of May was out in North Winnipeg practising the track. During this year, however, there had been a diphtheria outbreak, and, unluckily, Bill caught it as a result, he thought, of drinking impure water. At the time he was living in the Delta Upsilon fraternity house because the Deke house was closed for the summer, and the DUs were upset because their entire house had to be quarantined. However, Bill soon became too ill to stay there and was admitted to King George Hospital, which he described as "a real old-fashioned pest house." Diphtheria was cause for alarm. Called the "strangling disease" because it attacked the throat and obstructed breathing, it could be fatal if the antitoxin was not administered early on. Mitchell said his throat looked like "a spider web,"[15] and the danger was that the mucus build-up would close off the throat completely. Because diphtheria is extremely contagious, Bill was put in isolation in the hospital.

What Bill recalled most through this ordeal was his loneliness. Presumably his mother did not visit because of the quarantine. But one of his fraternity brothers braved the quarantine, as well as the gated and fenced-off hospital, and appeared at his window one day: "Dan had got through and then his face was at the window – and that was the only contact I had with the outside world."[16] His sense of isolation was further reinforced by his nurse. Bill was fascinated by the way in which she could manoeuvre herself into her hospital gown by touching only the inside of it and could change his sheets without ever touching the contaminated side. While he was amazed by these "incredible acrobatic feats," he was puzzled by what seemed to him to be an overfastidiousness about cleanliness and human contact. She believed that people would not catch diseases if they avoided touching one another, and she admonished him for his carelessness. She was, however, an "Icelandic" beauty, from the Gimli area of Manitoba, with black hair and incandescent blue eyes, and he said that "even in the grip of diphtheria I guess I fell madly in love with her."[17] Mitchell later drew on his bout with diphtheria for *The Vanishing Point*'s exploration of how puritanical attitudes can prevent people from "bridging" and, in an interview about *Ladybug, Ladybug . . .* , said that the isolation he felt during his diphtheria quarantine made it easier for him to write about the kind of desperate loneliness that Kenneth Lyons feels when he is abruptly retired from university teaching, when age removes him "from the living whole."[18]

The recovery from diphtheria is quite slow, and although Bill was hospitalized for just ten days to two weeks, he was advised to take it easy for the summer. This put an end to his dreams to go to the Canadian diving tryouts in July and on to the Olympics. He got out of the hospital in time to join the rest of the gang who were going across the prairies selling magazines – "sheet writing" as it was called in the trade. As Mitchell put it, "This was the beginning of my illustrious career as a con man."[19] His savvy for selling his own books was first developed during this summer when he went door-to-door selling magazines.

The lead member of this group was Al East, a seasoned sheet writer who knew all the angles. Six of them travelled "in this big Graham Page touring car" from Winnipeg to Saskatoon to Edmonton and blitzed many small towns in Alberta: "You were like termites hitting a building – you ate a town up pretty quick." Al, cleverly, would take the business district and give the greenhorns the residential area, so he always finished quickly with "a roll of bills" whereas they had little to show for their efforts. Bill did much better when Al taught him more effective tracks, one of which, even fifty years later, he could reel off word for word:

> Al went up and knocked at the door and said, "Hi, my name is Al East and I'm with the Canadian Advancement Board and I'm just checking to make sure that you got your little blue card. Good day." And he started walking away. And the woman would say, "What little blue card?" He'd turn around and say, "I just wanted to make sure that you had been reached." "No." And he would say, "You've heard of the Canadian Advancement Board based in Ottawa?" And it's natural everyone would say

sure. He would say, "Fine, that's all I'm checking on. You've got all the information on the little blue card. Goodbye." Well, that was too much and they'd say, "What little blue card?" Then he would come back and start in. "These are hard times and the Canadian Advancement Board believes that the most effective way they have found to encourage people to support their fellow Canadians in times of depression like this when everybody is out of work and everybody is scratchin' – I'm scratchin', you're scratchin', everybody's scratchin' – is to promote through advertisement. What that little blue card would have told you was that you had agreed to accept free of charge, at no cost to you, copies of *Maclean's*, which contains only Canadian advertisement, advertising products made by Canadians for Canadians. Now isn't that a smart way to improve the economy? You get it free for three years. But you wouldn't expect them to handle the wrapping and postage charges, which come to three cents a week – that's all. And if I could I would like to ride around on my little red bicycle and collect your three cents every week but we can't do that. So just sign this and go to the cookie jar and get me three dollars and ninety-five cents." ZAP!

Sometimes it worked and sometimes it didn't, but Al's advice was that "you didn't improvise and try to fart around, you just delivered that track as often as you could. You didn't stay and argue. If there was resistance you just said goodbye and went and did the next one."[20]

Bill spent some time working the Edmonton area, probably in late May or June, and was able to use the Deke house in Edmonton as his base. There he met Wilbur Bowker, who had just completed his law degree and was spending the summer looking for a place to article. Bowker recalls how "thin-going" it was that summer for many. Another of Bowker's friends who was studying law and staying at the Deke house (Douglas McDermid, who became a justice in the Court of Appeal for Alberta) could only get a job selling Wear-ever aluminum. These salesman jobs were "a tough racket," said Bowker, and you could only survive at them if, like Bill, you "had enough hustle."[21]

This summer job *was* tough and Bill "got pretty streetwise." When he returned for his second year, he was "much more sophisticated," even though he never lost his "openness."[22] He may have matured, but he did not gain anything more tangible, as he had hoped. He was only able to break even with this job, and his mother had to finance his second year.

— "A WONDERFUL DISASTER": 1932 TO 1933 —

Bill registered again in Science, signing up for Chemistry, Botany, and Zoology. However, he also took Philosophy III, the first term of which was Social Psychology, and the second term the History of Philosophy. Sometime in the fall term Bill began having serious problems with his wrist and simply could not use his right hand to do the lab work required for his courses. As a result he was becoming increasingly disenchanted with his science program. In fact, the only science course he took an interest in was Chemistry because the lab was taught by Louis Slotin. Bill liked Slotin and would often visit with him over a coffee after class. Some of Bill's fraternity brothers, however, did not approve of his association with Slotin because he was Jewish, exemplifying another characteristic of fraternities that bothered Bill. But Bill was to remember Slotin for a remarkable act that took place fourteen years after he had him as a lab instructor. Slotin, who had been brought up and educated in Winnipeg, went on to work at Los Alamos, New Mexico, where he "built the explosive mechanism for the world's first atomic-bomb test," which took place on 16 July 1945. A short time after that, while adjusting the mechanism, "tickling the dragon's tail" as Slotin referred to it, his hand slipped. He reacted quickly and stopped the action. What stayed with Mitchell throughout the years was the story of how Slotin used his own body as a shield to save others from the radiation. Within days he died of radiation and his body was shipped home to Canada in a lead-lined coffin.[23]

Bill did not return to his diving during this year for a number of reasons. His wrist was a problem, but also Judy had become interested in someone else so the extra impetus to practise every day was missing. But the main reason was a run-in Bill had with a member at the Winter Club:

> The following fall when I came back I'd go down and go through my compulsories and optionals. One time I went down and went through to go to a locker and one of the other divers whose family did belong said, "What are you doing here, Mitchell?" I said, "I'm coming in to dive." He said, "What do you mean? You don't have a membership – or your family – in the Winnipeg Winter Club." And that was very hurting.[24]

Bill felt "humiliated" and, since the Winter Club had the only pool in Winnipeg with a three-metre board, he had no alternative place to go. Although it was not amusing at the time, he later satirized such elitist attitudes in "All Westerners Are Snobs." Here he described Manitobans as prone to first-family snobbery: "Unless you are a descendant of one of those who ran barefooted through the snow from Portage La Prairie to the relief of Fort Garry, came out with Lord Selkirk, [were] an original member of the council of Assiniboia, you can't consider yourself one of Manitoba's elite."[25]

Crucial to his second year at Manitoba was Bill's association with the Lehmann family. Peter Lehmann, like Bill, was in pre-med. He lived with his family in Winnipeg and would invite Bill over to his house on the weekends for meals. This was a great pleasure for Bill, who was no longer living in the fraternity house but in a rooming house on Wardlaw Street. The home-cooked meals and Peter's three interesting sisters (one went into drama) were enough to draw Bill to this household, but, even more, he was fond of the parents. He always called Mrs. Lehmann "Mother Lehmann." Peter's father was a doctor, and Bill and Dr. Lehmann would get involved in conversations about philosophy and human relations. Peter recalled that Bill would "talk and talk" with great excitement to his father about the things he was reading at university. Peter seldom joined in these conversations; in this regard he detected something "different" about Bill, who was more intense than most of his university friends.[26]

His wrist had now become quite swollen and painful, and Bill decided he had to do something about it. He made an appointment to see Dr. MacKinnon, whom he had not seen for about two years, and was told that he would have to start wearing his aluminum brace again. As Dr. MacKinnon readjusted the splint he asked Bill what he was taking at university: "I said, 'I am taking medicine.' And he said, 'What the hell are you talking about?'" It was then that Dr. MacKinnon told him that a career in medicine was impossible because of his tubercular history. Tuberculosis! Bill was shocked. He had never suspected that his mother had not told him the true nature of his wrist condition: "My mother didn't tell me, or didn't choose to tell me, because in her eyes to have TB in the family – that was limited to Indians and people from the London slums or Birmingham or somewhere – and was only slightly less reprehensible than congenital syphilis."[27]

Dr. MacKinnon explained that Bill had contracted bovine tuberculosis from drinking unpasteurized milk.[28] When he had initially injured his wrist the tuberculosis bacilli attacked the synovial membrane and then spread to the bone. The medical treatment prescribed for his condition – rest, prolonged and complete immobilization of the joint, cod-liver oil, as much sun as possible – was generally successful in causing the tuberculosis to go dormant and preventing it from spreading. But with excessive movement or stress, the dormant bacilli in a joint could become active again and spread to other parts of the body. Dr. MacKinnon urged Bill to have the bone fused in order to avoid further problems with his wrist. This treatment, anchylosis, involved scraping the two ends of the wrist bones and fusing them together, which would leave the wrist with no vertical movement and little if any lateral movement.

Bill was worried by this news. It did not help that he had learned the last year they were in Florida that his childhood hero

George Agnew had died as a result of bovine tuberculosis. Agnew had originally developed the disease as a result of a knee injury playing football at Princeton. It had been dormant for years but again flared up in his late thirties. Although he moved down to Arizona, it was too late. It had already spread to his stomach.[29]

Bill decided to take Dr. MacKinnon's advice and have his wrist fused. One evening when he was over at the Lehmanns' for dinner, he told Dr. Lehmann and Mrs. Lehmann what he was planning to do. After dinner, Mrs. Lehmann took him aside and had a chat with him. She had clearly been coached by Dr. Lehmann, who, Bill guessed, felt it would be unprofessional for him to directly disagree with Dr. MacKinnon's advice. Mrs. Lehmann persuaded Bill not to act too hastily, explaining that it was not just the movement of the wrist that she was concerned about. The danger was that the surgical intervention of scraping the bones to fuse them together could stir up things, or, in Mitchell's words, "echo through the rest of the body" in which case "I would end up like George in my late thirties dying of either TB of the stomach or of the bowel or it could have hit the spine, which is the other thing. So Mother Lehmann and Dr. Lehmann saved my life."[30] Bill did not get his wrist fused. But he had to give up his labs and failed to complete his science credits.

Bill, fortunately, had begun to enjoy philosophy and his arts courses more than the sciences. This was largely due to Professor Rupert Lodge, who taught him philosophy.[31] Like Miss Murray, Lodge made a lasting impression on him and was instrumental in altering his career direction: "It was Lodge who introduced me to the excitement of the inquiring mind, who helped me to discover that, philosophically speaking, I am an idealist."[32] Lodge was a Platonist who, like the fictional Dr. Millet in "The Alien," told his students that they had to choose a stance, that they could not be dualists and adopt more than one philosophy: "He [told] them that there were three broad ways to approach life in this universe, that they had their choice of the materialist, the phenomenalist, the realist – that the second of these was – untenable – illusory – that they could not travel on one, switch to another – change their minds." The first position, he goes on to remark, is blind hedonism. Rather he "invited them to the good life of the spirit, called them from the wild horses of appetite and passion" (A 72-73). Although Bill did not remain an idealist all his life, he described himself as a "Lodge boy" in the larger sense of having adopted a passion for philosophical inquiry.

Lodge's sense of humour and ability to make difficult concepts relevant attracted Bill. In "The Alien," Carlyle's enthusiastic description of his favourite philosophy professor, Dr. Millet, reflects Bill's feelings for Lodge: "His lectures were alive with illustration and energy; he was a good performer with a feeling for climax and dramatic surprise. He stung his students into statement, then backed them from premise to qualified premise . . ." (A 71). Stimulated by these lively debates, Bill did extremely well in Lodge's class, obtaining 86 per cent in his second term.

Lodge had definite views on the role of the university in educating the imagination. In the fall of 1931 various people debated in the editorial pages of the *Winnipeg Free Press* whether or not science and literature were "parallel functions of the human mind." Some argued that science was a body of fact to which new information can be added as acquired, but that literature was something else and that new writing did not make older authors obsolete. Another debater argued that literature courses at the university should not deal with older writers but with new writers in the way that science deals only with the newest ideas. Lodge disputed that science was simply a body of fact: "Science thus represents an adventure of the spirit, quite as much as poetry, and has quite as much power to thrill the imagination and liberate the mind from instinctive and local prejudices." He believed that a student of science should study the history of science in order to "acquire background and culture." He did not believe that either Science or Arts departments at universities should turn out technicians, but that "the primary function of our university departments is, surely, to enlighten and liberate the minds of our students so that, whatever their professions or interests in after-life, they may be able to bring an educated and cultured outlook to bear upon their problems."[33]

Although Bill took a principal role in *Spring*, a light, entertaining play which was the choice of the Science faculty, his wrist problem curtailed other activities this year. Yet it was his wrist which was also responsible for a significant change in his ambitions. He was forced to give up his plans for a career in medicine and, luckily, philosophy and Professor Lodge were there at the right moment. As he later put it, "My aborted medical career had been a wonderful disaster for it led to my discovery that as well as logic logic [that is, scientific logic] there is artistic logic, the logic which is the thematic foundation for play, poem, and novel structure" (*Eve* 256).

– EUROPE: SUMMER OF 1933 –

It was during the summer of 1933 that Bill discovered that he wanted to be a writer. Like many university students he decided to travel in Europe. His mother, a little concerned that her young-looking, unworldly son was setting off on his own, insisted that he write her frequently, so Bill began keeping a diary:

> I began every night in my tent, with a candle wherever I went, writing down whatever floated across my vision. And this, in turn, when I returned to the University of Manitoba, was a series for the literary quarterly, the *'Toban* [sic]. . . . And I suspect it was about then that I consciously said that I might be a writer. It would be at about nineteen.[34]

These diary pieces, excerpted in weekly letters to his mother, became the basis for his first publication. "Panacea for Panhandlers," which appeared in three parts (November 1933, February 1934, March 1934) in the *'toba*, the newly formed arts journal at the university, is the most immediate record of his travels that summer. As well as an introduction and a conclusion, there were twelve entries, dated from 4 May to 30 July 1933. Unfortunately the original note-book and letters to his mother were not kept.

When he later recounted to friends the adventures of this summer, he added many details that he had not dared write about to his mother or print in the *'toba*. In the 1990s he returned to these experiences and used them as the basis for Arthur Ireland's adventures in *For Art's Sake* (1992). In April 1991, after completing what is now chapter three of that novel, he wrote, "This probably is the most autobiographical thing I've ever found for my fiction. With very slight changes it is actually my summer of 1933."[35] Unlike Ireland, Bill was not going to the Sorbonne to study, but Ireland's travel adventures are very close to what actually happened to Bill.

With a hundred dollars, a gift from his mother, Bill set off for Europe right after exams. He caught a cattle train bound for Montreal and then was booked on a cattle boat to London. But he never made the connection, and that was only the first of a number of interesting – and sometimes dangerous – mishaps that occurred this summer.

Somewhere in northern Ontario Bill met Mr. McPhee, a "professional hobo" who sold egg boilers made from baling wire. He would twist lengths of wire into a contraption that had a handle and five half-spheres, each of which could hold one egg. Bill helped him make some, and at one of the train stops McPhee persuaded him to pick up some extra cash by helping him sell them. By the time they got back to the train yard the train had gone and they had a rough ride in the next train out: "We rode the coal tender through to Montreal, and it ain't very tender lying on that."[36] But, by the time they arrived in Montreal, the cattle boat had gone, and Bill had to find passage on another ship. This was difficult, for he did not have the proper union papers. Finally, he settled for a Greek tramp steamer, and on May 4 signed on as galley boy.

The *Onassapinellopi* was a "floating league-of-nations" with a crew composed of a Dutchman, Italian, German, and Turk and some Greeks, English, and French. Bill was put to work cleaning the deck:

This afternoon I worked with the deck hands, stoning down the bridge with sand and caustic. The Bos'n himself washed the deck down with the hose – he was like a little boy playing in a mud puddle, with his nose running, his feet sopping and his cap on the back of his head. He cursed the stones, he cursed the pails, he cursed the deck, he cursed the hose, the caustic of his tongue put on a new and shiny cleanliness on the deck.[37]

As galley boy he helped the cook, an old Turk, peel potatoes and do other galley chores. There were nine sheep on board to be used as food and, every three days, he had to help slaughter one: "The cook's helper would slash the jugular of a sheep, skin and disembowel it on the deck between the galley and the rail. Blood and guts were very resistant to soogey and holy stone" (*Art* 52). For the rest of his life Mitchell's stomach turned at the thought of mutton stew or lamb curry. One tense moment occurred when the trimmer, known as the Liverpool Rat, attacked the coal passer with a butcher knife. The trimmer was pinned down, put in irons, and taken off to a mental institution when they arrived in port.

The *Onassapinellopi* docked in Purfleet on the Thames down-river from London. Bill skipped ship and took lodgings in a place that had been recommended in the first pub he visited. He was taken in by Mrs. Sage, a white-haired, vulnerable-looking landlady who seemed to be quite afraid of him. Her refrain was, "Mind. You don't do me no 'arm – I don't do you no 'arm" (*Art* 56). Seemingly sweet and motherly, she offered him a cup of tea before bed. The next morning he woke up late feeling very groggy. When he went back to the pub to get a meal, he discovered that his wallet and money were missing. Mrs. Sage "had broken her promise to do him no harm" (*Art* 64). She had spiked his tea with "knock-out drops" and then robbed him after he had passed out.

Bill, fortunately, had secreted away some traveller's cheques. He used two pounds to buy a used New Hudson motorbike, "immediately christened the Rock of Gibraltar – neither would move if you essayed to push them."[38] He made his way to the coast without any problem, and from Dover he took the ferry to Calais. Halfway to Paris, his motorbike stalled on the railway tracks and, unable to push it off the tracks quickly enough, he had to jump aside and helplessly watch as it was demolished by a train.[39]

Now on foot and hitchhiking, he stopped the first night at a farm and asked the farmer if he could camp in his field. As described in *For Art's Sake*, his first-year-university French amazed the farmer:

> "Bon soir, Monsieur. Je suis un étudiant canadien qui fait la tour de monde pour étudier et je porte à dos ma petite tente. Je veux permission d'employer un de vos champs pour monter ma tente."
>
> "Eloise – Eloise! Viens vite! Nous y avons un fou canadien!"
> The farmer's wife came running.
>
> It seemed that he had pronounced "champs" as "chambre," "tente" as "tante," so that the farmer thought he'd said: "I carry my little *aunt* on my back, and I would like permission to use one of your *rooms* to mount my aunt. (*Art* 61)

By June 10 he was in Paris, where he took a place in the Latin Quarter. Each night as he returned to the hotel from his sightseeing he was accosted by one particular prostitute: "Eh, Chéri, est-ce que tu veux une tranche, une belle tranche?" She did not take kindly to his refusals. After attempting to engage him three nights in a row she became aggressive and tried to physically manoeuvre him into the hotel. When he swore at her and called her "un sale cochon," she attacked him: "She let me have her kneecap in the nuts and I dropped down." She gouged his face and eyes with her long nails and tore off his shirt, calling him, among other things, "Verte écume de pissoire!"[40] He had chosen, apparently quite innocently, a hotel used by prostitutes. Indeed, L'Hôtel Espagnol, he claimed, was a *famous* whorehouse known throughout Europe.[41] He did not include this incident in his diary – nor did his mother ever hear about it.

He visited the Louvre and climbed to the top of the Eiffel Tower, but these were not the experiences that formed the usable past for his fiction. He was slightly more interested in the cafe and street-life scenes that had been described by Hemingway and Fitzgerald in the 1920s. Morley Callaghan and John Glassco had been in Paris about four years earlier than Bill, and they would write about their Parisian adventures in the early 1960s. Bill went to the Folies Bergère, but "the true end of all innocence" came when he went to the Folies de Paris, where he witnessed "the priest and his religious-rite copulation with the nun – dog fashion!" (*Art* 65). Already Bill's instinct for burlesque and eye for telling detail were at play when he described the "Madame Butterfly" routine:

One scene – the dance of the butterfly – depicted the birth, life and death of a beautiful butterfly. It was so grotesque that it was impossible to refrain from laughing – and I've never felt guiltier. . . .

Seven of the dancers appeared as leaves blown hither and thither to the tune of "Alouetta." But the very scantily clad leaves had unfortunately forgotten to erase the lines left by their garters.

There came a lull in the flurrying of the leaves and the butterfly was ushered in with a resounding crescendo of the piano. Two of the leaves then took up positions at the back, standing very much like horses on a hot day – resting with one hip out of joint and arms in Egyptian fashion. The others arrayed themselves around Madame Butterfly, who, with her coy, mincing steps, her pirouettes and whirls, was quite entrancing. Madame Butterfly, artistically fluttering her wings, carried on the good work while the light changed from different shades of bilious green to an anaemic yellow and blue, imparting an almost human expression to the blank faces of the semi-nude leaves.

It was difficult to decide whether it was meant as a burlesque or not – in any case, upon the death of Madame Butterfly, I lost any vestige of self-control that had kept me from going into fits of laughter. As Madame Butterfly drooped dying to the floor, there ensued a shuffling and stamping of the leaves, resembling nothing so much as people on a cold day trying to keep warm by flinging their arms about and stamping circulation back into their feet.[42]

One of Bill's fraternity brothers, Blair Ferguson, had come to France to improve his French and was living in a *pension* in Tours. One day he noticed a "scruffy-looking" figure looking in one of the shop windows. Noting "Canada" written on the knapsack he approached and was amazed to discover that it was Bill. He offered to take him back to his *pension* to clean up. While Blair went off to check things with the two sisters who managed the *pension*, Bill was left standing in the vestibule. One of the staff mistook him for a tramp and when Blair returned he found Bill being chased away with a broom. But by dinner that night Bill had "charmed" them all with descriptions of his adventures. Blair was amused by the force of Bill's charm. Not only did the staff fix up a cot for Bill in Blair's room, but they took his clothes and washed and mended them, "all free of charge." Bill spent about a week with Blair, cycling around the Loire valley and visiting various châteaux. Oblivious to social conventions, Bill did not realize he had overstayed his welcome, and Blair recalled that he "practically put him on the train" to get rid of him.[43]

On the outskirts of Tours, Bill started hitchhiking again. He always found someone interesting to hook up with, first a young Austrian who was cycling with a small monkey and barrel organ, then a priest who drove him through — and almost off — the Pyrenees, and then a truck driver taking cows to a Basque version of the bullfight. The truck driver dropped him off on the outskirts of Pau at two in the morning, and Bill headed into the city to put up his tent:

After crawling from my sleeping bag this morning, I peered forth from the interior of the light-weight dwarfed French army tent I had pitched on the darkened and deserted lot the night before. I had emerged halfway out into the tropical noonday sun before I realized that my deserted island of poplars was in the center of a semi-busy boulevard. A batoned Gendarme was directing occasional traffic some 150 yards away, and a cafe through the trees to the left was preparing for its noonday clientele of aperitif drinkers. I clutched the tent flaps shut, pulled on my trousers after unrolling them from the form of last night's pillow – and after coming into the open again spent the most embarrassed ten minutes of my life taking down and packing away the tent for the day. I felt like nothing so much as a nudist fanatic practising a bit of applied "nudistry" on his way to the office one fine morning. . . .

Allah be praised! I didn't back out into civilization, into Paw [Pau], city favored of the kings of Navarre.[44]

On July 30 he reached Biarritz, the famous seaside resort of kings and queens and of the rich and famous. Hemingway, Picasso, and movie stars like Charlie Chaplin made this a favourite resort in the first half of the twentieth century. Bill's last *'toba* instalment relayed his excitement at seeing the Bay of Biscay from the clifftop overlooking Biarritz:

> Below, at the foot of the plough-shared cliff, it laced its blue green into foam with the same quiet rhythm, and then slipped noiselessly back down the gentle slope of the sandy beach, leaving behind hesitating white semi-circles that finally slipped silently into the next line of surf. Description of impressions is impossible.

As he lay "on the ferny crown of the cliff," captivated by the scene, two young men greeted him. An identification card worn around their necks explained that they were German Swiss just returning from a trip of two years to Africa and Greece:

> Neither could speak French or English – I couldn't speak Spanish or German. Then with a sudden brain wave I bravely

blurted out, "Venio ab Canada." The chubby fellow's eyes lit up and he replied with – "Sumus studiosi" – and finally as I made no reply – "Potio?" As I silently cursed the rashness of expecting assistance from a three-year dead high school Latin – Caesar tipped an imaginary bottle to his mouth by way of demonstrating. A few minutes later we were passing my litre of wine around and eating their bread and my sausage.[45]

Bill found in his travels to France something quite unlike the mood of disillusionment and the broken relationships pervading the expatriate fiction of Hemingway, Fitzgerald, or Glassco. In fact, what is striking about this last scene in "Panacea" is its sense of making contact or, to use one of Mitchell's fondest metaphors, "bridging" across barriers of language and culture.

When a friend rediscovered "Panacea for Panhandlers" and showed the three pieces to Mitchell sometime in the early 1970s, he had a good laugh: "When I looked at that stuff, it sure made me hang in there with young writers. It was a cross – sort of between Christopher Morley – Robert Louis Stevenson – *Travels With a Donkey*. And it was pompous! It was mannered! It was phoney!"[46] The "Panacea" pieces have an unusual mix of the pretentious and the casual. The sophisticated man of the world vies with the earthy prairie boy. On the one hand he can unremarkably describe signposts as "pointing desultorily" and a priest walking in "religious quietude," but then he notes with more individuality the "tang of forest mold and husky pulsing beat of insects." Slightly more forced is his description of the trees, "like green inverted ice cream cones minus the ice cream, of course."[47] But, with freshness and an un-tourist-like eye, he describes "a walnut-coloured woman in sabots" who had "a little black moustache hardly distinguishable from the dark hue of her lip."[48]

Bill stopped his "Panacea" articles at this point in his journey even though he went on to spend another month in Europe before returning to Canada. On the beach at Biarritz he moved into a hotel which was run by a Basque family, the Pennes. Bill and the Pennes' son, Roger, were lifeguards on the strip of beach in front of the hotel. Adjoining the hotel beach was, much to Bill's surprise, a semi-nude beach. He quickly became used to it, and was highly amused by one irate American woman who ordered him to remove from the beach one of the bare-breasted women who was attracting her husband's attention and who had come over to the Pennes' hotel beach.[49] He also quickly became comfortable wearing *un slip*, the skimpy bathing suit worn by French men. Later, when he wore his *slip* back home in the Weyburn pool, his cousin Monty described it as brief enough to fit in a thimble.

He had worked for two to three weeks when he and Roger decided to hitchhike to San Sebastian, just over the border in Spain. On the way back they were thirsty and stopped at a waterfall by the side of the road. Although he had been warned about polluted water and had been very careful up to this point, Bill persuaded Roger that this water could not possibly be contaminated as it was falling through rock. He was wrong. They both came down with severe cases of Spanish flu and were bed-ridden for a while. Bill's illness put an end to his summer adventures. He made his way back to Paris, where he was apparently well enough to take his fraternity brother, Blair Ferguson, to the Folies. In London he stayed with a friend of the family for a few days until his mother sent him fare for the steamer back to Canada.

Bill's return voyage on the *Empress of Britain* was a far cry from his trip over on the Greek tramp steamer. Although he was in steerage, he took full advantage of the ship's amenities, including its swimming pool and springboard (although the lifeguard reprimanded him for wearing his *slip* and ordered him to get into something more appropriate). On the boat he met Margaret Beattie, a student from the University of Manitoba he had known from one of his classes. She had gone to England that summer with her parents to attend her brother's graduation from Oxford. Margaret and her father noted immediately how thin Bill was and invited him to eat with them on numerous occasions.[50] The Beatties were in a higher-class section, and Mitchell recalled sneaking up to attend the dances which were held in the ballroom. Here he recalls "doing the Charleston" with Margaret, although "not well."[51] However, he must have impressed her in some way, for back at university they started dating.

For Arthur Ireland in *For Art's Sake*, this summer of 1933 represented a "necessary loss of innocence." Perhaps that is both too grand and too suggestive a phrase to describe Bill's own experience. But certainly his trip to Europe opened his eyes to people and attitudes unfamiliar to his Presbyterian small-town sensibility, even though his California and Florida experiences had already taken him a long way from Weyburn. But in Europe things happened *to* him. He was conned, robbed, and propositioned – by both sexes; he learned to drink wine – and had been violently drunk; he had been without money and hungry; he had been left speechless by the stunning natural landscape and left laughing by the unnatural grotesquerie of the Folies. He loved the adventure of it all and knew he could use these experiences to "get good laughter mileage" (*Art* 65) – and more. He thought he could be a writer.

— THIRD YEAR: 1933 TO 1934 —

Bill changed over to Arts in his third year, taking Economics and Philosophy. Academically this year was the highlight of his university experience. He achieved mid to high 70s in his economics courses, but he excelled in philosophy, which he again took from Rupert Lodge. He received 88 per cent in the first part and 80 per cent in the second part. Mitchell claimed that he won the gold medal in philosophy for that year. He never saw it but remembered being told by another student that he had been awarded the honour. The award is not listed on his transcript, but that may be because he did not complete all of the course requirements for his B.A. degree and therefore did not graduate. The switch from Science to Arts left him short two arts course credits.

The campus had been in transition during his second year, with the senior students attending classes at the new Fort Garry campus, south of the city. Bill now had to take his classes there, so he joined a car pool. Margaret Beattie was in that group and probably drew him into the artsy crowd she was going with. Frank Pickersgill drove the car. Frank, who later joined the secret service, was involved in many literary activities. He wrote editorials for the new arts magazine and some items for the literary supplement that came out with the student newspaper, the *Manitoban*.[52] Bill remembers being in Moliere's *Le Malade Imaginaire* with Frank that year, both in supporting roles.[53] The group often gathered at Frank and Jack Pickersgill's house on Sunday nights where there were "pots of coffee," "mounds of sandwiches," "crazy games," and "real conversation."[54] Bill may have attended some of these evenings, but was not a regular. Two of the people in this group, Mary Lile Love and Frank Jones, were involved in the establishment of the *'toba* and likely encouraged Bill to submit something on his travels in Europe for the first issue, due out before Christmas. The first issue "met with a very enthusiastic reception" and sold out in two days. Bill, with his "travel talks," is noted in the 1934 yearbook for making the *'toba* a "very successful magazine."[55] Among the other contributors who later gained recognition were Marshall McLuhan and J.W. McInnis.

Bill and Margaret went together for a short time and she remembers him as interesting and sophisticated. Like some of his other friends, particularly his female friends, Margaret recalled that they would go on long walks during which Bill told her stories about his adventures in Florida. It is possible that he took her to the first dance of the new term, the Pi Phi Prosperity Prom, which rather too optimistically took "Prosperity" as its theme.[56] Another fall event was University Day, held on Thanksgiving Day, October 9. Prime Minister R.B. Bennett addressed three thousand university students on the topic "Don't Lose Your Ideals."[57] The closing event was a dance at the new Students' Union building, and Bill and Margaret were both on the list of those who attended.

At the end of February, Bill also attended the dinner and dance in honour of students graduating from the Faculty of Arts even though he would not be graduating. He was now dating Jeannie

Bell, an Arts student who was a year behind him, and he invited her to this dance. Bill had the usual excitements and disappointments in love during his university years, but none of his girlfriends became serious interests. In "The Alien" he presents very convincingly a couple of exchanges between characters on the subject of love and loss of virginity. One of the fraternity brothers was concerned "with the problem of being a virgin at almost twenty" (*A* 128) and spoke to his friends about "visceral tensions, mental conflicts, sublimation" (*A* 129). But Carlyle preferred to be discreet about his love life. Even with his best friend, Rosie Betton, he resented "the prospect of a warm little talk about sex secrets" (*A* 135). In spite of Carlyle's warning, "Oh, spare me, Betton!" Rosie goes on to tell Carlyle about his first sexual experience.[58] Bill no doubt participated in such "bull sessions" (*A* 130), but his own love life was more cerebral than physical. Mitchell recalled that "until Merna [his wife] most girls threw me over,"[59] although elsewhere he revealed that one of his girlfriends was heartbroken when he decided to ask Jeannie Bell to the dance and not her.[60]

Mitchell used this graduation dance and his actual date with Jeannie Bell as the basis for a scene in *Since Daisy Creek* in which Colin Dobbs, the protagonist, gives his fraternity pin to his soon-to-be wife, Sarah Halstead. The fraternity dances as Mitchell described them here and in "The Alien" took place in one of Winnipeg's prestigious hotels. The custom was to rent a number of hotel rooms where the boys and their dates could do their drinking. The actual dance took place in the crystal room of the Royal Alexandra Hotel. Bill did not have good luck with his dance dates. Jeannie Bell, like her fictional counterpart, Sarah, in *Since Daisy Creek*, had a plantar wart on her foot and was unable to dance more than the first dance. So Bill took Jeannie out to the fire escape and "read her all of the Song of Solomon from the Gideon Bible" (*SD* 79). As Mitchell ironically commented, "You know I had great promise as a seducer."[61]

If Bill was a bit of a "talker," he put this talent to good use as a debater at the Arts Debate held in March. The issue was "that no censorship would be preferable to that now in force." Bill and Margaret Adamson argued for the negative, defending censorship against the affirmative team, Leonard Levi and Elsa Lehmann (Peter Lehmann's sister). Bill and Margaret were successful. Bill's argument was that "censorship did represent the will of the people." According to the reporter, Bill, "to give more life to his debate, brought out an empty beer mug and showed how people blew the froth off their beer to illustrate that man would get that which he wanted no matter what the consequences were."[62] No doubt Bill's prop created more of a stir than his opposition's book of Shakespeare's censored sayings.

During his final year at Winnipeg, Bill became more avidly involved in theatre. He did not act in the Science Faculty's one-act play this year, which was again being directed by Tommy Tweed, but Tommy introduced him to John Craig, the director of Winnipeg's Little Theatre. John Craig and his wife, Irene, were very important to Bill in those years. He recalls visiting them in their apartment and, although cast lists do not indicate that Bill had any significant role in the productions between 1931 and 1934, he claims that he became involved in at least two of their plays.

John Craig was a talented director. His first season at the Winnipeg Little Theatre began in September 1930, and by the following year it was reported that "the Winnipeg Little Theatre is looked up to as 'something first rate' by other similar bodies in Canada."[63] Craig encouraged community involvement in the theatre, and there were often newspaper notices requesting those interested in acting to audition. His aim was to create a genuinely Canadian theatre. A few years into his tenure there it was obvious that Craig was making his mark, and he was instrumental in creating the Winnipeg Little Theatre as "a model which cities both east and west would like to copy."[64]

Mitchell remembered playing the young Northern spy in Craig's production of William Gillette's *Secret Service* in December 1933. He also said that he had a role in *Prunella* but dropped out before it was performed in March 1933. *Secret Service*, subtitled "a

*Bill's doodlings on his economics textbook while
he was attending the University of Manitoba in 1933.*

romance of the Southern Confederacy," was about the attempt by
Union forces to capture the city of Richmond during the American
Civil War.[65] There was a huge cast of thirty-five, and Bill's role must
have been too small to warrant specific mention among those named
in the *Winnipeg Free Press*. Bill did not shine on stage this year as he
had in St. Petersburg, but he got a taste of good amateur theatre and
also met people with whom he would work later in his career, such
as Tommy Tweed and Esse Ljungh, who was later to direct some of
the CBC *Jake and the Kid* radio episodes.

During these three years Bill had pursued his dreams – medicine, diving, acting, and writing. And, a bit by luck and a bit by
choice, he discovered where his real interests and talents lay. In his

third-year textbook, *Principles of Political Economy,*[66] Bill drew a caricature self-portrait with a narrow face, crooked smile, and owlish glasses hung over big ears. Over this page and the next he tried out variations of his name in printed form: "Billy," "Willie," "Bill," "Will," and "W.O. Mitchell." He also experimented with his signature, "Mitchell," and then, three times, "Bill Mitchell." On the next page he wrote "Wm.O. Mitchell." He may very well have been searching for the name he wanted to be known by. On all three instalments of "Panacea for Panhandlers" he opted for Bill Mitchell. Seeing his words in print, his name on the cover, and experiencing the "applause" from his readers, he knew then that he might be a writer. This early writing perhaps revealed "the earnestness of youth slightly drunk on its own articulate dignity" (*A* 153), but it was a heady beginning.

All of W.O.'s writing, except for "Panacea for Panhandlers," was published under the name W.O. Mitchell. Initials had a special significance for him. His father had commonly been called O.S. and his Uncle Jim was called J.T. R.W. God is the name he chose for Brian's fantasy playmate in Who Has Seen the Wind, *another echo of his own father. As Brian says to his father, "I call him R.W. like you do with 'Judge' Mortimer – E.L. and Mr. Hoffman – S.F. and like that" (*WW 46*). So "W.O. Mitchell" linked him with his father, and it had a more sophisticated sound to it than plain "Bill" Mitchell.*

Around 1969 W.O. made another clear decision about naming. When we returned from England, the first grandchild greeted his grandfather at the airport: "Hello, Grandpa." Not only was W.O. shocked that his Canadian-born grandchild had picked up an English accent (he looked at us and asked, "What the hell have you done to my grandson?") but he had called him "Grandpa"! W.O.'s reply, "I'll break your jaw if you ever call me 'Grandpa' again," was a joke that came to be passed down through the family and served as a firm warning to subsequent grandchildren. Not one of his six grandchildren called him "Grandpa."

Although this was said jokingly – albeit in his typically dramatic way! – W.O. had a serious explanation for not wanting to be labelled Grandpa or Grandfather. He thought labels interfered with the one-on-one relationship he wanted with his grandchildren. He did not want to be cast in the old-grandpa stereotype, to be dismissively thought of as a grey-haired, cane-carrying, rocking-chair-ridden, crotchety old man.

The first grandchild called him "W.O." – and it stuck, not just with the children but with the rest of the family. By the mid-1980s he was known throughout the country as "W.O."

8

DEPRESSION YEARS

— 1934 to 1939 —

I N WINNIPEG, Bill saw some of the effects of the worst years of
the Depression. Crops had been destroyed by grasshopper infes-
tations (the worst occurring in 1933) and drought. In the spring
of 1934 the "worst drought since 1894" set in with severe dust storms
and long dry spells. Hundreds of thousands of acres of land lay
waste.[1] Thousands of transients moved across the prairies for har-
vesting time and then out – to Vancouver or back East – for the
winter season. In the fall of 1932, Bill's second year, there was a daily
average of 150 transients moving in and out of Winnipeg.[2] The
downtown location of the university and fraternity house meant
that Bill would often see the unemployed lining up for food, for
work, or hanging around the train yards. In *Who Has Seen the Wind*,
Mitchell describes the fall of 1932 and the culture of the transients:

> Fall brought another crop failure to the district; the land was
> dotted now with empty farmhouses, their blank windows
> staring out over the spreading prairie, their walls piled high
> with rippled banks of black dust. . . . Freights were dotted with
> unemployed, many of them young boys who had never had jobs
> in their lives – "gay cats" and "scenery hogs," who had left the

East to find work in the West, or the West to find work in the East. In winter-time they worked for five dollars a month on farms, or lived in ten-cent "scratch houses and pogies" in Calgary, Regina, Winnipeg or any of the prairie cities, standing on street corners and "dinging" passers-by for the price of a cup of coffee. According to their vices they divided themselves into: "McGoof Hounds," "junkers," "winos," "canned-heat artists," "rubby-dubs," "wolves," "proosians," "gazoonas," "gazeets," and "gazats." According to their way of getting food: "winter christians and mission stiffs," "ding-bats," "dinos," "lump and stew-bums." Some carried "bindles"; all hated "the mounties, harness bulls, and town clowns"; they spoke patronizingly of farmers as "hoziers and johns." They left their pencilled marks on doors of generous people: "Champ 32," "CPR 10," CNR Jos"; "21-Circle." (*WW* 197-98)

The university community and his mother's financial support cushioned Bill from the Depression. On his journeys in the summer of 1932 across the prairies and then in 1933 riding the rails to Montreal, he began to experience what the Depression meant. But over the next five years he was for the most part on his own and discovered first-hand the impact the Depression had on people's lives.

— SEATTLE: 1934 TO 1936 —

Knowing how tough it was to find work and not wanting to go back to the University of Manitoba to complete his last two credits, Bill decided to do some more travelling. He and Connie Benson (his friend from Carlyle Lake summers) planned to ship out together to South America as deckhands on a freighter leaving from Seattle. Connie lived with his grandmother in Bellingham, Washington, and had just graduated in Engineering from Washington State University. Bill hitched rides to the States with various people, including his summertime pal Bill Cameron, stopping in Cranbrook, B.C., for a few weeks to make some money picking strawberries.

While working his way down to Seattle Bill did something which he always looked back on with some embarrassment. During the previous year when he had acted for John Craig at the Winnipeg Little Theatre he had acquired some skill in the application of make-up. He decided that a moustache was just the thing to make himself look older and, unable to grow one of his own, resorted to theatre tricks. He soaked and straightened braided lengths of crepe hair, tinted and cut them into one-inch bunches, then, after applying them with spirit gum, trimmed his "moustache."[3] This was not a one-time exercise. He wore this guise for a few months, replacing it whenever he had a shower. It was so realistic, though, that even his cousin Mildred (his Uncle Jim's daughter and his former grade-two teacher), with whom he stayed for a few weeks at her home near Aberdeen, Washington, did not know that it was fake.

While at cousin Mildred's he took on another pose. He began dating a girl whose father was French Canadian, although she herself did not speak French. Much to Mildred's amusement, he assumed a French accent in order to impress her.[4] Mitchell recalled that part of the impulse behind this subterfuge and the "careful pretense" of the moustache was a desire to look more grown up and sophisticated, "but at the same time I was wishfully kind of thinking I'd like to be an actor." He never told his cousin Mildred, or the girl, that the moustache was not real. As with his childhood interest in magic, Mitchell took delight in fooling people. But this was also a deception in the name of vanity and perhaps that is what embarrassed him most: "I wore a false moustache, for Christ's sakes, for three months. I'm not comfortable with that. I think I'm ashamed of that kind of phoniness."[5]

He met Connie in Bellingham, but a longshoreman's strike interfered with their plans to ship out to South America. The strike was not settled until the end of July, so Bill spent most of July on Orcas Island fly fishing and cliff diving with Connie and one of his friends. The diving meant the end of the fake moustache. It was while cliff diving here that he did his highest dive, of some ninety feet. They were all quite fearless, and they kept going up higher and

higher on the cliffs only quitting when Bill "just missed an underwater deadfall in a new place."[6]

With his travel plans thwarted, Bill decided to stay in Seattle
for a while and attend university. In September 1934 he enrolled in
the Journalism program at the University of Washington. His performance in the first half of term was abysmal and he was "reported
to the dean" and put on probation. Of the four courses he enrolled
in he received a passing grade (C) in only one, News Writing.[7] He
failed Short Story Writing, a course geared towards journalism rather
than creative writing, which he took from Vernon Mackenzie, a
Canadian who had worked for *Maclean's* and been an editor of
Cosmopolitan. Bill wrote a number of short stories at this time, one
which he recalled:

> The third short story was of a cowboy who went over to France.
> Guess where? The south of France. Guess what he ends up in?
> In a bloody bullfight. He decides it's very interesting. He's trav-
> elled rodeos and things back in Canada – but that's kept for a
> surprise. He gets a picador's horse and what he does is – I didn't
> know anything about what I was doing about either one of the
> things – he bulldogs the bull instead of using the thing prop-
> erly. Even as I look back it was pretty imaginative.[8]

Obviously "imaginative" stories were not the ticket for a pass in this
journalism course.

In the second half of the term (winter 1935) he took three more
courses in Journalism and one in Applied Psychology, passing three
of the four. But the highlight of his time in Seattle was a play-writing
course he sat in on, gratis, thanks to the kindness of the professor,
Glenn Hughes. Hughes, who taught English and Drama at the university from 1911 to 1961, was the originator of the Penthouse Players
Theater in Seattle. Hughes's course was an important influence.
Mitchell said that Hughes approached writing with "pragmatic and
practical suggestions" which had a "levering effect" for him.
Hughes's advice about conflict and the balancing of antagonists and

knowing "what your play was about, where it was and who it was" were useful, but in the end "they just simply were not enough."9 It would be another five years before Bill would meet a creative-writing teacher who was much more helpful. In the meantime, he put in a lonely and frustrating apprenticeship in which he churned out "one-cell deep" mechanical pieces which only resulted in a sheaf of rejection slips. But Hughes's groundwork in play writing was very useful to him and is partially responsible for Mitchell's success in developing a full-fledged career as a playwright as well as a novelist.

Mitchell wrote three one-act plays for Hughes. The first one involved "a wimp, a stereotype," coming into a psychiatrist's office:

> And he was telling the psychiatrist about how his wife dominated him in everything. But it was a clever thing because I ended up with him switching the roles of ascendancy/submission and getting the psychiatrist then to unload. And the ironic ending was the psychiatrist is in worse shape than this patient.10

The second play, set on board a ship, was about a cockney who was obsessed with a "pillow 'is mother give 'im." The third was called "Cabin Fever":

> It was about two old Scottish guys living in the bush and they can't stand each other. And it ends up with them fighting with each other and divvying up everything. And then they get to the canoe and they get the crosscut saw, one on each side, and saw the canoe in half and then they can't decide who gets the front end, the bow end, or who gets the stern of it.11

Hughes was impressed enough by Bill's plays that he suggested submitting them to Samuel French's, which publishes plays in chapbooks for professional and amateur theatre groups. Bill did not act on Hughes's advice. While he appeared to have dismissed and forgotten about them, some of the ideas from these plays lay dormant and sprouted years later. In 1951 the situation dramatized in "Cabin

Fever" surfaced in a *Jake and the Kid* radio drama, and in 1974 the ironic reversal of patient and psychiatrist became the central situation in a television drama which was adapted into a major stage play, *Back to Beulah*.

Bill's other preoccupation during this time was Margaret Laird, from Norfolk, Virginia, who was enrolled in first year. Bill and Margaret, along with two other university friends, Proctor Melquist and Archie Taft and their girlfriends, would go out: "We used to go into the Blue Danube or the Club Victor there. This is when the beer halls came about. Fifty cents and you got a gallon jug and each of you took a turn." On one of these outings they celebrated Bill's birthday:

> It was a lot of fun and indeed for my twenty-first birthday we went in and I think Margaret was only seventeen or eighteen. And I remember the waiter came up and said, he spoke to me, "How old are you?" It was the only time I ever did get checked out down there. And I said, "I am twenty-one today," because twenty-one was the age you could go in. He said, "Outside." And I was the only guy there who was twenty-one – Archie and Proctor weren't. And it didn't do any good explaining this *was* my birthday.[12]

Margaret returned to Norfolk after spring term, and Bill saw her off on the train: "It was 'heart-rendering' – I say 'heart-rendering' deliberately because I've got my tongue in my cheek as I look back. I remember going out and walking up and down and being dreadfully sorry for myself." Bill looked forward to seeing Margaret when the fall term began. He thought of this relationship as quite serious, serious enough that he wrote home to his mother about Margaret and sent her a photo.[13]

In the spring and early summer Bill spent a great deal of his spare time boating with Proctor Melquist and Archie Taft. The three of them invested in a boat, christened *The Banshee and the Canshee*, which they would tell prospective girlfriends was their yacht: "It had been a large ocean-ship lifeboat, big double-ender, and it had a lug sail on it and a cabin had been built on it. Archie found it – seventy-five dollars – and we paid twenty-five dollars down on it. Proctor's dad was head of a paint company out there and had a lot of leftover black paint so we painted it black."[14] On weekends the three of them would hitchhike from Seattle through Lake Union and the canals to get out to the sound where they would pick up jugs of beer and sail.

Bill had managed to survive the fall and winter by doing odd jobs and working as a houseboy at the Deke fraternity house. But steady summer employment was difficult to come by. He tried selling space-rate classified advertising for the *Seattle Times*, but this was a commission job and as a rookie he was unable to earn much. He worked briefly in a salmon cannery pasting labels on cans. That, too, did not last long. Then, fortunately for Bill, his fraternity connections paid off again. Don Callison, a Deke fraternity brother, invited him along to his father's summer house on the Hood peninsula to help tend the extensive grounds. Don's father, known as the "Cascara King," had made his fortune marketing cascara bark, the main ingredient in laxatives.[15] Bill was offered room and board in exchange for his work. The grounds were so large that it took the boys more than a week to mow the grass, and then they just started all over again. They spent a lot of their spare time springboard diving on the Hood Canal.

When Bill crossed the U.S. border in June 1934 he had been granted a six-month visitor's pass. By now he had been in the States for fifteen to sixteen months and for most of that time he worked illegally. He made no attempt to hide the fact that he was a Canadian and "there were cracks always floating around about Mitchell's one of the aphids on the maple leaf kind of thing."[16] Some time near the end of October the immigration authorities paid him a visit at the fraternity house:

> Somebody must have squealed on me and the immigration
> people got in touch with me and they were very decent about
> it. They said, "Why don't you go on back into Canada and then

come back down here and come in properly under a visa and we'll forget about the fact that you're over the length of time and you've been working more or less while you were here." So I returned to Canada.[17]

With about one hundred dollars in his pocket (which his mother had sent him) and a bus ticket to Weyburn, he was all set to return. As it turned out, it would be four years before he got back to Weyburn.

His fraternity friends had a going-away party for him at the Blue Danube. That night they "practically poured" him on the bus: "I woke up on the bus. I'd passed out, I guess – just beer. I discovered that while I had been asleep, euphemistically speaking, somebody had rolled me and I had twenty-seven cents." He found himself in Fernie, B.C., without a ticket and without cash, and it was late at night. By hanging around the beer parlour and helping clean up at closing time, he persuaded the night man to let him stay. Things didn't look much brighter in the morning:

> I had a cup of coffee for a nickel and that left me twenty-two cents. I had nothing to eat that day and I couldn't get a ride out (I'm headed for Weyburn) and that night was Halloween night and there was a big Fernie party at the Legion Hall. And I went late to it. They weren't taking tickets. I was a classy dresser in those days – I had a topcoat, a hat, and a suitcase, and so when they had sandwiches I ate quite a few and then I made several trips out to the cloakroom and stuffed sandwiches into my topcoat pocket. And then I slept that night on the beer-parlour tables again.
>
> I still had twenty-two cents, and I went into the cafe to get a cup of coffee. I remember the waitress was blonde, not unattractive but not all that good-looking. I said, "Can I have a cup of coffee?" She said, "Okay," and she came back with bacon and eggs and coffee and toast and I said, "Hey, I can't pay for this."

She said, "I know you can't, I saw you. We catered that party last night and I saw you stuffing sandwiches in your topcoat."[18]

After his breakfast Bill went to the Fernie filling station to see if he could catch a ride out. Finally he got one. Relating the event some forty-eight years later, Mitchell recreated it all again in precise detail: "I saw a car stop that had California licence plates on it and I asked him where he was going and he said Calgary. His name was Elijah Barron, the Christian Jew." Elijah was coming back to Canada, because "he had got exported, kicked out." Mitchell interrupted himself at this point to say, "You know, I get accused of being too romantic and exotic and everything else, but in fact life is colourful and I notice it":

Well, out of Fernie a ways we stopped and I am hearing him quoting Corinthians 1 and 2 and not saying anything because I got a ride to Calgary. And we go into this place to get a fill-up. There was a grizzled old guy and he was from Somerset or somewhere. There were two of them sitting there and Elijah said, "Bless you, brother," and this old guy looked at him and he turned to his partner, and he says, "We've got another Christer." He said, "Yes, I have drunk of the fountain of life." Then this old miner began to quiz him and he says, "And you believe in that stuff about 'eaven and everything do you?" And he says, "Of course I do." "You believe in an after-life?" "Yes, I do." He said, "Well, and just by gettin' saved, eh?" And Elijah said, "Yes, that is the way." And he said, "Well, I know a lot of miserable sons-of-bitches that if they got saved could they then go to 'eaven?" And he said, "Yes, they could." And then he says, "Tell me something, I've wondered about it a lot." And he says, "Do they have dogs in 'eaven?" And Elijah said, "No." He said, "Well, there you are." He says, "That's not the place for me." He says, "I've known some pretty fine dogs and I've known some sons-of-bitches that was humans and you tell me them sons-of-bitches is gonna be there but there won't be one bleed-ing dog in 'eaven."[19]

Like most writers Mitchell always did "notice," and what frequently took his notice was the unusual and eccentric. Rather than being wary of such characters, he was drawn to them and fixed them per-manently in his memory – their accents, expressions, dialogue, situ-ations, and particularly their humour.

— CALGARY: NOVEMBER 1935 TO 1939 —

When they got into Calgary later that day, Bill asked Elijah Barron to let him off in front of the *Calgary Herald* office, where he hoped he could talk himself into a job:

> I wasn't smart enough to realize it was closed up tight being a Sunday and there was nothing doing. So I then walked over, and it was so goddamn cold, and I had no mitts or gloves, that I opened my suitcase and I took out a pair of socks and put them on my hands. And then I went over to the YMCA and the night man there was a sweetheart of a guy, Percy Witt. So I helped him do his night work and then he let me sleep on the gym mats in the gym. And he was breaking the regulation. The superintend-ent was putting a stop to it, because this was by the railroad tracks and a lot of guys would come in, and you see they could use the showers to get the coal dust off them. But Percy was still letting them in and keeping it quiet.[20]

The prairie provinces were hit hard by the Depression. Alberta's cattle industry had been crippled in 1931 when the United States closed its border to Canadian cattle. In 1932 the price "for prime beef at the Calgary stockyards dropped from $7 per 100 pounds to $2." This winter of 1935-36 was "the dying end" for the ranchers of Alberta. Thousands of head of cattle perished in the winter and in the summer the federal government bought and slaughtered fifteen

Bill and Al East sheet
writing, summer 1932,
and University of Manitoba
portrait, 1934.

Bill and George Humphries as Metitia the Educated Horse, Drumheller,
August 1939.

Bill and Merna at Southside pool, Edmonton, summer 1940.

Merna Hirtle publicity photograph for *Love on the Dole*, Edmonton, 1939.

Top: Cast picture of the University of Alberta Dramatic Society's production of *What Say They*, February 1941. Merna (*left*) as Ada Shore and Bill (*right*) as Dan McEntee. *Above*: Merna (*second from right*) in the University of Alberta Philharmonic Society's production of *Pirates of Penzance*, February 1942.

Above left: Bill and Merna, Edmonton, spring 1941. *Above right*: Professor F.M. Salter, Edmonton, 1942. *Right*: Bill and Merna. *Below*: Dr. G.F. McNally, Mrs. Margaret Mitchell, Bill and Merna, Mrs. Evelyn Hirtle and Rev. S. Hirtle, Edmonton, 15 August 1942.

Bill, Orm, and Merna,
1944; Merna, Bill, and
Orm, New Dayton,
1944.

UNIVERSITY OF CALGARY

Above: The house in High River, 1947. *Right:* High River post office in the 1940s.

MUSEUM OF THE HIGHWOOD

GLENBOW

High River, Fourth Street West, with the *High River Times* office in the background, in the 1930s.

Left: Orm and Bill, High River, 1947. *Right*: Merna in High River house living room, 1947.

The living room with the "gen-you-wine Eyetalyun carvin' - Renny-saunce-Eyetalyun walnut" chairs on either side of the fireplace.

thousand starving cattle to get them off the market. At the same time the Alberta government was asking for help to move four hundred thousand starving cattle from southern Alberta to pasture in the north.[21] In June 1935 the jobless number had hit a record, and in mid-November the *Calgary Herald* reported that there were 8,597 men registered as unemployed in Alberta. The government was easing the situation by placing men in work camps or in farm-relief jobs.

So Bill's prospects of finding a job in Calgary were not promising. But on Monday he shaved, washed up, had some of the remaining sandwiches he had stuffed in his topcoat at Fernie the night before, and called on the news editor of the *Calgary Herald*:

> The editor then was a guy named [Clarence] Stout and I told him I'd worked for the *Seattle Times*. I didn't tell him I was selling classified advertising. I didn't tell him I didn't even know how to use a typewriter – yet. I didn't have a typewriter. And he said, "Well, I haven't got anything." And I hung in and I said, "Look, I'm a pretty good feature writer. I can do colour stories. Will you let me bring in stuff space-rate?" And that was twenty-five cents a column inch. And he said, "Okay." And it was just good-heartedness.[22]

For the next few weeks Bill continued to sleep on the gym mats at the YMCA, and survived by doing freelance pieces for the *Calgary Herald*. He first did a highly fictionalized "colour story":

> With Percy's help I got a typewriter. I knew I had to turn it in typewritten, and that was the first I'd ever typed. And I typed out the goddamndest short story that was six inches. By god, that was one buck and a half. I did this beautiful thing with a snapper ending about a drunk cowboy on this horse. The reason the horse wouldn't budge for this drunken cowboy (who kept falling off it and wanted to get home) was it was the wooden horse outside of Riley and McCormick's Saddlery. Oh, Stout

knew it was bullshit. He could have been paying me out of his own pocket. And he gave me a buck and a half. And he said, "How come you're such a god-awful typist?" And I said, "Well, I've got an old wrist injury. I've been having a tough time. I got rolled coming through from Seattle and I haven't been eating very much. When I get low, the damn thing flares up again, but it will get a lot better." And it did. I learned to type in one week.[23]

Bill did a series of two or three stories on Gypsies who were squatting "in an old empty building on 9th Avenue." He visited them a couple of times and talked with an old fortune teller:

And I got three stories out of those Gypsies. They had a phrenologist's head in the window and actually they were blessing money. These guys would come in and they'd get them to bless the money, and they'd wrap it up and they'd bless it. And then they'd say, "But don't open it for twenty-four hours because if you do there will be a curse on your money and you won't win a crap game with it or anything else." They'd open it up and then they'd find it stuffed with newspaper that was cut out like dollar bills.[24]

Bill had obviously made some kind of impression on Stout, for within a few weeks Stout hired him to sell classified-ad space for the Christmas season. He could now afford a room at the YMCA. Although Bill's employment prospects were looking up, his love life received a setback. Margaret Laird wrote him a Dear John letter – she had fallen in love with a navy man and was about to be married.[25]

When he started selling Christmas advertising space, Bill met Bill Spencer, a fellow Deke, who was also selling classified advertising for the *Calgary Herald*. His father was O. Leigh Spencer, the publisher of the *Herald*. Bill Spencer met Bill at the Avenue Grill, where the owner and cook would frequently give Bill a meal or allow him to wash dishes or sweep floors to pay for one.[26] The Spencers felt sorry for Bill and gave him some of their son's winter clothing and invited him for Christmas dinner. Mitchell recalled with some emotion that Christmas evening at the Spencer home: "After dinner, when we went into the living room, Leigh said, 'There's something on the tree for you there.' And there was an envelope for Bill Mitchell. And it was a ten-dollar bill. Now that would pay for my YMCA room for a month." Spencer, knowing that Bill's seasonal employment with the *Herald* had finished, arranged for a job for him at the *Herald*'s affiliated radio station, CFAC:

> In January I started to work selling for CFAC at fifteen dollars a week, sixty bucks a month. Oh, that was great because I went down to Hudson's Bay and bought a grey double-breasted suit. It cost me fifteen dollars – and that was a top price. Later that summer Mother came out to visit me and she came out to dinner at Spencers' and she spoke to Mr. Spencer and she said, "Bill looks so thin." And Leigh Spencer said, "That's why he is such a great salesman – he's got that lean and hungry look."[27]

Bill's job at CFAC involved calling on Calgary businesses and selling them spots on various transcribed programs such as "Tarzan of the Apes" and "Pinto Pete and His Ranch Boys," as well as other shows featuring personalities: "I remember all those people – there was Yogi Jorgensen, there was Tizzie Lish, there was Senator Fishface, there was Popeye." These programs would arrive on huge disks, which held fifteen-minute segments, and the local announcer would write an introduction to each show with an advertisement for a local business. Bill's job was to sell the advertisement spot. As with his magazine selling, he developed a very effective "track." He would talk his prospective buyer into visiting the studio and sit him down with a cup of coffee. He would already have written an introduction for one of the transcribed shows and have arranged for one of the CFAC announcers in the control room to read the ad, followed by the announcement of an episode of one of the shows.[28]

Within a few weeks Bill moved out of his YMCA room and into a basement suite at Ma Cavanagh's boarding house on 14th Avenue (where he paid eighteen dollars a month for his room and board). Madeline Austin, who had taken a job as continuity writer at CFAC in January 1936, said that when Bill joined the station he looked as if he was starving. Madeline was living at home with her parents, whose house was on the same block as Bill's. They would walk to work each day, and talk and talk – about "life and philosophy"; he was a "marvellous conversationalist." For a while things went quite well at work and, as Madeline recalled, they "had a lot of fun together."[29]

Both Bill and Madeline recalled the CFAC office intrigue that soon emerged. The secretary was dating the sales manager, Eric McLeod, and she kept turning over the jobs to him rather than sharing them out. Since everything was on commission, this made it very tough for Bill. But he did have a big success. He discovered that nobody had tapped Calgary's beauty parlours. CFAC's only beauty-parlour spot was for a Madame Maxine, who owned a chain of beauty parlours in Oregon, Washington, British Columbia, and Alberta: "She was a carrot-haired old woman with tremendous make-up and she had a sort of verbal diarrhea." Once a year she came up to Calgary for a two-week period and bought two or three hours of radio time: "She would do Madame Maxine's beauty hints and she would roll on and on and on. She had a voice like a crow calling the others to gather together for the fall and go south."

Bill took the initiative. He went around to other Calgary beauty shops and sold a lot of one-minute spots. He made a big sale to Marvel Beauty Schools: "It was daily for a year. It was a big contract running into thousands of bucks. But the owner insisted on a certain time and I got it, signed it up."[30] There was a new manager at CFAC, Gordon Henry, who did not know that the spot Marvel Beauty Schools contracted for was, in fact, Madame Maxine's time. When Madame Maxine made her yearly visit to Calgary and discovered that the Marvel Beauty School advertisements were running in her spot, she was furious. Bill was called in by Gordon Henry "and bawled out in front of Madame Maxine" and fired. But Bill thought that this was all a big show put on to mollify Madame

Maxine. He went back to his desk assuming that everything was sorted out. Then he discovered that Eric, the sales manager who had been getting most of the commissions from the start, was in collusion with Henry:

> I went out and I was at my desk and Eric McLeod came by. He said, "Why aren't you cleaning out your desk?" And I said, "What do you mean, cleaning out my desk?" And he said, "Didn't Gordon fire you in there?" And I said, "Well, he said I was fired." "Well," he said, "you *are* fired." And that asshole had just been waiting for an excuse to do it. That was when I really learned about business. That was rough.[31]

Bill later believed that Gordon Henry and Eric McLeod had been using him all along. McLeod had also been living at Ma Cavanagh's, and Bill had originally helped Eric learn the ropes of selling CFAC spot advertisement. Bill felt betrayed and was particularly bitter over this firing. Because he had a strong sense of loyalty and lived by an old-fashioned kind of honour, Bill's ingenuousness often got him into trouble in the business world.

Bill had worked for CFAC for about three months. His next job, the most steady and best-paying job he had during the Depression, was selling insurance for Prudential Life: "That was twenty dollars a week and commissions. I must have been making at least $125, maybe $150 a month. I would go around and collect nickels and dimes selling industrial insurance and everything." He bought his first car, a 1927 Pontiac, which cost him $115. At this time he also tried to sell oil-well royalties. Although it was a "very exciting" time with a lot of potential for making "anywhere from twelve hundred to as high as five thousand bucks," he was not lucky at this game and soon gave it up.[32]

Just after landing his job at Prudential, Bill began dating Marie Dixon. It was not too long before he gave her his Deke pin, and they were considered engaged. Marie had taken two years of Pharmacy at the University of Alberta in Edmonton, but because of hard times had taken a year off school from late spring 1936 until September 1937. She was living with her parents and grandparents and working at a drugstore. Her father was a dentist, whose practice was not flourishing, and he and his family lived with his wife's parents, Mr. and Mrs. McLachlan, in their house on 6th Avenue East. Mrs. Dixon's sister was married to R.A. Brown, who at this time was profiting from the Turner Valley oil boom.³³ So Marie had connections and moved in what Mitchell referred to as "that whole top-drawer bunch that went to Palliser supper dances." The Palliser, Calgary's stately Canadian Pacific Railway hotel, held weekend supper dances which were popular among the city's high society. With his job at Prudential, Bill had enough money to take Marie, on occasion, to the Palliser and even to the Banff Springs Hotel.

Bill had written home to his mother telling her about Marie and, on April 3, Mrs. O.S. arrived in Calgary to visit with him and look over her prospective daughter-in-law and her family. She had not seen her son since the summer of 1934 when he left for Seattle. Mrs. Mitchell stayed at Ma Cavanagh's, where Bill was boarding, and she met some of the Calgary "top-drawer" people during this visit, including the Leigh Spencer and R.A. Brown families. When Bill drove her over to visit the Dixons, McLachlans, and Mrs. R.A. Brown, she also had an opportunity to observe some of Calgary's lower-drawer people, much to her son's amusement and surprise:

> As we drove this spring Sunday afternoon up 6th Avenue East, which was the red-light district of Calgary, it was a beautiful, beautiful spring morning, and the windows and screens were open and the porches, and all the whores were looking out the window and standing in the front. And Mother noticed there was something out of synch here. And Mother said, "What's the score here?" And I said, "Mother, that's Calgary's red-light district. Those were prostitutes." She said, "No! Really?" I said, "Yes, Mother, you must have seen something like this when you were in training in the big city of New York." And I said, "Now here's Dixons'," and she said, "Drive around the block again." I

said, "Sure," and this time much more slowly. And that proper Victorian woman was looking at these ladies of ill repute![34]

Bill's mother had a very pleasant visit with Mrs. R.A. Brown: "They really hit it off. They were classy." She was not, however, impressed by Mrs. Dixon: "Mrs. Dixon wasn't feeling well – she wouldn't even come downstairs for the tea that was held. Mother considered this very, very tacky of Mrs. Dixon."[35]

On Labour Day weekend, Bill joined his fraternity friends for an outing at the Banff Springs Hotel. Because of the Depression it was not fully booked, and the young people from surrounding areas were let in free just to establish a lively and full dance floor. Wilbur Bowker, who had met Bill at the Deke house in Edmonton in 1932, and was at this time a young struggling lawyer, described the atmosphere and excitement of this weekend:

> Bob Brown, Jr., arranged a weekend at the Banff Springs Hotel. He had a new Cadillac, I think it was. We all happened to be in the same fraternity. He got two rooms. There were six of us but we had beds for five – sixteen dollars for the two rooms. But hell, there were more waiters at the Banff Springs Hotel than there were guests in '36! We walked into Mart Kenney playing in the ballroom and as long as you were respectable-looking they didn't even charge. We started off around dusk, I suppose it was a Saturday – there was Bill, [Douglas] McDermid, Harry Rose. We got there in time for the supper dance – oh, it was quite a wingding.

In comparison to his friends, Bill was "very poor and very proud but wouldn't talk about his impecuniosity. He was really strapped and carried it off stoically." To this group of friends, Bill was still boyish-looking, quiet, and gave no indication that he was an aspiring writer: "He was rather retiring. He wasn't a showman – except when it came to the diving board, and boy!" Bowker remembered, as others have, the rapt, self-absorbed poise of Bill performing one of his dives:

"The next morning, which would be Sunday, he went swimming in the outdoor pool. And I remember the incredible style in diving – he might have even been a candidate for Olympic-level diving. Here we were standing looking at this outdoor pool, and I can still see this – what style diving! This was an eye-opener to me."[36]

In August, Bill responded to an audition call for a role in *Recipe for Murder*, the first play of the season for the Calgary Theatre Guild. They had recently acquired a new director, Frank Holroyd, who had been co-founder and director of the Edmonton Little Theatre. *Recipe for Murder* was a mystery by Arnold Ridley. Bill's role was minor, as suitor to the leading man's sister, but he played it with "pleasant assurance."[37] The next production, Elmer Rice's *See Naples and Die*, was staged in October and was the major play of the season. Holroyd both directed it and designed an attractive set with the Bay of Naples in the background. The play was a comic love story. Bill played the lead's former fiancé and was congratulated for the "natural ease" with which he acted and for displaying the "ready wit" of his character's personality.[38] In January he had a minor role in the pantomime, *Aladdin*.

Just when life was on a steady course for Bill, things went wrong again. He had paid off his debt on the 1927 Pontiac Cabriolet and traded it in on a Willis Knight, a "pretty fancy" car. But on his way back to Calgary from a selling trip in Bowness he rolled it. He was not hurt, but without a car he was obviously at a disadvantage in his job. Shortly after this he was fired. Mitchell claimed he was fired because the manager, Frank Spink, thought he was too young and did not have confidence in him. Mitchell admitted that at the time he was "a jolly sort of young kid" and perhaps his "jolliness" translated into irresponsibility for Spink.[39]

Mitchell's Depression years are difficult to chart. He simply said of these years, "I'm confused about when exactly events happened because it was such a thing of flux."[40] Three or four months of hardship must have seemed like a year, and one good year, like that with Prudential, could become exaggerated into two years. He worked at about eight different jobs, and there were many times when he was without work, money, and food. When the jobs gave out he would move out of his rooming house and back to the YMCA for cheaper accommodation. Pierre Berton described this period in Bill's life:

> Bill Mitchell . . . found that if necessary he could go without food for three days. Mitchell disciplined himself never to eat more than one meal daily while on the road. In cheap restaurants, where you could get a three-course meal for a quarter, he'd take all the extra bread and pats of butter and save them for the following day. No matter how hungry he was, he never removed the five-dollar bill he kept hidden in his sock. When charged with vagrancy he could produce it to prove that he did have "visible means of support."[41]

For a short period Bill did some sheet writing, as he had in the summer of 1932. He moved from the boarding house to the YMCA, and his brother Bob may have stayed with him for a while. He then turned to selling *Colliers Encyclopedia*, something he did between "real" jobs for the next two years. Being a "book man" was a step up from sheet writing: "When you were a book man you weren't like a cheerleader guy working his way through college selling *National Home Monthly* door to door. As a book man you wore a topcoat and had a shoeshine and your pants creased and wore, perhaps, a homburg roll-brim hat. And it was dignified." The "pitch" was easy for Bill, who was an experienced actor, and the lines were so ingrained that he never forgot them. He travelled to dozens of Alberta towns and got very experienced selecting likely prospects:

> Priests were good, lawyers were good, doctors were good. Grain-elevator operators were good for some damned reason and lumberyard owners were good. So you call on them and you avoided bomb words. You didn't say encyclopedia, just as in sheet writing you never said magazine. You said this fine periodical. You didn't say subscription – that was another bomb word. You said reference library. The pitch was, "I am calling on

– well, I hate to use the word – opinion moulders. I'll put it bluntly to you – prestigious people in Hairy Hill. There are about ten of you. And you are one of them. You're on my list right here. Do you want to see my list? To put it as simply as I can, I want to ask you to accept from Collier Press a complete reference library in colour, beautiful illustrations, marvellously designed and cross-referenced. Now wait a minute, don't get me wrong. We want you to have it at no cost. And that may seem too good to be true but we ask for two things. First, this is in the nature of promoting a brand-new reference library set of books and the best way we know of is word-of-mouth advertising. So if we pick people who stand out within their respective communities, and it is a select few, then we ask you to recommend this reference library. One other thing, we do expect you to write a letter of testimonial which you will then give us permission to use – like this. Here's a letter speaking in glowing terms of *Colliers Encyclopedia* – signed Franklin Delano Roosevelt. Do you think you could write a letter like that?"

If the grain operator of Hairy Hill fell for this slick track and agreed to accept the "free" twelve-volume reference library, Bill would sign him up. Then, almost as an afterthought:

"You do understand, in our modern contemporary times, change comes pretty quick historically, economically. And there are new science discoveries every day. And what worth is a reference set that is out of date? So Collier Press would ask you to pay for the annual update. In order to make sure it goes on for a long time they would like you to agree that you will keep it updated with a new volume every year for ten years. It comes to about seventy-five cents a week. Okay?" You hadn't stopped to think that seventy-five cents a week times fifty-two comes to $39 per year and for ten years that comes to $390. And then, "You wouldn't expect me to ride around every week on my little red bicycle to collect seventy-five cents from you for this, so we would just like you to take care of it." So you end up selling a set of encyclopedias that cost $390 for $390. It was never updated – he never got another damn book. But after that, it was a year, so what the hell.[42]

Mitchell later ascribed this experience to his evangelist Healy Richards, in *The Vanishing Point*, who, in his early days, was a successful encyclopedia salesman: "Wasn't another book man in North America was pumped back in the barber's chair every morning after breakfast – had his face swathed in steaming towels and the mint smell of shaving-cream . . ." (*VP* 271). Bill did not pamper himself in this fashion, but he did survive at this con game for four or five months.

His brother Bob was now lifeguarding at Lake Louise and Bill occasionally visited him, perhaps at the end of July when their mother came to Alberta to visit both the boys. Bob and Bill, in fact, worked and lived together off and on for the next two years. Although they were close as brothers, they were quite different in temperament as well as physique. Bob was more like his father, O.S., shorter and more muscular than Bill. A good-looking fellow, he was featured, poised on a diving board, in a *Liberty* magazine ad for Lake Louise.

One weekend when Bill went up to visit Bob, he ran into some trouble. According to their younger brother, Dick, Bill and Bob got drinking at a bar one Saturday night:

Bill took a fancy to this girl who was with a guy. So Bill went over and started making up to this girl and this guy was getting a little uptight. What happened was, Bill could always talk himself out of anything, you know. And Bob was kind of watching. This guy invites Bill outside. So Bill says, "Oh yeah, fisticuffs!" And this guy's ahead of him and Bill's following along behind him. And he still figures he can talk him out of it, but his guy turned around and let Bill have it right in the chops and knocked him out. And as he started putting the boots to

Bill, Bob came around the corner. That guy's lucky to be alive today. Bob was a bull. He just physically picked this guy up and Bill says, "I looked up and there he was and he was pounding this guy and his head was coming off the building." Bill had to stop him.[43]

It might have been around this time that Bill surprised Bob by getting into another compromising situation. He and Bob were living together at the YMCA dorm again. Marie had returned to university in Edmonton, and Bill was working for London Life, but not having an easy time of it. He had signed on for Frank Holroyd's fall pantomime, *Sinbad the Sailor*, in which he played "the pessimistic Uncle Sinbad."[44] While acting for Holroyd during the previous year, Bill sensed that Holroyd's interest in him went beyond his acting talent. On one occasion Holroyd bought him a cup of coffee and made some comments which made Bill slightly uneasy:

> Then he said, "You know, it's a funny thing times like this – young men are approached. I know a young man in tough circumstances like you and he was approached by a guy and he made a proposition to him and said I'll pay you ten bucks." He said, "You know, that damn fool didn't take him up on it, and yet he had gone without eating." And I said, "Why are you telling me this, Frank?" He said, "Well, it's just as an interesting thing." He also told me about *The Well of Loneliness*, which I'd never heard of before – the first time anybody published a book about lesbian relationships.[45] And I don't know – I didn't recognize this as a preparation.

Holroyd invited Bill and two or three others who were in *Sinbad* to a private party following the cast party. Everyone was drinking a lot, and Holroyd, who was an amateur artist, decided to do some sketching. He asked some of the men to undress for him and do some posing:

Holroyd said, "Oh be nice, hey, Bill? Why don't you take off your clothes and you pose and make it more interesting for all of us?" I said, "No thanks." And Gerald said, "Oh he's too shy –" the idea was I was too chickenshit to do it. And I was drunk enough I said, "Oh Christ." So I stripped and then Holroyd said, "All right, now bend down there, now you get there and you get there." And the next thing I knew Doug had his arms around me. And I pushed him away and stood up. He came up and came at me and I ploughed him right in the mouth. And I grabbed up my shorts and my pants and two bottles of Scotch and went out. I went back to the dormitory and Bob was there and I woke him up. He said, "What the hell?" I said, "Well, we've got two bottles of Scotch." And he said, "What happened?" So I told him. And strangely for him – he was looking and looking at me. And finally I said, "What's the matter?" He said, "Why did they invite you there in the first place?"[46]

Bill now understood the motive behind Frank's invitation, but he did not feel at all threatened by Frank and his friends. Bob did, however, and he judged his brother's tolerance as a potential sign of homosexuality. In fact, Bob himself had been propositioned earlier when he was watching one of the rehearsals, and when Bill asked him what he did, Bob responded, "I was going to give him a shit-kicking, but I didn't." Unlike Bob, Bill had got to know a number of homosexuals, primarily through his acting. He simply did not imagine, on this occasion, that they were interested in him. He had always felt secure about his heterosexuality, but he had that writer's deep curiosity about new experiences and interesting individuals. He was, of course, drawn to Holroyd because of his talent and energy as a director and set designer.[47] And, like many of his contemporaries at this time who were "on their uppers," he enjoyed a good party – especially if there was free food and drink to be had.

In December, a month after *Sinbad*, Bill played the lead in a one-act comedy, *Birds of Passage*, which the Calgary Theatre Guild entered in the subregional provincial drama festival. This was his most successful role, and the adjudicator said, "The production was remarkable largely for the very good comedy acting of Stewart Frankland, played by W. Mitchell."[48] There were six plays in this competition. *Birds of Passage* and another play, *The Hand of Siva*, were chosen to go forward to the Alberta regional dramatic festival, which was held in Calgary's Grand Theatre February 17-19. The adjudicator for this event was Malcolm Morley, "English dramatic authority." Morley was more critical of Bill's performance than the previous adjudicator, although he, too, thought that Bill and his female lead were "good as a comedy team." The characters they played were strangers to one another and the humour revolved around their having to spend the night together in an English cottage. In Morley's view the "keynote of Stewart's part was embarrassment." However, he thought that Bill played the role as if he "enjoyed the situation more than he was embarrassed by it."[49]

Soon after this play, in February 1938, Bill went up to Edmonton for a weekend to take Marie to the Deke formal. They had now been engaged for almost two years. His performance at this event was hardly as accomplished as that in the play. He was staying at the Deke house. He drank far too much and passed out:

> And then I came to again and I pulled myself together and went over to the Delta Gen house. Marie was there and she was pretty unhappy because it's about midnight that I had made it, instead of ten o'clock or nine to pick her up. And I remember she was wearing a brown velvet dress and it wasn't her own, it was one of her fraternity sisters'. And I apologized profusely and went back home to Calgary. The next day her mother calls, and about two weeks later I received my Deke pin back in the mail with a letter saying it's all over.[50]

Later, in the 1950s, when Mitchell was working on a section of "The Alien" that deals with Carlyle's fraternity experiences, he resurrected some of the details of his relationship with Marie and their break-up. Carlyle drunkenly misbehaves at a fraternity formal partly because he believes Grace, his girlfriend, may be carrying on with one of his fraternity brothers. Bill, in fact, thought that Marie had fallen for one of his fraternity brothers, John Sturdy, who Mitchell said was "a very charming rascal who moved in on me" and eventually married Marie.[51] Carlyle behaves even worse than Bill, punching out his fraternity brother (Melquist) and starting a brawl. Grace breaks off their relationship:

> It was Grace, who truly mattered. At the thought of her he felt his heart constrict. She had every right to return his pin. Why – why had he done it! It was no use saying he'd always hated Melquist, that he'd got too drunk – that the thing had got out of control. Lots of people before him had pounded someone they hated when they were liquored up. But that wasn't the answer. It was his own damn fault. He should have stayed miles away from Melquist. Then there would have been no little square box in the mail. (*A* 170-71)

Partly it was Bill's "own damn fault" that Marie threw him over and partly it had to do with his being financially strapped. He was becoming less interested in moving with the moneyed crowd, and much more interested in theatre and writing. He admitted that it must not have looked to Marie as if he could offer her much of a future:

> I think she had decided that she didn't want to spend the rest of her life living on 6th Avenue East next to the fire hall. My clothes bothered her. I mean, my shoes weren't shined. I at this time had a lead in [probably *Birds of Passage*], and I would come over to see Mrs. Dixon the odd time because the theatre was in that part of town. And I'm pretty sure her mother wrote her and said that Bill was here and his collar was just a dreadful mess. What it was – the collar was a mess because I had to wash my own shirts and press my own pants. But it was probably a hell of a lot of make-up around the collar during the run.

Mitchell never told Marie about his writing: "I never once confided in her that this was what I did on weekends and when I had spare time."[52] Perhaps he sensed that his writing and acting ambitions would not be met with approval.

By July, Bill and Bob were both out of work. So they cooked up a clown and high-diving act and for about three weeks worked for Red River Shows while it was performing in Calgary, Medicine Hat, and Cranbrook. Red River Shows was a carnival-type midway which wintered in Brandon, Manitoba, and then travelled to various prairie towns and cities during the summer. This particular summer in Calgary it was sponsored by the Rotary Club to raise funds for sports in the city. It was a "modest cheesy little carnival" that could not even boast a freak show or a Ferris wheel. In 1946 Mitchell gave a brief description of his diving act on the biographical form he filled out for the Atlantic Monthly Press:

> At one time I did a high diving act for a Midway (Red River Shows) with a brother for double dives. Our canvas tank was between the Hula Show and the Chinese Magician with Crown and Anchor in front of us. After two towns and two weeks we came to the conclusion that it was only a matter of time before we completed a dive into the Hula Show, the Multiplying Pigeons act, or the cent of spades on the Crown and Anchor board.[53]

Their act was introduced by a barker and began with a clown routine off a three-metre springboard. In the "Mae West dive," Bill, wearing a skirted suit and a woman's bathing cap with a big red rubber peony on the side of it, would perform a high swan dive in which he "shimmied [his] ass the whole way down." One of their most popular routines, "The Dumb Swede," began with Bob expertly executing a few fairly difficult dives. Then Bill, pretending to be one of the audience, would call out in a Yogi Jorgensen accent, "I vood like to doo that too." An argument ensued which ended with Bill stripping down to wildly coloured boxer shorts and climbing the three-metre-board ladder. Awkwardly he would run and leap high to hit the end of the board only to have one foot completely miss it. With a yodelling yell he went off the side of the board and into the pool. He would come bellowing out of the water insisting that he could "doo it too." After a few more attempts, all the while muttering Yogi Jorgensen imprecations he would suddenly lose all gracelessness and effortlessly leap high up into a tight tuck and complete a cut-away one-and-a-half somersault towards the board, ending with a clean entry into the pool.

Following some professionally done singles and doubles dives, the climax of the show was Bill's high dive off a platform:

> They dug out a hole for a pool and lined it with a canvas liner. They hooked up to the nearest hydrant – and that water came out at roughly a couple of degrees above freezing. The ladder tower was just a narrow ladder that went up with guy wires and a little postage-stamp thing on the top of it and I did a back layout off the back of it which is a back full somersault out in the swan position, or, as I like to think of it, the crucified position. It would be ten metres, which would be about thirty-three feet. But I think they said it was about seventy or ninety feet – because that's what it looked. It's strange – people have not got a good judgement of heights. When you've got a narrow ladder with guy wires up there and a little postage-stamp platform up there, it looks as though it could be seventy feet or ninety feet. So it wasn't a true high dive.[54]

Mitchell recalled the barker's spiel to the audience: "And now, ladies and gentleman, Mr. Bill Mitchell will perform his death-defying high dive from the seventy-foot platform in full back layout into what amounts to not much more than a wet sponge." It may not have been a true high dive, but from a height of thirty-three feet he was travelling at a pretty good speed when he hit the water. His entry into the water was feet first. After one incident, when he almost hit the water astraddle a floating crackerjack box, he made doubly sure that his legs were tightly clamped together.

They moved with the Red River Shows to Medicine Hat and then to Cranbrook. After Cranbrook, however, they decided they had had enough of the "big time" life (earning only twelve dollars a week), and they left the show to look for work in Calgary. Mitchell recalled paying rent for the basement suite and getting a little frustrated with Bob, who appeared to be simply having a good time: "Bob and I were close, let's not make any mistake about that. But by the time Calgary hit and everything, he pissed me off."[55]

For the rest of the summer of 1938 through to the summer of 1939 Bill had a series of jobs – sheet writing, selling encyclopedias, working for London Life – but things were very tight. They moved to a cheaper room at the YMCA, and Bill told his brother, "getting a job is a job – start cracking and find yourself a job." Bob could get a job when he tried and always "astonished" Bill with the ones he found. At one point he worked as an adviser of personnel for the Hudson's Bay Company. He joined Bill in sheet writing, but that soon petered out. Finally, in the spring, Bob went on the road with a partner "peddling photographs."

Subsequently Bill met up with Bob and his partner in Brooks, where they had a falling-out. Bob and his partner were not doing well, and at the end of a day's subscription selling Bill came back to his room to find they had skipped town leaving him with the week's hotel and cafe bills. Bob "had left a note for me saying that he was going home and that would make it easier for me." This left Bill in a bind. Earlier that year he had bought a Harris tweed topcoat and fedora in order to look presentable as a salesman. It was about all he had that was worth anything. He got fifteen dollars for the coat and hat from "the guy that ran the beer parlour," but managed to pay off only the cafe bill and part of the hotel bill. He explained to the hotel owner how he had been left "holding the bag" and that he had already worked the town for subscriptions: "I said I had to move on, but I would pay him and he trusted me and didn't turn me in to the Mounties."[56]

Bill ended up in Drumheller for the summer of 1939 giving diving lessons at the city swimming pool. He did not get a salary, only his meals and a dollar for each diving lesson he gave.[57] But he and the other staff made some money from galas for which they charged admission. The last gala, on August 16, did very well and went on to play at Carbon. Bill did his "Dumb Swede" routine and, in Carbon, an underwater escape act in which he was handcuffed, tied up in a canvas bag, and dumped into the deep end of the pool. When he did not appear after a couple of minutes, "the guys would start diving and showing panic and when everybody was shitting themselves for fear I had drowned myself I would come strolling up from the other end saying, 'Could I help you guys?' "[58] The *Drumheller Review* reported that "one of the hits of the evening" was "Metitia the educated horse (Bill Mitchell and George Humphries)," who, after "mounting the three-metre diving board and doing different stunts at this great height, made a real high dive into the water below."[59]

Once when my father was showing me and my brother how to dive, he told us about the horse diving act he and his partner devised for the Drumheller gala. My father was the front end of the horse and his partner was the rear. The "horse" would come out from the dressing room neighing and prancing, climb up the ladder to the three-metre board, strut out and rear up on the end of the board, and do a double dive. The timing of the two halves of the horse had to be perfect. At one of the performances in Carbon, the audience roared with laughter even more than usual as soon as the "horse" stepped out onto the board and then again as it went through the preparatory motions for the first dive. His partner was hamming up this part of the act and getting tremendous laughs but my father could not figure out what was going on. Every time he tried to look back or between his legs the audience laughed louder. When the act was over and they went back to the change room, which was also used for the hockey rink in the winter, my father asked, "What the hell were you doing back there?" His partner, who had had a bit to drink before going on that night, grinned and pulled a red-and-white striped hockey sock stuffed with toilet paper from the hind end of the horse costume. During the act when the "horse" pranced and reared on the board he had dropped the hockey sock out of the costume between the "horse's" hind legs. Whenever my father tried to see what was going on, he pulled the sock back in. So during this Carbon performance Metitia was a studhorse.

In late August the swimming pools were closing down for the summer and Bill had to look for work elsewhere. Over the next two years he would spend his falls stooking and on threshing crews pitching or spiking bundles or skinning a team. He was in a field stooking for a farmer named Anderson in the Carbon district in early September 1939 when he heard over the radio that war had been declared. When he finished stooking for Anderson, he joined a custom threshing crew in the Red Deer area and travelled with it from farm to farm for the rest of the season: "Generally farmers would put together their own crew but then there were some guys with behemoth big bloody machines and crews and they would do it for a farmer and charge a flat rate."[60] It was hard work. In an article, Mitchell recalled an old seasoned pitcher's advice on his first bundle-pitching job:

> I met him during the depression years of the thirties on top of a very badly stacked rack of bundles beside a thirty-six-inch threshing machine with its slant plume of chaff. I was at the time undergoing those initiation rites which come to a prairie boy when he works on his first harvest crew, and I wasn't doing at all well because, whenever I went to spear a bundle with my fork, I happened to be standing on another bundle which was across that bundle, which was then, therefore, binding that bundle. This man took the fork from my hand and smoothly and effortlessly began, almost negligently, to fork the bundles

into the feeder. "There's the way to do it," he said. "Don't git your muscles all harled up. Just grab the handle loose and easy an' let her slip through your hand easy. Do it so she looks easy but remember she shure as hell ain't."[61]

Custom threshing crews played, as well as worked, hard: "On Saturday night you had to go into Drumheller or Red Deer or something and fight the other custom crews. There was a Billie Mitchell that never went into town on Saturday night. I just went into the chicken house or the granary or wherever we slept, and I slept from Saturday through Sunday." But there was a price to pay for not going into town. Since they were feeding crew members who stayed around on Sunday, farmers expected some work in return:

> You always had a goddamn farmer who let the cow shit and horse shit accumulate until it was just packed in those barns – a whole year's accumulation. You'd be in there with your eyes watering from ammonia. And those farmers used you since you weren't working on the gang and they were feeding you. And I think that's why some of the guys went into town on Saturday. I forked an awful lot of horse shit and cow shit in my time.[62]

When threshing finished, Bill was feeling flush, for he had managed to accumulate about eighty dollars from his diving lessons, galas, and fall stooking and threshing. He paid off the hotel owner in Brooks and got a ride up to Edmonton. He stayed in Edmonton until Christmas selling the *World Book Encyclopedia*, a job which was eventually to lead to a very important event in his life.

– WEYBURN: CHRISTMAS 1939 TO EASTER 1940 –

Around Christmas time of 1939, Bill went back to Weyburn and stayed until Easter. He had not been home since leaving Weyburn in the summer of 1934. His brother Bob had just joined up with the South Saskatchewan Regiment and was in training. Dick had come home for the holidays from the University of Saskatchewan (Saskatoon) and Jack was managing the skating rink in Weyburn. In the 1920s the city had consistently lost money on the skating rink and owed a substantial amount on a mortgage held by O.S. Mitchell's estate. In the spring of 1931 a deal had been made with the city, and the title of the rink was turned over to Mrs. O.S. Mitchell, so Jack had a ready-made job.

It was on this visit home that the mystery of the missing glider wings and parts was finally cleared up. Bill received a large bill from the CPR in Brandon for storage of crates of glider parts for nearly nine years. He confronted his mother about this in one of their are-there-any-new-developments talks:

> I used to talk a lot with my mother. Generally when she had gone to bed I'd go in and sit on the edge of her bed and talk with her – especially if I had been away for a long time. And I said, "All right, Mother, I got an interesting letter from the CPR in Brandon." And she burst into tears. She told me, "Billie, I never thought you would do it. I underestimated you." And then she said, "My heart sank. Every afternoon after school, weekends if you weren't down at the spa doing your compulsories and optionals, you were in that darned back yard working on that darned hydroplane. I knew you would kill yourself. So I just told them to hold it in Brandon until they heard from me." God, what she must have gone through. It must have been awfully tough on my mother knowing all the time I was making these fruitless trips in there, that she had got the CPR to hold it in Brandon at the divisional point until further notice.[63]

Bill felt his style a little cramped during this six-month stay at home. He loved his mother dearly, but as a young man of twenty-five who had established an independent and rather nomadic life and was returning to a household run by a strong-willed matriarch, there was bound to be some friction and frustration – on both sides. Mitchell used the frustration he experienced during this stay in Weyburn for his character Hugh in *How I Spent My Summer Holidays* (1981). Hugh remembers returning home after a long absence when his father died. He, too, is twenty-five years old: "That summer was not an easy time for either my mother or me, not only because of our grief, but because with the years we had both lost some of the small talent we'd ever had for patience. My mother still tended to come on too strong, right through neutral territory and into my own" (*SH* 215). Mitchell, commenting on the mother-son relationship in *Summer Holidays*, said that unlike Hugh's father, "his mother has unforgivably exceeded the territorial imperative and has crossed him up, denying him, cautioned him, out of love. Every time he wants to do something his mother for the best reasons denies him – she is the best example of that interfering, trespassing good guardian." This invasion of territory was very close to what Bill felt:

> And *that* mother is so close to my own mother and his impatience with his mother is so close to my impatience with my mother when she denied me or disciplined me. Which I now see – especially after reading these goddamned texts on stored past and the explosion of the id coming through and something from early childhood being bounced off somebody else through transference. And as Merna can tell you, my impatience and my crankiness explode when somebody says – and it's so goddamn trivial and so immature – to do this or do that or I want this. And I keep telling you to come on, keep to your own territory – you're moving in on me too strong – just don't do it. And I think *that* mother personifies and captures probably in feeling, anyway of impatience, my relationship with my own mother.[64]

No doubt the frustration affected them both. On at least one occasion Bill outraged his mother when he was carried home half-unconscious from a night of drinking with some soldiers from the South Saskatchewan Regiment. According to Jack and Dick, "he heaved up everything in the centre of the living-room rug. And a friend had fed him a gallon of tomato juice and he brought every goddamned bit of it up. Mother came down and she said, 'He's bleeding to death!' She wanted to call a doctor and I had a hell of a time keeping her off the telephone."[65] While his mother may have been concerned about Bill's health that night, she was not the following morning:

> I woke up and I was on my back, under the bed, my head just out. And I guess I had blood from the fight and vomit. And Mother's face looking down at me. And Mother's two words, "You animal!" And she went into the bathroom and she put in a hot bath. She came back in and said, "Your bath is drawn." That's all she said.

Bill's brothers did their share of drinking as well and, as Mitchell said, "we're not very different from most people of our generation, I often think. You *all* went to a party, you *all* got stoned and plastered and you all talked about it afterwards."[66]

There were other ways in which this winter was not an easy time for Bill. Although he was now writing a novella, it was lonely work with no one to talk to or encourage him, and his attempts to get something published had been fruitless. He co-managed the Weyburn skating rink from Christmas to Easter with his brother Jack. This, too, led to some friction. Jack was a flamboyant and strong individual and still treated his younger brother as a kid. Bill, who had been supporting himself for the past five years in very tough times, did not take kindly to being ordered about. Bill himself could be just as volatile as Jack, so Mrs. O.S. had her hands full trying to keep calm in the family.

Bill organized a carnival at the rink in order to raise a stake to go back to Edmonton. According to Mitchell, Jack was for some reason unhappy about this carnival, and he deliberately tried to scuttle it by locking the rink up the night of the performance. That did not work and Dick described the carnival as a big event, like the

Ice Follies of our times, with dancers from a local dance school and Bill's clown act:

> He had billboards all over town. It's the only time the rink was
> filled that winter. Bill got up in the box above the goalkeeper,
> and they put the spotlight on him. He was playing a clown, you
> know – he was pretty near falling out of this thing and saying, I
> don't care if you call Jack Mitchell. And then he got out there
> and he did his clown act on skates. You know, all over the place.
> And he was pretty good. He couldn't skate anyway – he didn't
> have to. He packed the rink. And that's where he got the money
> to get out of town.[67]

Dick recalled another incident in which Bill threw a hammer at Jack: "It had something to do with flooding the ice – I don't think he was going to hit him, but he threw a hammer at him he was so mad." Mitchell himself did not go into detail about these confrontations and simply referred to running the Weyburn rink "in spite of Jack."[68] Bill, with his flair for the theatrical, attracted crowds to arena events in a way that may have undermined Jack's sense of his position as manager. But it must have seemed to Bill, who had been living a hand-to-mouth existence for five years, that Jack had it easy. He had stayed in Weyburn, and while one of his "jobs" was looking after his mother it was, in turn, a way of looking after himself. Dick admired Bill's self-reliance: "And Bill was in lots of places working. And he never, or very seldom, wrote or got bailed out. Well, you can tell the way he got out of Weyburn – a preview of the Ice Follies. He didn't go to Mother – he could have gone to Mother and got money. But he was on his own. That tells you something."[69]

The skating rink was the scene of another confrontation. Père Athol Murray, who was in charge of Notre Dame (a very successful reform school for hard-to-handle teenage boys), was legendary for his feistiness and his hockey team. The Hounds of Notre Dame had developed quite a reputation, not only as Murray's main pedagogical tool in straightening out young men, but also as a perennial contender for the provincial playoffs and finals. Late one Friday afternoon Père Murray and his team rolled into Weyburn for a game that evening with the Weyburn Beavers. The rink's public skating hours ran to seven p.m., but Père Murray wanted his boys to have a practice. So, he simply told his boys to get dressed and he pulled the nets out onto the ice in the middle of the public skaters. When his players stepped out onto the ice he announced to the public skaters a practice had been scheduled for his team at five and that they would have to leave the ice now. His air of authority and his stubbornness were rarely challenged. At this point Bill came on the scene and got into a heated argument with him. Père Murray simply refused to take his players off the ice. Bill realized that he could not physically eject the whole team and knew that Père Murray was very handy with his fists. Inwardly raging, he went to the rink office, unlocked the fuse box and threw the main switch so that every light in the rink went out. He then waited for Père Murray and his team to exit the rink and the scheduled public skating resumed. Mitchell claimed that this was one of the few defeats Père Murray suffered in the Weyburn rink.

⁓ BILL'S APPRENTICESHIP AS A WRITER ⁓

Many years later, Mitchell said the dullness of Depression jobs was in a way a blessing: "I turned to writing for surcease every chance I got."[70] During these drought years he wrote about twenty short stories and a novella, but they reaped only a bumper crop of "little printed rejection slips." He finally "smartened up: I suddenly realized there must be some reason, so I quit sending them away after about five or six years and I would put [the stories] in my dresser in whatever boarding house I was living in."[71] He looked on this period from his diary writing in the summer of 1933 to the early 1940s as his early apprenticeship years. He rarely confided in anyone, even his close friends, about his writing ambitions. As Mitchell recalled some thirty-five years later, "The creative frustration of a writer trying to break free from the solitude of the writing act is probably most intense during young apprenticeship. The loneliness can never completely leave him; indeed, this is quite likely the main reason that so many potential artists give up too soon."[72]

None of this apprentice work has survived in manuscript form. However, the kind of characters in some of these stories is revealed in a letter Mitchell received from Virginia (Scott) Bue, who wanted to interview him about his insurance days when she had known him in the 1930s. She wrote that she enjoyed *Who Has Seen the Wind* "enormously – it's a far cry from the bindlestiffs you used to write about. They were wonderful characters – nevertheless. I recall them quite clearly. . . . You may be subjected to a grueling probe into that era of your life when you sold insurance and lived at the Y; your stumble bums and bindle stiffs; your career as an actor."[73] So some of the stories Bill was writing in the late 1930s were about the single unemployed, perhaps in the style of Steinbeck's *Tortilla Flat* or *Of Mice and Men*, which were published about this time.

In a 1962 CBC interview with Harry Boyle, Mitchell described with some amusement the stories he wrote just after his Europe trip – romantic adventures involving "Russian counts and blondes." He also refers to a "bad surreal novel" he had written.[74] This was "Mr. Twill," a novella about a man who is dominated by his wife. It grew out of the one-act play he had written four years earlier. Mr. Twill takes refuge from Marge, his domineering wife, in a fantasy world. He spends more and more time watching and talking to Marge's goldfish, which can neither talk back nor order him around. Mr. Twill is finally driven to commit suicide by jumping off the Edmonton high-level bridge. Bill probably worked on this novella over the fall and winter of 1939-40, and finished it by August 1940. In retrospect Mitchell was both amused and slightly embarrassed by it:

> It was written in Edmonton, really, because I used the high-level bridge – Mr. Twill and the goldfish which bugged him. And the

goldfish may even have been in the first piece [the one-act play]. And how he committed suicide by leaping off the bridge. And then, real clever this time, because through transubstantiation and reincarnation there's another goldfish in the bowl where Marge is playing bridge with the girls and it's got a nick in its left front fin as Mr. Twill had from offering a sugar lump to a milk-wagon horse which has bitten off his thumb and finger. It goes even further back to my interest in abnormal psychology and intention of taking psychiatry at one time.[75]

Bill was working on this novella when he was living with his mother in Weyburn. For the emotional frustration Mr. Twill felt in his relationship with Marge, Mitchell drew on his memories of how he felt as a child and an adolescent, and on his immediate feelings as a twenty-five-year-old man during this visit, when his mother was "moving into his territory." It is possible, since Bill was a fan of James Thurber's stories and cartoons, that he had in mind Thurber's "The Secret Life of Walter Mitty" (1932), a story about a weak husband who engages in fantasies of heroism because of a domineering wife. At any rate, female domination quite early took hold of Mitchell's imagination and is a thread that runs through much of his work, from some of the early "Jake and the Kid" short stories to *How I Spent My Summer Holidays*. Hugh quotes a particularly resonant line from Hesiod: the silver-age heroes are " '. . . eaters of bread, utterly subject to our mothers, however long they lived' " (*SH* 3). Female domination is only one variation on the theme of ascendancy and power in relationships which Mitchell explored in his work.

These were drought years as far as Bill's getting published was concerned, but he reaped benefits in other ways. His experiences as a harvest hand during the fall of 1939 led directly to his first "Jake and the Kid" short stories, although they owe something, as well, to his younger years in Weyburn on his Uncle Jim's farm. But there were other intangible benefits gained from this period, having to do with the shaping of his personality. These experiences affected the way he looked at and responded to his world and people, and ultimately determined the way in which he peopled his fictional towns.

Bill did not suffer as much as many who lived through the Depression, but even some fifty years later when interviewed about this period, he called them, with noticeable pain in his voice, "dreadful years."[76] Apart from the physical discomfort of going without food (for three days on occasion), there were emotional and psychological discomforts. The periods of loneliness spent in cheap dorms and boarding houses, the failed relationships, the continual struggle to survive by working at jobs that never lasted for more than a year or from which he was fired, the rejection slips, all inevitably led him into periods of depression. He even contemplated suicide a few times during these years, but was quite aware, in retrospect, that these suicidal thoughts were fleeting and were prompted by physical, external forces, in contrast to a later period when he began to question his inner worth:

> Now this was not a depressed period at all [in comparison to the early 1960s]. I was flying high, wide, and handsome. I had [two good jobs]. But I would always get fired. And then – dreadful. During those Depression years there were, I think, about three times I talked to myself about suicide. I recognize *now* how shallow that was. I don't think I came within a country mile of ever contemplating it. But I remember thinking of it, and with pain. And one of the things I would remember was, not once but a number of times, when I would walk all the way out to the Mission Bridge [in Calgary] and the snack shop and chat with the owner and be charming and then say, "Hey, I'm kind of broke but I'll pay you later – I'd like, ah – can I have a hamburger and a cup of coffee and a piece of pie?" And I think he knew. I think he knew [that I had been three days without food]. He was a hell of a nice guy.[77]

One night, when W.O. was about eighty years old, we went for dinner to a Greek restaurant in Calgary. His memory went back to the time he first came to Calgary in 1935. On that cold November day, without a job and without money, he went into a restaurant near the Calgary Herald *office and the owner, a Greek, realizing his situation, set down before him bacon, eggs, coffee, and toast at no charge. And then gave him discount coupons for the next five meals. W.O. explained that that's how it was during those hard times, and, he said, it was the immigrants and the hard-pressed workers who were the most giving, who with little themselves, gave so much. W.O. never forgot the ways in which people reached out to help him during those Depression years, and he repaid this debt in his own way by helping the underprivileged who came to him. In Mitchell's last novel,* For Art's Sake *(1992), Arthur Ireland establishes a haven of "sanctuary and friendship" (Art 21) out on Tongue Creek for four men who are down on their luck. He invites them to "stay there until you get back on your feet" (Art 19), a phrase that evokes some of the generous-spiritedness that W.O. himself experienced during the Depression years.*

These years also made him keenly aware of the community spirit that pulls people together in such times. The Depression was a great leveller. Through this decade Bill came in contact with people in all kinds of "circles" – from Gypsy fortune tellers, con artists, carnies, threshing crews, bindle stiffs, travelling evangelists to the "top-drawer" elite circles of "substantial" people. The Depression nourished his egalitarian sensibility. He was befriended and supported as much by the small cafe owners, the waitresses, the cooks, and the janitors as he was by his "top-drawer friends." His small-town upbringing, coupled with this experience of the 1930s, enabled him to form friendships with people from all walks of life. One of the direct results of this would be a fictional world filled with a rich range of characters in the tradition of Charles Dickens and Mark Twain.

These years toughened him mentally and taught him something about surviving in an extremely competitive job market. He had to be versatile, deal with job rejection, and sell himself. In the NFB interviews Mitchell described how the Depression freed him from a kind of Protestant ethic of work, money, and stability:

> I have seen lots of people ruined by the Depression, and I have
> seen people of my generation mean-spirited, niggardly, careful,
> gutless . . . as I said [the Depression] could either free you or
> enslave you. I think it freed me. I had some bad moments,
> waking up beside Merna with a year-old son . . . and I would
> wake up and think, Oh my God, I haven't got a steady job. I
> think that went back to the Depression.[78]

But, he explained, if you have been through the Depression, "if you
go that low and you get in that tough a position, to hell with money,
who cares about it." The Depression taught him to take chances and
he thought of himself as "a fast guy with a buck." But his attitude
towards money was more complex than this suggests. Whether it
was Depression or Scottish genes, he was not free with his money, at
least when it came to practical things like clothes, eating out, essen-
tials for the house. Yet he would think nothing of lending money
to help someone out and he could be extravagant when it came to
buying art objects such as antiques, paintings, or fine carpets –
although with these he loved to wheel and deal.

Bill never experienced personally any of the violence or social
injustices that radicalized some of his contemporaries. He was fortunate in having various safety nets like his home in Weyburn and
his fraternity house and brothers in Seattle, Calgary, and Edmonton.
He never had to go on relief. He was single and could afford to treat
this time of his life as an adventure. He was not then, nor did he ever
become, a political activist:

> I was terribly politically unaware at that time – I still am, I
> guess. I saw the unemployed lying in front of the buses and
> there was unrest – but I didn't really sense it.
>
> Perhaps it's because I've never been interested in groups, it's
> not that I hate humanity, but rather a case of being interested
> in individuals. . . .
>
> All I thought about [during the Depression years] was my
> stomach – jumping off a train after three days on the rails with

nowhere to go – ten-cent meals and ten-cent rooms – I don't see how the hungry revolutionaries survived – they couldn't have been that hungry – when you are, the only thing that matters is the ache in your guts, not some ideal or philosophy.[79]

Although he declared himself "terribly politically unaware," he did have a philosophical curiosity about the political scene.

In 1966, about a year after this interview took place, I recall having a discussion with my father about Steinbeck's novel In Dubious Battle *(1936). On one level this novel is a starkly realistic portrayal of a communist agitator and his protégé attempting to organize a strike in the apple orchards of Salinas Valley in the early 1930s. I had been very impressed by this relatively unknown Steinbeck novel and felt that in some ways it was a more powerful exploration of the plight of migrant workers in the Depression than* The Grapes of Wrath. *I recall my father saying that during these troubled Depression years anyone who was really worth their intellectual salt knew something had gone dreadfully wrong with the capitalist status quo and flirted with, if not subscribed to, communist and socialist remedies – was a "fellow traveller" to one degree or another.*

Mitchell's politicization was more in the sense of becoming concerned about human-rights issues as, for example, in his participation in the Stoney Indian land claims in the 1940s. He rarely used his writing as a didactic platform for a political or ideological message, although he did, like Steinbeck, often use it to dramatize and expose "political" issues in which individuals' freedoms, rights, dignities, and personal or cultural identities are encroached on or "vanished," the word he uses with multiple implications in *The Vanishing Point*. Mitchell, whose father had been a Conservative candidate, never took that route of active politicking.

In his interview with Harry Boyle, Mitchell referred to himself as "a watcher and observer." What could be termed Bill's political naïvety was a direct result of his essentially artist's frame of mind, which was instinctively attracted to the individuals and situations he encountered with an innocent and wide-open sensibility unencumbered by political party lines or ideological preconceptions. This is not in any way to detract from his entrepreneurial initiative in finding ways of surviving these difficult times – nor from his patient persistence in following through on his desire to be a writer for some seven years without any financial support or audience encouragement. Given his particular circumstances and his frame of mind, he moved through this decade as both a privileged observer as well as a participant.

9

EDMONTON

— 1940 to 1942 —

B ILL LEFT Weyburn and returned to Edmonton at Easter
1940 where he continued selling the *World Book Encyclopedia*
and working on "Mr. Twill." He lived at the Strathcona
Hotel on Whyte Avenue through the summer and into the fall,
paying twelve dollars a month for his room. Both his writing and his
love life up to this point had been apprenticeships characterized by
rejection. The first domino to fall in the sequence of events which
led to his being fully indentured as lover and writer took place in
May when he sold a set of the *World Book Encyclopedia* to the wife
of the minister of Strathcona Baptist Church, Mrs. Evelyn Hirtle.

One of the sales angles used by *World Book Encyclopedia* was to
obtain lists of social-studies students' names and addresses from
school principals. In return the schools would receive a free reference set of encyclopedias for every ten sets sold to their students.
Mitchell said that the *World Book Encyclopedia* was a good reference
set and "was the cleanest book or sheet-writing job that I was ever
in."[1] Bill got the student list for the King George Junior High
School, and a teacher went over the list pointing out likely prospects.
One student, Spurgeon Hirtle, was dismissed, described as "an odd
one" by the teacher, who added that his father was the minister of

the Strathcona Baptist Church. But Bill decided to try out the track he had used on prominent opinion moulders of the community during his previous stint selling *Colliers Encyclopedia*. So, decked out in a topcoat, creased pants, a homburg roll-brim hat, and a shoeshine, he called at the Baptist parsonage, which was only a few blocks from his hotel: "Mrs. Hirtle answered the door and I went through my pitch and my illustration. Shit, did I ever sell that *World Book Encyclopedia* right there and I made forty bucks on that."[2]

Mrs. Hirtle was an ideal prospect for Bill's track. She was British-born and, although not upper-class, put stock in a good education. Also, she was concerned about her son's poor performance in school (which Bill knew about from the teacher) and hoped that the encyclopedias would help him improve. Mrs. Hirtle was very impressed by this young but obviously discerning encyclopedia salesman who assured her that her son's academic performance would show miraculous improvement if only he had the *World Book* reference set.

Bill must have been pleased with his success. His commission from this sale would look after his meal and room expenses for about a month. But he had no idea how beautifully he had scored, for this sale led to the most important event in his life. When he delivered the encyclopedias the following afternoon, Mrs. Hirtle was not there, but her daughter, Merna, was. Merna was completing the last two high-school credits for entrance to university in the coming fall. They described their first meeting:

> w.o.: And this little cookie met me at the door and then I had
> to sit down and show how the encyclopedia set worked so
> she would be able to tell her brother how to use it. And –
> you put me off a little bit because those big dark eyes were
> so goddamn sincere and so intense and we sat down on the
> couch together there and while I was explaining it, "Oh
> yes," you were saying, "Oh yes, yes." And here's this kid
> because – how old were you in 1940, Merna, in the spring
> of 1940?

MERNA: I was twenty.

W.O.: You had just turned twenty and I was twenty-six and I had not been leading a sheltered life the previous eight years, I can tell you. And she got talking about how – you had just been in *Love on the Dole*, hadn't you?

MERNA: The year before.

W.O.: Oh well, but anyway you had been in it. And she had discovered that I acted and she insisted on my reading with her the love scene on top of the hill from *Love on the Dole*. What I haven't told you was, Merna, I was embarrassed.[3]

Walter Greenwood and Ronald Gow's play *Love on the Dole* (adapted from Greenwood's 1933 novel) is about the devastating effects of unemployment and hard times on a British working-class family. Sally Hardcastle and her lover, Larry Meath, a factory worker, are in love, but without hope for any economic security:

SALLY: Larry, we've got to get out. . . . Ne'er mind Hanky Park! We'll be wed soon. It's you an' me . . .

LARRY: That's it! You and me and to hell with the others. Oh, what's the use of talking? I love you, Sally, better than anything else on earth . . . but it's no use . . . God, it's no use![4]

Near the end of the scene Sally "impulsively throws her arms round" Larry, and, at the end, he "buries his face in her hair." On the surface it looked like a boldly flirtatious act on Merna's part to ask Bill to read this scene with her. However, in their retelling of the event, the motivation appeared to be an enthusiastic sharing of a common interest in drama. This play, and this scene in particular, was the high point in Merna's acting career. Their impromptu performance illustrates the spontaneity that characterized both Merna and Bill and that drew them to one another.

Bill left the parsonage with mixed feelings. As well as feeling slightly embarrassed about reading the love scene from *Love on the*

Dole with this "little cookie," he probably felt some guilt about wrapping up his "con" encyclopedia-sale performance with those sincere and intense eyes watching him. At the same time, although he saw her as a "kid," he was intrigued by her, attracted to her wide-eyed interest in his pitch and in acting. Merna's initial impressions of Bill were similarly mixed. She already knew something about him. When she had come home from school the previous day, her mother had told her about his visit and commented that he was "just the kind of young man I'd like to see you go out with."[5]

Merna thought that Bill was too old for her, and was not really interested in him until later that summer. She was giving swimming lessons at the Edmonton Southside pool when Bill arrived one afternoon to work out on the three-metre board:

> W.O.: I didn't see Merna until June when I showed up at the Southside swimming pool and at the far end was this compact little girl with black hair in a black wool bathing suit with about – what would you have, thirty, fifty kids?
>
> MERNA: Oh they were broken up. Of course there were wee little ones – I could have had up to twenty or twenty-five at a time.
>
> W.O.: Telling them to put their faces in the water and blow bubbles. And of course I get up on the springboard and start to work the board and, you see, the quality of diving in Canada compared to Florida was not up to much, and I would be doing dives, some of them they hadn't even seen – a cut-away backward spring forward one and a half.
>
> MERNA: Oh yes, we'd seen Phyllis Harris –
>
> W.O.: [interrupting] Phyl Harris couldn't do a cut-away one a half, for Christ's sakes! All she could manage was a one and a half – that was the top of her degree of difficulty. And some gainers. But she could not, she was not doing a cut-away swan – it was a back jackknife. She was certainly not doing even a single cut-away one, let alone a one and a

half. That's back to the board, you jump backwards and
then you do a one and a half against the board when you
go in. And I guess that's when Merna fell for me. I don't
know, that's up to her.

MERNA: No, I didn't fall for you then. We used to talk, you
know, at the end of the pool. There were bleachers outside
the fence that people could come and sit and watch people
swim, and then they also had these bleachers at the other
end of the pool and we'd take towels and we'd lie and sun
on those and Bill and I would talk. And I thought he was
just being kind to me and that's about the time that Bob
McDermaid and Elgin Brisbin came and suddenly I was
getting a lot of attention. Now Elgin wasn't as old as Bill
or Bob but I thought Bill was just being kind.

W.O.: [wryly] This old guy![6]

This is typical of Bill and Merna's exchanges through the years. Bill
exaggerated, Merna qualified – and suffered being interrupted. In
interviews, Mitchell frequently dramatized this event even more,
saying that he and Merna "met under water." And while her version
of why she "fell" for him – they "would talk" – is less dramatic, it is
more revealing about the reasons for, and depth of, their initial
attraction for one another.

Bill was now captivated by this "girl with black hair" and
intense eyes, and he moved in on Elgin Brisbin and the other young
men who had begun to call on her. Merna "was really flattered"
when he asked her to go to a show at the Princess Theatre on Whyte
Avenue. His goodnight kiss, as he remembered it, was a rather
formal affair, a flourish and a kiss on the forehead. Merna recalled
that her mother was watching from the window and was "pretty dis-
approving."[7] When Merna alone was interviewed and cast her
memory back to this evening, she responded that Bill had been very
considerate: "He wasn't too fast coming on, if you know what I
mean. He was – he was – really nice. Really nice."[8]

Bill started seeing Merna regularly and by the beginning of August they were deeply in love. Two of Bill's love letters to Merna have survived, both written to her in August 1940, when Merna went with her parents to Banff to take a drama course and then to Jasper for a camping holiday. The first letter is handwritten on Strathcona Hotel letterhead:

Dearest:

It's no use. I told myself before you left that I wouldn't write you a slushy letter – that I'd only write once a week. Here I am writing again after having sent one last night. As to the second rule I'm afraid that feeling as I do tonight any letter I write would have to be shovelled through the mail. Well they can just bloody well shovel because Myrna when I'm in the mood to write a slushy letter – I write a slushy letter.

In the first place dear, I love you. I don't mean that I just 'love you'. I mean that you've packed your overnight bag and moved into my heart – or maybe it was a steamer trunk because I have a feeling you'll be there for a long long time.

I hope you remembered to bring your tooth brush and have a room with a nice view of the lungs and liver. I have to add things like that because if I don't I'll be saying extravagant things like "you're part of me" and "I miss you horribly" and things like that. I have to watch myself on it because you are part of me now and I do miss you horribly. When you remember that I love you too you can see I'm in a bad way. I've found a way to help that though. The hotel lobby is a great place for strangers to pass through. I just sit in one of the chairs and when a stranger begins to pass through I stop him –

"Lovely day," I say brightly, or "Dull day," dully if it is a dull day.

"Been to Banff at all lately," I usually say.

If they say no I tell them you're there and I say I miss you. I tell them all about you and then show them your picture.

"She's one of the kind with black hair and dark eyes. Vest pocket edition and with the nicest _____ well you know dearest – shocked?

One fellow said, "Yes, I know her. Daughter of the minister of my church. I agree heartily with you on that last. I noticed it myself numerous Sundays."

"Oh you did, did you," I said. He looked kind of funny walking out of the lobby, wearing a spitoon [*sic*] on his head.

I ran out of strangers to talk to about you last night. That may explain why I'm so full of love tonight, dear. I love you, Myrna – so damn much it hurts. Good night my dear.

Bill[9]

Mitchell used his first impressions of and feelings for Merna during their courtship as an emotional base for his description of Digby's interest in Miss Thompson in *Who Has Seen the Wind*. When Digby first meets the new teacher, Miss Thompson, he is immediately drawn to her, and one of the first things he notes, as Bill did with Merna, is the age difference, although here it is a much larger gap of thirteen years. There are considerable similarities between Merna and this attractive, energetic, and feisty schoolteacher, and Mitchell attributed a great deal of his own lovestruck obsession with Merna to Digby. Like Merna, Ruth Thompson was "a young woman with quick and definite features" and had "blueing-black hair." Bill had always been attracted to dark-haired, dark-eyed women, and Ruth "had the sort of dark eyes that seem all pupil, so deep is the brownness of the iris." But, beyond physical attractiveness, Merna, like Ruth, had that positive, welcoming enthusiasm that Bill admired. Miss Thompson's response to Digby's hope that she will like her new school is applicable to Merna: "She assured him that she would; the sudden expressiveness of her face, the girlish quality of excitement in her, warmed Digby to her immediately. He was positive that this was an honest woman" (*WW* 153). Later on, Digby realizes that he wants to marry Ruth:

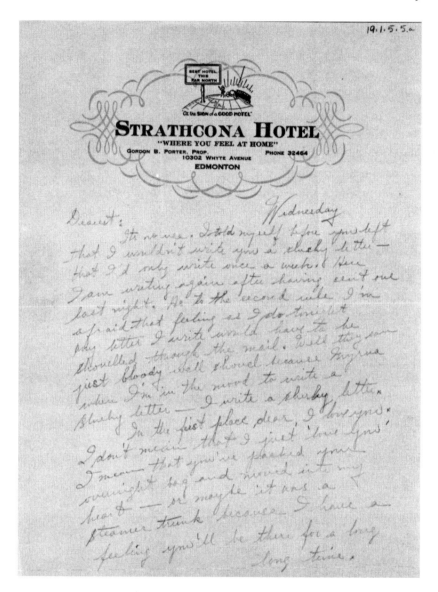

The first page of Bill's letter to Merna, 11 August 1940.

As they talked Digby felt, as he had a hundred times the delight of just being with the woman. Just as simple as a drink of water on a hot day, except, he reflected, that the thirst was ineffable. Her gaze was so direct sometimes as almost to disconcert him; in her eyes now was a look that told him plainly she understood him, a look that established complete and intimate understanding. (*WW* 245-46)

Miss Thompson is not sure that they are meant for each other and turns down Digby's proposal. Merna, too, was to call off her engagement with Bill. In *Who Has Seen the Wind,* as in all his fiction, Mitchell explores the difficulty of arriving at that "complete and imitate understanding" with another, and discovers that it is as elusive as the wind, as difficult to sustain as Brian's "feeling." Although he and Merna were to marry within two years – and stayed married for their lifetimes – Mitchell was often to say how "lucky" they were, indicating the fragility and mystery of such connectedness.

⁓ MERNA AND HER FAMILY ⁓

Merna adored her father and had his openness and enthusiasm. Spurgeon Maskell Hirtle was born at Mahone Bay, Nova Scotia, on 26 August 1897 into a staunchly Baptist family who named him after a great Methodist evangelist: "He was called to the ministry in early childhood, and the fact that the name 'Spurgeon' was chosen for him by his parents betrays the thought and the atmosphere that influenced his life as a child, and explains, in part at least, the spiritual authority and power of his ministry."[10] At seventeen, when he began his B.A. at Acadia University, he was already preaching. When war was declared, he felt it his duty to join, and on 10 March 1916, when he was eighteen and a half years old, he enlisted. Six months later he arrived in England and was then sent to France. In January 1918 he gained the rank of lieutenant and was to be promoted to the rank of captain just as the war ended. He showed great bravery and leadership at the front and in 1919 was awarded the Military Cross. The citation reads:

> For marked gallantry and good leadership of his platoon during the attack on the Canal de l'Escaut, at Escadoeuvres on the morning of 10th October 1918. At a critical moment his platoon

was held up. He rushed an enemy machine-gun post in the face of intense heavy machine-gun fire, putting them out of action. On arriving at the objective he took charge of a reconnoitring patrol and obtained information of great value to his company commander.[11]

In France he met Evelyn Steele, an English girl who was serving with Queen Mary's Army Auxiliary Corps. Evelyn had been raised in West Hartlepool in the north of England. Her mother and her father (who had been a silversmith) had died when she was eight, and she had been shuffled around amongst her older brothers and sisters. It would appear that she had not been given very good schooling, for Merna can recall that, later in Hudson, her father would teach grammar to her mother. The insecure life she had had as a youngster later took the form of a great dependence on her husband, and then on Merna. In France, Evelyn was assigned to mess duty and there she met Spurgeon (who was called Spud). She was a genteel-looking young woman, small in build (about five foot two). Merna said that it was probably her mother's looks, kind-heartedness, and sense of humour that first drew Spud to her. She was just what Spud needed during those tough times, and, perhaps, he was intrigued by her hearty sense of humour because he, himself, was serious and fairly straitlaced. They were married in France on 3 March 1919, returned to Mahone Bay in May, and Merna was born on 11 February 1920.

Spud resumed his studies at Acadia in the fall of 1921 and completed his B.A. in 1923. He did very well, with most of his grades at 85 per cent or higher. He was an excellent athlete, and was involved in hockey, tennis, pole-vaulting, and rowing. He was captain of both the track team, which won the intercollegiate championship in 1923, and the hockey team. His agility, not his stature, accounted for his athleticism, for he was a small man, about five foot five. Later, when they moved to the Boston area, he was invited to try out for the Boston Bruins, which had just been established as a National Hockey League team.

Ancestors of Merna Lynne Hirtle

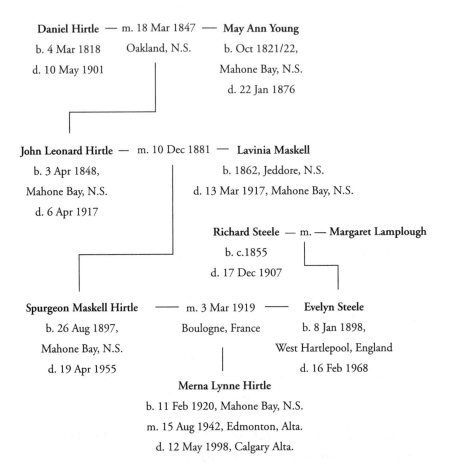

Daniel Hirtle — m. 18 Mar 1847 — **May Ann Young**
b. 4 Mar 1818   Oakland, N.S.   b. Oct 1821/22,
d. 10 May 1901   Mahone Bay, N.S.
                                   d. 22 Jan 1876

John Leonard Hirtle — m. 10 Dec 1881 — **Lavinia Maskell**
b. 3 Apr 1848,   b. 1862, Jeddore, N.S.
Mahone Bay, N.S.   d. 13 Mar 1917, Mahone Bay, N.S.
d. 6 Apr 1917

Richard Steele — m. — **Margaret Lamplough**
b. c.1855
d. 17 Dec 1907

Spurgeon Maskell Hirtle —— m. 3 Mar 1919 —— **Evelyn Steele**
b. 26 Aug 1897,   Boulogne, France   b. 8 Jan 1898,
Mahone Bay, N.S.   West Hartlepool, England
d. 19 Apr 1955   d. 16 Feb 1968

Merna Lynne Hirtle
b. 11 Feb 1920, Mahone Bay, N.S.
m. 15 Aug 1942, Edmonton, Alta.
d. 12 May 1998, Calgary Alta.

Merna's brother, Spurgeon Steele Hirtle, was born on 1 March 1923 in Wolfville. A few months later, Merna's father graduated from Acadia and took the ministry of the Baptist church in Canso. However, he wanted to further his career in the ministry and, when Merna was five, in the fall of 1925, the family moved to Newton Centre, a suburb of Boston. Here Mr. Hirtle entered the Andover Newton Theological Seminary, to which he had received a scholarship to do post-graduate studies. After graduating with his B.D. degree in 1928 he became minister of the First Federation Church in Hudson, Massachusetts.

Life in Hudson, a small town near Boston, was very happy. Merna described a lively household and good childhood friendships. She went on trips to Boston with her father and mother and holidays on the coast at Marblehead. Merna's mother, however, was not the typical Baptist minister's wife. She enjoyed the secular life – playing tennis, attending movies, dancing, and even taking a glass of wine, which Spurgeon himself never did, although he never denied her one. Even before they left Hudson, Merna's mother had started leaning on her, asking her to prepare food for the many visiting parishioners.

Had it not been for a difficult political situation that erupted in 1935, they might well have stayed on in the States for many years. Rev. Hirtle was well liked by his parishioners. He was not an evangelistic, fire-and-brimstone preacher, but one who was rooted in reality and concerned about everyday problems. He put great stock in common sense, in an ecumenical community of faith, and took an active interest in the political and economic issues of the day. In fact, Merna recalled one of the parishioners saying that he was "quite socialistic."[12] He was very disturbed by the closing of the Firestone plant in Hudson and was a supporter of President Roosevelt's many plans to make work for the unemployed. But he felt it increasingly difficult to speak out from the pulpit on political issues. Finally, one issue allowed him no room for compromise.

In the spring of 1935, as fear of an approaching world war gathered momentum, a bill, sponsored by the American Legion and endorsed by the Senate of Massachusetts, was put forth requiring all teachers, professors, and instructors in educational institutions to swear allegiance to the constitutions of the state and of the federal government. The bill was seen by educators as an invasion of freedom of speech (particularly academic freedom), and a "wedge for a Fascist regimentation of schools and churches."[13] There was intense debate about why teachers (including church teachers) should be singled out to swear allegiance, and why schools should be subjugated to the state. Sixteen colleges and universities in Massachusetts, including Harvard, strenuously opposed the bill.

Andover Newton Theological School, Rev. Hirtle's school, passed a resolution stating that the oath "violates the spirit of our American tradition of a free church in a free state."[14] Perhaps Rev. Hirtle had a hand in writing it. At any rate, he was very involved in the debate, and Merna vividly recalled that her father joined forces with the Harvard professors to fight the bill. She remembered that he was called the "fighting parson."[15]

He felt strongly that, if he were to stay in the States and take out citizenship, he would be unable to take the oath of allegiance. He could, in good conscience, support the taking up of arms to defend the nation against an aggressive attack (as he had done so gallantly during the First World War), but he would not swear to support a government that initiated the aggression. In fact, he advocated changing the wording of the oath to reflect that qualification.

In March 1936 there was a three-day hearing before the Legislative Committee on Education at the State House. In spite of a slate of speeches against the bill, the State House of Representatives on 6 April 1935 refused to repeal the ruling. Disillusioned by the failure of the repealers and unable to take the oath as it stood, Rev. Hirtle felt he had only one recourse – to resign from his church and leave the States. So, after eight years in Hudson, he and his family left for Canada. Merna was immensely proud of her father's stand and was marked by his example. She was always interested in political events and nothing animated her as much as a good rousing political debate, whether local or global.

Before the Hirtle family moved to Edmonton, Merna had almost completed two years of high school in Hudson. She enjoyed school but her English class was her favourite. She remembered that one of the assignments was to write in a kind of impressionistic manner, similar to what Mitchell himself was later to characterize as "freefall" writing. This early encouragement, as with Bill's English program at St. Petersburg High, helped to build in her a confidence in self-expression and fostered a willingness to try new things. She was on the college course stream, and, although her mother was less encouraging about her schooling, her father had expected that she would attend Wellesley or Smith. Merna had also shown a musical talent and, until she was twelve, was given piano lessons and sang in the church choir. Her father encouraged her to perform readings, in the same way that Mrs. Mitchell encouraged Bill, and Merna was often "in demand" to do recitations.[16]

Rev. Hirtle accepted the ministry of the Strathcona Baptist Church in Edmonton and drove his family (Merna was sixteen and her brother Spud was thirteen) from Boston to Edmonton at Easter 1936. The Edmonton Strathcona High School was a difficult adjustment for Merna because the school insisted that she start at grade nine, so she was nearly two years older than most of her schoolmates. Probably because of this setback Merna turned to other ways of expression. She made friends with Betty McNally, who attended the same high school and the same church, Strathcona Baptist. Betty's father, Dr. G.F. McNally, was a powerful man, not only at the church, where he was treasurer and on the board of deacons (and probably responsible for hiring Rev. Hirtle), but as the deputy minister of education for Alberta from 1935 to 1946. The two girls had similar interests: both were headed for university and both were interested in music. They sang in the church choir and together they began doing recitals, with Betty playing the piano and Merna singing. Right from the start Betty thought Merna was "very neat . . . always a little bit different from the average south Edmonton girl."[17]

Through a parishioner who knew of Merna's interest in drama, she was invited to audition for CKUA, the University of Alberta's broadcasting station. In her first fall in Edmonton Merna started taking roles in a radio series, "New Lamps for Old," for the CKUA Players and, over a period of two years, she played most of the young female parts. She then became involved in the series "Building of Canada," which was written by Elsie Park Gowan and ran for a year. In his book on the Banff School of Fine Arts, David Leighton describes how Merna became involved in this series:

> There was a very talented girl from Edmonton in the drama class that year. Her name was Merna Hirtle, and Elsie [Park

Gowan] was so impressed by her she later used Merna in many of her radio plays. "The first series I had on the CBC was called 'The Building of Canada', and Merna was every heroine from the seige of Quebec to the discovery of radium in the north. She was awfully good. I remember her telling me she had a good friend who was trying to write short stories." [18]

Merna then became involved in the Edmonton Little Theatre, coincidentally around the same time that Bill was acting for Calgary Little Theatre. Her first stage performance, in May 1938, was as the fiancée of the son of an over-possessive mother in *The Silver Chord* by Sidney Howard. The reviewer commended her for "excellent command" of the role, "particularly in some stormy scenes which might have failed to convince if sincerity and conviction bolstered by the right touch of restraint had been lacking."[19]

In the spring production (March 1939) she played the young heroine in *Love on the Dole*, the play she asked Bill to read with her on their first meeting a year later in May 1940. It had been a challenge to learn the Lancashire dialect for her character, but she did it well, and her reviewer said that she "richly earned the special plaudits she received for a performance adorned by tender insight and intelligence. Her scenes with the doomed Larry were profoundly affecting and persuasive." Fourteen hundred people attended this performance, which was pronounced "one of the most noteworthy and commendable efforts in the ten-year history of the Edmonton Little Theatre."[20]

It looked as if Merna was headed for a career in theatre. Indeed, through her acting roles for "The Building of Canada," she was offered scholarships to pursue an acting career at Iowa State University and with the Provincetown Players (Rhode Island).[21] As well, a visiting British director, who had heard some of her radio work, urged her to go to Britain to train as an actress.[22] But more interesting to Merna was an acting school in Seattle that had been started by Florence and Burton James, with whom she had studied at the Banff School of Fine Arts during the summer of 1938. They had founded the Seattle Repertory Playhouse and, in conjunction with that, a drama course which trained young actors. Unfortunately, there was no scholarship for that school, and Merna decided she could not afford to go. Furthermore, the war, her family commitments – and Bill – interfered with these plans.[23]

When they met in the spring of 1940, although Bill was six years older and Merna was still in high school, Merna was not really the "kid" Bill saw her as. Although small and girlish in stature, she was neither retiring nor unsophisticated. In fact, as their friends of the time noted, Merna was a steadying influence on Bill, who could appear quite "flighty" at times.[24] About the time that Bill was introduced to the Hirtles, Merna's home life was growing more complicated. Her seventeen-year-old brother, Spud, who was not doing well at school, and had always been spoiled and protected as a child, was becoming more and more of a problem. He was rebellious and had a temper, and he resented his mother's interference. Mrs. Hirtle was alternately hysterical and defensive about him. Never one to participate energetically in her husband's ministry, she had become preoccupied with Spud. So, many of the household and social duties fell on Merna's shoulders. In some degree the mother–daughter roles were reversed, and Merna treated her mother as "dear little Mother." The church people knew the situation and made allowances for Mrs. Hirtle. Although she was well liked (as one parishioner noted, "she was just a darling"[25]), Mrs. Hirtle was also self-centred and naïve.

Rev. Hirtle was highly thought of by his parishioners. Merna's best friend, Betty, "just worshipped him," and Dr. McNally was one of Rev. Hirtle's chief supporters. Betty described Rev. Hirtle's sermons as very emotional and very powerful: "Never a sermon went by that he didn't weep."[26] Bill, too, admired Rev. Hirtle, and even though he had given up attending church he would frequently take a seat in the last pew, beside Mrs. Hirtle, and not just to see Merna, who was singing in the choir at the time. Merna said that her father and Bill immediately connected: "Dad really loved Bill, he really did. He knew what Bill was like, that he was a man of integrity and that he could trust his daughter with him, and they got along beautifully."[27] Mitchell said that he and "Pop" had "an awfully nice flow between [them]":

> Pop and I talked a great deal. Pop was uncomfortable with the emotional, mindless approach – the charismatic emotional quality of the Baptist religion compared to Presbyterian, Anglican, or Catholic. And he quoted a section from the Bible in which it said, "Thou shalt love the Lord thy God with all thy heart, with all thy soul," and, he said, they are forgetting the third one, "with all thy *mind*."[28]

As in his sermons in Hudson, Rev. Hirtle sometimes addressed contentious social and political issues of the day. Bill admired his resoluteness in taking up positions which raised the hackles of some of the businessmen who were influential church members. Mitchell recalled one Sunday in particular when he was sitting with Mrs. Hirtle directly behind Chester Gainer, "a porcine type of guy with his neck bulged over the back of his collar." Gainer was a deacon who took up collection and was a brother of the owner and founder of Gainers Meat Packing. Bill, fascinated, watched the effect of the Reverend Hirtle's sermon:

> I didn't know what was going to happen with Pop when he got up in the pulpit. Intelligent as hell, he was articulate and he was caring. It was the late end of the Depression years and his sermon for the day was, "What do you think Christ, who threw the money-changers out of the temple, would think today of an administrator or corporation head or somebody hiring people for a sixty-hour week at eight dollars per week?" Now, I'm looking at the back of Chester Gainer's neck – Pop knew it, and Pop was pissed off with the whited sepulchre of this guy active in the church, passing the collection plate and paying eight bucks a week – [Gainer's neck] became more and more porcine, it became pinker and pinker – the skin under the little stubble bristles on the back of his neck became scarlet.[29]

Merna inherited her father's social conscience and caring nature, and later she was often the advance antenna that drew Mitchell's attention to social and political issues. In *Who Has Seen the Wind*, Miss Thompson's outrage at and condemnation of Mrs. Abercrombie's racism and power politics at the school-board meeting may owe something to Merna and her father. Indeed, Mrs. Abercrombie herself is modelled on some of the upright members of Rev. Hirtle's Strathcona Baptist congregation.[30]

Bill's relationship with Mrs. Hirtle was more guarded than that with Rev. Hirtle. While he was pleasant to her and called her "Ma," he found conversation more limited. Merna said he was particularly troubled by the way in which her mother controlled and imposed on her: "Bill would have the odd run-in with my mother because she was still trying to manipulate me as if I were a child and he resented that, and maybe there was a bit of tug-of-war for my position on both their parts."[31] While some of this was simply a mother's fear of letting go of her daughter, there was a more serious personality conflict between mother and husband-to-be. Always protective of his own inner territory, Bill resented Mrs. Hirtle's moving in on Merna's territory, just as he had resented his own mother's invasions. In particular, however, he disliked the way Mrs. Hirtle played on what he came to call "Merna's Baptist guilt." Bill felt that Mrs. Hirtle spoiled Spud at Merna's expense and generally took advantage of her. By the time she was in her teens, Merna was doing most of the cooking and housework. According to Mitchell, Mrs. Hirtle enjoyed a life of leisure, listening to the afternoon soaps on the radio or attending matinees at the movie theatre. Early on in his courtship of Merna, Bill and two of her other boyfriends (Elgin Brisbin and Bob McDermaid) sarcastically referred to Mrs. Hirtle's laziness in a letter to Merna when she was holidaying with her parents and Spud in Jasper: "Nous espérons que tu ne laisse pas votre mère travailler trop durement ou somme[s] nous trop comme les chats quand nous dison[s] des remarques comme ça?"[32]

At one point in their courtship Bill got caught up in the Hirtle family politics. Merna was doing some housecleaning and trying to get Spud to do his homework when he threw one of his tantrums, turned on her, and called her a "bitch." Outraged, Bill threw a glass of milk in Spud's face. Spud started bawling and Mrs. Hirtle, who heard the commotion, came rushing hysterically to Spud's defence. When Mr. Hirtle arrived on the scene, his wife accused Bill of bullying their seventeen-year-old son. Bill explained the situation, and Mr. Hirtle reprimanded Spud. This incident illustrates the nature of the Hirtle family dynamics, which were only to grow more tense as Spud grew up.[33] Later, Bill would often have to mediate between mother and son and even protect Merna against herself when she got wrought up about her family situation.

⁓ ENGAGEMENT ⁓

During this first summer in Edmonton, Bill was able to get only occasional work as a lifeguard. He did not tell Merna that at times he could not afford to have one, let alone three, square meals a day. Merna learned about this only after they were married: "He would come home from the pool, and I would give him bacon and eggs. I didn't know it was the only food he had. He never told me. I was furious when I found out."[34] Finally, in August, he got work as a harvest hand in Rabbit Hill. He borrowed young Spud's bike and cycled the twenty miles or so from Leduc to the farm where he worked as a spiker and field pitcher:

> I was what was called an alternating spike or field pitcher. Each guy had a rack and would fill it and when he had it half-filled the field pitcher, to speed things up, would come along and help finish that. As soon as he finished one he'd go to the next rack, of which there would be six to eight in the field pulling up to the thrashing machine with their team. So the field pitcher got no load rest while he waited for his turn to come up. This was a man killer. The spiker was the guy on these two racks on either side of the feeder who would get up and join a

guy and help unload. He got no rest either, but you got an extra fifty cents a day.[35]

On the weekends he would ride Spud's bike back to Leduc and then make his way to Edmonton by bus or by hitchhiking.

One of the weekend social activities, established before Merna met Bill, was to get together to listen to classical music. Merna, Elgin Brisbin, Bob McDermaid, and Bob Kerr (who was later a host on a CBC stereo program) were the regular participants in these music evenings. Occasionally Betty McNally dropped in and, when Bill started taking Merna out, he met the group. This was one area of interest which Bill did not share with Merna:

> I would be just plumb dead after a week, and I would come back and sit beside Merna, whom I was in love with now. I was even kissing her by this time. And they would be playing *La Bohème*. So I would sit there bathed in this goddamn music. This is why I hate opera so much today. It's a bastard art of melodrama, no restraint, predictable, excessive, and awful. If there's anything Merna hates to see me do is to sleep at an unusual time in a room with other people. And I would fall asleep.[36]

By August, two of Merna's suitors had given up the field and were standing by to see if Bill's victory was final. When Merna was in Banff during the first part of August attending drama school and holidaying with her parents, Bill, Elgin, and Bob got together to write her a letter. The first part of it is in French and Bill explains that he and Elgin (who was studying for a French course) and Bob have gone on a "drinking binge" ("grands quantités du lait") because they all miss Merna so much. He thanks Merna for the photographs she sent him: "J'en ai donné une à Elgin. La reste sont à ma chambre à côté des cela de ma famille dans la miroir de ma bureau." The letter is predominantly teasing, but Bill tells her that he loves her: "Good by mug. I still insist that I love you and this isn't Elgin." The other serious moment is when he tells her that he has sent off "Mr. Twill" (his novella) to a publisher and has been working on a new story, "Jake and Frobisher."[37]

Merna was the first person in whom Bill confided in any detail about his writing. She recalled reading "Mr. Twill" and some of the early "Jake and the Kid" material and described "Mr. Twill" as a "fantasy or science-fiction story which didn't sell." She said, "Very few people knew that he wrote and wanted to write when I met him. He didn't talk about it that much."[38] In fact, Bill was at this time quite despondent about his failure to sell any of his stories, and his sharing the news about "Mr. Twill" with her indicated the depth of his feeling: "Of all the girls I had ever gone with – and I had been writing all through those years [in Seattle and Calgary] – Merna's the first one I told I had written."[39] In November Bill gave Merna an emeraldine ring, and they were engaged.

What Bill needed at this point in his writing career was what he had found in his diving coach, Pep Smith, when he first began to learn high-degree-of-difficulty dives in Florida: a sympathetic yet critical eye to tell him what his performance looked like, where it was going wrong, where it was succeeding. In later years, remembering his own frustrating and lonely years of apprenticeship, he would tell his students that no one could teach them how to write:

> Writing is like playing a dart game with the lights out so that the writer has no way of knowing whether his darts are coming anywhere near the centre or are missing the board entirely. This is a cruel analogy, a first-rate nightmare for all writers. Even though the light comes on and readers may indicate he has scored, the next time the artist plays the game it will be in the dark again. Imagine the frustration of a learning young writer who has no one to turn on the light for him – no one whom he can trust. Blood relatives, wives and lovers, dearest friends are all compassionately untrustworthy.[40]

However, an experienced mentor can turn on some lights for the beginning writer. And Merna, in some ways, was an exception to Mitchell's general rule about lovers and wives, for she was always able to dispel some of the dark with her intuitive and critical insights: "From the time I first met Merna I shared with her my writing and early discovered that Merna's critical judgement was important to me. She's my first editor."[41]

– UNIVERSITY OF ALBERTA –

In September 1940 Bill was admitted into the third year of the B.A. program at the University of Alberta.[42] He took the four arts courses he needed to complete his degree, and he enrolled in Philosophy for interest's sake. Although he dropped it sometime after Christmas, he submitted two essays, "An Understanding of St. Francis of Assisi" and "In Defense of Idealism." These essays have survived and throw some light on Bill's thinking and reading at this point in his life.[43]

"An Understanding of St. Francis of Assisi" gives a lively biographical portrait of how "the head of a band of young spendthrift troubadours became an ascetic." The statements at the end of his essay are presented in first-person and the conclusion Bill arrives at, that "sincerity – intelligence – sympathy . . . are the virtues of civilization," is a reflection of his personal philosophy. The essay is enlivened with an easy informality and with metaphors he will use in *Who Has Seen the Wind* (on which he may have just begun to work): "Francis no more reasoned his way of life than a tree does its growth or a sheet of lightning, the brilliance with which it winks up sharply and clearly the landscape over which it plays."

Bill began "In Defense of Idealism" by saying that every human is a potential philosopher who should strive to "clarify his thoughts" to "find out what he really is" and thereby "add sureness and vigor to his life and through it to the community in which he lives." His "faith in the idealist way of life" has recently been shaken by the "pragmatic viewpoint as articulated by Bode, James, and Dewey," and he says he is writing this essay to test the idealist and pragmatic views and thereby reorient himself. Referring to his own life, Bill says that he cannot accept the pragmatist's view of empirical time:

> Imagine a writer who devotes two hours of his waking day to writing. Empirically two twelfths of his life are devoted to writing while the other ten twelfths are made up of some other occupation, say that of insurance salesman. In time then, the man is two twelfths writer, ten twelfths insurance agent. Such a division is convenient, but it is not true, for if the writing is more important to him than the activities concerned with the selling and explaining of Twenty Pay, Pension at Sixty, Double Indemnity, then the writing becomes more than a mere episode in his life. It is his whole life – his life as a whole. And if his writing warrants it, the two twelfths of his life may become part of all time. He is at home with all writers, past, present, and future.

Bill concludes his essay by reaffirming his faith in the efficacy of idealism and its transcendent abstractions. The pragmatist's accusation that the idealist is "an aristocratic Lady of Shalott" living in an ivory tower is false, for "the idealist . . . does look at the river of life, and unlike the pragmatist, looks not just at that section before his window, but up and down stream as well." Far from isolating him in an ivory tower, the idealist's "dissatisfaction with the actual" leads to growth and expansion, to "an essentially progressive movement akin to everything which is truly alive." Later, Bill will use this same argument when he is accused by his Toronto writer friends of escaping to an ivory tower in High River.

As at Manitoba, academic performance took a back seat to other activities. Bill had discovered what he really wanted to do – write – and he was writing. And, of course, he still had to make money to support himself, so he continued to sell the *World Book Encyclopedia* during the school year. In January, for the University of Alberta Dramatic Society's annual spring play, he played the male lead, Dan McEntee, in James Bridie's comedy *What Say They?* Merna played the female lead, Ada Shore. Merna did not like the play itself and one reviewer commented that it "was a most difficult play to produce." It required Scottish and Irish accents, but Bill could do that well given his bond with Grandma McMurray. According to the reviewer for the *Edmonton Journal* Bill's "accent at all times was most authentic."[44] The audience, however, must have had difficulties understanding the actors, for the *Edmonton Bulletin*, although noting that Bill was "completely natural and at his ease," commented that "the words were obscured by his accent."[45] Merna also received contradictory reviews from the two papers: the *Bulletin* commented that she "put vitality and reality into her part" whereas the *Journal* noted that "she did not appear to be at ease" in the role.

Merna, too, had a mixed degree of success that year with her university courses. She did very well in her French and received a second in her German. But her other course marks (Philosophy, Zoology, and English) were all in the 50s. With little encouragement from her mother for continuing in university, and, on the other hand, some success in theatre, and marriage on the horizon, she thought that university was not for her.

– PROFESSOR F.M. SALTER –

Merna had met F.M. Salter, an English professor at the University of Alberta, through the historical dramas she was acting in at CKUA. Salter was interested in CKUA as a possible market for some of the writers in the creative-writing course he had started the year before. Early in September, through Dick MacDonald, a friend of Merna's who was a director at CKUA, Bill was urged to show some of his material to Salter.[46] An appointment was set up, and Bill went to Salter's office with his portfolio, which included some finished short stories and the just completed "Mr. Twill." As he was pulling out work from his portfolio, he paused over a short piece he had written a few nights before and said, "I won't give you this." Salter assured him that he'd like to see all the work. When Bill responded, "No, no, it's just handwritten," Salter insisted, "I read a lot of crappy handwriting."[47]

A few weeks later at his second meeting Salter more or less dismissed most of the finished stories Bill had laboured over for the past few years, but was fascinated with the short handwritten piece. Bill recalled the meeting: "Salter said, 'This is vulgar, this is very clever, this is publishable, but *this, this!*' – and here were these about four pages of handwritten recall, and he said, 'I'd love to know what happened to that boy before this and after it.' And that was the true genesis of *Who Has Seen the Wind*."[48] "*This*" was the first of Bill's experiments in what he would later call freefall, a kind of spontaneous writing in which he set down as quickly as possible whatever floated to the top of his consciousness without any attention to technique or theme or structure, with no story or novel destination in mind. What he had handed Salter were four pages of recall about standing in the cemetery at his father's grave and seeing his mother cry. This was the first writing that had come unbidden from the heart. Here was a dart Bill had thrown in the dark which had hit the bull's eye. Mitchell never forgot the moment Salter excitedly turned on the lights for him.

Fuelled now by Merna's and Salter's encouragement, Bill began writing about the young boy Salter was so intrigued by. He had written enough by late November or early December that he decided to submit two stories, "Spalpeen" and "Ants Don't Care," to *Queen's Quarterly*, an academic journal which published serious fiction alongside its literary criticism. *Queen's Quarterly* acknowledged receipt of these stories on December 30 but subsequently rejected them. Although the original manuscripts are missing, it is likely that these stories were early versions of episodes in what are now chapters one and three of *Who Has Seen the Wind*. It was probably one of these stories that Robert Blackburn (who had taken Salter's 1939-40 creative-writing class) recalled hearing Bill read at the Hirtles' one evening. This impromptu workshop was engineered by Merna:

> One night some of us were invited over to Hirtles'. I can't remember what the occasion was but it turned out to be a reading. Bill was reading something that he had written. . . . Mrs. Hirtle brought us some cookies and tea. There were perhaps a dozen of us sitting around. Bill was reading and Merna was saying, "No, you can't say *that*," or, "You can't say it *that* way." This was from one of the chapters of *Who Has Seen the Wind*.[49]

Even though Salter himself modestly suggested that he only "straighten[ed] [Bill] out a little,"[50] his role was much more significant. In fact, from 1939 until his retirement in 1960, Salter was the midwife for a great deal of Western Canadian writing when Canada's literary culture was really beginning to come of age. Among some of the notable writers he worked with were Henry Kreisel, Christine van der Mark, Rudy Wiebe, and Sheila Watson, whose *The Double Hook* may never have been published without his help. He had a gift for inspiring beginning writers and worked tirelessly behind the scenes, encouraging them and giving them detailed critiques. In some cases he played a key role in getting their work published and he was directly responsible for two of his writers being *Atlantic Monthly* "firsts." One of these, Robert Blackburn describes Slater's workshops:

> In the classroom he read to us from our own work or from other sources either good or bad, and through comparison and example he passed on to us his love of the right word and accurate detail, his ear for apt expression, his impatience with anything shoddy. . . . He taught us that the most important things to wonder at and write about were those within our own experience.

He assigned no topics, but required each of us to write something every week. He handed our papers back promptly, marked in red with a fine nib, and some of our pages returned more red than black. His annotations could be stern but never unkind or discouraging, and sometimes ended with an invitation to go to his office for a talk; altogether we took much more than a reasonable share of one man's time. In our excitement as "makers" many of us wrote far more than was required, went on writing even after the course was ended, and years later continued to fill the Salter mailbox with our manuscripts and our hopes.[51]

From fall 1940 to spring 1942 Bill met regularly with Salter, occasionally sitting in on his writing classes and Shakespeare lectures. He was doing a great deal of freefall:

More and more often I found myself travelling back into my stored past to find someone I had loved or hated, dramatic incidents, sights, sounds, feelings, smells. I wrote them down in detail. It wasn't writing; it was finding. When I would touch base with Salter almost weekly I would give them to him to read. In a way it was an imposition, for I was not enrolled in his creative writing class. We often met in his backyard after he had put aside the lawn mower or the hoe – or in his living room or office at the university. At the end of almost six months in one of our meetings he said, "Bill, this stuff you've been showing me is autobiographical chaos. You've got to start behaving. I've been going over all of it to see if there's any possible literary order suggested."

He pulled the great pile of papers across his desk. With Scotch tape tabs he had singled out page parts. "Let's consider these." (*Eve* 257-58)

Salter then pointed out how much of this material suggested a "strange pattern"[52] of "birth, then death, then birth, then death" and asked Bill if he noticed "anything promising in the way of a novel." When Bill responded that he could not see any "plot," Salter said, "Forget plot. Think symphony" (*Eve* 258). Once Bill's attention had been drawn to the underlying motifs in his freefall, the shaping process "became deliberate and that is the genesis of the symphonic structure with the refrain effect and the increasing birth and death moments" of *Who Has Seen the Wind*.[53]

As well as drawing Bill's attention to shaping his freefall into "literary order," Salter reinforced for him the importance of the quality of grace achieved through restraint:

> I came up with a very clever, I think connotative, phrase that was so bloody smart, shockingly, unusually, unpredictably, vividly great. When I talked with him afterwards, sure enough he had marked this particular thing and he said, "That's pretty clever." I can't even remember what it was. I'm sure it would be a connotative word that through a cross-fertilization suddenly made something stand out vividly. I said, "Yeah." He said, "I wonder what Katherine Mansfield would think of it?" And my heart just sank to the bottom of my boots. I knew right away what he meant. It was so bloody clever, so unusual that it called all attention to itself and it therefore was flawed because it was not gracefully done. It was done with self-congratulation – see what a smart boy am I.[54]

On the dedication page of *Since Daisy Creek* (1984) Mitchell lists F.M. Salter as the fourth mentor to whom he owes "IOU's." One of the characters in this novel, Professor Lyons, is in part modelled on F.M. Salter (along with Rupert Lodge at the University of Manitoba): "He'd taught him to write. He'd taught him to teach. And what a tricky teacher *he* was. With what cunning sleight-of-hand he palmed truths and insights and hid them in his students without their knowing it, to appear magically years later" (*SD* 71).

I remember meeting Professor Salter in the fall of 1961 when my mother and father drove me up to Edmonton for my first year of university. My parents had not seen him for about fifteen years, and I remember their excitement about meeting him again and their pride when they introduced me to him. It was then that I learned that my father had spent the night with Salter when I was born and that Salter had wakened my father, who had fallen asleep on their couch, to tell him the hospital had called and that Merna had had a boy. In the fall of 1961 Salter was suffering a great deal of pain in his elbow and his hip from arthritis. He now had to lecture sitting down. I recall being a bit puzzled by the way my father was with Salter during this visit. He obviously admired and respected this man and felt a great deal of gratitude for what he had done for him. But there was a reserve, a formality, about the way he was with Salter that was unlike the way my father was with his close friends. When he introduced us he said, "Professor Salter, this is our son Orm," and throughout our visit he called him "Professor Salter." I visited with Professor Salter and his wife a number of times that year and acted as a messenger for my father, who gave me orchid blossoms from his greenhouse to give to Mrs. Salter and their daughter Elizabeth. I recall one visit in particular. I had received very poor grades on my first two English essays and at my father's prompting went to see him. The topic I had chosen for my next essay was "The Role of the Fool in King Lear.*" Salter talked with me for well over an hour but he did not* tell *me anything – he simply asked me questions. When I responded to his questions I would get a noncommittal "Perhaps," or another question. I was disappointed when I left his house because I felt that I had not learned anything. But as I reread* King Lear *and worked on my essay over the next week I realized that I had learned a great deal. His "cunning sleight-of-hand" questions turned on some lights for me and helped me learn how to discover insights on my own. I received 80 per cent on that essay, my first first-class university grade.*

Salter thought of Bill at this time as a "boy" who innocently got himself into dreadful scrapes and had to be looked after. Soon after they met, he was giving Bill "fatherly" advice, not only about writing, but about the direction his life should take. During the summer of 1940 Bill had made up his mind that he was going to complete his B.A. and then go into law. However, Salter quickly advised him against this plan. He felt that Bill was a "born teacher" and convinced him to go into education, arguing that a teaching career would enable him to salvage more free time for his writing.

Twice Salter had to rescue Bill from scrapes. In the first instance, Bill ran afoul of a professor who was teaching him English 53. Although he did well enough on assignments, according to a classmate Bill missed so many of the classes (because he was working on his novel) that the professor threatened to flunk him.[55] Salter intervened in some way, and Bill received credit for the course.

The second mess that Bill got into was more serious. At this time the university required male students to take the Canadian Officers' Training Course (COTC), which involved twice-weekly sessions of small-arms practice and parade drills. Mitchell attended COTC throughout the fall of 1940. By Christmas, however, his wrist was "inflamed and puffed" from the small-arms drill. He went to see Dr. Cantor at the university student-health services and told him about his tubercular wrist. Dr. Cantor said it was "ridiculous" for him to be doing COTC (because his tuberculosis meant that he was not eligible for service) and told him to stop going.

In the spring he discovered that his final marks were not listed. He went to see Mr. Ottewell, the registrar, to find out what the problem was, and was told that for every time he was absent from COTC practice he should have filled in a slip:

> "Well," I said, "okay, we'll make out a lot of absence slips. I've told you now." And I remember his very words. He said, "When you go out into the world after you leave university" – he's talking to a son of a bitch who has been without food for three days and slept in pogies and scratch-houses and sheet wrote – "you are going to discover that if you do not get to the train on time and the train leaves the station you cannot call it back."

Bill tried to argue his case, but Mr. Ottewell only offered Catch-22 alternatives:

> Ottewell said, "I see by this that because of your medical record you can't enter the army. One way you could make this up, you could go to" – and he named the camp where soldiers trained in the summer. "But," he said, "I see you are too old to qualify for that." I was at the cut-off age or something. "So those are your two possibilities."

Mr. Ottewell's patronizing observations about missing trains and impossible "possibilities" were too much for Bill's patience and he lost his temper:

> And that's when I said, "Thank you for your goddamn alternatives that aren't alternatives." I'm standing in front of him and I said, "I've been a radio salesman, I've been an insurance salesman, I've been an oil-well royalty salesman, and I have never called on anybody in an office where they were rude enough to keep somebody standing in the goddamn office while they told him dreadful, ridiculous news." He said, "Get out of my office." Now that is a verbatim thing (but I didn't say "goddamn" at that time of my life).

Bill was lucky that Salter overheard this conversation (probably quite deliberately) and he cornered Bill as he was leaving Mr. Ottewell's office:

> I came out and do you know who was standing out in the hall? Great big dark-eyed Mr. Salter. He said, "All right, what have you done now?" I said, "I just told Mr. Ottewell he was the rudest person I've ever known in my life." He said, "I see. I guess you are never going to learn, are you?" I said, "Well –" "Now," he said, "you've got to learn to eat humble pie." He said I had to, and I had to do it weekly.[56]

Salter coached Bill on how to go back to Mr. Ottewell every third day and plead for a solution to his predicament. After some eating-humble-pie meetings with Mr. Ottewell, Bill was told that he would have to go to see Dean Smith. But Dean Smith told him that the decision rested with the registrar, Ottewell. So Bill alternated his pleadings with the two men through most of May and June until, finally, Dean Smith told him that if he took a summer-school course he could attend the COTC sessions provided for summer-school students. He had to do COTC five times a week during the summer, which was the equivalent of a full year of the training, even though he had taken the training up to Christmas the past fall.

Through the summer Bill also worked for the City of Edmonton as a lifeguard at the west-end swimming pool. He had to do some fast footwork to keep up all three activities:

> I used Spuddy's bike and I would ride to my shift at the swimming pool. Mattie [his boss] always had a sleep in the afternoon, thank god. And I would get on the bike and ride it clear across town and over the high-level bridge and then take army in my goddamn lifeguard ducks, putting the bloody rifle up and everything else, and then ride back. I cautioned Obie if Mattie wakes up and says, "Where's Mitchell?" tell him I'm in the filter house either doing chlorine or, better still, because Mattie was hung up on it and we had a key machine, tell him Mitchell's grinding keys.[57]

Bill's University of Alberta transcript indicated that a letter was received 16 August 1941 "from Dean Smith stating that Mr. Mitchell has completed all military training as required by Senate. Credits may therefore be released." He completed History 4 that summer and needed only to complete French 2 to satisfy all of the requirements for his B.A. degree.

In the fall of 1941 Bill enrolled in three education courses and French 2, which he had dropped the year before. He was impatient with the education courses (which he found neither challenging nor useful) because of the time they took from his writing. But by the late fall of 1941 his life had settled down and taken on a clear direction. He and Merna set their wedding date for the following summer. Merna decided to work full-time to save money towards their marriage, and she got a job with the Department of Agriculture.

By November, Salter's intuition that Bill was a "born teacher" proved correct. In response to a concerned letter from Mrs. O.S. about her son, Salter replied, happily, that he had settled down:

> I hear golden reports of Bill in the College of Education. This year I have a little one hour job of teaching there myself, so that it is possible to know something of what is going on. Bill has also told me of some of his experiences in practice teaching. I think he has "found himself" at last – he seems to have a real gift for teaching. . . . I am most anxious that he keep out of the dreadful mix-ups that dogged him last year, anxious also that he should come through the year so well that he may be able to get the best job going with the solid recommendation of the whole College of Education behind him.
>
> Writing is better as a hobby than as a job. When he gets into teaching, I hope he will have time for the hobby, and there will always be plenty of material to write about. A lad like Bill just naturally picks up ideas everywhere. . . .
>
> I feel confident that Bill's progress from now on will give you nothing but happiness – and you may be very sure that I share your pleasure.[58]

Salter's observations about teaching as a job and writing as a hobby should be qualified. Mitchell would be committed for the rest of his life to the vocations of writing and teaching, and he would look on neither of them as hobbies – except insofar as a hobby is an activity passionately, intensely, and obsessively pursued for its own sake. At first he would see his teaching as a necessary financial support for his primary vocation, writing. But throughout his life teaching held a special attraction for him and, as Salter foresaw, it afforded Bill some extremely rich material for his writing.

– FIRST ACCEPTANCES –

By the summer of 1941 Bill had been coached by Salter for almost a year, and he had written a substantial amount on his novel "Spalpeen." Two stories from it had been rejected by *Queen's Quarterly*. In late summer Bill finished another short story, "Ab and Annie." Salter, beginning his stint as Bill's "literary agent sans 10%," suggested that they try *Maclean's* this time. In his covering letter to Jack Paterson, the fiction editor, Salter praised the story's humour and depiction of prairie farm life. On September 23 Paterson wrote Salter rejecting the story because it was based on "human afflictions" (Ab has a club foot and Annie has a "cock eye"). Paterson was worried it might "misfire" with their readers. "Ab and Annie" explores the idea that "very frequently we love the dependent or the thing with a flaw in it."[59] The narrator, a young boy who visits his uncle's prairie farm, tells how he saves a runt pig from being killed by Ab, the hired man, and how he helps Annie arrange to get glasses to fix her cock eye so that Ab's romantic interest in her will be clinched. Ab, however, loses all interest in Annie when she gets her glasses. This episode basically remained intact in the final version of *Who Has Seen the Wind*.

Although Paterson rejected "Ab and Annie," he was impressed by Mitchell's "sense of humour and splendid . . . sense of atmosphere and character," and he asked Salter to submit more of his work.[60] Mitchell recalled that "when they turned down 'Ab and Annie' Salter said, 'those [the characters] are interesting people.'" At this point Salter suggested transforming the story, and the main characters "became Jake and the Kid instead of Ab and Annie and Brian."[61] Bill promptly set to work on this story and within three weeks gave Salter "Elbow Room" – and this was "the genesis of the 'Jake and the Kid' series."[62] A few years later Salter described to Dudley Cloud, managing editor at *Atlantic Monthly*, how "Elbow Room" had grown into a story:

> And I said, "Well, you're far enough along to make *Maclean's*. Would that please you?" It would. Very well, then. You must use the prairie, and you're good with youngsters. You need a good character. Let's try the tall-talker – nobody has ever done much with him. Farm, of course – tall talker and kid. Since it's war time, the kid's father is overseas and this tall talker fellow runs the farm. Now what? There's that German prisoner who escaped the other day; we'll send him to the farm – thrashing time, and he gets a job stooking. What effect would the prairie have on him? The freedom. All that space. Elbow room. I thought of a symbol, a fly stuck in amber in a paper-weight: "All my life I haf that fly been." It was a good story, and *Maclean's* took it.[63]

This was Mitchell's first acceptance, on 28 October 1941. Salter's letter, which shows the sort of one-on-one workshopping sessions that he and Bill had, does not accurately reflect the history of this first "Jake and the Kid" story. The Jake character, his colloquialisms and his tall tales, did not materialize in a short two- to three-week period just after the rejection of "Ab and Annie." Ab (glum, taciturn, God-fearing) and Jake (sociable, colourful, down-to-earth) are very different characters. More than a year earlier, Bill had told Merna that he was working on "Jake and Frobisher." It probably originated during the Calgary years from 1935 to 1939 when he was writing stories about the Depression. Jake grew out of the transients, bindle stiffs, and farm workers Mitchell encountered in the 1930s. So Mitchell had created a character named Jake before Salter came on the scene. Probably Jake already had some of the characteristics of the tall-tale teller, although it was through Salter's suggestion that Jake became the hired man of the "Jake and the Kid" stories.

Salter quickly identified Bill's strengths (his feel for the prairie, his interest in the "tall-talker," and his ability to recreate the inner world of children), and pushed him towards a plot and theme. In fact, Salter gave him the conflict for the story – what will Jake and the Kid do when they discover that they have hired an escaped German prisoner to do their stooking? Already in this first story the place (Crocus, Saskatchewan), the time (the war years), and the main characters (the Kid, his mother, and a hired man) are established. As well, Jake's signature characteristics are well developed here – his tall tales ("He's the only man ever threw Looie Riel three times in a row"); his malapropisms (referring to a dead body as "corpus delicious"); his figuring ("yer Ma's . . . drunk twenty-seven five-hunerd-gallon bar'ls of tea"); and his prairie-isms ("my tongue swole up and cracked like summer fallow after four years drought"). As in most of the stories to follow, it is the Kid who tells the story. His language, like Jake's, is colloquial and down-to-earth ("our stooker had Jake skinned a mile at the dinner table"), and, more than anything, he wants a "Little Daisy twenty-two rifle" to "touch off" gophers. However, his sensitive, at times poetic, side shows itself in his many descriptions of the prairie landscape:

> A person feels very sort of peaceful lying on their back under a whole lot of sky. I could hear the wind going like when you blow on tissue paper – somewhere a gopher squeaked – a meadow lark let go a few notes. But the gopher and the meadow lark sounded funny; they didn't sound real – not alongside all that quiet. She was kind of numb out there, like the prairie bumped its funny bone.[64]

"Elbow Room" contains rich imagery, yet what distinguishes it from the others is its political topicality. The trigger for it was, as Salter indicated, a news item. In September and December 1940 and February 1941 the *Edmonton Journal* ran reports about escaped German prisoners of war.[65] Although Mitchell dealt later with racial prejudice and community issues in his "Jake" stories, they more frequently concerned human foibles and relationships. But in "Elbow Room," the advantages of democracy over the horrors of dictatorship are didactically and sentimentally spelled out. As a result of the prairie's "elbow room," the escaped German prisoner comes to the realization that "in this world there is no room for dictators. You in Canada know this – it is not so clear to some who have never known the prairie, and the friendships it breeds. . . ."[66] While the Kid, Jake, his tall tales, and the prairie descriptions are all Mitchell creations, the stooker, including the image of him as a fly trapped in amber, was Salter's idea. The plot, with its political overtones, is not the best aspect of the story. To be fair to Salter, the theme of reforming a Nazi was made more didactic through the insistence of Jack Paterson, who was afraid that it would not "pass with the reading public" at this time unless it was made "*very* clear that the Nazi had been reformed through his encounter with 'elbow room' and genuine friendship, something unknown to him before."[67] Mitchell made the required changes without protest. Interestingly, Salter, who thought of the "Jake and the Kid" stories in general as popular, not serious, literature, proclaimed this story better than any other of the "Jake" stories, an assessment, perhaps, more personally biased than critically sound: "I don't mean that there is anything wrong with the Jake and the Kid stories; we have had fun out of them – I've suggested quite a few of them – but the best of them all was the first. And that's bad."[68]

Although "Elbow Room" was Mitchell's first acceptance (he received eighty-five dollars for it), it was almost eleven months before *Maclean's* published it, on 15 September 1942 (a month after they published "You Gotta Teeter"). Perhaps they were still uneasy about "Elbow Room"'s "borderline theme" and felt their readers would be more receptive to it if they had been first introduced to Jake and the Kid in another story. Because of this delay, it was *Queen's Quarterly* that first published Mitchell. In February 1942 he sent them "But as Yesterday," another story based on an episode from "Spalpeen." *Queen's Quarterly* accepted it May 29, and it was published in their 1942 summer issue. Their fee of fourteen dollars was his first payment for close to eight years of writing. But Bill was particularly proud of being published in this quality periodical, especially alongside Sinclair Ross, whose short story "Cornet at

Night" was also in this issue. Here was the first tangible sign that his work was being taken seriously.

"But as Yesterday" is a moving story about a grandfather's last days. It involves a situation and characters which attracted Mitchell's imagination numerous times over his writing career – the exchange of a gift that symbolizes the link between the young and the old. The grandfather, who lives with his daughter-in-law, makes a top out of a wooden spool for his grandson, tells him tall tales about his early life as a pioneer coming out West, and reflects on the transience of his life in the face of impending death: "Now that eighty years had imperceptibly declined, moment by moment piling up their careless weight, the old man knew his life for a firefly's spark in much darkness."[69] The grandfather's death, suggested only through the image of a twig breaking off under the "careless weight" of falling snow, is juxtaposed to the young boy sitting on the floor, learning to spin the top. At first it falls, but finally he gets it to spin, just as his life will spin out its days like his grandfather's. This story was altered for *Who Has Seen the Wind*, where it is Brian's grandmother who is dying and she knits him a pair of hockey socks as she tells him the same tall tales as the grandfather told. Mitchell will come back to this situation in his novel *The Kite* and in his stage play *For Those in Peril on the Sea*.

"Elbow Room" and "But as Yesterday" represent two different strains of writing that Mitchell continued to pursue throughout his career. There were the pieces, predominantly comic or humorous, written for popular media or for public performance, and, on the other hand, there were his novels and stage plays, the more literary works. This generalization must be qualified, for "Elbow Room," like many of the other "Jake" stories, has a serious theme, and all of his novels contain humorous episodes. Salter was quick to recognize the danger of Bill's facility in the comic mode, warning him early on about being lured into writing "tripe" for the popular-magazine and pulp market.[70] Mitchell did not completely escape some of the demands and traps of this slick market, both early and late in his career – partly because writing was how he made his living, not just a hobby. Therefore he had to make compromises, but it is also true that he was inherently drawn to comedy and to writing for performance.

In December Bill had an attack of appendicitis, and it was, said Merna, her father who "saved his life": "He insisted that Bill go to the university doctor to be examined and they put him in hospital right away and operated on him. And then he spent a week with us recuperating before he went back to his boarding house."[71] Around this time Merna was rehearsing for *The Pirates of Penzance*, a Gilbert and Sullivan production put on by the Philharmonic Society of the University of Alberta. Merna had been asked to play the lead even though she was not a university student. However, when it came to the opening, it was decided, at the last minute, that the understudy, a university singer, should take the lead. The performance then moved to Calgary and Merna played the lead role in the Friday-night and the Saturday-matinee performances. Unfortunately she had a bad cold and was very disappointed with her performance; the newspaper review was less harsh: "Miss Hirtle has a light, pleasant soprano, though not always completely adequate for the role's extensive vocalizing."[72]

There was drama behind the scenes too. Merna had fallen for one of the actors in the musical. Around the end of January she broke off with Bill "because I thought – well, I was so damned innocent that I thought if I could be interested in somebody else I wasn't really interested in him, and my god did I miss him! I soon found out. It was a good experience. It was good for me because then I knew for sure."[73] Bill was devastated, but it was only, said Merna, a "brief crush." Soon she and Bill were back together, and they set their wedding date for August 15.

Bill passed his three education courses and was hired as a life-guard at the Edmonton Southside Pool beginning in June. During May and June he spent time on his writing, and his second "Jake" story, "You Gotta Teeter," was accepted on May 13, for which he received a hundred dollars. *Maclean's* was now interested enough in Mitchell that they wanted to have another look at the "Ab and

Annie" story. But in early June they decided that it was still too risky a piece for their readers.

The next six weeks were frantic. Bill had two courses to make up. During the fall session he had once again dropped French 2, so this was his last chance to take it to complete his B.A. requirements. He was also taking Educational Psychology to complete his Senior Diploma and High School Teaching Certificate. Once again he was bending university regulations. Only one course was allowed during summer session, and he was not supposed to have a job. He borrowed Spud's bike for the summer and pedalled furiously four times a day between the pool and the lectures for his courses at the university.

He had to cut a few corners. Because of his fluency in French he thought he would be able to slide through French 2 with a minimum of effort. He simply decided not to read about half the texts on the course and hope that he would get lucky on the final exam. He was not. One of the main questions was on a novel he had not read. He decided to be creative; he answered the question, in French, based on characters and a plot he made up as he went along. He must have charmed his professor with this ploy for he scraped through the course.

The major paper for the course in Educational Psychology was required during the second week of August, and he had done no work towards it because he was so preoccupied with writing his novel. But he came up with a bright idea which not only saved him some time but afforded him some useful research for the novel. He was particularly fascinated with Jean Piaget's work on child psychology, which helped him to crystallize insights he had already arrived at through observation of children at play. Bill asked the professor of this course if he could do a variation on one of the topics. Rather than writing a descriptive summary and analysis of some of the standard educational psychology theorists on the course, he would do an essay reversing the process. That is, he would begin with their abstract theoretical conclusions about the various stages of the child's psychological development and attempt, through the fictional devices of dialogue and stream-of-consciousness narration, to create a child's world dramatically illustrating the ways children view their world, use language, learn, think, and fantasize. According to Mitchell, the professor thought this was a "wonderful creative idea"[74] and told Bill to go ahead with it. Mitchell admitted later that, at least in part, he was doing a con job on his professor. Over the previous twenty months he had already written a great deal of this kind of material for "Spalpeen." And much of it had been based on first-hand observation:

> I am staying at Florence O'Neill's boarding house and listening to little kids across the fence in the sand pile and that's where I got my conversations for the wee little ones and learned about their asocial nature – that one kid says something and the other one is on another course. And the "song-ones" that Brian called them – they're the echolalian things. I'd be out there with a notebook all the time. They were dear little children.

Bill felt that he had done "the most beautiful paper"[75] – and he received a respectable 74 per cent for the course.

It was just the day before he was married that he completed all of his course assignments and exams. He loaded the library books he had used during the summer into a wheelbarrow. As he was wheeling the books up to the return counter, he passed Professor Lazerte, dean of Education:

> Dean Lazerte came out and saw the wheelbarrow and the books and he said, "It looks as though you spent a very busy summer." I said, "Yes." He said, "Taking that French course from Dr. Sonet" – which I wasn't supposed to. And I said, "Yes." And he said, "And working at the Southside swimming pool as well." Dean Lazerte had known through the whole goddamn summer![76]

He managed to keep his head above water in his two courses, but lifeguarding proved to be more dangerous. This was the summer that he almost drowned attempting to save a "pool-crawler," a non-swimmer who ventures into the deep end of the pool by hanging on to the gutter and pushing himself along the side of the pool with his hands and feet.

This is the way I remember my father telling the story: There was this one guy, a fat Greek, that I kept warning to stay out of the deep end. He must have weighed at least three hundred pounds. But he persisted. Sure enough, one day he crawls down to the deep end, is holding on to the gutter with one hand, and next thing you know he's floundering and bellowing about ten foot out from the edge. I get in the water behind him and wait for him to go under a couple of times, and then try to get an arm around him, and the next thing I know he's grabbed me and is pulling me under with him. And he's strong, probably a goddamned Greek wrestler. I managed to get partially free and surface for a good breath before he pulls me under again and we sink to the bottom of the pool. By this time he's managed to get me in a leg-scissors hold around my waist and pinning one of my arms. So I figure I've got a good breath and I'll wait him out and we lie on the bottom of the pool for a good minute. Well, he still isn't letting go so I helped him along a bit – I hit him with my free hand as hard as I could in his Greek balls. He let go then. When I came to the surface I grabbed the edge of the pool and I'm seeing sparkly lights and sucking down air and Jimmy, the pool manager, is yelling at me and I can't make out what he's saying and I'm looking down trying to see the bugger on the bottom of the pool. And then I hear what Jimmy's saying: "Let the son of a bitch drown, Bill! Let him drown!" Well, I didn't. I waited another minute and then dove down and pulled him back up by his hair – I wasn't going to get any closer to him than I had to. Jimmy banned him from the pool for the rest of that summer. I don't think he'd have come back again anyway.

Merna was having her own problems during the few weeks before her wedding. Spud, against his parents' wishes, had enlisted in the army in June 1941 and had been sent overseas in December. It was quickly apparent to those in charge that he was not suited for army life, and after a couple of incidents he was hospitalized in May 1942 in England. The original complaint was a stomach problem, but, on undergoing a complete assessment, he was diagnosed with chronic anxiety neurosis. He was deemed unsuitable for further military service and sent home. The Hirtles had been informed of his arrival back in Canada and of his admission on June 18 to Ste. Anne's Hospital in Montreal, but they had been given no other information. In July, one month before his daughter's wedding, Mr. Hirtle wrote to the minister of National Defence complaining that he and his wife had been kept too long in the dark about their son. It had only been through a friend that they heard he was suffering from nervous exhaustion. Rev. Hirtle requested that Spud be sent to a hospital closer to home where he could benefit from family care. Finally, on August 1, Rev. Hirtle was given the official diagnosis that his son was suffering from schizophrenia and that within the week he could be transferred closer to Edmonton.

Just one week before Merna's wedding, Rev. Hirtle went to Montreal to accompany his son home by train. When Spud arrived home on August 13, it was clear that he was still very confused and disruptive. When he started referring to Mrs. O.S. Mitchell as Hitler, Rev. Hirtle decided to commit him to the Provincial Mental Hospital at Ponoka, where he underwent a series of shock treatments. Merna did not know all the medical details at the time, and it would be typical of Rev. Hirtle to shoulder most of the responsibility himself so as not to spoil her wedding day.

~ MARRIAGE ~

On Saturday afternoon, 15 August 1942, William Ormond Mitchell and Merna Lynne Hirtle were married at the Strathcona Baptist Church. "August 15," said Merna, "was hot – it was absolutely beautiful."[77] Merna looked dramatic in her floor-length bridal gown, her dark long hair rolled to shoulder length, showing off to great effect her headpiece wreathed with orange blossoms. Bill, whose ideal woman was dark-haired and dark-eyed, must have been immensely pleased. In unofficial photographs they look smiling and adoringly into one another's eyes. It was a marriage that lasted a lifetime – and adoration and laughter were key to its longevity.

Merna's father officiated and a close family friend of the Hirtles, Dr. McNally, gave the bride away – reluctantly, as Merna would always add! Dr. McNally made it quite clear that he thought that "our Merna" could get a much better man than a beginning teacher with a crazy obsession to become a writer. Also, Dr. McNally may have thought that Bill at twenty-eight was too old for Merna, who was just twenty-two. His daughter, Betty, who was Merna's best friend, was to have been bridesmaid, but she had recently married and was out in Vancouver. So, Billie MacDonald, a friend from church, was her bridesmaid.

Chet Lambertson, with whom Bill had become friends through an English class and Salter's composition course, was the best man. Bill, in fact, was Chet's best man before the favour was returned, and Merna had sung at Chet's wedding. Well known in the university circles as the composer of the University of Alberta's official varsity song, Chet was a talented musician and was fast becoming respected in professional musical circles as the leader of a very fine band, one that was compared to Mel Hamill's and Guy Lombardo's.

In the official photograph of the wedding couple and their parents, Bill stands rather stiffly beside his mother, who is slightly ahead of the group and turned, as if to show her best profile to the camera. She looks sophisticated, but austere, in her long navy gown with ecru lace on the bodice and her wide-brimmed navy hat. Overshadowed by Mrs. O.S., Mrs. Hirtle in her floral silk dress stands relaxed and unassuming beside Merna. Rev. Hirtle and Dr. McNally stand at either side of the group. Following the photograph session was a reception for sixty held in the Hirtle home, at which Dr. Salter gave the toast to the bride.

Bill and Merna loved the coincidence that this was the day that Bill's first story appeared in *Maclean's*, and that on the cover of this issue was a painting of a little white church. The story, "You Gotta Teeter," is an endearing "Jake and the Kid" story, less didactic and political than "Elbow Room" and with more Jake colloquialisms. It is set during the war years in Canada, and the Kid has been asked to give a speech to raise money for refugee children from Belgium, France, and England. As he prepares for it, he discovers that his pup, Mr. Churchill, has been killed on the road. Although the Kid is devastated, Jake convinces him to make the speech. His advice to the Kid is that to be an effective "orator" you have to "teeter." According to Jake, "Wilf" (Sir Wilfrid Laurier), Canada's greatest orator, told him that "if 'tweren't fer teeterin', there wouldn't have bin no Canada" (*JK* 6). Although "teetering" obviously refers to the physical gesture of rocking back and forth while pondering the next illuminating words, Jake implicitly suggests that there are other requirements for a successful speech. Teetering also suggests a kind of keyed-up state with the "stumick all squoze up" (*JK* 9) and a sense of responsibility so as not to "turn quitter" (*JK* 7). When the Kid gets up to speak he stumbles around, talking about the loss of his pup, but finally connects pups with kids and relates his feelings of loss to the lonely feeling of the refugee children who are in Canada without their parents. The speech, of course, is a great success, marked by the donation of ten dollars by "the tightest man in the district" (*JK* 13).

Perhaps on this day, 15 August 1942, Merna had little idea how great an "orator" Bill was going to be, but she must already have sensed that he was something of a "teeterer," living his life on the edge. The Depression years proved that he was no quitter, and the next two years were going to see the two of them teetering between a relatively stable career in teaching and a risky career in freelance writing.

Their honeymoon had the comedic drama of a Charlie Chaplin movie. They left for Sylvan Lake by bus in the late afternoon. They had a miserable trip seated next to a drunk, and when they arrived they discovered to their dismay that their room was on the west side of the second storey – and this was one of the hottest mid-August days on record. The next day Bill went looking for cooler accommodation and discovered a small cottage. As usual he bargained and got the landlady down in price – although she had the last laugh.

Because of the reduced price she had refused to clean the cottage, which was "filthy," so Merna and Bill spent the morning cleaning. Their every move – including their trips to the backhouse – was watched by a little three-year-old boy from the next cottage who "kept pressing his nose against the screen door so that his little nose got flattened" and who kept repeating, "Wha' chu doing, wha' chu doin'?"[78] Then, it turned out, their bedroom had two single beds – not simply single, but single hospital beds on wheels! At night they rolled them together but this caused more hilarity and their second honeymoon night was spent on the floor. Finally, to cap it all, Mrs. Hirtle decided that she would like to join Merna, so she, Rev. Hirtle, and Mrs. O.S. drove to Sylvan Lake and kept Merna and Bill company for the rest of their honeymoon. Castor, where they went by train after their week's honeymoon, must have been a welcome relief.

10

CASTOR

— 1942 to 1943 —

T HE MITCHELLS rolled into Castor Monday, 24 August 1942. Their arrival was announced in a lengthy article, reprinted from the *Edmonton Journal*, on the front page of the September 2 issue of the *Castor Advance*. Castor, like most small prairie towns, had been devastated by the First World War and the Depression. Its population had dropped from 1,659 in 1911 to 625 in 1941. For fifteen dollars a month the Mitchells rented the Anglican manse, which was no longer needed because several of the churches had combined. They had little furniture with which to fill this large house: two trunks covered with some velvet drapes (from Mrs. O.S.) which they used to sit on, a table Bill made, two kitchen chairs, and springs and a mattress for which Bill built a box frame. When the cold weather came – and it was a particularly cold winter, with temperatures dropping as low as –50 degrees Fahrenheit – they discovered that the furnace had been repaired in a haywire fashion by welding a piece of galvanized metal over the draft. When they tried to regulate the heat and it got too low, "we'd have to open all the doors and windows because the house would fill with the smell of coal gas."[1]

One of the first friendships the Mitchells formed was with another couple newly arrived in Castor, Cec and Marg Hewson. He had just finished his Ph.D. at Berkeley, California, and was the new superintendent of schools for the large division (the Castor school board had resisted joining the larger unit, so Bill's school was not under his jurisdiction). Marg Hewson, who had dreamed of living in a small American university town, recalled, "I practically had a nervous breakdown when I learned I was going to have to live in Castor." They had no water supply, electricity, or telephone. She said Merna's dream of having maple furniture "remained strictly a dream." But Merna wanted a bathtub more than anything else and, after Bill sold one of his stories to *Maclean's*, the Hewsons remember looking out the window and seeing Bill marching home with a large tin bathtub on his head which had to be filled with water heated on the stove.

The Mitchells were soon involved in Castor's social life. Merna played the organ for the United Church. With the Hewsons they took up curling. According to Cec Hewson, Bill did not take curling as seriously as Castor's seasoned curlers would have liked. Playing in a bonspiel "was serious stuff" but Bill "sloshed around" in unbuckled overshoes that he never did up. Once he was sweeping a rock and one of the buckles fell off and got caught under a rock, which had to be thrown off. On another occasion, when his team was conferring about the next shot, Bill said, "Why don't we just throw a rock into the middle of that mess and see what happens?"[2] But curling in Castor gave Bill first-hand experience of the importance of curling in prairie-town culture and politics, which would later figure in a number of his "Jake and the Kid" stories and *The Black Bonspiel of Willie MacCrimmon*.

The Mitchells also joined a reading club, which met monthly, and they took up bridge. Their circle included Dr. Cousineau, who was Merna's doctor during her pregnancy in Castor, his wife, the Hewsons, the Coppocks, and the Matthiases. Merna became an excellent bridge player but Bill made a reluctant fourth. The discussions on these evenings often turned to the friction in the community between the Catholics and Protestants and to the school board's and the Catholics' resistance to joining the larger school division. Mitchell recalled that the common refrain was, " 'The Catholics are taking over this community. Do you realize that, if they go on reproducing the way they do, they're going to be in a majority and they're gonna call every shot.' "[3] Bill himself became one of the main sources of entertainment for this circle. Marg Hewson and Pearl Coppock fondly recalled listening to him tell stories about his Florida years, his trip to Europe, and his adventures during the Depression.

Early in the fall the Mitchells organized an evening of entertainment to help raise funds for parcels to be sent to soldiers overseas. The evening consisted of "skits, blackouts, music, and readings," but the main event was a production of Thornton Wilder's *The Happy Journey from Trenton to Camden*.[4] Admission was thirty-five cents. The Mitchells directed the play and acted the parts of Ma and Pa and three of Bill's students played the son and two daughters. Doris Thomson, who played the older daughter, recalled "the pleasure of working with them" at rehearsals held in their home. She also remembered the way Merna and Bill worked together: "The play was . . . directed by W.O. (with, I might add, frequent advice from Mern – accepted either graciously or Un!)."[5] Kathleen Davies, who played the younger daughter, also recalled the rehearsals:

> Bill was fun to work with but insisted you learned your lines and learned to do "things" his way. I remember learning to go down pretend stairs with your back straight. How to travel in a stationary car and make the audience believe you read the road signs as you passed, how you turned a corner and reacted to a bump in the road. He made you feel good when the play was coming together as he wanted.[6]

These kinds of projects were quite new for Castor, and the Mitchells must have appeared quite unusual to the community. Bill, certainly, came to be perceived as an eccentric. Kathleen Davies thought they were a romantic couple: "It was known that the couple were newly-wed, that this was Mr. Mitchell's first teaching assignment, that the couple were to live in the Anglican Church manse. This to junior high school girls meant romance. Mrs. Mitchell was so charming, pretty, petite." However, Kathleen also noticed the dynamics in their relationship:

> Even then, I think, we sensed that she sort of kept him on track and was the one to smooth ruffled feathers that Bill had knowingly or unknowingly ruffled. I'm sure the adjustment to living in a small town with its lack of conveniences was rather overwhelming but she was soon involved with church choir and organized a junior girls' choir. Looking back, Bill's attitude was more "I'm here and you're here and that's the way it is."[7]

Marg Hewson felt that "Bill was so unconventional that he didn't fit into Castor very well" and "there were a lot of people in Castor who were not broad-minded, shall we say, and didn't appreciate what he had to offer: I think they were just waiting for a chance to throw him out."[8]

‑ SCHOOL ‑

The Castor public and high school, a three-storey sandstone building, had been built in 1910 to handle a much larger student population than Castor and area now had. Grades one to four, taught by Miss Velma Caddey, and grades five to eight, taught by Miss Jessie Campbell, were on the first floor. The principal's office and high-school classes were on the second floor. The third floor of the school had been closed down. The vice-principal, Mrs. Annie Sparrow, and Bill taught the thirty-five high-school students in two rooms. Bill's first visit to his new office was not auspicious. A week before the school opened, on a particularly hot day, he was met by a foul stench when he walked into the office. He opened the windows and began searching for dead animals. Velma Caddey came in with her pupil lists as he opened the bottom drawer of his desk and discovered "this great big turd" left, a week or so earlier, by a student for the new principal.[9] Bill was both shocked and, later, amused by this act. When school opened he discovered who the culprit was and had to strap him.

Bill got along well with the teachers. While they may have thought that he neglected the administrative details of running the school, they were won over by his friendliness and respected his abilities as a teacher. He had a good rapport with the school janitor, Charlie Bullington. Kathleen Davies described Charlie as "the furnace room philosopher, teller of tales" who "shared owner-ship and management of the school with Bill." He was probably the first of many "informants" – store owners, tradespeople, town gossips, secretaries, janitors – Mitchell would tap over the years for his writing.

Bill taught French, Drama, Social Studies, English, Health and Phys. Ed., and Creative Writing. Kathleen Davies said that "this was the first class in the history of the school to have oral French."[10] She remembered Bill describing his travels in Europe and that one of his more difficult assignments was to tell a joke in French. In his drama class he did pantomime and had his students produce a class play. But it was his creative-writing class, a new optional course, that he most enjoyed teaching. In fact, he found it difficult to keep his inter-est in writing and aesthetics at bay when teaching his other subjects. Doris Thomson recalled, "In other subjects he would often ramble on in his search for descriptive words, then shake himself and say, 'Oh, yes, this is supposed to be Social Studies or something.' I don't remember any facts I learned from him in Social Studies or English but my love of literature gained new dimensions and other times and other places became real to me."[11]

Twenty years later, in a talk to Alberta teachers, Mitchell recalled his first creative-writing class in Castor and how his students' creativ-ity impressed him:

One of my students said he had a little pig and I said, "Well bring it in a cardboard box, a shoebox or something." So he brought it in. Then the children began to write to try to capture this animal exactly; what it was and what it was like. I can recall today that one little girl . . . pointed out that its ears were exactly like elephant's ears (and they are too, if you look at them) and another said the thing stood on the very tips of its toes like a woman in high heels. If you can get your children to focus on the actual smell, the actual sound, the actual taste, the actual feel, the actual emotions, they have the foundation for the creation of the illusion of reality.

Mitchell urged the teachers "to get the child to write about his own experiences, his own life, his own feelings, his own days, these are the unexciting things – until the attention is focussed on them."[12] This insight, validated by writers he admired, such as Thomas Hardy, Virginia Woolf, and Katherine Mansfield, had taken Mitchell years to discover for himself, but now it had become a fundamental aesthetic principle in his writing.

Bill was a particularly effective teacher in drama and creative writing. Doris Thomson recalled a typical day in his grade-twelve creative-writing class:

Nine o'clock bell. All classes in session – except ours. Record player at full blast, lots of socializing, one (usually me) hovering by the window to announce, "Here he comes." Hands deep in overcoat pockets, fur hat pulled down over ears, he trudged across the snowy schoolyard seemingly unaware of route or destination. Eventually the creak of the stairs caused us to silence the record and assume semi-attentive positions at our desks. In comes our teacher with eyes looking beyond us and room. He stands, bundled in hat, coat, and scarf, and breaks the silence to say, "How would you describe old men's mouths?" Various suggestions come forth and he appears to ponder over each and finally says, "Do they look like bubbles breaking on porridge?"

Many times like this he shared with us. I'm sure we all feel that
we are part owners of *Who Has Seen the Wind* although I know
our suggestions were facile.[13]

Bill's success as a teacher stemmed from a number of qualities.
His authority in the classroom grew, paradoxically, from his avoid-
ing the usual kinds of authority wielded by teachers and principals
(a quality for which some school-board members and other townspeople faulted him.). He worked *with* his students rather than *over*
them. He told stories to illustrate a point, capture attention, and
communicate his own enthusiasm for literature. And he took his
students seriously, making them feel that they were partners in *his*
creative process. He further legitimized writing for his students by
having some of their work published in the local newspaper.[14]

⁓ "ROUGH LUMBER" ⁓

During his ten months in Castor, Bill found "rough lumber" for a
number of characters and events he was soon working into
"Spalpeen." The China Kids and their father Wong Tae, the Ben
and the Young Ben, and Saint Sammy began with people Bill met
in Castor and grew into fictional characters with complex lives of
their own.

Bill was warned by one of his teachers to watch out for a trou-
blemaker in grade six who ran a poker game in the back of his
father's closed-down cafe using milk-bottle caps as poker chips.
Eddie Wong, eleven years old, was one of nine children raised by his
father, Wong Tae, who had come to Castor in the early 1920s and
opened the City Cafe. Mr. Wong was born in Canton in 1870
and emigrated to Canada (Victoria) in 1890. He married in 1901 on
a visit back to Canton and settled in Trail, B.C., then opened a cafe
in Rossland, B.C., and finally moved to Castor. His business deteriorated as a result of the Depression and the death of his wife in 1937
and he was finally forced to close it down. When the Mitchells
arrived in Castor, Wong Tae was working as a cook for the cafe next

door and struggling to raise Eddie, Kathleen, and Norman, the three of his nine children still at home. They could afford only enough fuel for the pot-bellied stove to heat the ground floor of their two-storey building. Eddie remembered sleeping on one of the cafe booth tables and how cold it was in the winters. And he also recalled, with some chagrin, how he ran wild in the town with a gang of other kids. One of their gambits was to wait outside the beer parlour when it closed for an hour at six o'clock. Pete Stoller ("he was kind of like the town drunk – the kids really liked him – he was like a Pied Piper") would come out feeling particularly magnanimous and give the kids nickels and dimes ("a lot of money for us then").[15] Mitchell recalled a trick Eddie and his friends would play on Pete:

> The kids all loved him – and maybe there was derision. But he would be drunk, walking down that main street, and the kids would come up behind him and he would talk to them. Then he would start out and do his Cossack march down the street. But the kids had a game on. As soon as he would turn and get started they smoked out of there and they left Pete thinking he was leading an army of children down the streets of Castor.[16]

Eddie and his gang also "helped" the station agent unload the freight trains when they came in – when the agent was not looking they helped themselves to various goods. This led to Eddie's first meeting with the new principal of the school. Eddie and his friends were caught stealing boxes of cookies from one of the freight trains: "Next day at school we were taken into the principal one by one. Everybody that came out, came out crying – just sobbing. We took it for granted that each one that had been in there had been strapped." But when Eddie's turn came he got a story, not the strap. Mr. Mitchell described to him how his father was struggling to support his children and give them an education so that they could live happy and successful lives. In return Eddie was letting his father down. Mr. Mitchell graphically described the kind of life Eddie was heading for, which would inevitably lead to jail, and how he would miss his family. Eddie, too, left the principal's office in tears. He recalled this as a turning point in his life which prevented him from being caught up in a life of "small-time crime."

Although Eddie remembered being ostracized and looked down on by the Castor community, he did not feel this was caused by racist attitudes. He sensed that it was more a class and economic snobbery that was operating, that they were simply from the "wrong side of the tracks." Merna, however, believed that some in the Castor community felt that there was no need to help the Wongs because the Chinese had their "tongs" and could look after themselves.

In November, the Mitchells were watching the kids play hockey on the outdoor rink and noticed that Eddie was the only kid on the ice without skates. He was sliding around in his shoes and was behind the play most of the time. Yet when he did get his stick on the puck, he was clearly the best stickhandler and shooter on the ice. So the Mitchells struck a deal with Eddie – they would pay him so much a week to save towards a pair of skates if he cleaned the ashes out of their furnace. Eddie described how he got his first pair of skates (second-hand) and how he was "taught" by Bill and Merna: "I had to work for it, you know."[17]

Every Saturday morning – "the only morning we could sleep in!" said Merna – Eddie would appear at the back door with his younger brother and sister shadowing him. Eddie would go down to the basement to clean the ashes out of the furnace and Norman and Kathleen would ask Mrs. Mitchell, "Can Mr. Mitchell play with us?"[18] And more often than not, he would. He did magic tricks for them (such as palming nickels and miraculously pulling them out of their ears and noses), made them "tractors" (from wooden spools, matchsticks, a piece of candle, and an elastic band), and, in the spring, he made them newspaper kites.

I was about seventeen when I first became aware of the special place Eddie, Kathleen, and Norman held in my father's and mother's hearts. They had neither seen nor heard of the Wong children after leaving Castor, but in 1960 received a phone call inviting them to Wong Tae's ninetieth birthday. My parents later introduced me to Eddie as their "numba-one son" and I remember meeting Kathleen at the Purple Lantern restaurant in Calgary. In going through papers after the deaths of my father and mother, we found the following one-page toast which my father had given at Kathleen's wedding:

> *I would like to say that I saw her first. But I was already married to Merna. Also she was eight years old. The first thing that caught my eye was her smile. The word smile is not good enough, for it was more than radiant – it was incandescent. The next thing I noticed was that she had a tight hold on somebody by the back of his collar. That was her little brother, Norman. We had no children of our own that year in Castor, though Merna by then was carrying our first son and I think that for quite a few years Kathleen thought my wife was the shortest but the fattest woman in the West. The Wong children were our first children, but the more important thing is that Kathleen was my first daughter. She still is. In* Caesar and Cleopatra, *Shakespeare said of another beautiful woman: "Age cannot wither nor custom stale the infinite variety of her charm."[19] And if Mi-Tang [Kathleen] had been unrolled from a rug at Caesar's feet, he would have fallen for her just as hard as he did for Cleopatra.*
>
> *A toast to Kathleen.*

Bill loved to entertain children. In fact, one of his teachers at Castor believed that his run-in with the school board was in part caused by the perception that he spent too much time watching and playing with the elementary-school children when he should have been teaching in his own classes and running the school:

> . . . he left his classroom too often in order to spend time with the very young pupils. He enjoyed watching them, visiting and playing with them. Little Norman Wong was a special favourite and Bill used to ride Norman around on his shoulders and even give him small amounts of money. This made Norman

somewhat of an object of envy, such partiality being unfair to the other youngsters.[20]

He closely observed the children and their community politics in the school and the schoolyard. While his vision and portrayal of the child's world in his writing was influenced by Wordsworth's poetry, he was acutely aware of its darker aspects and how it mimicked that of their parents. The shunning of Norman and Kathleen Wong moved him to pay more attention to them – a response he later ascribes to Miss Thompson in her treatment of the China Kids in *Who Has Seen the Wind.*

On Kathleen Wong's eighth birthday, 20 January 1943, an incident occurred that deeply bothered Bill. He had overheard some of the children talking about Kathleen and her birthday party, to which they had been invited. After school, when he dropped by Wong Tae's cafe, he discovered that he was the only invited guest to show up. Eddie Wong recalled Mr. Mitchell arriving and giving Kathleen a small bottle of perfume. He also remembered his sister's embarrassment when Wong Tae brought out the birthday "cake," a pie with whipped cream on top – "she didn't even have a cake!"[21] Bill began working this incident into "Spalpeen" and within a year had shaped it into a short story, "The China Kids," which Salter submitted to *Atlantic Monthly.* They turned it down, saying that it was good, but "we must give our readers a rest from racial intolerance."[22] One of the readers' reports on the "China Kids" is more blunt: "This story is so shocking in its details of character that we can't use it – couldn't, probably, even if it were completely successful. Mitchell is better when he's being amusing."[23]

This story and its characters finally became a part of Mitchell's portrayal of small-town bigotry in *Who Has Seen the Wind.* Here Mariel Abercrombie, "a full-faced little sadist of ten years" (*WW* 165), instigates the "whispering campaign" (*WW* 181) against Mi Tang. When Miss Thompson confronts Mariel and asks if she is going to Tang's party she responds, "'No. . . . Mother says not!' The answer was triumphant" (*WW* 184). Mitchell ascribes to Miss

Thompson some of the details of his experience at Kathleen's party. While Wong Tae goes back to the kitchen to make more sandwiches and pots of cocoa for the invited children, Miss Thompson gives Tang her gift:

> They were in one corner of a tilting settee, quite close together; Tang had her arm around Vooie's neck; over the top of the stove with its elbowed pipe disappearing into one wall, Miss Thompson could just see the boy's black, chrysanthemum head. She stepped around the stove.
>
> "Happy birthday, Tang."
>
> The tan, flat planes of their faces tilted up to her; their dark eyes stared.
>
> "Thank you." Miss Thompson barely heard the words.
>
> She held out the bottle of perfume with the card tied to it. . . . "Thank you," she whispered again. Her hand dropped to her lap. (*WW* 187-88)

Miss Thompson, who discovers that Tang and Vooie are suffering from malnutrition, takes up the Wongs' cause and badgers a reluctant town council into giving them relief. But it is only temporary until the town arranges to have Tang sent away to an Uncle in Vancouver and Vooie to a home in Winnipeg. Two weeks after his children are sent away, Wong Tae despairs and hangs himself.

The real Wong Tae managed to regain financial solvency and raise his children. At his ninetieth birthday (attended by eight of his children, nine of his fifteen grandchildren, and thirty family friends), Mitchell gave a speech which began, "A great part of man's immortality is in his children. I had not appreciated until tonight just how immortal Mr. Wong is."[24] Wong Tae lived to be 107.

Wong Tae was "immortalized" in another way. In January 1970 Eddie Wong brought the movie actor Dustin Hoffman over one afternoon to meet the Mitchells. Eddie was the Calgary location manager for Arthur Penn's film adaptation of Thomas Berger's novel Little Big Man. *All of the Battle of Washita scenes were shot on the Bow River just west of Calgary. At one point in the conversation, W.O. and Hoffman started comparing notes on how similar the acting and writing processes are – W.O. explaining how he drew on his own inner world and his observation of bits and pieces of actual people for his fiction and Hoffman describing how he worked in a similar fashion as an actor in creating his characters. Hoffman described what a wonderful fluke it was that he had met Wong Tae, who was now a hundred years old. During the two weeks he was in Calgary, Hoffman spent hours visiting with old Wong and watching him as part of his character building for the 121-year old Jack Crabbe sequences which frame the film's narrative. In the opening and closing scenes we see a character whose physical characteristics and mannerisms owe a great deal to Wong Tae – we are watching his arthritically gnarled fingers as he haltingly smokes a cigarette (which at one point slips out of his fingers onto his lap), we are listening to his raspy voice as he narrates his life, we are watching his at times amused, at times distant, primordially ancient stare.*

What had been a long-standing but more or less quiet racist attitude towards the Chinese and Japanese in the Western provinces and British Columbia became more openly hostile when legitimized by a renewed "yellow peril" scare following the bombing of Pearl Harbor in 1941. Mitchell used the Wong family episodes in *Who Has Seen the Wind* as one of the main threads in the "heart of darkness" motif that runs through the novel. The natural destructive element of the birth-life-death cycle of the prairie is counterpointed against the darkness of "civilized" behaviour exemplified by the likes of Miss MacDonald, Rev. Powelly, Bent Candy, and Mrs. Abercrombie. Miss Thompson, referring to the community's treatment of the Wongs, chastises Mrs. Abercrombie, saying, "You've shown me the heart of darkness" (*WW* 328). The China Kids and their father were the first of many marginalized individuals who elicited Bill and Merna's sympathy. Mitchell's creative imagination was attracted to outsiders and eccentrics who do not fit conventional society's norms. His fiction and drama turned again and again to explorations of such individuals and groups who struggle to lead meaningful lives in the shadow of the ascendant majority culture.

During his year in Castor, Bill met three more outsiders: Old Ollie, Pete Stoller, and his son, Young Pete. Bill and Merna had heard stories about an old prairie recluse nicknamed Ollie Behind the Rock, who lived in a piano box on the open prairie east of Castor. The Mitchells went to meet him with a cattle buyer who was going out to Ollie's place to buy some of his cattle. Bill was fascinated by this prairie eccentric who talked to his cows and had a few unbroken Clydes he paid pasture for and kept to pet for company. Merna remembers Ollie's bed, a nest of sheep's wool and binder twine. His clean pink skin, which showed through the holes in his pants, made her wonder how he washed. He had very red cheeks, white hair, and startling blue eyes, and "had a funny free kind of walk that was almost like a dance."[25] Ollie showed them some of the things he collected, including underwear labels in matchboxes and a tin of salted cod which Bill remembered was one of the things that was sent out during the Depression to farmers on the prairies. Ollie said that even though it was more than ten years old, if you "put it in water it would taste just as shitty now – but not be harmful – as it did back in the Depression."[26] The Mitchells heard years later that Ollie had frozen to death in a particularly bad winter.

Bill was also fascinated by the Stollers. Pete Stoller was "the most undisciplined man I have ever known – a late middle-aged Cossack who lived with his wife and son in a coulée on the edge of our town. He had a magnificent capacity for alcoholic beverages. This he slaked by operating a still, now and again selling a bottle to those who had been born without taste buds. Locally it was known as Pete's Own or Old Wolverine."[27] Bill frequently chatted with Pete, drunk or sober, because "he looked promising" as material for his fiction. He remembered one exchange they had in Jessie's cafe:

> I remember looking across the counter. Pete was up against the opposite wall and I said, "Pete, when are you coming up to see me and have a beer at my place?" "Oh, some day, Raverand."

And I said, "I'm not a reverend, I'm a teacher – you know, from Vladivostok." See, Pete was Russian. "I like you – I was born on the steppes of Russia." I shouted this in Jessie's cafe. And he said, "Front steps or the back steps?"[28]

Pete Stoller's son, Young Pete, was a fourteen-year-old "who was a contradiction of Rousseau's faith in natural man."[29] Early on, Bill was warned by various people that Young Pete was a hopeless student who spent more time running wild on the prairie than he did in school. Although he was officially in grade four, he could neither read nor write. When he did come to school he sat with the grade-seven students "so that the disparity in size was not too noticeable," but he did not participate in the class exercises: "He stared always through the side window to the prairie stretching wide from the school yard edge."[30] On one occasion Young Pete's teacher came to Bill with some concern because he "had carved his initials on the back of his hand with his knife."[31] Charlie Bullington, the school janitor, told Bill that Young Pete never took part in any of the school sports and that the only reason he came to school at all was because his father had been threatened with the law. In Charlie's opinion, Young Pete needed school "like I need a handful of horse manure under my cap."[32]

⇀ BILL AND THE SCHOOL BOARD ⇀

The secretary-treasurer of the public school board, Mr. F.T. Tucker, was a late-middle-aged man who wielded a great deal of power in the town and kept his eye sharply focused on the way the school was run. A stickler for rules and details, his aura of power was in part created by his use of legalese and his ability to quote the School Act at the drop of a hat. Bill quickly developed an antipathy for him. Merna recalled him as a "terrible little man."[33] In a piece written in 1948, Mitchell described his first meeting with Mr. Tucker:

In his office sweet with the smell of alfalfa, green feed, and hay, he said, "You're going to have your hands full with the Young Pete." He said this slowly and portentously as he handed me a regulation length of britching harness strap and a Gideon Bible from the hotel. "You'll be needing that Bible for reading 'em the Scriptures every morning – School Act – section four – paragraft 10A."[34]

Mr. Tucker had developed quite a reputation as a scrapper and Bill heard a number of stories about him, particularly from Charlie Bullington. Mr. Tucker became pugnacious after a few hours in the beer parlour and, on occasion, ended up stepping outside, removing his glass eye and carefully placing it under one of the planks in the boardwalk, and then squaring off with whomever he had picked a fight. Following the fight, Mr. Tucker would retrieve his glass eye, replace it, and return to the beer parlour.

Bill used his school office in the evenings and on weekends to work on his short stories and "Spalpeen." He kept his correspondence and manuscripts in the office desk. After supper he would walk the four blocks to the school and work for three or four hours. One evening he went up to his office and discovered Mr. Tucker sitting at his desk reading material he had taken out of the desk drawer: "I told him if he didn't keep his nose out of my correspondence I would flatten it across his face. I said, 'I really mean it – get the hell out of here. This is my office.'"[35] In retrospect, Bill felt that this run-in with Tucker had a great deal to do with the school board's subsequent behaviour towards him.

The 13 January 1943 edition of the *Castor Advance* included an item about the high-school students holding a party at the school: "Talks were given by Edna Ulmer, Sally McMurchie, and Mr. Mitchell. The party was well supervised by Mr. and Mrs. Mitchell and Mrs. Sparrow. A good time was reported by all." This was the first of the Friday-night "lits" Bill and Merna organized following the success of their production of *Happy Journey* in December. They felt that the junior-high and high-school students needed some form of chaperoned entertainment of their own that would be safer than the community dances, which attracted an older, drinking crowd and could get pretty rough. The lits comprised various forms of entertainment – skits, readings, talks, music, and other performances. On one occasion some of the students, whom Bill had been coaching after school in the community hall, put on a tumbling and acrobatics exhibition. On another, Bill had a group of grade-nine students put on a puppet show. These evenings would end with some light food and a dance.

The lits proved to be quite successful and the Mitchells planned to hold them regularly. However, in early February when Bill announced to his grade-twelve class details of the upcoming lit, one of his students interjected that her father, who was on the school board, said that there were not going to be any more lits. The next day Bill received a curt letter in officious legalese from Mr. Tucker notifying him of the school board's decision: " 'Henceforth from this day forward there will be no social functions held on any part of the school property whatsoever.' Signed by the secretary-treasurer."[36] Bill took the note to Mr. Weaver, chairman of the school board. Mr. Weaver, who ran the town butcher shop, was a devout Mennonite. When Bill asked him to explain why the school board had made this decision and why he had not at least been consulted, Mr. Weaver brusquely responded that the letter was self-explanatory and " 'there ain't going to be no dances held.' "[37]

Bill immediately wrote a letter of resignation, which began by regretting the lack of confidence in him shown by the school board. He explained why the lits had been started and how they were well chaperoned and fulfilled a need for the town's teenagers: "I ended up by saying that I am much younger than any of the members of the school board, but even though I have many more years left than they have, I still have not enough remaining years to waste any time with such rudeness, pettiness, and meanness of spirit and that I therefore respectfully suggest they take their three-storey brick schoolhouse and shove it up their collective school-board asses. I resign, sincerely,

W.O. Mitchell."[38] Bill decided to go ahead with the planned lit in spite of the school board's edict and the February 24 *Castor Advance* reported a successful high-school party that Friday evening with Fleet High School in attendance.

On March 10, some examples of penmanship appeared in the *Castor Advance*. Jessie Campbell, perhaps mischievously, had her students write applications for the vacant position of principal at Castor Public School. Two days later the school board considered Mitchell's letter of resignation and the following day Tucker wrote Bill:

> Dear Sir:
>
> This acknowledges receipt of your letter of the 12th ultimo which contains your resignation as Principal of The Castor High School effective at the end of June, next.
>
> Your letter was presented to our Board Trustees at their regular monthly meeting held last evening and the resignation therein contained was accepted by them.
>
> Yours very truly,[39]

In late April, Mitchell's work at the school was inspected by H.C. Sweet, "a quite forbidding man, as most school inspectors were because they held the power of life and death over a teacher." However, behind the forbidding exterior he was "gentle and compassionate." He gave Bill a glowing report, particularly on his teaching of Drama, French, English, and Creative Writing. Sweet's only suggestions were that he use his time more efficiently, insist upon effort and response, and use brief tests. Sweet was so impressed by Bill's work that he urged him to reconsider his resignation. Bill invited Sweet for lunch and, with Merna, described his run-ins with Tucker and the school board. Sweet persuaded Bill to reconsider staying if the school board were to reverse its acceptance of his resignation. According to Mitchell, Sweet did not get very far with Tucker:

> He wasn't gone a half-hour. When he came back, he was no longer "sweet." He was quite upset and said, "Don't! Don't!

People like that do not deserve a teacher of your calibre. Forget what I said about reconsidering your resignation." What I found out was that he had gone to see Mr. Tucker and had mentioned that I would probably withdraw my resignation and this thing could be smoothed over. Mr. Tucker got very hostile with the inspector and said, "I'll show you what kind of fellow he is – just read this insulting and obscene letter." Dr. Sweet continued to reason with Mr. Tucker, who began shouting at him and ordered him out of his office.[40]

This experience with the Castor school board affected Bill deeply. He drew on it for Miss Thompson's confrontation with the school board in *Who Has Seen the Wind* (giving her some lines from his own letter of resignation) and later for Carlyle's conflict with the school board in Part II of "The Alien."[41]

Bill's resignation became a *cause célèbre* and also became caught up in two larger conflicts which divided the community: the Castor district school board's resistance to joining the larger provincial division; and, the Protestant and Catholic division in the community, which Mitchell claimed was almost as fractious as that in Ireland. Mr. Tucker and the school-board members were opposed to joining the large division because they felt it was a threat to their power; the leader of the Catholic faction in the community, Father O'Halleran, was opposed because joining would mean that the Catholic separate school's Monfort boarding facilities, run by the nuns, would lose a number of out-of-town student boarders.

Bill took some satisfaction in helping to foil the school board's desire to keep Castor out of the larger division. When Dr. Cousineau, who had just been elected as the new mayor, asked Bill for advice about the larger division, he strongly supported joining it. In early June, a month before the Mitchells left Castor, the rate-payers voted in favour of joining. However, the school board refused to comply with this vote and sign the necessary papers. Bill and Merna advised Mayor Cousineau to contact Dr. McNally, deputy minister of Education (and a close friend of the Hirtles). According to Mitchell, McNally wrote a letter to the school board ordering them to sign the papers. When they still balked he threatened to come down and dissolve the school board. The chair and school-board members all resigned, a new board was installed, and the Castor school became part of the larger division.

Towards the end of his first year of teaching, in spite of the delight he got working with students, Bill was having second thoughts about teaching. He was beginning to feel hedged in and frustrated by the routine, the rules, and the administrative details. Early in the spring he was forced to deal with Young Pete Stoller in a way that intensified these reservations:

> With spring it was only natural that the Young Pete's truancy increased. With blandishing chinooks honey-combing the snow, with the song of the first meadow lark, I found myself becoming irritable and unreasonable at times; I wondered if I had chosen the right profession; I wondered if I could stand another day of the dry smell of chalk dust and sweeping compound, the snufflings, the foot-scrapings, the herding trivia of classroom sounds.[42]

Mr. Tucker brought Pete's truancy to Mitchell's attention and told him to do something about it:

> Mr. Tucker stopped me outside the post office, pointed out that he had heard the Young Pete was spending more time down at the livery barn or out on the prairie than he was in school.
>
> "What do you think I should do about it!" My tone was brusque.
>
> "You're the teacher. He needs beltin'."
>
> In deference to Mr. Tucker and the town opinion, I strapped the Young Pete, while he lifted one hand high after the other. I did not strap him again.[43]

A few weeks later, even though according to the School Act the Young Pete had to continue in school, Bill let him go.

It is interesting the way Bill drew a parallel between his own trapped feeling and that of Young Pete. Although his quarrel with Tucker and the school board must have depressed him, his disillusion perhaps had more to do with a loss of faith in the efficacy of teaching and in an educational system which failed children such as Young Pete. For him, the school had become a prison and place of physical punishment. A few weeks after strapping Young Pete, Bill saw a caged owl in the back yard of the town lawyer's home, its "grey wing shoulders . . . weaving tirelessly from side to side in a frantically uneasy glide." The caged owl crystallized Bill's misgivings: "That night I lost a little faith in the validity of teaching; I wondered if Wordsworth had mentioned teachers at all in *Intimations of Immortality*; I considered the advisability of taking up carpentering or butchering or insurance selling for a living."[44]

Within a year, in New Dayton, Alberta, he would again find himself forced to use the strap on a student. In this case, a teacher punished a student who had been bumped off the double-desk seat into the aisle by making him sit in the aisle for the rest of the morning. When she tried to make him sit in the aisle again after lunch, "he got at her and then she came whining to me and I had to strap him for it."[45] Ever since Bill had been a child he had resented any kind of authority which wilfully "moved in" on individuals, especially on the vulnerable young. As principal he felt uncomfortable by the demand that he at times act as the punishing authority.

I don't recall as a child ever being physically punished by my father. In High River our family had a reputation for being a "shouty bunch" and my brother Hugh and I were frequently yelled at, but never belted. I do remember one occasion when Hugh and I thought we were going to get "the belt." I was about nine. Hugh and I slept in the same three-quarter bed in a room just off my father's office and we usually went to bed around eight. My father would lie down on one side of the bed, tell us a story, and then go into the office and start typing. He did a lot of his writing at night, working into the early morning hours. It was a summer night and stayed light until ten so Hugh and I did not want to go to sleep. We started horsing around, tickling and shoving each other. First came a yell – "Settle down!" Five minutes of silence and his typing started again. More giggling and horsing around. Another yell: "One more time and I'll give you the belt!" Ten minutes of silence. Typing. Then again stifled giggles which broke out into a shoving match with Hugh thudding out of bed onto the floor. Our bedroom door banged open as the light snapped on and there was our dad looking furious. "Okay! I warned you. Both of you, out of bed." No giggles now as we stood by the bedside looking up at him. As he slipped his belt out of the loops on his pants, he said, "Turn around!" Now we knew we were really in for it. "Take your pyjama bottoms down!" We did. "Lie over the bed!" We did, our bare butts vulnerable, tensing for the first stinging whack of the belt, tears welling in anticipation. Instead, we felt the tickle of his moustache as he kissed our bare buttocks. "Now, get into bed and go to sleep. Next time it will *be the belt!"*

Merna had also come to feel uneasy in Castor, to sense that both she and Bill were looked on with disapproval. As her pregnancy developed she ignored the conventional behaviour of pregnant wives, which was to stay out of the public eye. She was a small woman and by March, her sixth month, she was obviously very pregnant. Bill teased her that the fetus had opted for a horizontal full lay-out rather than the normal tuck position for its first dive into life. She had to give up playing the old pump organ for the United Church because there was not enough room between the bench and the keyboard. Marg Hewson insisted that she exercise every day and took her for brisk walks around the town. Merna hated these cold winter walks and bucking through heavy snowdrifts after a late-April snowstorm, her short legs and extended belly making it impossible to keep up with Marg. But she enjoyed getting out of the house in the warmer spring weather of May and June. Doris Thomson said that the town was scandalized by Bill's "easy reference to his wife's pregnancy and even more that she showed herself in public – 'right there on main street as big as brass, I saw her myself!' "[46]

Mayor Cousineau, like Sweet, tried to persuade the Mitchells to change their minds and stay on in Castor now that a new school board was in place. They were touched by his offer but also amused that he thought that they would love to stay in Castor. They had both been relieved that Sweet's earlier efforts to smooth things over had been unsuccessful. They politely turned down Dr. Cousineau's offer. Merna recalled, "We just wanted to get out of there."[47]

Bill had experienced life in many small Western towns during the 1930s, but from a limited point of view. As a farm labourer or sheet writer or encyclopedia salesman, his stays in them were brief and he was essentially an outsider. As a newlywed man and principal of the school in Castor, however, his inside view of Castor's, and later High River's, community life gave him access to a very different kind of information. It is commonly assumed that Weyburn is the only template for Brian's prairie town. But Castor was also the factual basis for Mitchell's vision of small-town life and was an essential part of the rough lumber which went into the building of *Who Has Seen the Wind.* The fictional prairie town of Crocus is, for the most part, only a name in the early "Jake and the Kid" stories. But as Mitchell lived in and absorbed more of prairie and foothills small-town life, Crocus became incorporated as a richly detailed place inhabited by dozens of town characters.

In the last week of June, Bill completed his school duties and finished packing up. Merna, now eight and a half months' pregnant, had gone to Edmonton to be with her parents. Dr. Cousineau had grown quite concerned about Merna's size and wanted her to deliver at the University of Alberta hospital in case of complications. On July 1 Bill "made a grand finale" at the Coronation swim meet, where his high-diving act at the end of the program was a big hit.[48]

The following day Bill left for Edmonton and spent a worried ten days waiting for Merna to give birth. In January, when she was only about three months' pregnant, Mitchell had written a "Jake and the Kid" story, "Gettin' Born" (published in the May 1 *Maclean's*), which probably reflected his own concern about Merna's pregnancy. The Kid becomes very worried about his Aunt Margaret, who is about to have a baby. He senses that Jake, his mother, and other adults change the subject whenever he asks what's wrong with his Aunt Margaret because they do not want to alarm him. He concludes that "getting born must be awful if they won't even talk about it" (*AJK* 31). Although the story ends with a life-affirming birth, there are dark undercurrents in it which surface in the Kid's worries about how things can go wrong. He thinks about Archie, his best friend, whose mother died when he was born, and he asks Jake if his runt pig will have a second chance, will "get born over again" (*AJK* 30). Out on the prairie he comes across a gopher that he had killed a few days before and he is filled with a foreboding of the finality of death:

> He had his paws held out ahead of him like when a person prays. His eyes were open; they were more like dead black beads. I didn't feel so good.

> I was remembering about a train I had once — the kind that winds up with a key — and how she wouldn't go after I busted the spring. I couldn't make her move at all till Jake fixed her with some solder. That was a funny thing for a person to think about when he was looking at a dead gopher. A person sees a lot of dead gophers. Only this one was different. He was dead, and the prairie wind was whispering careless, and another gopher hidden off somewhere was squeaking like he didn't care either. . . . Jake couldn't solder this. (*AJK* 34)

Merna went into the University Hospital on July 10. Bill spent the evening at the Salters', a short walk from the hospital, anxiously waiting for news. There had been some talk about a Caesarean. Late in the evening he fell asleep on the couch and was awakened by

Salter early the following morning with the news that he had a son and Merna was fine. The baby was named Ormond Skinner, after Bill's father. For the rest of the summer the Mitchells lived with the Hirtles and Bill worked as a lifeguard at the Southside swimming pool to supplement their income. Bill put in a productive summer working every spare minute on the novel – and Salter was right there looking over his shoulder.

II

NEW DAYTON

— 1943 to 1944 —

ARLY IN SEPTEMBER 1943, the Mitchell family left
Edmonton for New Dayton. The Hewsons offered to drive
them to Calgary but were alarmed when they discovered Bill
had been unable to ship Taffy, a cocker spaniel Bill had given Merna.
Their car was packed with Bill, Merna, their two-month-old baby,
their dog, and luggage. At Calgary, Merna and the baby continued
on the train. According to the Hewsons, Cec drove Bill and Taffy
to the Calgary city limits so that he could hitchhike to New
Dayton. By wrapping Taffy in one of the baby's blankets and
holding her in his arms, he got a ride immediately. Bill and Merna
stayed in New Dayton's small hotel the first few nights while they
waited for their furniture.

New Dayton, about thirty miles southeast of Lethbridge, was a
much smaller community than Castor, with a population of about
ninety. Bill and Merna lived in the teacherage right beside the
school, which was on a knoll on the edge of town. There was little
snow that winter but "that wind – my God!" recalled Merna.
Mitchell joked, "That's what added the wind dimension to *Who Has
Seen the Wind*, I'm telling you!" The house was heated with a big
kitchen wood-and-coal stove and a Quebec heater, which they had

to bank up at night to keep the house warm. But it could not be properly dampened down, and when the wind came up, the stove-pipe "would be cherry red clear up to the ceiling."[1] Once, when Bill banked the fire up so the house would be warm when they came home from a trip to Lethbridge, the temperature had risen so high that the thermometer had burst and there were little puddles of beeswax under the antique chair and settee which Bill had refinished earlier that fall.

Living conditions in New Dayton were not, as they had hoped, better than in Castor. The cistern they had insisted on being built so that they would have soft water was outdoors "and you would see dead mice floating around in it." The kitchen pump water "was so bad that the lab in Edmonton said it was fit for neither man nor beast – it was full of salts of some kind. The kids at school used to deliberately drink that water when a test was coming and then they'd get the trots." Merna bought an aluminum cream separator with a tap at the bottom for water they got from the CPR. And the "indoor" plumbing had its drawbacks:

> And of course this house also had an outhouse and what they called a "convenience" in the basement – it was a can you had to empty. The stairs were like a ladder and so help me Bill would let the can fill to the brim before he would empty it and I would get out of the house and up the road three hundred feet away from the back door when he came up the stairs with that can because I could see him dripping and slopping that stuff all over my kitchen floor.[2]

Bill and Merna were not as active in the community of New Dayton as they had been in Castor, partly because it was so small. But also they had other more important things on their minds – their baby son and Bill's writing, which was more than ever taking over both of their lives. The doctor made a trip from Lethbridge once every two weeks to check over the baby. On occasion they would take the bus into Lethbridge for a break. But on the whole, Bill and Merna found life in New Dayton, particularly during the long and cold winter evenings, desperately boring. Merna recalled, "Orm was the one that made our life when we were in New Dayton."

During our 1996 Christmas visit with W.O. and Merna in Calgary, we were going through some boxes in the basement and came across two small samples of petit point. One design has a red rose in the centre of green leaves, the other blue, red, and yellow pansies in leaves. We asked Merna what they were. "My God! That's petit point your father and I did when we were in New Dayton!" She excitedly showed it to W.O., who muttered, "Shows you how goddamned bored we were on most winter nights there." We asked which one he had done and he shrugged. Merna said, "Look at the backs of them and you'll know right away." The stitches on the back of the pansies are small and tight and outline a fairly clear reverse image of the front. The stitches on the back of the rose are a mess.

The Mitchells became close friends with their nearest neighbours, Harry and Ruth Gorrill, who owned the farm next to them. New Dayton had no library but Ruth was a member of the Book-of-the-Month Club: "She had all these books and that's what saved my life," Merna recalled. Ruth and Harry were an early version of the Humane Society. Ruth had bottle-fed a ram which, now full-grown and quite large, followed her wherever she went: "The ram loved her so much it kept butting her in the ass and practically knocking her on her chin when she wasn't aware of him and couldn't sidestep." On one occasion Harry brought over a bird from a nest that his plough had disturbed, saying, "It's a little meadowlark for you, Merna." She recalled that it was a big bird that "looked like a vulture."[3] He was pulling her leg: it was, in fact, a ground owl. Harry also taught Merna and Bill to horseback ride, which Merna in particular enjoyed. He started her off bareback riding on his horse Shorty, which on one return trip refused to rein in and cantered into the barnyard and right on through the partially opened barn door, peeling Merna off its back, as Harry put it, "like the skin off a grape." "God, Shorty was a mean little son of a bitch!" Merna recalled.[4]

Harry was a master of tall tales and the source for a number of Jake stories. Mitchell said that Harry particularly enjoyed unloading his tall tales on innocent Merna:

> I remember one time Harry looking at me and winking and then, with this innocent look, he started talking about the Depression drought years and how awful it was and how the worst thing was the grasshoppers. "They just et everything, the grain, the leaves, anything green. Didn't just have to be green. They et the handles off the forks, the bundle forks." And Merna is sitting there taking in everything he's saying. "They consumed four treads and risers – well no, just the treads. No risers of course in them days on a back porch. They et that whole back-porch steps and old man so-and-so had no way of knowing and he stepped out and went right on his ass." And that's about the time Merna wised up to this.[5]

Merna recalled one of his tall tales, in which he described a herd of wild horses stampeding at night through a canyon – "you could see it lit up like day because their hooves set off sparks" against the rocks.

It was through Harry Gorrill that Bill first became aware of the Hutterites, "these people of the gentle persuasion." There were a number of colonies in the New Dayton district. Harry was "very good friends with them at a time – I suppose it's still true in Alberta – when Hutterites did not have many non-Hutterian friends." The Hutterites often paid visits to Harry's farm because he had a farm-implement dealership. Many of the implements came in parts and Harry would get young Hutterite boys to help assemble them. Bill would drop over and talk with Harry and the boys as they worked, and on occasion he went with Harry on his visits to the colonies. He recalled in particular a conversation he had in Tom's Cafe in New Dayton:

Two young Hutterite boys – probably fifteen, maybe sixteen – were standing and looking down in the glass case in the cafe. They were looking at a lovely harmonica in its box. I said, "Pretty nice mouth organ, hey?" And they agreed it was. "I guess you'd like to have one of those?" Each of them said no, he wouldn't. I said, "Why not?" They said, "It's the Devil's instrument – you would risk your immortal soul." I was fascinated. "What would be wrong with blowing through a mouth organ?" They said, "Well, it says in the Bible you've got to love the Lord your God with all your heart and all your soul. If you had that mouth organ you might love blowing that mouth organ too much. It would be wicked because it would diminish your love for God." It was interesting to me – I hadn't thought of love as a diminishable or exhaustible quantity. These guys had, or had been told so. I said, "Well, that means you mustn't love anything except God." They said, "Yeah, that's right." I said, "Well, a girl? Your wife? If you loved her you would diminish, take away from the quantity of love you had for God." They said, "Yes."[6]

This exchange was the inspiration for a story Bill began to work on about a year later, "Peter and the Goose Boss," which eventually grew into an unpublished novella, "The Devil's Instrument."

⏤ THE STONEYS ⏤

School did not open until October 1. Because many of the men were away at war, the high-school boys were needed to help bring in the crops. While he was preparing for the opening, Bill took on an article assignment from *Maclean's* on the fall cattle round-up in the foothills country west of High River. In the last week of September he took the bus to High River and dropped into the *High River Times* office. Here he met Mrs. Hughena McCorquodale, the associate editor. She advised Bill to join the round-up at R.R. Macleay's ranch, the Rocking P, west of Nanton. She and her husband, Alec, a lawyer, were driving out to the Macleays' the following day on some business, and she invited Bill to come out with them.

At the Rocking P Bill got the material he needed for his "Cow Heaven" article. He was also introduced to the Stoney Indians. About twenty-four Stoney families were camped on the Macleay ranch. Bill was told about the petition they were preparing. The Stoneys had been lobbying the government for about five years for additional land suitable for agricultural purposes. The land at the Morley Reserve (ninety thousand acres that had been granted to them by Treaty Number Seven in 1877) was no longer able to sustain their hunting culture. It had become hunted, trapped, and timbered out and was unsuitable for grazing and agricultural purposes.[7] As a result, the Bearspaw sub-band of about 175 people had left Morley and were scattered through the foothills to the south. They barely managed to survive by doing seasonal work, such as haying, stooking, round-ups, brandings, fence-pole and rail cutting, and fencing. They camped in canvas tents wherever they could get permission, and for a number of generations had been living a "nomadic life in the foothills west of High River."[8]

Rod and Maxine Macleay were particularly concerned about the plight of the Bearspaw band and, with Hughena and Alec McCorquodale, had taken up the Stoneys' cause and were helping them with a petition to Ottawa to obtain more suitable land. Rod Macleay was the main organizer behind it, Alec McCorquodale acted as legal adviser, and Hughena wrote a series of front-page articles in the *High River Times* covering and promoting the Stoneys' land claims.[9] Senator Dan Riley, a prominent southern Alberta rancher and politician, was also an active supporter of the cause.

Bill, full of excitement about High River, the foothills, and the people he had met, returned to New Dayton to begin the school year. He told Merna that they should consider moving to High River the following summer. In mid-October Bill was invited to attend a council meeting held on the Macleay ranch where the Stoneys would discuss their case and sign a formal petition to the federal government, requesting that land be purchased for them in the foothills country lying between Sheep Creek and the Oldman River, their traditional territory. Bill got a ride out to the Rocking P with the McCorquodales and Senator Riley. At the meeting King Bearspaw and Amos Wesley acted as interpreters for the few whites who were present. Among the many speeches made by Stoney tribesmen at this meeting were those of John Lefthand, Peter Dixon, and John Dixon:

> JOHN LEFTHAND: Before white people came, Indians had good living, hunting in fall, put up dry meat and berries for winter. Sometimes 200 or 300 move into shelter for winter, and stay safe. Make buffalo hides, windproof for cold. These days we got canvas, wind blows through. We can't stay in one place, must look for job, people get sick out of it.
>
> PETER DIXON: We promise we live in peace way but we suffer too much in our own country. If we stay all year round at Morley, more hard for all of us. If we get starvation then government will know.
>
> JOHN DIXON: When government tells me to do things I keep doing. Now I am in a sack, can't get out. Happy days are lost.[10]

Bill was moved and impressed by the various Stoney speakers. A number of their images and phrases later found their way into his fiction.

After the formal business of the afternoon meeting was over, the Stoneys set up a tent for the dance that evening at which Bill, apparently, enjoyed himself very much. A few weeks later, Hughena McCorquodale jokingly suggested in a letter that his enthusiastic participation in the festivities may have been viewed by Mr. Macleay (who was a Methodist) as diverting attention away from the main cause (the petition to Ottawa): "We still carry the picture of you sitting in the Indian teepee at 1:30 a.m., or bowing and capering with little Rain-in-the-Face. That was quite a night and I'm afraid

Mr. Macleay will think I haven't done his cause justice. He is a man of one idea, and he does concentrate."[11] Bill was powerfully affected by the dances, particularly the prairie chicken dance, and his interest in the Stoneys obviously went beyond their land claims. During this first brief encounter he began some lasting friendships as well as a long-standing fascination with and concern for the Stoney culture.

Back in New Dayton, Bill completed a final draft of "Cow Heaven" and sent it to Mrs. McCorquodale to check over for facts.[12] He also began working on a partially fictionalized article, "What's Ahead for Billy?" This story-article dramatizes the proceedings of the October council meeting from the point of view of a fictional character. A young Stoney called Billy peeks through the window of the cabin in which the meeting is being held and listens to his elders. After Billy hears the speeches of King Bearspaw, Johnny Lefthand, Peter Dixon, Ezra Lefthand, Howard Rolling-In-The-Mud, John Dixon, and Amos Wesley, "the old, blind chief" is helped to his feet:

> "We been here first our color people. At Treaty Number Seven we were promised help if we need it – as long as water flowing in the Bow River. We need help. Water still flowing in Bow River. I very anxious to hear answer from Ottawa. That's all."
>
> And that was all that Billy heard, for at that moment his deaf-and-dumb mother had pulled on his shirt, had taken him back to the camp with her in the buckboard. That afternoon he had watched the squaws set up the dancing tent, and that night he had watched the dancing, had himself danced the Prairie Chicken dance after all the men had signed the piece of paper.
>
> And, though Billy did not know it, the piece of paper that was to go to Ottawa, concerned him; it asked for new land for all the Stoneys, but it concerned Billy, all the Billies of the Stoney people, and those who were Billies ten and fifteen years ago – it concerned these most.

One wonders what is ahead for Billy, and for the 715 Stoney people, who live from day to day on the edge of starvation, acquainted with all it stands for, and, in spite of that, a loyal and peaceful group of people.[13]

Mitchell's choice of the name Billy for his representative Indian child in this scene suggests one of the central paradoxical themes he will later explore in "The Alien" and *The Vanishing Point*. Giving the Indian child his own childhood name suggests Mitchell's desire to fully understand and identify with the Stoneys. But at the same time the scene implicitly reveals his sense of being on the periphery. Mitchell is an alien white watching from outside. Both protagonists in "The Alien" and *The Vanishing Point* grapple with the twinned but conflicting tensions of alienation and bridging. They have an overwhelming sense of the impossibility of communication yet a deep desire to connect: "Out of my skin and into yours I cannot get – however hard I try – how ever much I want to!" (*VP* 216).

"What's Ahead for Billy?" dramatizes the Stoneys' dilemma. The younger generations are perilously caught between the old ways of their hunting culture and the new ways of the "civilized" white culture. The strategies for untying the "sack" in which they are caught include education for their children and opportunities to achieve an adequate standard of living. Metaphorically, as well as literally, the younger generations must learn to speak and hear the language of this foreign white culture in order for their own to survive within it. Mitchell concludes the article by emphasizing the obligation of white Canadians to help the Stoneys and drawing a parallel between them and the oppressed minorities for whom Canada was then fighting a war:

It can be said that the choice of land made by the Stoneys themselves sixty-seven years ago, was an unwise one. . . . The fact that they made their own choice should not mean that they must continue to regret their bargain and suffer more. An obligation for Canadian people exists, all the more imperative now that we are engaged in a war to establish the rights of oppressed minority groups.

The Stoney people are one of these.[14]

Bill hoped his piece would help bring public pressure to bear on the government to help the Stoneys. Unfortunately, *Maclean's* rejected it. N.O. Bonisteel, the assistant editor, felt that the mixture of fictionalized story and factual article did not work. He asked Bill for a pure story "with a good plot forgetting the little Indian boy but using this reservation atmosphere and background."[15] Bill sent "What's Ahead for Billy?" to *Canadian Forum*, which published a much shortened version of it in July 1944. Much of the fictional material was removed from this version, including a detailed description of Billy taking part in the prairie chicken dance, a scene Mitchell would rework and expand at least four times over a thirty-year period.[16]

Seven months later Bill and Merna were invited by the Macleays to stay for the Easter weekend of 1944. The Stoneys were having another council meeting. Bill persuaded Merna to come with him and, reluctantly and for the first time, she arranged for a babysitter for three days. They attended the Stoneys' Easter Sunday church service, and on Easter Monday Bill attended the council meeting. Again at this meeting a number of Stoneys spoke eloquently of their plight. Isaiah Rider, a great-grandson of Chief Bearspaw, who had signed the original treaty of 1877, said, "In future if we could get land like this round about us now, we don't even want to go to heaven, just stay right here and be happy."[17] One of the other speakers was Peter Dixon, who spoke of his hopes and fears for the future of his baby son and other Stoney children. The whites were also invited to speak. Senator Riley spoke of his long friendship with the Stoneys and then explained that the government, although it understood their needs, was at present involved in a war. He promised to continue to lobby the government for their land claims. Alec McCorquodale then reported on the response to the Stoneys' petition from the minister of the Interior and the Department of Indian Affairs. While the Stoneys' claims were viewed as legitimate, the government could do nothing about them while the war continued. Bill was also called on to speak:

> W.O. Mitchell, writer, said: "Yesterday, my wife and I went to your church meeting. It was a good service. I noticed Peter Dixon's baby at the end of the tent. Peter's baby is eight months old and has four teeth. My son is nine months old and has four teeth. Both babies are Canadians, Peter's just as much as mine. I'll do everything I can to see that my baby eats, and I'll do everything I can to see that Peter's baby gets his chance too for the right food."[18]

Mitchell vividly remembered this occasion. He felt that he had really "bridged" with the Stoneys. He certainly connected with the Dixons that afternoon.

As a child and teenager in the 1950s, I recall the regular visits Stoney families made to our High River home — there were the Shotcloses, the Rolling-In-The-Muds, the Dixons, the Lefthands, the Bearspaws. They would pull up in front of our house, their old cars burning oil and packed with adults and kids. The men would get out, slowly walk to the front door, and talk with my father. More often than not they would shyly refuse an invitation to come into the house. My father would walk back to the boulevard with them and visit with the rest of the family through the open car doors. On most of these occasions they had dropped by to see my father because they were in a bind or to ask him to sell some of their beaded jackets and moccasins and white doe-skin shirts with brilliant flowered needlework.

After visiting and catching up on the Eden Valley Reserve news, he would come back to the house with an armload of Stoney dry goods, which he would sell over the next few months to anybody who happened to drop by the house. But on two of the visits from the Dixons, they had come to see me and not to drop off goods for my father to sell. I was about nine years old the first time, and I vaguely recall my father introducing me to Mr. and Mrs. Dixon. But I remember in detail the gift they had brought me. Mrs. Dixon, her husband grinning and looking on, handed me a smoked buckskin jacket, fringed and with beautiful beadwork across the back, on the front, and on the two side pockets. After the Dixons had left, my father and mother told me that this was a very special gift. They told me about the council meeting some nine years earlier and that the Dixons' first son, to whom my father had compared me in his speech, had died from pneumonia when he was about three years old. I vaguely remember something about his father having ridden on horseback to a neighbouring ranch or to Longview for help, his son bundled up in blankets in his arms, but arriving too late. The Dixons had "adopted" me because of my father's little speech and his continuing interest in them and the Eden Valley Reserve community.

About six years later, the Dixons called by the house again – this time with a smoked moose-hide jacket. The beadwork was less elaborate and it was too large for me. I was small for my fifteen years. I remember more clearly the giving this time. We sat in our front living room, the Dixons looking a little uncomfortable. My father joked that Stoney boys grow faster and that I would have to eat more to grow into the jacket. This broke the formality and the Dixons laughed and spoke to each other in Stoney, now smiling constantly as they watched me trying on the jacket and thanking them. My father offered to pay them for it but the Dixons simply smiled and shook their heads. I wore this jacket throughout my high-school and university years, at first with the cuffs rolled back. And I still have it. The smoked hide is as supple as the day I got it, in spite of being soaked on a number of occasions. Chewed to softness. It now has only a trace of its original pungent smoke smell, a smell which I always loved and which had come to have a special meaning for me.

Some time early in 1944, Mitchell had salvaged the fictional material from his original version of "What's Ahead for Billy?" for a short story titled "Billy Was a Stoney." It begins with Billy getting a ride in a democrat to a nearby ranch with Mrs. Rider. She is grieving over the death of her young son and is going to the ranch to have a "burying box" made for him. Billy watches as the ranch hands build the coffin and then paint it with green kalsomine. He is given the small amount of remaining kalsomine, which he uses to paint himself "green from the blue-black bowl of his head to the soft, buck-skin soles of his moccasins" for the dance that evening.[19] The last four pages of the partial manuscript describe Billy's first awkward rounds in the prairie chicken dance. In August 1944, Salter sent "Billy Was a Stoney" and "The China Kids" to *Atlantic Monthly*, and in his covering letter commented on Mitchell's interest in the Stoneys: "He is a lad of enthusiasms – and 'Billy Was a Stoney' is one of the new ones. He has been very much interested in the Stoney Indians – and the terms in which he condemns governmental treatment of the Indians would curl your hair. You may take this Billy story as authentic stuff; he knows what he is talking about."[20] *Atlantic Monthly* readers felt that, although both stories were "talented performances," the magazine could not use them because "we have had, for the moment, enough race prejudice in the magazine" and "Billy Was a Stoney" depended too much on atmosphere and needed more action.[21]

For the next four years the Stoneys continued petitioning the government for more land. Finally, in the fall of 1948, the Department of Indian Affairs bought the Eden Valley ranch, forty miles west of High River, for the Bearspaw band. The property had ranch buildings and a swing bridge over the Highwood River that gave access to the small acreage on the north side of the river which was bounded by the main road into the Eden Valley from High River and Longview. The Eden Valley Reserve started operating as a sub-reserve in the summer of 1949. The ranch buildings were used as a school, a hospital, a community hall, and a residence for Rev. Roy C. Taylor and his wife: "Mr. Taylor is the resident official and will conduct the day school and the missionary work which is under United Church auspices. Mrs. Taylor is a registered nurse and has charge of the hospital." The Stoneys had already put in a few acres of garden, and work was under way on log homes for some of the families. It was expected that when "the wanderers are gathered in for the winter," the reserve population would be about 140 people. Hughena McCorquodale concluded her last article on the Stoney land claims as follows: "First impressions incline Mr. Taylor to believe that the Eden Valley experiment may develop very beneficially for these Stoneys of the foothills, who have been voluntary exiles from the non-productive Morley reservation, but have suffered the handicap of lack of school, lack of hospital care, or constructive attention. They now have a home."[22]

— CAREER DECISIONS —

Bill and Merna's four-day visit to the Macleay ranch enticed them even more to move to High River. Merna, too, fell for the foothills country and its people – particularly Mrs. McCorquodale, with whom she would develop a deep and lasting friendship. Bill had been telling her all about Mrs. McCorquodale for months and had begun writing an article on her for *Maclean's* called "Prairie Editor."[23] This love affair with a new place and its people, along with Bill's growing success at selling his stories and articles, led to Bill and Merna's taking stock of their financial and career options.

Bill had thought seriously about leaving teaching in February 1944 when Harry Clark, associate editor of *Maclean's*, arranged to meet him in Lethbridge and offered him a job. Although tempted, Bill turned down the offer. He explained why in a letter to his mother:

> I have just seen Harry C. Clarke [*sic*] of *Maclean's*; they seem to want me for an Associate Editor, a special article staff writer to go on assignments, to expect a salary of about $300 a month, at least that's what I said I would expect if I took it, and then I said I didn't think I would. He explained that I would likely draw one half to that much more besides on manuscripts they published – a matter of $5400 to $7200 a year, and believe it or not I don't think I'll be taking it. Look at the income tax! Seriously, the thing is all wrong; I have no ambitions toward becoming a

popular magazine writer; I have ambitions but they're a little
higher. A magazine staff editor is not an *author*; he is a hack
writer, a business man out to make money, to manufacture
wordage, and that's selling your birth right for a mess of potage.
Besides, although it's a longer road, there's a hundred times the
money in novels, in quality writing.

He then described the writing he had managed to do over the past
few months – twenty-five thousand words on the novel and four
stories – and how publishing a story in *Maclean's*, *Saturday Evening
Post*, or *Colliers* did not have the same effect on novel sales as having
a story in *Queen's Quarterly*, *Atlantic*, or *Canadian Forum*. He excitedly told his mother that Salter was going to send two of his stories
to *Atlantic* and that "one click there and the novel is a sure seller."
He felt the *Maclean's* job would interfere with his real ambitions:

> I know that if I were filling a job on *Maclean's*, meeting dead-
> lines, doing story reading, doctoring scripts, I wouldn't have the
> time for improving my style, and no amount of money can pay
> for that loss. I like teaching; it gives me spare time, long holi-
> days and weekends, and keeps me here where I'm with the
> people and the country I write about. If I wanted to, I could
> make just as much money turning myself into a hack-writing
> machine, without having to go East to do it.[24]

Although Bill appeared in this letter to have made up his mind
to turn down the *Maclean's* offer, he wrote Salter asking him what
he thought about it. Salter answered that he was "in two minds
about the *Maclean's* offer" but had told Clark that Bill could handle
the job. He outlined the advantages and disadvantages of taking it
on, but finally said, "I just don't know, and wouldn't advise."[25] Salter
was in fact very anxious that Bill *not* take this job and was gambling
that he would make the right choice. This must have been difficult
for Salter. Over the years their relationship had taken on a father–
son dimension and he knew that Bill would probably do as he

advised. But Salter was a consummate teacher who instinctively knew not only when to come on strong but also when, and how, to hold back. In the end Bill opted, with Merna's support, to turn down the *Maclean's* offer and stick with teaching.

Six weeks later, however, shortly after their April visit to High River and the Macleays, Bill and Merna changed their minds about his teaching career. They decided to move to High River and try to survive on what was coming in on the "Jake and the Kid" stories and articles and what might come in on the novel. This was a big risk and Salter was cross with Bill for making what he considered to be an irresponsible decision. He tried to persuade Bill to continue teaching, but to no avail. In a letter to Dudley Cloud a year later, Salter referred to Bill's career decisions: "He is about thirty, married, and he refuses to do anything but write. Last year he chucked school teaching – and told me he had ulcers of the stomach! That is, he knew I wouldn't approve. Since then, he has been offered a job as the desk editor of some sort with *Maclean's Magazine*. I refused to advise – they came to me first – and I held my breath, but, thank God, he turned it down."[26]

— "JAKE AND THE KID" STORIES —

From the beginning, the "Jake and the Kid" stories were a hit with *Maclean's*. After the first four were published, Jack Paterson answered a letter he had received from Bill's mother, saying, "the arrival of a Mitchell manuscript in this office is a blessed event. . . . Bill's stuff is new proof that no matter how cynical and brittle the reading public may at times appear to be, there is always a pay-off on sincerity. Bill's people are real people, his atmosphere is real Western, and I hope, with you, we'll see much more of it."[27] By March 1944 Bill had sold six "Jake" stories to *Maclean's* and written four more. They had become one of the most popular fiction offerings in the magazine.

At this point, however, Salter sensed that Mitchell's treatment of the "Jake" stories was getting sloppy. Bill was focusing his energy on the novel, now titled *Who Has Seen the Wind*, and writing the "Jake and the Kid" stories to bring in extra money. A week after Bill had written his mother about his ambitions to write quality stories, Salter wrote Bill with a warning:

> If I were you, I wouldn't neglect or skimp work on the Jake stories. And I wouldn't be too cavalier with *Maclean's*. In the first place, *Maclean's* did give you a break. In the second, there's no reason why the world's best short story shouldn't appear in *Maclean's*; it's just as likely a place as any other. Our friend Shakespeare was able to suit *every* taste, and there is no reason why a popular story should not have all the fine workmanship that would appeal to anthologists. When you get enough of these Jake stories together, a book of them would do you some good if they were worth reprinting. Make sure they are. Make sure that anybody who has read even one of them would want to get the lot together.[28]

Salter's attitude towards the "Jake" stories was ambivalent. Although he scolded Bill about getting sloppy (and gave a detailed critique of "Old MacLachlin Had a Farm" illustrating his point) and argued that fine workmanship should go into the writing of these popular stories, he clearly distinguished between the writing in the "Jake" stories and the writing in Bill's novel. A year later, in a letter to *Atlantic Monthly*, Salter described his role in suggesting the first "Jake" story, "Elbow Room," but then explained that Bill was capable of more: "But Bill has *good* stuff in him. Long ago I talked to him seriously about these things. I am not interested in developing writers of tripe. Besides, I said, you can have a run with that sort of thing and die before you're dead. Or may be forced to write stuff that revolts your own soul. You had better choose before no choice is left. Bill chose right. . . ."[29] But the choice between writing "*good* stuff" for a serious reading audience and writing popular stories for a mass audience will prove to be a more complex and continuing issue in Mitchell's writing career than Salter suggested in this letter.

Mitchell's work attracted both a highbrow and lowbrow audience, and his best writing, as Salter's March 8 letter suggested, will make its appeal to a mixed audience, will "suit *every* taste."

The popularity of the "Jake" stories was in part due to their use of the tall-tale tradition. The Kid tells us that Jake Trumper invented hay wire, "made Chief Poundmaker give in at Cut Knife Crick," (*JK* 3), was a close friend of Wilf (Sir Wilfrid Laurier), "drunk Catawba wine with Sir John A," and "made Looie Riel say uncle three times – once in English, once in Cree, and the third time in French" (*JK* 177).[30] Many of the "Jake" stories are literary tall tales which aspire to be much more than a collection of simple tall tales based on an oral tradition. These stories depict and humorously satirize a small prairie community that becomes a microcosm of the Canadian community. They also dramatize and explore the process of the Kid's moral and imaginative education, a process in which Jake (a surrogate father for the Kid, whose father is killed in the war) and his tall tales play key roles. One of Jake's rivals in this process is Miss Henchbaw, the Kid's schoolteacher. The Kid often finds himself caught between Miss Henchbaw's historical facts and Jake's imaginative tall tales. Miss Henchbaw sees Jake as a historical liar and tells the Kid that the history books do not mention Jake and that Riel and Poundmaker "were way before Jake's time." The Kid dismisses this – "All Miss Henchbaw knows came out of a book. Jake, he really knows" (*JK* 3). When Jake describes how he invented the buffalo jumping pound (based in part on the tall tale of the stampeding horses that Harry Gorrill told Merna), the Kid says, "Jake . . . that's real hist'ry. That's – hist'ry!" (*JK* 69)

In the early "Jake" stories, and in "The Liar Hunter" in particular, which was written in New Dayton, Mitchell first explored two issues he would often return to in his work: what lies behind the need to tell stories and what is the nature of the relationship between fact and fiction, reality and stories. In a later "Jake" story, "The Golden Jubilee Citizen" (1955), the pedagogical approaches of Jake and Miss Henchbaw are paradoxically complementary: both tall tales and history are stories and both are legitimate ways of understanding the truth, of mediating between ourselves and reality. While "The Liar Hunter" on the surface appears to be simply an entertaining story composed of tall tales, on a deeper level it explores the nature, strategy, and rationale of tall-story telling. Mitchell had noticed "how much of this exaggerated tall-tale telling involved dangerous things, like an extremely bad winter, or pests, grasshoppers, sawfly, or drought."[31] He ascribes this insight to Mr. Godfrey, an anthropologist from the East who has come West in search of folklore and to court Molly Gatenby. His courtship runs aground because Molly becomes angry with him when he encourages her father and Jake to tell their tall tales which she, like Miss Henchbaw, views as silly lies. He wins her interest again when he confronts her with the following impassioned justification:

> "What I do is important. Important as history is important. . . . Not the history of great and famous men . . . but of the lumberjacks and section men, hotelkeepers and teachers and ranchers and farmers. The people that really count. . . . Their history isn't to be found in records or books. . . . Their history is in the stories they tell – their tall tales. . . . And I can tell you why they lie. . . . This is a hard country, I don't have to tell you that. There are – drouth, blizzards, loneliness. A man is a pretty small thing out on all this prairie. He is at the mercy of the elements. . . . These men lie about the things that hurt them most. Their yarns are about the winters and how cold they are the summers and how dry they are. In this country you get the deepest snow, the worst dust storms, the biggest hailstones. . . . Rust and dust and hail and sawfly and cutworm and drouth are terrible things, but not half as frightening if they are made ridiculous. If a man can laugh at them he's won half the battle. When he exaggerates things he isn't lying really; it's a defense, the defense of exaggeration. He can either do that or squeal. . . . People in this country aren't squealers." (*JK* 99-101)

Godfrey's defense of what he does and the tall-tale teller's role is a thinly disguised statement of what is at the heart of Mitchell's conception of the story-teller's strategy and aim. His story illusions, which are made up of bits of true autobiographical and factual detail, are lies, lies which invite the creative-partner reader to explore fundamental and universal truths in order to make sense of and cope with the existential dilemma of being human.

~ SALTER FINESSES *ATLANTIC MONTHLY* ~

One of the exercises Salter used in his University of Alberta creative-writing class in 1943-44 was to have his students critique some of the *Atlantic Monthly* short stories. *Atlantic Monthly* was then the leading North American magazine for current serious fiction. On 10 January 1944 Salter wrote the editor of *Atlantic*:

> Dear Sir:
>
> This year I have been using the Atlantic in my class in Composition. Last month, you had a story by Freitag called "The Golden Horn." My students objected to this story. Peter Offenbacher said you "must have made a mistake: it is not modern writing, just bad writing."
>
> I was not surprised, therefore, to receive the enclosed manuscript, "The Golden Horn Fleeced." Needless to say, I must not tell an editor his business! But it does seem to me that if the original story was worth printing, this one is not less worth printing. Indeed, as it has a medicinal value, its value is probably greater.[32]

Salter's letter was handled by Miss Dorothy Boyce and, not too far under the surface of her polite answer to Salter's challenge, one can sense annoyance: "We are surprised that such a simple human story as 'The Golden Horn' should arouse the ire of a reader. . . . We are glad to have seen Mr. Offenbacher's parody, even though we cannot spare the space for it. I should add that we have received a great volume of correspondence as warm in praise as your students have been in dispraise."[33]

Salter must have sensed that he had his "mark" on the defensive, and in his next letter he increased the pressure. In the *Atlantic Monthly* files there is a three-page summary of this initial exchange of letters which reported that Dorothy Boyce's letter

> was like waving a red flag in front of the bull. Mr. Salter's letters grow. The prickly Mr. Salter wrote back at length: "What astonishes me is that you attempt to defend such a vapid and specious piece of writing. Tell it to the Horse Marines, Miss Boyce, or to Sweeney. . . . What am I to tell my students: that this story was no mistake but the level of the considered taste of the Atlantic Monthly? You and your 'simple human story'! Simple human tripe!"

Atlantic did not respond to this last attack and Salter feared that he had put them off. He wrote to Bill on March 8 asking him to send copies of "The China Kids," "The Ben," and "Billy Was a Stoney," which he would try to sell, but he explained that *Atlantic* is not a likely prospect: "At the moment, *Atlantic* doesn't like me. One of my lads wrote a burlesque of one of their stories. I sent it in for the fun of it, and they were very self righteous in trying to defend the original. So I 'tore off a strip,' told them it was indefensible tripe, and they haven't answered. But *Atlantic* isn't the only ocean."[34]

Salter was wrong. *Atlantic* were simply regrouping after his last assault. Apparently, Dorothy Boyce had had enough of Professor Salter and passed him on to *Atlantic Monthly*'s managing editor, Dudley Cloud. Cloud wrote Salter March 24 explaining *Atlantic*'s editorial policy on its fiction and thanking him for taking the time to express his opinion. But Cloud, obviously intrigued by this "prickly" Canadian professor, concluded by asking Salter what he thought of Mrs. Osborne's story "Maine" in the February *Atlantic*.

Salter resumed fishing in the *Atlantic* ocean. He had now succeeded in getting his foot in the managing editor's door and launched the next stage of his "track," a masterful two-page single-spaced letter sent May 19. He apologized for his "ill manners," but the apology was camouflage for another bash at "The Golden Horn" and more criticism: *Atlantic* lacked "a sense of proportion, or sense of humor," failed to encourage "a young fellow who has a future as a humorist," and has attempted "to defend the indefensible." Salter finished the first part of his letter saying that his apology has "an ulterior motive!"

But before moving on to it, he questioned the motive behind the concluding paragraph in Cloud's March 24 letter. He asked if Cloud's question regarding his opinion of Mrs. Osborne's "Maine" was "rhetorical, a flourish to wind up a letter and parade a receptiveness to criticism adverse or other?" He then gave a detailed and perceptive critique of her story. This was followed by Salter's concluding paragraph, the "snapper":

> Now for my ulterior motive. I try to follow my students after graduation. On my desk at the moment are an armful of stories some of them have done. May I send along two? Both are authentic; that's all I can say. I mean only that they are true to the parts of this province in which they are set. One of the writers has published perhaps a dozen stories, the other none. The one who has not published is, to me, the more interesting. I need not indicate which is which; you will note the difference in slickness. If you should find either or both of them suitable or useable, I shall be most happy to pass on the word to the authors.[35]

What Salter was doing in this letter, quite consciously, was keeping Cloud off balance. If Cloud's concluding question was rhetorical and meant to simply show that *Atlantic* was open to criticism, Salter's detailed comments on "Maine" made it impossible for Cloud to continue corresponding "rhetorically," hoping that Salter would simply go away. Salter's letter demanded a serious response on the level of one editor to another. But it also pushed

Cloud into agreeing to have a look at some of Salter's students' writing and giving that writing his personal attention. It is a safe bet that very few young writers taking university creative-writing courses in the 1940s had their work looked at by the managing editor of *Atlantic Monthly*.

Cloud answered Salter's letter May 23 saying that his "analysis of Mrs. Osborne's story certainly puts the finger on the sore spots." He invited Salter to submit some of his students' stories, adding, "We like to think that the *Atlantic* is the most hospitable magazine in the country to the work of new writers."[36] Salter immediately sent Cloud two stories, "Burns Night in Forsinard" by W.T. Cutt and "The Owl and the Bens" by Mitchell.

Bill had started working on this short story about a year before in Castor. A number of years later, in a talk he gave to the English Council of the Alberta Teachers' Association, he used the "The Owl and the Bens" to describe his aims and method of writing:

> There is a special kind of truth that is the writer's truth. It is not so much a scientific truth or an economic truth, a sociological or a political one, as it is a *human* truth. There are actually certain of these human truths which can be communicated in no other way than through the creation of characters, their conflict and their success or failure, because only after the reader has identified himself with them can he receive the particular truths to be communicated. . . . The artist must manipulate the characters, their sights, sounds, tastes, feelings, wonderings, hopes, disappointments in such a way that they embody insight into order and significance. Life doesn't very often present the artist with the people and the events harmonizing in chronology and meaning and climax.

He then described Pete Stoller and his bootleg business, the Young Pete and his resistance to schooling, and how these and other disparate elements from his Castor experience coalesced into the meaningful pattern of "The Owl and the Bens":

[Young Pete's] teacher came to me quite concerned about him. In an arithmetic class this child had carved his initials on the back of his hand with his knife. I believe that both of us thought of a wild animal in a trap, gnawing off a leg to free itself. (Here, had I used restraint, I would not have mentioned that to you but would have let it ripple in your own mind.) Early in the spring of the same year [1943], one Sunday morning when nothing would float to the surface, I recall leaving my typewriter with a notebook and pencil and visiting the chicken coop at the back of the local lawyer's house. There I took 20 pages of notes on a young owl that wove back and forth on a perch there – the unblinking lemonade eyes, the bird of prey with down-curving beak, the talons. This all went into a filing case, as did notes upon this boy I mentioned, and as did notes upon his Cossack father. It was a year or more later that all three of them came together in a short story and then later the larger pattern of a novel. All three and the events of their lives were used to articulate a truth – that to people, wild and human and otherwise, life is unsupportable without freedom. This is the way the writer does it in a short story.[37]

Mitchell reflected that one of his weaknesses as a writer was to delay getting down to the final stages of shaping his work: "I tend to – because of apprehension, lack of confidence in my skill or talent, abilities – to keep the thing open-ended, keep going in there and not put a finish on it too soon. Let it grow. I overdo that." Bill had sent Salter a great deal of freefall writing growing out of his Castor experience in the summer and fall of 1943. He urged Bill to "bring order out of this stuff" and suggested that he take some of the rough material he had written on the Stollers and the Wongs and "put a finish" on it.[38] Bill did so and in February 1944 sent Salter the "The Owl, the Ben, and the Young Ben" ["The Owl and the Bens"] along with "The China Kids" and "What's Ahead for Billy?" He wanted Salter to try these out on *Atlantic*. Salter, in his March 8 letter, critiqued the stories and said that

"'The Ben' . . . isn't the thing for *Atlantic*."[39] His comments on form and structure were, as usual, succinct and right on the mark. He sent all three stories back to Bill for reworking.

"The Owl and the Bens" is about the Ben, an alcoholic boot-legger who is jailed for three months when his still is discovered, and the Young Ben, his son, who is a wild prairie boy unwillingly forced to go to school. The Ben has an owl that he trapped and keeps caged in a chicken coop. The story ends with the principal releasing the Young Ben from school. The Young Ben stops by the jail to talk, through the basement jail window, with his father, who has three days left in his sentence:

> The Ben's head appeared, with its gray hair standing out in two tufts from his temples; then his hands with their chicken-foot knuckles and their spade nails gripped the bars. His eyes stared out at the Young Ben from raw rims red as meat, eyes that by their fixity had stopped being anything but things by them-selves. The Young Ben could hear his father's breathing, harsh with a shrill edge to its rough rhythm.
>
> He told his father that he had dropped school. He stood there in the slanting rays of the fall sun and rubbed the back of one leg with the bare instep of the other. The Ben's head and its two eyes moved slightly from side to side with impatience, as though to move the bars from his line of vision. He said nothing.
>
> Finally the Young Ben said he'd better be getting home; there were chores; the cows had to be brought in and milked; feed had to be thrown down; the owl had to be fed.
>
> Low along the prairie sky the dying sunshine lingered, faintly blushing the length of one lone, gray cloud there. The Ben said: –
>
> "Let that there goddam owl go."[40]

Mitchell recalled that in his first version of "The Owl and the Bens" the story did not end here. It continued with the Young Ben enlist-ing, going overseas, performing heroically at Dieppe and returning as a hero. The community, which had looked down on the Bens, now holds them in respect. But at a ceremony in honour of the returning hero, a very drunk Ben appears. He "didn't know what all the fuss was about and tore the whole thing apart by stumbling out in front of the grandstand and puking into the goldenrod."[41] Salter told Bill that he was "all hay-wire on the structure" of the story by "trying to drag in the war and every-thing else that doesn't belong." He advised ending the story before the war material: "When Ben says, 'Let that goddam bird go,' the story is finished. All the King's horses and all the King's men couldn't get you past that. Curtain; the story is over; fini." Salter advised that the rest of the material belongs in another story, "'Hero of Dieppe,'" with a very different Young Ben: "For, actually, that young Ben does not enlist. Not as you describe him. Or if he did enlist, he went AWOL long ago; he deserted, and now he's in the tall timber. As you describe him. But a slightly different character can certainly be used for another story of the local boy made good, brass bands, and father drunk."[42] Bill rewrote the story following Salter's advice, and two months later "The Owl and the Bens" was on its way to *Atlantic*. He did not follow up on Salter's advice to work the cut material into a "Hero of Dieppe" story.

Salter was right about this story's structure, but his sense that it was not right for *Atlantic* proved to be wrong. Cloud and three other readers were impressed by "The Owl and the Bens" and Cloud decided Edward Weeks, editor of *Atlantic Monthly*, should see it. After a three-month lapse with no word from Weeks, Salter wrote a short peremptory note on 11 August 1944 requesting a report on "The Owl and the Bens" (and pointing out he had enclosed return postage with it!). He also mentioned he had another writer, Christine van der Mark, in whom *Atlantic* might be interested. Cloud replied August 17 that Weeks wanted to read "The Owl and the Bens" but he was waiting for "the proper moment to slip it into his crowded reading schedule."[43] He also asked to see anything else by W.O. Mitchell. Salter responded saying he is grateful "and a little shamed"[44] – probably because he had doubted that Cloud was genuinely interested in his protégés and would not really give their work a serious look. He promised to send two more Mitchell stories ("Billy Was a Stoney" and "The China Kids") and one by van der Mark and gave a short biography of Mitchell. Cloud returned "Billy" and "China Kids" September 21 saying that they were very good but not for *Atlantic* and that he was still holding "The Owl and the Bens" for Weeks.

Edward Weeks was indeed a busy man. As well as editor of *Atlantic Monthly* (for which he wrote a regular review page), he was the chief editor of Atlantic Monthly Press, the coterie press of Little, Brown. His editorial work was highly regarded among American publishers and writers, and he had worked with such authors as Mazo de la Roche, James Hilton, Agnes Newton Keith, Walter Lippmann, H.E. Bates, and Walter Edmonds – an impressive list at this time. When Weeks got around to reading "The Owl and the Bens" in early December, Salter's persistence and "track" (and of course Mitchell's talent) finally scored. On December 6 in a hasty note, Weeks wrote Cloud, "You did well to keep the boy on ice. The story has the raw authentic vigor of Canada." Weeks went on to say he would like cuts: "It tries to take in the whole village. We don't have to insist on the cuts but I think you'll agree that they point up the narrative."[45] The other readers had also felt that the story tried to cover too much ground. They did not realize that what appeared to be extraneous characters and events were the result of the story being part of the larger canvas of the novel *Who Has Seen the Wind*.

Dudley Cloud set to editing the story, claiming that he read it aloud in the office to whomever happened along, with great response. Cloud was so impressed with Mitchell's work that he sent the story to his friend, Wallace Stegner, who had been raised in southern Saskatchewan but was now writing successfully in the States. A few months later Cloud added the following to one of his letters to Bill: "P.S: I showed proof of THE OWL AND THE BENS to Wallace Stegner. He said, 'It's a better story than I could write!' A swell guy, is W.S."[46]

Atlantic Monthly bought "The Owl and the Bens" for four hundred dollars (more than one-fifth of Mitchell's principal's salary in New Dayton in 1943-44) and it was published in the April 1945 issue. Up until the acceptance of this story, Bill had left Salter to act as his agent with *Atlantic Monthly* and, apart from the March 8 letter in which Salter explained why he thought *Atlantic Monthly* was cross with him, Bill knew nothing about the details of the "track" Salter had used. Soon, closely coached by Salter, Bill began to deal directly with Atlantic Monthly Press in the selling of his next short story, "Saint Sammy," and his first novel.

⁓ WEYBURN ⁓

While Salter "shilled" and *Atlantic* mulled over "The Owl and the Bens," Bill completed his teaching duties at New Dayton by mid-July and with Merna packed up their belongings in preparation for their move. They took the train from Lethbridge to Weyburn for a short visit with Bill's mother, but when they learned that the house they had contracted to rent in High River had been rented to someone else for a higher rent, they ended up living with Mrs. O.S. for six months. In retrospect, this was exactly the reprieve they both needed. Going back to Weyburn for a sustained period gave Bill the opportunity to confirm and sharpen the prairie and community landscapes he was creating in his novel. He revisited old haunts and was inspired to create fresh scenes and characters and to add more details to Brian's prairie-town world. This was, he said, "the first time in my writing life that I was only writing so I had time to indulge myself." His workplace was the glassed sunporch of his boyhood home which "next to the coal room, or the attic, or the root cellar, I loved." It was "a special place and took me back to the magic of when I was Brian's age." He walked out on Sixth Street as he had as a boy, and he remembered "looking at a dried-up slough bottom and suddenly realizing that it was like a pocked human face." It was at this time that he "thought of the lovely connotative phrase of a cater-pillar making a parade of himself" and of the childhood rhyme, "step on a crack and break your Grandma's back – and of stepping on every possible crack."[47] He visited Knox Presbyterian Church "to see what the stained-glass windows were," which inspired Brian's description of the Christ depicted in them as "all grapes and bloody" (*WW* 26). He heard again the many wind voices that had stirred him as a child. He renewed old acquaintances and experienced again the prairie rhythm of life.

The six months in Weyburn were a necessary rest for Merna as well. That spring, X-rays showed that the cold she had had that winter had left some scarring and might well have been pneumonia. A small woman to begin with, she was down to ninety-four pounds. Looking after her very active son, Orm (who, she claimed, weighed thirty pounds at eight months), was not helping her condition. The doctor was worried that she was susceptible to tuberculosis and advised her to get plenty of rest and sun. Weyburn provided exactly what she needed that summer and Merna found it a leisurely stay, entertaining young Orm during the day while Bill wrote, and then playing bridge with Mrs. O.S. and her friends in the evenings. The only "disturbing" time occurred when Bill decided, against her better judgement, to buy some Italian antique furniture from an old couple who had travelled in Italy before the First World War: "It was Italian walnut and it was very peculiar furniture – tremendously ornate with carved griffins and mythological figures."[48] Bill paid three hundred dollars for the set – that was half of their savings.

Buying and restoring antique furniture had become a passion for them both, although after this instance it would always be Merna who made the selections. They made a good team, for Merna had an excellent eye for quality and style while Bill loved to bargain and described himself as a "wheeler-dealer." This extravagant purchase paid for itself in the end, for it inspired a new "Jake" story, "Auction Fever," which Bill sold to *Liberty* for four hundred dollars.[49] Jake and the Kid go to an auction to buy Ma a stove and, the Kid hopes, a colt. As they look over what is on offer, they notice a strange couch:

> One of her legs was off, so she leaned to one side like a horse resting on a hot day; she was all scuffed up and carved up and

battered up. Springs hung out of her bottom; they were poking out her top. I guess she was a couch.

. . . . Her back was curved out in two places. . . . Along the front were baby angels with their cheeks blown out, and in the middle of the top were two black hawks. They must have been mad at each other, because they were pointed in the opposite direction. (*JK* 106-107)

Jake is tricked into buying this "shaganappy" couch. However, all turns out well because Mrs. Fotheringham, one of the town's elite, has been waiting forty years for what Jake now proudly calls his "Gen-you-wine Eyetalyun carvin' – Renny-saunce – Eyetalyun walnut" couch (*JK* 117). Jake gets enough money to buy not only the stove for Ma but also the colt that the Kid wants so desperately. This couch reappears in *Who Has Seen the Wind* as the proud possession of Mrs. Abercrombie, the mayor's wife: "stiff and uncomfortable evidence of the Abercrombie *vandervogel*" (*WW* 57).

— "SAINT SAMMY" —

Early in February 1945, the Mitchells left Weyburn for Edmonton, where they spent a couple of months with the Hirtles. Mrs. Hirtle once again needed Merna to help her. Rev. Hirtle had decided to give up the ministry and move to a small farm holding on Vancouver Island because he believed that the farm would be a better environment for Spud, who at this time was in the mental institution at Ponoka. Bill, nearing the completion of the first draft of *Who Has Seen the Wind*, was pleased to be near Salter again and was seeing him regularly.

Cloud, now corresponding directly with Bill, wrote January 24 asking him to send any other stories he had. Four days later he sent the galleys for "The Owl and the Bens" and again asked for more stories, adding that if he had a novel in progress they would like to consider it for publication under the Atlantic imprint. A month later

Bill sent Cloud "Saint Sammy," a story which grew out of his encounter with Ollie Behind the Rock in Castor.

Bill's letter to Dudley Cloud showed that he had developed a confidence and a critical reflectiveness about his own work:

> I have made liberal use of religious symbolism in the prairie descriptions before and after the Lord's coming, a device suggested by Keat's [*sic*] *The Eve of St. Agnes*. My aim has been to create in the reader the same feeling of incongruity he would feel in talking with an actual dementia praecox case, hence the frog, the pun on hail, the deliberate unseating of dignity from time to time.
>
> Not all of my characters are odd; I like to think that my work is not simply regional, but the nature of "Who Has Seen the Wind" has dictated these particular people. It is a story of the influence on a boy of the prairie and his search for God. The Young Ben is used as a foil for him, and his acquaintance with Saint Sammy comes at a time when his conception of God is much that of Sammy's.[50]

In the last paragraph of this letter Bill reported that the completed first draft of *Who Has Seen the Wind* was being read by Salter and that he would send it to Cloud after putting in "another couple of months" fine-tuning it. His eight months of concentrated work on the novel in Weyburn and Edmonton paid off.

Salter was pleased with "Saint Sammy," particularly because it showed Bill's increasing independence and maturity as a writer. He wrote excitedly (with Mitchellesque rhythms in the first sentence) to Cloud:

> It's honest-to-God stuff; every prairie town has one or more of these crazed hailed-out, droughted-out, grasshoppered-out, frozen-out farmers, and not a few of them are religious-cracked as well – and the God of the prairie is a good Old Testament

Presbyterian Jehovah. But what I especially liked about "Saint Sammy" was that it was entirely Bill's – the whole thing was a surprise to me, and I was not aware of ever having made the slightest suggestion toward it. That is, Bill is getting beyond me and can go his own gait.[51]

Bill's apprenticeship was nearly complete and Salter was prepared to let go, for Mitchell had now developed that judgement about his own work that Salter had urged a year before. The uniqueness of expression and authentic portrayal of prairie and character had been evident in his work from the beginning. But both "The Owl and the Bens" and "Saint Sammy" showed his growing ability to bring craftsmanship to the finishing stages of his work, and a critical awareness and thoughtfulness about the construction and thematic implications of his material.

Cloud's opening line in his April 30 letter to Bill was "Saint Sammy is a wonder!" He enclosed a cheque for $450 and noted that Weeks had increased the payment so that the damage from the tax deduction would be less painful. He added, "Truly, we are burning to see the novel that comprises such varied souls as the Schoolmaster, Saint Sammy, and the Bens."[52] Here, finally, was the "click" Bill had been waiting for. Five days later Salter wrote Bill: "Well, I'm very pleased. And you have a right to feel some confidence in yourself. Just that, quiet confidence. But Merna can be proud if she likes. Only, tell her to talk about OS instead of her husband when she's out with the neighbors!"[53]

12

WHO HAS SEEN THE WIND

~ 1945 to 1948 ~

N EARLY APRIL 1945, Mrs. McCorquodale announced in the
High River Times the arrival of the Mitchells: "With a wide
choice of locations for a home, Mr. and Mrs. Mitchell have
selected High River as an attractive place in which to live. The town
extends a warm welcome."[1] In fact, the Mitchells were drawn to
High River as much by Mrs. McCorquodale as by the town itself.
Small, red-haired (in her younger days), and of Scottish descent, she
was an energetic, intelligent woman with a sense of humour.
Although sixty-four years old when Merna and Bill came to High
River, she had not slowed down much and was to continue to write
for the paper until her retirement in 1957. As associate editor of a
small-town newspaper she wrote every variety of column, from
chatty human-interest stories and witty editorials to strongly worded
political pieces. In 1937, along with some other Alberta newspaper
editors, she wrote editorials and letters protesting censorship of the
press by William Aberhart's Social Credit government. Their struggle to preserve the right to speak out against his policies won
them a special Pulitzer Prize, and the citation recognizing the newspaper's achievement hung on the office wall of the *High River Times*.
Mitchell used Mrs. McCorquodale as one of the models for Matt

Stanley in *Roses Are Difficult Here*, the novel which is most strongly modelled on High River, and in the opening page he refers to the citation: "Beside the masthead photo was the first Pulitzer Prize ever won outside the United States" (*RD* 7). *Roses Are Difficult Here* is dedicated to her.

To recognize her twenty-nine-year contribution to the newspaper and to the town, a "Mrs. McCorquodale Day" was organized in 1956, and Bill and Merna put together a series of readings that celebrated her life and activities in the town. Bill noted that she was often depicted as the spiritual successor of the infamous hard-drinking newspaperman Bob Edwards, who had started the first High River newspaper, the *Eye-Opener* (first called the *Chinook*), but, unlike him, she "never caricatured a foothills human in all her writing life." Her "sense of responsibility extend[ed] far beyond that of Edwards'."[2]

Aside from her public role, she was probably the most influential and most loved friend in Merna's life: "She was like a mother to me. We built our home across the street from her to be near her."[3] Davie, as Merna called her, was a female version of Mr. Hirtle, having his strength of conviction and his generous spirit. Merna, years later, thought so highly of Mrs. McCorquodale that she considered writing a book about her. Over a cup of coffee and hand-rolled cigarettes, Merna and Davie would discuss current community and political issues, some of which ended up in "Jake and the Kid" stories. Merna valued and trusted her opinions, and there were times during these early years in High River when Merna turned to her for comfort. During the next eighteen months, when Bill was fighting to keep his head above water financially, and when he was upset with his Atlantic editors over *Who Has Seen the Wind*, Merna would sometimes become the substitute target for his emotional outbursts. As Merna recalled, Mrs. McCorquodale was a tremendous "ally." She had no qualms about ordering Bill to behave himself – and he apparently listened to her.[4]

High River had other features to recommend it. Bill, by nature, was firmly rooted in the land and the small town, and High River, although of a different personality than his prairie town, Weyburn, offered that "poetry of earth and sky" that stimulated his imagination.[5] The Rocky Mountains, thirty miles away, were always a presence, sometimes just a thin pencil line on the horizon, sometimes so close they seemed only a few miles away. To the east and south, though, the land was flat, marked by the grain elevators of the small neighbouring towns. To the north, less than an hour's drive away, was the city of Calgary. Like other foothills towns High River's "streets [were] softened by cottonwood trees," a "chill and crystal" river flowed "down from the high ranges," and the "benign chinooks" offered a blessed reprieve from a harsh winter.[6] With the Highwood River running through the town and many mountain streams not too far away, Bill could indulge his new-found passion for fishing. Rather than walking out onto the prairie as he had as a child in Weyburn, he walked a block away to the Highwood River to fish. High River, with less than two thousand people, was smaller than Weyburn, but it afforded a similar kind of rural freedom and small-community stability and closeness that Merna and Bill wanted for their family. The friendliness, slow pace, and relative cheapness of High River life enabled them to bring up a family in a way that would not have been possible in a larger city. With an understanding bank manager and obliging grocery and hardware-store owners and with the occasional stint as a substitute teacher, Bill was able to freelance, something rare in Canada at that time. Bill would proudly tell his children, when they complained about not getting things other children got, that he could count on one hand the number of true freelance writers in North America and, though that meant that they were hard up, it was worth it. Bill and Merna truly believed that they had found the perfect spot for their family:

> In this town both my boys have grown up with the poetry of earth loud in their ears. They have flown their kites from what was once the Shorty McLaughlin horse ranch just west of our home, floated dry flies over the riffles of the old Blackfoot Crossing, played Tarzan in bush that once sheltered beaver

trappers and wolfers during their spring rendezvous. They've "bottomed it" and "made the moon rise" in a Highwood river swimming hole near the old whiskey trading post set up by Akers and Liver-Eating Johnston in 1870 on the MacLeod Trail.[7]

High River was a gold mine of stories and provided many plots and characters for Mitchell's radio plays and novels. It had some of the wild-west mystique about it, for in the early days it had been a trading post, a centre for cattle drives from the United States, and a whisky trading post. Originally a Blackfoot settlement (Ispitsi) on the Highwood River (Ispasqushow), it became known in the 1870s by the white population as The Crossing.[8] By 1910 it had settled into respectability, serving a large farming and ranching community. Bill soon soaked up the local history from the old-timers who congregated at the post office every morning. He called this his trapline, for if he did not get the cheque he was hoping for from *Maclean's* or *Liberty*, he always went away with some story of interest. There he picked up the stories of Liver-Eating Johnston, of Six-Shooter Joe and Shorty McLaughlin, of Bob Edwards, and of Guy Weadick, who started the Calgary Stampede. Bill's daily visit downtown was "the lifeline to our living," explained Merna: "He got to know people and he was able to talk to people from all walks of life without being patronizing or looking down. And he seemed to entertain them and was able to elicit information from them. This was how he picked up so many cultural expressions and ways of talking from these old, old guys."[9] Sometimes he would stop in at the St. George Hotel, where the old cowboys with their "high-heeled boots, spurs, faded blue levis, [and] stetson hats" would be resting in the large brown leather chairs in the lobby. There Senator Dan Riley, who had lived in the area since 1883, would "recount over a glass of Old Parr the ways in which a horse race could be fixed,"[10] stories that triggered the plot for the "Jake and the Kid" story "Two Kinds of Sinner." Senator Riley, who had been everything from a dispatch rider in the North-West Rebellion in 1886 to a senator (appointed in 1925), was much admired by Bill and was one of the models for a character in *Roses Are Difficult Here.*

High River was not all cowtown. The Count and Countess de Foras had settled in the area, and their daughter Odette became an internationally-known opera singer. Edward, Prince of Wales, was so taken by the scenery of the foothills country that he purchased a ranch, the E.P., which he visited from time to time, causing quite a stir in the community. In the early days, "ladies used calling cards, held afternoon musicales; there were formal balls such as the Polo Ball welcoming home the High River boys and ponies who had played off for the North American championship." However, by the time the Mitchells arrived, social life was more informal. Occasionally theatre and musical groups came through High River on their tours and, after 1951, when they had a car, Bill and Merna could easily get to Calgary to take in any arts event of interest. But the truth was that Bill enjoyed the time to himself that this small town afforded. Though an ordinary town in many ways, High River was special for Bill: "I cannot tell what sets this town of mine apart from the others in my affection, any more than I could analyze the stresses in a spider's web or one woman's special and immediate charm."[11]

They arrived on Good Friday, 30 March 1945. Since Merna's parents had just moved to Victoria, there was no place for them in Edmonton, so they simply decided to gamble on finding a place to rent in High River. This, in fact, was quite a risk: there had been no houses for rent for nine months, and they had only forty dollars in their pockets. For a while they had to take a room at the St. George Hotel, known for its bar frequented by the cowmen who came to town to celebrate on the weekends. To add to their concerns, Orm came down with measles. Bill remembered that those first few weeks "were the toughest then [that] we have known. . . . I used to wake up in a cold sweat, wondering what on earth I was doing here."[12]

Not long after this, walking down to the *High River Times* from the hotel, Bill noticed furniture out in front of the house right beside the *Times* office. The place was for rent and he took it immediately.

It was owned by Ernie Dart, a carpenter and handyman, who not only did a lot of construction work for the Mitchells in the next few years, but, as Merna recounted, "bailed us out again and again."[13] Merna returned the favour with her own sort of kindness – she gave Ernie a hot meal every day he worked for them.

The first month in High River was difficult and busy. In between bouts of bronchitis, a talk to the Alberta Teachers' Association in Calgary on "The Canadian Novel," and setting up the family in the rented house, Bill kept writing, trying to get enough material for a volume of "Jake and the Kid" stories to send to Macmillan, a book which he thought would bring in grocery money more quickly and more easily than the novel would.

Salter had other ideas for Bill, though, and at the end of April once again came to the rescue. He knew Bill was having a tough time financially, he knew that "*Maclean's* [was] easy money," and he knew that if *Who Has Seen the Wind* was to be finished soon and finished well then Bill would need a sizable advance from Atlantic Monthly. He wrote Bill saying he had assured Dudley Cloud that the "novel is a safe bet if he cares to gamble."[14] To Cloud on the same day he wrote a lengthy letter extolling Bill's talents: "Bill has the promise in him of a genuine artist. Canada has never had a writer like the writer Bill Mitchell might be." He then urged Cloud to make an offer and "make it worth his while." He hoped that Cloud was getting the message: "Is all this clear, or am I being metaphysical or something?"[15] Here again Salter was acting as Bill's agent sans 10%, making a pitch for an advance large enough to give Bill the next six months free and clear to write.

Salter must have been beside himself during those ten days of deal-making (from April 28 to May 9) when he contrived to make everything come together – to get Bill back to novel writing and to persuade Atlantic to send an advance. But this was just the kind of challenge that fired him up. In his April 28 letter to Bill he came on strongly – urging him three or four times to "drop everything else and get the novel finished": "But do it! Go at it in workaday fashion and rewrite it straight through skipping nothing, from beginning to end. . . . In your letter you say you are joining up the Jake stories. Chuck it. Jake will not help the sale of your novel; but the novel will help Jake."[16] He advised in his next letter, "Play canny, Bill," and suggested that although Atlantic was Bill's best bet it would not hurt to tease them a bit and let them know that Bobbs-Merrill and Houghton-Mifflin had shown an interest in the novel.[17] It worked. On May 9, Edward Weeks, through Salter, offered a thousand-dollar advance on the novel. This was enough to stop Bill from waking up in a cold sweat thinking about his family responsibilities. If it had not been for Salter's "finaigling [*sic*]"[18] as Bill called it, the novel might very well have been less carefully reworked and much longer in coming out.

Within five weeks of arriving in High River, the Mitchells' fortunes had dramatically increased from forty dollars (all spent on the house rent) to sixteen hundred dollars. In April *Atlantic Monthly* sent a cheque for "Saint Sammy" saying it was "wonderful beyond words."[19] Then came four hundred dollars from *Liberty* for "Auction Fever," and, finally, the thousand-dollar advance. Excitement ran so high that Salter advised Bill to "throw a rope around Merna and tie her down!"[20]

Feeling rich, they decided to invest in their first home. Salter, no doubt, was dismayed, for here was something else to distract Bill. Bill's mother came for a two-month visit, his brother Dick, who was between jobs and came out to help with the new house, stayed off and on for almost a year, and brother Bob and his wife visited as well. Typically, Bill seemed to thrive on all this commotion and kept on with his writing.

In June they heard from Mrs. McCorquodale about some small bungalows for sale in Turner Valley. For fourteen hundred dollars they found a ready-made house – it just had to be moved twenty-five miles to High River. They bought three lots for seventy-five dollars in the west end of the town right across the street from Mrs. McCorquodale. Bill and Dick dug out the basement by hand. This in itself was a novelty, for most people had their basements dug by machine. Merna did not sit idly by; she helped Bill finish pouring the basement walls – at two in the morning: "Mrs. Mitchell mixed and Bill wheeled and tamped. A neighbour who lent a hand remarked, 'First woman I ever saw mixing cement, when she dies she should have a cement tombstone with an inscription, "She Made It Herself." ' "21 By July the basement was ready for the house. The Highwood River was low enough that the house could be transported across just below the train bridge. Perhaps the Mitchells started a fad, for by the next spring it had become common in High River to see a house brought in like this. As the *Times* reported, it was a "quick and satisfactory method of getting a home and it [was] quite exciting to see a residence apparently dropped down out of the skies in the twinkling of an eye." 22

Bill's borrowing habits and his single-mindedness became legendary around High River, although he and Merna claimed that most stories were exaggerated. The joke around town, said Grace Clark, wife of the editor of the *High River Times* and a friend, was that "Bill built a house without even owning a hammer."23

Everyone we interviewed in High River had a Bill Mitchell story to tell, many of which concerned Bill's building projects. Former friends and neighbours felt compelled to tell funny stories, stories in which Bill was typically negligent, forgetful, or outrageous. Many of our interviewees began, "Have you heard the one about . . . ?" Bill and Merna had early on become characters in High River – and with some justification, for, with their spontaneous personalities, they attracted happenings. But colourful characters spawn even more colourful stories and some of these tales, as Merna and Bill were quick to point out, were simply untrue. One of these was about Bill, when he was substitute teaching. Apparently he had slept in and it was reported that he was seen dashing off to school with his pyjama cuffs sticking out of his trouser legs. But, as Merna used to retort, "He never wore pyjamas, so that couldn't be true!"

The stories about Bill's borrowing, however, did contain an element of truth – Bill was a consummate borrower. Jack Denny, a neighbour across the alley, lent Bill two pipe wrenches to do some plumbing for the greenhouse. When he came to retrieve them a few weeks later they could not be found. Fifteen years later, when the green-house was torn down, they were discovered sealed up inside one of the walls. On another occasion, Bill borrowed a cement mixer from George Harper, the high-school principal, and not only forgot to return it but lent it to someone else, forgetting it wasn't his. Mr. Harper, a formidable man, was so frustrated in his attempts to track down his mixer that he finally went to Don Blake's hardware store, bought a new one, and charged it to Bill Mitchell! One other borrowing story that was true according to Merna (though hotly denied by Bill) was that, when Charles Clark, the editor of the High River Times, *was taking the photograph of Bill for the back cover of* Who Has Seen the Wind, *Bill borrowed his pipe, since he had forgotten his own. The next time Charles saw his pipe Bill was smoking it.*

The proliferation of Bill and Merna stories highlights their comic magnetism. Very quickly Bill became for the people of High River bigger than life, and once he had been constructed as a comic figure in his own town, he could do little to tone down the exaggerations. But these stories expose more than the comic side of Bill's personality. He had a communal philosophy about property, derived from his small-town upbringing and from his travels during the Depression years when sharing was a matter of survival. He would loan as freely as he would borrow. In an aesthetic sense as well Bill was a borrower, for High River and its inhabitants provided the rough lumber with which he built his novels and short stories. He borrowed bits of character, colloquialisms, plots, and places and made them his own.

Merna, who was not as prone to exaggeration, described an incident that occurred one very hot day when she and Bill were up on the roof nailing down the shingles. Bill offered to get some lemonade for them. He climbed down, but was called over to the fence by his neighbour, Jack Kelly. When the conversation was finished – probably half an hour later, given Bill's talkativeness – he had not only forgotten the lemonade but had forgotten Merna. He returned to the house, moved the ladder, and went across the street to visit Mrs. McCorquodale. When Mrs. McCorquodale asked about Merna, Bill suddenly remembered that he had left her up on the roof. This was not to be the only time that Bill left Merna stranded.

In August, the living-room addition was begun. The Mitchells decided to celebrate with a neighbourhood party. Unfortunately it poured rain that night and their new basement flooded. Typically the Mitchells made a joke of it all, and Merna laughed as she recalled that one of their neighbours sat above the hole where the basement stairs were to go and pretended to fish into the basement water with a string and nail. Their carpenter, Ernie, decided they needed roof shingles immediately. When Bill said he could not afford them right then, Ernie pulled a wad of cash from his pocket, peeled off five hundred dollars and told Bill to pay him back when he could.

This house, which was to be their home until 1968, showed Merna's influence throughout. It was a Cape Cod–style bungalow nestled low on its foundation and painted white. She designed the living room, and helped to build the fireplace, which was "their love."[24] She laid out the pattern for the curving brick walk to the front door and later she put up brown shutters. She planted the cut-leaf birch trees in the front yard and planted flower gardens, Bill digging out by hand all the couch grass. They did not have an inside toilet or laundry facilities until 1951, but the house was luxurious to them. Bill's study was constructed a number of years later, so the final rewriting and editing of *Who Has Seen the Wind* were done partly in the little rented house and partly at a typewriter on the kitchen table in their new house. The work on the house was nearly completed by the end of February 1946 when Merna left to visit her parents. She was five months' pregnant with their second child and had left the interior finishing of the living room to Bill. He installed the hardwood floor and then painted the room – purple! Merna rectified this on her return. Overall though, as Merna defensively pointed out, Bill proved himself quite capable and practical. However, the process, as usual with Bill, was dramatic.

There was always some suspicion about Bill because he did not have a regular job, but he and Merna were soon accepted by most High Riverites. The house-building project immersed them immediately into the community, for the Mitchells were as comfortable with the plumber and the carpenter as they were with the doctor or the newspaper editor. And for their part, the neighbours and the various tradespeople were attracted by the Mitchells' openness and enthusiasm. One of their friends commented that, "Everyone in High River loved both of them, but we were all a little overwhelmed – they were different."[25] Merna had early on won over Dr. Harold Soby when he came to the hotel in those first few days in town to tend to Orm, who had the measles. She felt that they were accepted partly because they had become friends with him. Since he had a lot to do with setting "the town's social structure," they were immediately introduced around. But as Merna added, the people "liked [Bill] at parties because he was so entertaining."[26] Merna was "accepted into the bridge club, and into the book club – that sort of thing." Bill, for his part, joined the Rotary Club, although only for a short time, and gave speeches when asked, the first one on his rambles through Europe in 1933 and subsequent ones on writing. In a speech to the United Farm Women's Association in December 1946, he characterized the view of High Riverites towards him: "Mr. Mitchell said that he realized that writing as an occupation was regarded as something dubious, perhaps slightly immoral. In fact when he joined the teaching staff at High River this fall . . . the common greeting was, 'Well, how does it feel to be back to work again?' "[27]

Freelancing proved to be tough going. The sixteen hundred dollars did not last long with the house-building expenses, and both Ernie Dart and the Royal Bank bailed them out a few times. Bill had nothing more until March 1946, when he received a fifteen-hundred-dollar advance from Macmillan for the Canadian edition of *Who Has Seen the Wind*, and, as he wrote his mother, he had the "electricians, carpenters, lumber companies, banks, plumbers, and the like" after him.[28] In High River it was common to run up a monthly bill with the various tradespeople, but at times Bill's went far beyond one month. When the High River High School principal approached him to substitute teach in the fall for two teachers on leave, Bill readily agreed.

On June 1, 1946, Hugh Hirtle Mitchell was born. "The Mitchell family is emphatically male," wrote Bill to his editor on June 3.[29] Coming from a family of four boys, Bill had very much wanted a girl and, perhaps, was momentarily disappointed. The day after Hugh was born, when Bill was visiting Merna in the hospital, a minister appeared at the door, and, as Merna recalled, it was an uncomfortable situation:

> He said, "Mrs. Mitchell," and I said, "Yes." He said, "You're a Baptist." And the way he had said, "You are Mrs. Mitchell," I first thought, my gosh, have we done something wrong? Then I knew that Bill had probably put down that I was a Baptist on the hospital information record. And I said yes, I was raised a Baptist but my husband was a Presbyterian and that we compromised, at least I did, and we would go to the United Church. Well, I didn't want to really hurt him. Now that should have been the end of it, but Bill was fascinated and asked him to sit down and then he proceeded to have an argument (or a discussion really), and I can remember Bill saying, "You mean that you believe all those little newborn babies in that nursery are sinners?" And the man said, "Yes." And of course he was a fundamentalist Baptist. I got terribly, terribly upset and, as a matter of fact, after he left, I cried. And Bill apologized profusely.[30]

Bill had switched into a writerly mode. He had been intrigued by this person, and had simply satisfied not only his own curiosity but also his love of argument. Always fascinated, yet frustrated, by religious fundamentalists and, in his opinion, their literal and narrow-minded illogicality, he had forgotten Merna and her feelings. Bill's harangue was even more upsetting to her than the minister's intrusion. This obliviousness was a side to Bill that became more obvious as their marriage went on. Merna, however, quite forgivingly, concluded her account of this incident with the remark, "Out of that conversation he got an insight into what these fundamentalists believe and it was something that he tucked away for further use."[31]

— THE TRIANGLE: WRITER, MENTOR, AND EDITOR —

The history of the final stages of the writing and editing of *Who Has Seen the Wind* is unusually interesting because it turned into a battle over words – in fact, over nearly twenty thousand words. At the end of the battle there were two versions of *Who Has Seen the Wind*, the American Little, Brown version and the Canadian Macmillan one, which was about seven thousand words longer. At the root of the trouble were the strengths, and yet the different visions, of the three players in the editorial process. Bill had two first-rate editors, his friend and mentor F.M. Salter, and Edward Weeks, the highly regarded editor of Atlantic Monthly Press, the coterie press which published with Little, Brown. Both were excellent in different ways: Salter had known Bill for five years by this time and was in tune with his vision and his style. Weeks, on the other hand, although he had a sophisticated aesthetic sense, was the editor of a commercial press and was concerned about the cost of paper, the number of words, the attractiveness of the title, and the danger of offending or boring the reader. The other figure in this triangle, of course, was the author. Although this was Mitchell's first novel and he was anxious to get it published, he was not easily intimidated. So Mitchell himself was a strong force in this mix, and there were times when he would resist the advice of both his editors. Indeed, at the end of 1945 Salter wrote to Bill, "So far as I am concerned, I think you might be granted your degree now and graduate into the world of authorship. I cannot see that I can be of any further value to you; you are beyond the pupil stage."[32] After their first confrontation, Weeks also acknowledged Mitchell's maturity as a writer: "It is always a source of satisfaction to watch a narrator develop and defend the validity of his work. . . . and to say that is to give you honest praise."[33]

Salter edited the first draft of *Who Has Seen the Wind* between February and September 1945. In his first letter about the draft, April 1945, he did not mince words about what annoyed him, and he praised what delighted him. He was particularly frustrated by "pointless conversation" where people interrupted one another and did not finish their sentences. He argued that "real life and art are two things. Art must be true to life, but life is rarely true to art. Art must select the meaningful." This struck such a chord with Mitchell that in later years, when he was teaching creative writing at Banff, his own motto became "Life ain't art," a refrain he used so often that one class made him a red banner bearing the motto which he hung in his study. Mitchell's interrupted conversations, mimicking oral conversation, became a trademark of his writing. When they worked, as they did in his most successful novels and in the "Jake and the Kid" stories, they were remarkable; when they did not, as in some of his later work, they were as annoying as Salter had found them early on. Salter also reminded Bill that "minute touches," a half-line or a phrase, will be enough to make characters "real rather than flat," and urged him to keep working in all of his characters throughout the novel through these deft "touches." Indeed, Mitchell felt in later years that he had not been entirely successful with Mrs. Abercrombie and was also unhappy when his Atlantic editors removed the little touch about Miss MacDonald breaking down in tears after her confrontation with Maggie O'Connal. As an afterthought Salter added a handwritten note to the typewritten letter: "And keep *God* out as much as you can – that is, the name of God. The thing should be *implicit*, not *explicit*." Salter was to come back to this aesthetic point in subsequent letters, a point that Mitchell completely endorsed. It was soon to be at the centre of his disagreement with Mr. Weeks.

There was one more comment Salter made in this letter that is particularly interesting: "In one of the versions of the death of his father, by the way, you had the boy on the prairie coming to an understanding of what his mother must feel in the absence of her husband and going back to make up to her as much as he could for that loss. I may have slipped over it but do not recall seeing that bit in the draft. It *must* go in."[34] The passage Salter referred to takes place after the funeral when Brian walks out onto the prairie and finally breaks down and cries: "His mother! The thought of her had filled him with inexplicable tenderness and yearning. She needed him now. He could feel them sliding slowly down his cheek; he could taste the salt of them at the corners of his mouth" (*WW* 284). Salter, of course, would remember such a scene, for it was the father's death that had been the genesis for the entire novel. Although Mitchell had still retained in his manuscript the passage in which the family makes the ritual visit to the father's grave (*WW* 288), he had somehow eliminated this other one. Salter quite rightly felt it belonged, for it emphasized Mitchell's philosophy that man is saved from despair by human bonds. It is a sign of Brian's growth that he intuitively recognizes that he can be of some help to his mother, and it is a motif repeated in the final pages when Brian turns "back toward the town" (*WW* 343).

When Weeks sent through his offer, care of Salter, he commented that Salter and Mitchell were "a good team."[35] Little did he know then how close a team they were. While all the creative energy in the phrasing, the characters, the themes, and the incidents was Mitchell's, Salter was an immense help with technical aspects. He was the one who saw that the material might take shape as a novel. Mitchell, self-deprecatingly, described how this happened in his Margaret Laurence Lecture in 1996:

> Salter shoved the papers aside. "Do you notice anything promising in the way of a novel?"
>
> "I don't know."
>
> "Consider. First there's the just-born baby pigeon . . . then its death. Then there's the puppy, then he dies. Your father's funeral, the two-headed calf, your brother's birth, your grandmother's death. Get it?"

"No."

"Birth, then death, then birth, then death?"

"I don't know."

"It's a clear pattern. Could suggest a possible novel."

(*Eve* 258).

Salter in fact told Cloud, "I suggested the novel."[36] So Salter had a more than usual stake in this work.

Atlantic began pressuring Mitchell to send the manuscript immediately. Weeks, as Dudley Cloud noted, was simply the best in the business: ". . . the advantage our Press can give you is the careful, detailed editing that Mr. Weeks lavishes on his authors. At this job he is a wizard, as everybody in the business will tell you. The high proportion of book club choices from our relatively small Press is no accident."[37] It might have been a bit of editorial rivalry, or it might have been the hard sell, but Salter was slightly apprehensive about Weeks taking over and a couple of weeks later wrote to Bill: "[Cloud] seems fussy about Mr. Weeks as a critic, and it's nice that the organization should be so loyal to the commander-in-chief. And, of course, you may learn a great deal from Mr. Weeks."[38] Throughout May and June 1945, Bill worked hard on the manuscript, and he and Salter corresponded regularly. One aspect Salter greatly admired was the "townishness of the book,"[39] but he did have a problem with the swearing:

> Your problem is one that RLS [Robert Louis Stevenson] had, to give the *effect* of swearing without using any objectionable words. I wince a bit at *whore* and *bugger*. . . .
>
> You see, a very large potential group of buyers of your novel will be what are technically called *good* people, ministers, etc. Well, figure it out – who *would* be interested in the story of a child's development?[40]

In two areas Salter was to have a profound effect on the novel: in the repetitive and symbolic use of wind, and in the heightening

19.40.10.f10

Who Has Seen the Wind?   10

                                        simply
        Brian was not startled; he ~~xxxxxxixxxly~~ accepted
the boy's presence out here on the prairie as he
had,that of the gopher, the hawk, the butterfly.
He saw that the boy's hair,bleached as the dead
prairie grass, lay across his forehead in an all-
around cowlick curling under at its edge. Once
blue, now indescribably faded, his pants hung open
in two tears below the knees. He was bare-footed.
        "This is the prairie," Brian said.
        The boy ~~xxxxxx~~ simply stared at him, then turning
began to walk as silently as he had come, out over
the prairie. His walk was ~~singularly~~ smooth.
        After the boy's figure had become simply a black
speck in the distance, Brian looked up into the sky,
his eyes travelling over a soft expanse of clouds
reaching ~~xx~~ down to the rim of the prairie, the higher
edges luminous and startling against the blue. As
he stared, the pigeon-gray underside of one slowly
and imperceptibly thinning, the layers of cloud stuff
driffting over each other, carding apart to give him
the dizzying feeling of apartness that ~~xxxxxxixxx~~ he
was used to in dropping off to sleep.
        Through the clouds' softness was revealed a blue
well shot through with sunlight lighting the cool
and brilliant depth of it. And almost as soon as it
had cleared, a whisking of cloud was stealing over it,
lingeringly and relentlessly covering it.
        God, he decided, ought to be very fond of prairie.

                          -30-

Sample of F.M. Salter's editorial work on
Who Has Seen the Wind, *spring 1945.*

of the Young Ben as a mysterious representation of the prairie. Salter
suggested bringing together Brian and the Young Ben at some key
moments. Bill disagreed at first: "The difficulty is that Brian and the
Young Ben are not likely associates." In fact, replied Salter, they "*are*
likely associates," and he described the relationship as an "eerie and

unexpressed understanding or friendship" that often occurs with children, particularly "sensitive, thoughtful" children like Brian.[41] Bill needed only this nudge. He quickly and enthusiastically wrote the Young Ben into, or added more detail to, a number of scenes in which the two boys protect and comfort one another or share a sympathetic response to nature. The most striking change occurred in the gopher scene. Here Mitchell changed his perception about how Brian would regard the Young Ben after he beats up Ike, who rips the tail off the gopher. At first Mitchell thought Brian would be repulsed, filled with "a faint nausea and fright,"[42] but, on Salter's advice and employing some of his words, Mitchell aligns the feeling of "fierce exultation" (*WW* 148) to the "feeling" Brian experiences throughout the novel:

> And Brian, quite without any desire to alleviate Ike's suffering, shaken with his discovery that the Young Ben was linked in some indefinable way with the magic that visited him often now, was filled with a sense of the justness, the rightness, the completeness of what the Young Ben had done – what he himself would liked to have done. (*WW* 149)

The Young Ben was changed from an ordinary violent boy to one who has a mysterious relationship with the prairie. Five months later Mitchell would use Salter's arguments to defend the Young Ben with Weeks, who found him unbelievable.

Just as their house was being set on its foundation, at the end of June, Bill began work on the final copy of the novel. On August 31 he sent about half the manuscript to Atlantic. He had spent the last two months working on his own without Salter's input. And now he was ready for their perspective on his work: "Both Mr. Salter and I are so well soaked in the thing now that it is difficult for us to get a fresh view point on it."[43]

On September 13 he sent the last half of the manuscript. It had been a huge push and his mental fatigue showed in his letter to Cloud:

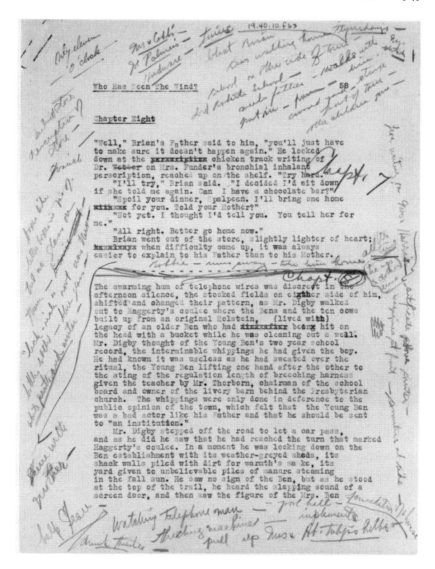

Draft manuscript of Who Has Seen the Wind
shows Bill's extensive editing, summer 1945.

Maggie O'Connal is not what I'd like her to be; the relationship between the two brothers is sketchy; I'm afraid that the Svarich-Thompson-Digby story needs more work. I'd rather like to see something in the way of a prairie bridge (as at the end of the first chapter and the last) between all sections. In addition to poor spelling and mechanical errors, you will probably notice time, name, and character flaws, that right now I am too tired to correct.

I think I shall now go out fishing.[44]

Bill did take a break. He joined the cowhands at the Macleay ranch southwest of High River for the fall round-up.

It turned out to be not exactly the brief weekend of escape that he had wanted. They were caught in the hills by a snowstorm and trapped in a small cabin for ten days. With nothing to do but play poker and nothing to eat but elk meat it became a tense situation. A small feud started between Bill and the cook, and Bill was goaded into trying to catch some fish to vary the menu. Much to the cook's amazement, Bill caught forty cutthroat – the creek had never been fished before! He also fished for stories and heard in detail the tale of the lost Lemon mine, the gold mine supposedly discovered by Lemon and his cohort Blackjack. They had come to Canada in the spring of 1870 with a group of prospectors from Montana. After leaving the main party, they prospected the upper reaches of the Highwood and discovered an "incredibly rich" vein,[45] but that night they had an argument, and Lemon murdered Blackjack. Unhinged by his evil deed, Lemon could never remember where the mine actually was. Two Stoney Indians had followed the men there, but when they returned to their chief, Jacob Bearspaw, he decreed the place evil and swore them to secrecy. Even as late as the 1960s people were still trying to find the lost Lemon mine. King Bearspaw, Jacob's grandson, claimed to know where it was and conned people into believing he could lead them there. Mitchell, looking ahead to a new novel and more "Jake" stories, tucked these events and characters away for future use.

— THE FINAL EDIT —

Mitchell was told in September that his book was being read with "whoops of joy,"[46] so he was completely taken aback by the list of revisions sent to him by Weeks in early December 1945. As he recalled later, he was "furious."[47] Although Weeks admired Mitchell's talent and wrote of "the exceptional pleasure" the manuscript had given him, there was an indication, even this early, that they had different visions of the book. There was a slight tone of condescension in Weeks's statement that it was exciting to "discover a man who can write," doubly so "when he comes from a region as remote and little known as yours and yet can write about that region in terms of universal truth."[48] That small hint that Weeks did not understand Mitchell's "remote" landscape was to show itself more blatantly in many of Weeks's suggested revisions. When Weeks questioned the mention of Louis Riel, Mitchell responded, "The fact that the novel is laid in Western Canada must necessitate differences of experience [and] background on the part of readers, for which I can't be responsible."[49]

While Weeks downplayed his requests for alterations as a little "fuss over certain details of revision" and "minor aspects," Mitchell rankled at many of Weeks's editorial suggestions and thought they showed a lack of understanding of the novel's theme and landscape. The opening sentence of the novel has become one of the most recognizable in Canadian Literature: "Here was the least common denominator of nature, the skeleton requirements simply, of land and sky – Saskatchewan prairie" (*WW* 1). "Cut it," Weeks bluntly wrote. He found it "full of dull words." After reading through the list of editorial suggestions it was clear to Mitchell that Weeks and Cloud disapproved of those very things that he, with Salter's support, had worked hard to achieve, particularly the symbolism of the wind and the characters of Brian and the Young Ben. Weeks thought that many descriptive passages were "over-decoration"; he found R.W. God, Brian's make-believe playmate, too fantastic a creation and somewhat offensive (in fact, one suggestion was to rewrite these sections from an adult point of view); he thought the Young Ben "implausible"; he felt Brian and the Young Ben were not punished enough for their misdeeds; and he thought that Brian should be an ordinary boy whose "feet must be planted on the earth."

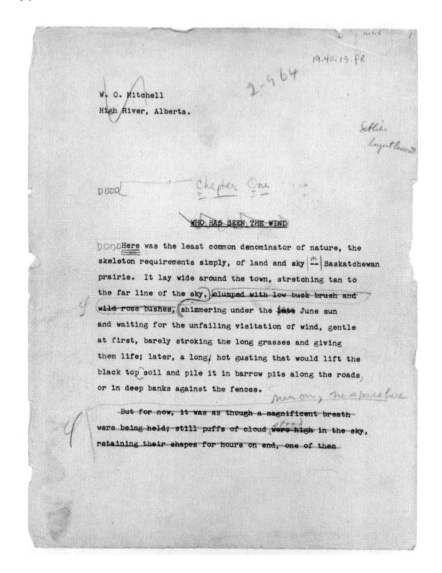

Atlantic Monthly's editing of the first page of
Who Has Seen the Wind, *spring 1945.*

Weeks also would have changed the title, not understanding how it was bound up with the theme. He appreciated, of course, that this was a story about a boy growing up, but he insisted that Brian needed to figure out what he wanted to be when he grew up – an engineer or doctor. What he did not understand was that the book was about questioning, not about finding answers. And he did not appreciate that the structure of the novel depended on a delicately varied repetition of images of wind, light, and dark. Of all the suggestions, however, it was Weeks's request to cut the last few pages of the novel – the description of the wind "wing[ing] on, bereft and wild its lonely song" (*WW* 344) – that most upset Mitchell:

> The ending is abrupt. It must be strong. It must be free and clear – with no chance for the reader to go wrong.
>
> The last two pages are now the weakest in the book, and they should be the best.
>
> The story in our minds will end with Brian, not the wind. What of his future.[50]

Utterly dismayed by these demands, particularly the last one, Bill turned to Salter for advice. Salter put the matter in perspective. First of all he assured Bill that he had written a good novel. Then he analysed the suggestions that Weeks and Cloud had sent through – and he was blunt: "I'm willing to bet that neither Mr. Cloud nor Mr. Weeks knows what this novel is about." But he wisely pointed out that if they did not understand what Mitchell was saying then neither would the common reader. Salter suggested compromising by "mak[ing] the theme a little more explicit throughout,"[51] exactly the opposite of what he had been suggesting earlier for aesthetic reasons. Two days later he wrote proposing a preface:

> Some time ago you showed me a quotation from the Bible about the wind. Put that in a Preface, and say that many interpreters of the Bible take the wind to be a symbol of Godhood, and then say, "In this novel I am trying to present sympathetically the struggle of a small boy to understand things that still defeat mature and learned men, the ultimate meaning of things and the cycle of life, birth, death, hunger, satiety, and eternity."

Mitchell used this idea and many of Salter's words and, although Salter thought that, with the preface before him, "surely Weeks will not ask you to end with Brian instead of the wind," that was not the case. Salter went through all the requested cuts and commented that "there is some value for you in a few of them, a shockingly small percentage," but urged Bill "to pretend to benefit by them." He apologized for catching Bill in the "cross fire" between himself and Weeks, then immediately added that he knew that he and Bill were really on the same side.[52]

To be fair to Weeks and Cloud, this was not an ordinary novel. Although most of their readers' reports were enthusiastic, one was negative and commented that Atlantic would not get its money out of this book. Certainly the plot was "tenuous,"[53] as Salter and Mitchell themselves knew, and there was an abundance of descriptive passages. Weeks and Cloud wanted a more explicit, traditional novel. Clearly impressed with Mitchell's talent, Weeks had assured Mitchell that his and Cloud's suggestions were "all tentative, and . . . you are the boss."[54] But Mitchell never felt as if he were. He intuitively understood that he was going to have to compromise to retain those aspects that mattered most.

At the end of January, Mitchell returned the manuscript with all his corrections. He mirrored Weeks's own approach, employing a grateful and conciliatory tone ("For the most part I have adopted your very helpful suggestions") to soften his more insistent demands that certain passages be reinstated. He did exactly what Salter had urged. He explicitly spelled out for Weeks what he was trying to do in the novel:

> I have not tried to prove anything with this book; I am too young yet for that. But I have worked hard for a quality of dualism: town and prairie; Brian and alter-ego Young Ben; birth and death. The latter concern me most – birth: the pigeon eggs, the puppy, the rabbits, the two-headed calf, the facts of human birth – death: Bobbie's early illness, the pigeon, the gopher, Jappy, the father, the grandmother. Love, hunger, the mystery

of sleep, are lightly touched. Only when the above realities are involved does Brian experience his intuitive moments of oneness with the world. The drop and the meadow lark's song are perhaps exceptions; in their beauty and perfection they are intended to contradict Milt Palmer, who senses only the brutal and frightening quality of the world. . . .[55]

He explained what he had tried to do in the final few pages of the novel where the wind, the prairie, and the cycle of seasons are lyrically evoked. He told Weeks that "the description of the prairie is not as objective as it may seem" and called his attention to words such as "seeking" and "truant." The prairie was not used to render a photographic, decorative description of the landscape, but to accent the "mood" running through the novel of "the transiency of man's days and the eternity of the prairie." In this regard he likens his own philosophy to that of Hardy and Conrad, who, although bleaker than Mitchell in placing man at the mercy of the gods, are similar in their emphasis of the bonding of humans against "the brutal and frightening" realities of the world.[56] He would cut what Weeks urged if it helped make clear the meaning of the book, and he insisted on reinstating those cuts that destroyed its fabric. On this first edit Weeks had asked for between fifteen hundred and two thousand words to be cut, and Mitchell obliged with about three-quarters of them. Weeks had certainly made some good suggestions, such as his request for a Christmas scene. Mitchell was tenacious, though, about preserving his ending and the beginning sentence and about retaining the unique, sensitive characters of Brian and the Young Ben.

Mitchell had given Little, Brown only the American rights to the novel and, as early as April 1944, had dealt separately with Macmillan of Canada. In January 1946, after making the first cuts suggested by Weeks, he sent a carbon of the manuscript to Macmillan, requesting an advance. Macmillan asked Frederick Philip Grove, author of *The Master of the Mill* (1944) and one of the most eminent Canadian writers at the time, to review Mitchell's manuscript. Grove was enthusiastic: "One does not often meet with a book which combines power and beauty."[57] Grove went on to praise the characterizations ("All this is very, very excellent") and the "atmosphere of Saskatchewan." He thought the manuscript over-long, with some passages that tried the reader with their poetic metaphors, a number of which, in his opinion, were affected. Bill was sent a copy of the report and was duly flattered. Just a year earlier, Bill had been introduced to Grove's work by an acquaintance in Weyburn, so he was amused by Grove's comment that "150 pages of the whole should be pruned out." When he sent a copy of Grove's report to Salter and to his mother he wrote in the margin beside that remark, "Have you read *The Master of the Mill*?"[58] for Grove's work, in Mitchell's opinion, could have stood some pruning itself. In spite of this criticism, Grove was very impressed with Mitchell, and writing to a literary friend he said, "Keep your mind open for a young Albertan; W.O. Mitchell, whose first novel I have just most strongly recommended to Ellen Elliott. There is all of Saskatchewan in it. Glad to see him coming along. To me he seems much better than myself."[59]

At the beginning of March, Bill wrote to his mother that "all hell popped." Macmillan agreed to publish his book, *Liberty* was interested in a condensation, and Weeks had sent through the con-tracts. Bill was exuberant:

> The royalty in both contracts is fifteen percent of the retail price – if there is a moderate sale – twenty thousand in Canada – forty – say in the States – it would mean close to $50,000 – and if it makes a book club circulation the returns would be astro-nomical. If Weeks sells the movie rights for me, it would be a catastrophe or something.[60]

He had cause for elation, and such optimism was characteristic of Mitchell throughout his life. But he was to be disappointed in the royalties, movie rights, and further advances he excitedly described to his mother.

Bill was acting as his own agent and, using his experience as a salesman, he began wheeling and dealing. He pushed his luck with Macmillan of Canada by asking for an advance of fifteen hundred dollars, arguing that the extra five hundred above Little, Brown's offer would "be compensation for whatever made me refuse *Little-Brown* the Canadian rights, three other American publishers, and finally two Canadian."[61] He won his argument and urged them to send the advance quickly so "I can get my wife and son and one unborn child home from Victoria."[62] Two months later he was using this settlement to bargain for another thousand from Little, Brown. He claimed that he naturally came by this inclination to bargain: "Everything's fair in business and I'm my Mother's son, and my Grandmother's too."[63]

In a letter that accompanied the contract Weeks asked Mitchell for "delicate power of attorney" for himself and Dudley Cloud to make "small cuts totalling from 10,000 to 12,000 words"![64] In fact, Jeannette Cloud told Macmillan just two weeks later that Mitchell had agreed to cutting fifteen thousand[65] and another reader had suggested cutting in excess of twenty thousand. On the surface Mitchell was surprisingly unperturbed about this request: "In view of the need for haste I have no hesitation in letting you and Mr. Cloud go ahead with the necessary cuts."[66] He asked only that they keep in mind the "concerns" he had already expressed, and requested that they make cuts in the beginning where he was "least sensitive."[67] Why he would be less concerned about cuts of twelve thousand words than he was about the original two thousand–word cuts is curious. Perhaps he was doing what Salter had suggested, pretending to comply in hopes that they would not cut so much. He was certainly bothered by their request to control the editing and in May wrote Cloud: "I have already made the greatest concession I can make and that is to let somebody else cut WHO HAS SEEN THE WIND; it was a darn sight harder than the matter of advance and that of the condensation rights."[68] Although he declared his concern, he did not agonize over these latest cuts as he had over the first. He was swayed by Weeks's arguments that with a shorter book the price would stay competitive at $2.50.[69] There was also the urgency of getting the book out for September publication.

On a less commercial note, he perhaps believed that Weeks and Cloud would not interfere with those themes, characters, and motifs of which he was so protective. And, finally, as was to be a pattern with later works, when he had a new work under way he completely turned his attention to it. In January, after he had finished with his first revisions for Weeks, he had begun writing a new novel, "The Alien." In April he indicated that he had been working for three months on it: "Chapters and narrative are blocked out; I have accumulated quite a stack of sensuous detail and character bits."[70]

On 5 April 1946, Bill learned that Martha Foley had selected "The Owl and the Bens" for *Best American Short Stories* of 1946. It would be sure to boost sales of the book, and he was flattered to be in the company of Vladimir Nabokov. At the same time "Saint Sammy" was taken by Desmond Pacey for *A Book of Canadian Stories*. There was much interest in *Who Has Seen the Wind* from magazines and from film companies, and Bill was kept busy answering requests for copies, including one from *Ladies' Home Journal*.

The galleys were sent in August. This round of editing had been done by Cloud. Mitchell was pleased to see that Cloud had done most of the cutting in the first part of the book; the ending was still sacrosanct territory for him. He generously indicated that he had located 107 lines additional to their suggested ones which he would cut and even suggested that he would be willing to cut an entire episode, such as the one about the China Kids, if necessary. However, he asked for seventy-two lines (approximately 650 words) to be reinserted: "I should be extremely disappointed if they didn't go back in."[71] Again, many were passages with the wind motif. One passage concerned Brian's night in the strawstack after he has run away from his uncle's farm. In this scene Brian feels frightened and alone: "He felt the wincing of his very core against it [the wind]" (*WW* 270). Unbeknownst to him his father has just died after an operation. Brian's feeling is conveyed by the "two voices" of the night wind, one which "keened" and one which "throated long and deep" (*WW* 270). Mitchell could barely control the sarcasm when he explained what seemed so obvious: "This is the wind again. The significance is that of an omen. I believe Shakespeare used them. The boy's father is being taken from him. Perhaps I don't achieve what I hope to with this sort of thing, then again I am afraid I'm being obvious. . . ." Throughout the editing process, from December 1945 to August 1946, he argued with Cloud and Weeks that all his descriptive passages were deliberate, that they offered "intellectual content" or, he added, perhaps "*emotional*" is a better word. He admitted that to many readers this may be "dead-wood," but, if so, "it will have to be,"[72] for he was not going to make cuts there. Cloud did not protest and restored the passages to the novel.

During this time, Mitchell also carried on a separate correspondence with Macmillan. Macmillan and Little, Brown, however, corresponded themselves, and it looked as if they were in agreement about the manuscript. In fact, Macmillan originally was going to buy five thousand copies from Little, Brown. By May Macmillan had decided they could print their own copies. Mitchell had not told them that he had allowed Cloud to make extensive cuts to his manuscript, and when they discovered that they asked to see the cut version. Perhaps it was too late for Macmillan to backtrack, or perhaps they preferred Mitchell's version. At any rate, in October he wrote: "I appreciate very much that the Canadian edition is to be much the same as the manuscript I sent you [in January]; although I have managed to get about half the cuts re-inserted, I do not consider the Little, Brown edition as good as the Canadian."[73] As a result, two versions of *Who Has Seen the Wind*, with about seven thousand words' difference, came to be published simultaneously in February 1947. After that, however, and again for financial reasons, the shorter American edition was used for subsequent editions until 1991. The Canadian version was all but forgotten.

~ LITERARY HEROES ~

Earlier in 1946, Atlantic Monthly Press asked Mitchell to fill out a form with biographical information, and on it Mitchell listed his literary influences: "I look to James for form, Katherine Mansfield and Virginia Woolf for sensuous detail, Dickens for technical tricks such as tagging a minor character, Galsworthy for restraint, and to Conrad and Hardy, who are my Gods, for all things."[74] These were the writers he had been brought up on in high school and university and who, philosophically and technically, influenced his writing.

He did not mention here Wordsworth, whose "Intimations of Immortality" ode had inspired him in Miss Murray's English class. In spite of his later dismissal of Wordsworth ("God wasted some wonderful insights on Wordsworth"), aspects of his philosophy influenced this novel.[75] In particular, Mitchell was drawn to Wordsworth's portrayal of the child's "primal sympathy"[76] with nature, when the child sees the world around him with a clear and fresh eye. Mitchell referred to these early years as litmus years, believing that a child is intensely open to and indelibly marked by his early sensuous experiences. He further believed that it was essential to carry into adulthood some degree of one's childhood responsiveness and connectedness to the world. All good guardians in his novels can summon up this "primal sympathy." The fact that Miss MacDonald, Brian's first teacher in *Who Has Seen the Wind*, has "complete amnesia for childhood" (*WW* 90) tags her as an ineffectual teacher. She has lost the capacity to see and feel with any vestige of childhood imagination.

The scene in which Digby mentions "Intimations of Immortality" (*WW* 340) was added during the last edit (September 1946) in response to Weeks's request to know what Brian's "future" will be, and, although it is appropriate for a schoolteacher to drag in this reference, it is apparent that Mitchell himself felt some reluctance to do so, not only because he did not want to suggest that everything has to "figure out" (*WW* 336), but because he did not want to align himself too closely with Wordsworth's vision of child-hood. For the same reason, although he thought of calling the novel "Trailing Clouds of Glory," he decided against it. He sensed in Wordsworth's ode an unhealthy nostalgic regret for a lost childhood and a rather dismal view that adults can hope to retain only the "embers" of the "joy" of childhood.[77]

Digby also refers to one of Mitchell's other literary heroes, Joseph Conrad. Digby is reminded of *Heart of Darkness* one evening just after a visit from the Rev. Mr. Powelly, who has come urging Digby to send the Young Ben to reform school. What Digby realizes is that people like Mrs. Abercrombie and Rev. Powelly, under the guise of Christian benevolence, often act for very selfish reasons. In this case they "had substituted a concern over the morals of the town youth for the real reason," which was a "distaste for the Young Ben's father" (*WW* 251). On a larger scale, this is what Conrad is dealing with in *Heart of Darkness*. Behind the European drive to reform or civilize Africa was the real motivation – materialistic greed for ivory and power. In citing Conrad as well as Wordsworth, Mitchell neatly counterpoints the Wordsworthian vision of the divinity of the child with the Conradian view of the innate darkness of the soul. Although in Mitchell's world, as in Conrad's and Hardy's, the gods have their sport – creating two-headed calves and too many rabbits – and although his universe can be just as indifferent as theirs – as it is in the final pages of *Who Has Seen the Wind* with their Ecclesiastian rhythms – his overall vision is more comic than bleak, and man, like the Wordsworthian child, is generally more in harmony with his world. But Mitchell's declaration that Conrad and Hardy are his "Gods" above all others is a reminder of the dark streak that runs through his work, all of his work, and a reminder that he does not offer sentimental, clear-cut answers to the human predicament.

For "all things," he said, he looked to Conrad and Hardy. His craft, like theirs, was to vividly and faithfully recreate charac-ters in their particular landscapes. Conrad outlined his aesthetic preconceptions in the "Preface" to *The Nigger of the Narcissus*: "My task which I am trying to achieve is, by the power of the written word to make you hear, to make you feel – it is, before all, to make you see. That – and no more, and it is everything."[78] Similarly, Mitchell believed that the writer must create the "illusion of realism." Echoing Conrad, Mitchell in one of his early addresses on the craft of writing said that it was most important to focus on the world of the senses, to capture by "word and by metaphors," the "provocative sensations of taste and of sound and of smell."[79]

The other writers mentioned in his biographical profile were also important models and later he referred to them when he was working with beginning writers. He had all of Virginia Woolf's work in his library, and he would frequently refer to Mansfield's short stories, particularly "Miss Brill" and "The Doll's House," for the subtle way in which they made the reader sensitive to another person's world. His nod to Henry James should be qualified, for he actually did not enjoy reading James. He did so only to comply with Salter's suggestion (in a letter of 27 June 1945) that he needed to learn more about novel structure. Mitchell, in fact, felt he was developing a new kind of structure in *Who Has Seen the Wind*, which owed more to Virginia Woolf than to Henry James. Later, when he read E.M. Forster's *Aspects of the Novel*, he completely agreed with Forster's view that James's obsession with neat mathematical structures restricted his characters from achieving spontaneous lives. Salter had referred to the plot and structure of *Who Has Seen the Wind* as "tenuous," "impressionistic,"[80] and symphonic (*Eve* 258). Mitchell adopted this latter term to explain that the novel is unified by motifs such as the wind, and light and dark. There is no structure of rising action and climaxes; rather it consists of "alternating high and low notes" (*Eve* 259). Certainly this was not in the traditional school of writing of the time, and Weeks wanted a climax in which Brian sorted out his life. The loose structure, ending with lyrical passages of the eternalness of the prairie, has continued to perplex critics, but it conveys Mitchell's philosophy that definitive answers are impossible, that "to see only things as cithcr/or and not realize the important harmony and amalgam of contradictions" is "the most damaging thing mentally that human beings do."[81]

Who Has Seen the Wind is decidedly Canadian in its region and in its characters, a feature that reviewers were to point to with nationalistic pride. Robertson Davies wrote that Mitchell "has so thoroughly captured the feeling of Canada and the Canadian people that we feel repeated shocks of recognition as we read."[82] And Frederick Philip Grove, in his reader's report, wrote that Mitchell captured very well the "freak religionists, nowhere to be found to the same intensity except in Saskatchewan where I know them by the dozen."[83] Mitchell was not the first writer, of course, to use this region literally and metaphorically. Both Grove and Sinclair Ross before him had written about the prairies, but their visions were more uniformly tragic and their landscapes were relatively dark and one-toned. In a speech given to the Canadian Authors Association in 1948 (which Mitchell attended) Merrill Denison complained that Canadian writers were not writing out of their own experience and "had failed to make Canada and Canadians interesting."[84] He went on to say that the two exceptions to his comments were Hugh MacLennan's *Two Solitudes* and W.O. Mitchell's *Who Has Seen the Wind*. Certainly Mitchell's prose was vigorous and colloquial in a refreshingly new way.

Mitchell was not much influenced by earlier Canadian writers. In fact, he confessed to not being particularly aware of or interested in Canadian literature in the 1930s and 1940s. He had thought *The Master of the Mill* surprisingly good when he read it in 1944 because he "didn't expect much from a Canadian [writer] at that time." Although he remembered quite vividly reading Sinclair Ross's "Cornet at Night" in *Queen's Quarterly*, around the same time that his own story appeared, and commented that Ross "was an excitement" for him, he had not read *As For Me and My House*.[85] Later Mitchell was often compared to Haliburton and Leacock because of his comic vision. It was Miss Murray who had introduced him to Leacock, but as an adolescent his favourites were the Americans, Mark Twain and Bret Harte. It was the Twain-like quality, the "raw authentic vigor"[86] of the prose, that Weeks first admired in Mitchell. Weeks, though, did not bargain for the philosopher side of Mitchell that applied a Hardy-esque and Conradian perspective to the prairies of Western Canada.

— CHAMPAGNE FROM "KITCHEN TUMBLERS" —

On Monday, 23 September 1946 a long-distance telephone call came from Philadelphia for Mr. W.O. Mitchell. Because the Mitchells did not yet have a telephone the town's telephone operator redirected the call to a neighbour's phone. With the neighbour and Merna hanging on every word, Bill heard from John Mabon at *Ladies' Home Journal* that they wanted to buy the condensation of *Who Has Seen the Wind* – for five thousand dollars! He and Merna were beside themselves with excitement. Mrs. McCorquodale made sure the entire town heard the news, placing it on the first page of the *Times*: "It isn't going to be long until the name of W.O. Mitchell of High River will be widely known in literary circles of this continent. The most recent appreciation of his writing comes from the Curtis Publishing Company. Last Monday this company talked to him by telephone from Philadelphia. . . ."[87]

On Saturday Bill and Merna went to Calgary to celebrate their good fortune. Even thirty-six years after the event Merna retold the story with breathless excitement:

> First we went to Heintzman's and there they had a grand piano and it had been used in Banff at the School of Fine Arts. So he bought the piano for five hundred dollars. Now, I didn't have a washing machine or a refrigerator or a vacuum cleaner, none of those things. He bought me a piano!
>
> Then we went to the Hudson's Bay and Bill said I was to have an evening dress and he had his own tux – God knows whose tux it was because it was pretty old and he had gotten it all pressed up and he was skinny at that time – and he picked

out a black velvet dress that came off the shoulders and the little girl, who got caught up in the excitement, said, "Go and get your shoes and I'll see this dress is shortened for you" – because Saturday night the Palliser Hotel had supper dances. So we went down and we got shoes, came back, and she pinned it and said, "We will have it ready for you in about an hour but I think you should have a little string of pearls to go on it." All the dress had was a little bit of fine lace around the cap sleeves.

Well, believe me, it was a beautiful dress and we went to the supper dance. And we stayed at the Palliser Hotel that night. And Bill actually danced. He didn't enjoy dancing very much but he did that night. We were on top of the world, you know.

Oscar Peterson, Canada's soon-to-be-famous jazz musician, was playing that night. Merna asked him to play some of her favourites. Many years later he still remembered this petite jubilant young woman – who really knew her music – standing behind him at the piano with request after request; he said that they were the two most excited people he had ever come across.[88]

They had to wait until the end of January 1947 for the actual appearance of the *Ladies' Home Journal* condensation. On February 9 they drove to Calgary again: "I have just received my author's copies: the Canadian Customs officials at Calgary's Department of Internal Revenue do not approve of people who rip parcels open before paying tariff, in their anxiety to see book jackets." That evening they celebrated with "a bottle of Heidsieck's drunk out of kitchen tumblers, saved for over a year and extra dry."[89]

The *Ladies' Home Journal* published their condensation in the February issue a few weeks before the release of the novel on February 18 in the States and on February 28 in Canada. Publicity and promotion of books was not the media show that it is today. In fact, Ellen Elliott, director-secretary of Macmillan, wondered how to promote Mitchell at all. Writing to publisher John Gray she regretted that there was not much to "play up" in this book – "If

Publicity display for the Ladies' Home Journal *condensation of* Who Has Seen the Wind, *February 1947.*

only Mitchell had a war record – he hasn't." She suggested some public appearances, adding what in hindsight is a highly ironic comment: "always supposing the man can speak."[90] Promotion consisted of a book signing at Eaton's in Calgary for the opening day of the sale of *Who Has Seen the Wind,* a couple of speeches in Calgary and Lethbridge and then, in June, the keynote address to the Canadian Authors Association in Vancouver and to the Canadian Library Association in Victoria.

Mitchell was disappointed with the publicity efforts on the part of Little, Brown: "They did not do nearly the job of pushing WHO HAS SEEN THE WIND that *Macmillans* did."[91] However, the American reviews were very satisfying. Joseph Henry Jackson, reviewer for the *San Francisco Chronicle* and, according to Dudley Cloud, one of the best reviewers around, set the tone by considering *Who Has Seen the Wind* a book with a "serious purpose," concerned with a young boy's "wonder[ing] about his own wondering." Unlike Weeks, he recognized that the uncertainty of the ending was deliberate and necessary: "Brian has not answered any of his questions, of course."[92] The common note of praise from the American reviewers was that Mitchell showed "unmistakable talent for beautiful, evocative prose."[93] Lloyd Wendt of the *Chicago Sunday Tribune* believed that "Brian O'Connal is destined to join the boy immortals of American literature" and placed Mitchell in the company of Mark Twain, Booth Tarkington, and Marjorie Rawlings.[94]

Almost all reviews in the Canadian press were enthusiastic. Two declined to review the book, finding distasteful the goddamns and the references to R.W. God. Samuel Roddan, who reviewed the book for *Canadian Forum*, criticized Brian as "a ridiculous little chap with an unhealthy interest in God," and added that he thought that Mitchell would "do some good work when he has exhausted his nostalgic interest in the delicious little world of the child."[95] Interestingly, when Earle Birney, who had met Mitchell in Vancouver during the authors' convention, wrote to congratulate Mitchell on his book, he remarked on this review: "I liked [*Who Has Seen the Wind*] for many things that the patronizing Samuel Roddan didn't note. . . . Most of all I liked the lyrical impulse that steadily recurs – it is what gives the book its unity for me."[96] Ethel Wilson, whose novel *Hetty Dorval* had just been published by Macmillan, was full of praise for *Who Has Seen the Wind*. She wrote to Ellen Elliott that his novel was "so well sustained, well-balanced, and of very great beauty" and noted, accurately, that "there's a lot of work and care in that book, and the simplicity that (I feel) can only be attained by the expenditure of time." She modestly expressed a wish that if there were to be an award or a prize this year that "Mr. Mitchell gets it."[97]

There were many favourable reviews by Canadian newspaper critics, but the most glowing review and the one which greatly pleased Bill and Merna was that by William Arthur Deacon in the *Globe and Mail*, who wrote that *Who Has Seen the Wind* is "one of the finest Canadian novels ever written," a work of "complete naturalism of presentation coupled with the insight of an uninhibited imagination."[98] Deacon praised *Who Has Seen the Wind* over Gabrielle Roy's *The Tin Flute*, which had come out at the same time (and which won the Governor General's Award that year). Bill wrote to Deacon saying that he felt that Deacon had come closer than any critic to understanding what he was trying to do in the novel, and what pleased him most was that Deacon had chosen to quote two passages that he had "to fight for with *Little-Brown* editors" and of which he was "very fond."[99] In his review, Deacon predicted that *Who Has Seen the Wind* would "be popular in the extreme and also win critical acclaim."

Certainly public acclaim by newspaper reviewers quickly came his way, but academic notice did not begin until the 1960s. Interest in the book was lively (with requests for translations and movie rights), but sales, both in the States and in Canada, did not match the expectations Bill had excitedly itemized in his 8 March 1946 letter to his mother. There was no movie-rights sale, and Weeks reported that, in the States, the overall book sales just covered the production costs. By mid-March Macmillan indicated that sales were approaching two thousand, but after that initial popularity sales slowed down, and in November only 3,293 copies had sold in Canada. John Gray, publisher at Macmillan, expressed discouragement at the slowdown in sales and urged Bill to accept a deal to export five hundred copies to the U.K. at only twenty-five cents because Macmillan had a lot of stock on hand. In the end they exported one thousand. A year later, Dudley Cloud reported that Mitchell had a debit account with them, that his book had not earned back the advance (overall it sold 4,051 in the States).

There was no further printing until 1960, when a new edition, as well as a school edition, were prepared, both using the American Little, Brown version. From then on the novel became a steady seller and a standard text in the classroom. Sales to date have reached three-quarters of a million copies. As Deacon had said in his letter to Mitchell: "*Who Has Seen the Wind* will sell in Canada, slower at the start than *Two Solitudes* but a darn sight longer. This will just go on and on, like *Sunshine Sketches of a Little Town.*"[100]

~ STRIKING ROOTS ~

During these first few years in High River, Mitchell began, like a chameleon, to change his colours from Saskatchewan prairie to Alberta foothills. *Who Has Seen the Wind* had been written over a six-year period and had been influenced by a number of different locations: "The town of this story has been called Weyburn, where I was born; Castor, New Dayton and High River, Alberta, where I have lived. It is none and part of all of these."[101] There was little of High River in *Who Has Seen the Wind*, but Bill's statement reflected how much a part of his life it had become. He was already at work on his next book, which would take place in High River and on the Eden Valley Indian Reserve in the foothills and mountain country of the Kananaskis.

Bill and Merna had settled into High River life. Although busy with a four- and a one-year-old, Merna still had time for bridge, the book club, and she was now singing in the United Church choir. Bill had developed a passion for fly fishing, and his letters to Dudley Cloud at *Atlantic Monthly* always contained a reference to tying flies or trout fishing. In June 1947 he reported that he had just returned from a trip "with a catch of nine brown trout, one of them four pounds"[102] although, reluctantly, he had had to use worms because of the high muddy water. He had been too busy with his schoolteaching to work on the new novel, but had sent a short story to *Atlantic* in April after they urged him to write something for their spring publication. The story, called "Catharsis," concerns an Indian father's grief over the death of his son. "It's a violent one, but by God it's true," Bill wrote to Cloud.[103] The readers' reports, however, were not favourable; they found it too unrelieved in its details about death and, in July, it was rejected.

Late in August, when he was out again on the Highwood, innocently fishing, a black Angus bull chased him, and he only escaped by jumping into the river, an episode that made news in the *High River Times*. By this time, though, Bill was being chased by more than bulls – he was financially struggling again to make ends meet and in September he wrote to Atlantic to ask for an advance against his new book. Stanley Salmen, who had taken over Dudley Cloud's office, responded with an offer of three hundred dollars, and asked Mitchell to send a plot outline and a tentative title for the new work. Two months later he wrote asking why Mitchell had not replied. Hurt by the low offer, Bill had decided to ignore Atlantic. In December he desperately appealed to Macmillan for money:

> Because of about five weeks off for that coast deal [the conventions], and because of my working on the next novel July, August, and September, and because I thought there would eventually be royalties from WHO HAS SEEN, which there weren't, – the wolf – not the kiyoot – wolf – has come in from the Porcupine Hills, past yon peak we call locally – Senator's Snoot – to howl and to whelp on the Mitchell doorstep. This is not good for a little girl reared in a Baptist Parsonage and unused to the howls of wolves.[104]

He said he had two-thirds of a rough draft done on his new novel: "my blue life blood is on every page." More optimistically he related that he had three stories, one novella, and one article out on the magazine circuit[105] and that these "forty thousand words" should give him "a four month breathing spell, in addition to relieving [his] banker's blood pressure." In January, Macmillan came through with a five-hundred-dollar advance.

In May 1948, Mitchell was awarded the IODE prize of five hundred dollars for *Who Has Seen the Wind*. The presentation was to be made at the annual dinner of the Canadian Authors Association in Ottawa on June 12. Others receiving awards were Gabrielle Roy, winner of the Governor General's Award for *The Tin Flute*; Dorothy Livesay, the winner of the Governor General's Award for *Poems for People*; and Paul Hiebert, winner of the Stephen Leacock medal for humour for *Sarah Binks*.

Bill, Merna, and Bill's mother left by train for Ottawa on Sunday, June 6. Bill had more than the award on his mind as he travelled east by train. He had just been offered the position of fiction editor at *Maclean's*. Once again he was presented with the dilemma – freelancing or a secure job. If he accepted the job he would have to leave the home he had just built in High River. Was the salary "high enough to lure him away from the quiet haunts of rural foothill Alberta," asked Mrs. McCorquodale in her Leacockian announcement of the offer in the *High River Times*:

> The salary offered to him ran into such heavy figures that he could not toss it off without a good deal of consideration. . . .
>
> In his opinion, it is no easy choice to make. . . . Counting up what he sacrifices by going east, he thinks of the joys of fishing from a mountain stream that flows almost past his door. He counts as assets an entrancing curve of woods . . . and the space all round him. He thinks it worth a lot of heavy sugar to have the fun of planting seeds in the ground and watch them pop up into flowers and garden stuff. . . . He thinks there is no end of satisfaction in having a house of one's own. . . . He likes the freedom of choice and action that may not bloom so freely for him in Toronto. Bill and Merna have their home – their own first real home – in High River and they've already struck roots.

So the last we saw of Bill heading east, he was low in his mind. He planned to settle down on the train and translate all the intangible joys of living here into terms of money, and then balance them against that sparkling salary offered him by Macleans.[106]

Bill had only a few short weeks in which to make up his mind. He was not sure whether he wanted to, or whether it was wise to, trade in "the green element" of the little foothills town for the bright lights of the big city.

ACKNOWLEDGEMENTS

W.O. and Merna first suggested this biography project to us in the late 1970s and generously gave us their support and time until their deaths in 1998. Our taped interviews with them spanned fourteen years – from 1981 to 1995. Between 1992 and 1996 they read over the first drafts of eight chapters and corrected factual errors. Always, they were helpful without interfering in our role as interpretive biographers.

We began interviewing relatives, friends, and professional associates in 1984. Their willingness to share experiences, anecdotes, and personal impressions has been invaluable to our project. We would especially like to thank W.O's brothers and sisters-in-law, Jack and Betty, Molly, and Dick and Mary Mitchell. Interviews with the following people played an important role in the construction of the narrative for volume one: Jack Andrews, Robert Blackburn, Harriette (Smith) Blackmar, Wilbur Bowker, Bill Cameron, Jessie Campbell, Emma Lee (Burke) Chilton, Grace Clark, Pearl Coppock, Kathleen Davies, Jack and Eileen Denny, Jim Duncan, Isabel Eaglesham, Blair Ferguson, Gary and Deb Frederickson, Jim Frederickson, Madeline (Austin) Freeman, Marg and Cec Hewson, Judy (Moss) Kennedy, Chet and Lois Lambertson, Peter Lehmann,

Helen and Earl Lewis, Betty (McNally) Love, William "Hodder" McConachie, Eleanor McKinnon, Margaret (Beattie) Pickersgill, Mrs. F.M. Salter, Bill Spencer, Doris Thompson, and Eddie Wong.

Because of the significance to W.O. of his family heritage, one of our first projects was to verify details of his lineage. We received considerable help in this endeavour from family, near and far. On the paternal side we wish to thank: W.O.'s first cousin James Mitchell, son of John Mitchell; his first cousin Anna Edgar, daughter of Alex Mitchell; the Willie Mitchell family in Ireland; W.O.'s second cousins Monty Adolphe and Beth Shupe, grandchildren of J.T. Mitchell in Weyburn. On the maternal side we wish to thank: Ina (Biggart) Young and Robbie Biggart in Dunlop, Scotland; his first cousin Jean (McSherry) Armstrong, daughter of his Aunt Josie. We are most grateful for the help we received from genealogical societies and from public-records offices: Nancy Kale, Mary McLeod, and Margaret McLean (of the Huron County Branch of the Ontario Genealogical Society); Beryl Simpson, Kathleen McLeod, and Marian Hertz (of the Hamilton Branch, Genealogical Society); the staff of the Register Office of Scotland in Edinburgh; the Public Records Office in Belfast, Northern Ireland. Further genealogical assistance and family-background information came from Ron Abel, Laura M. Begg, Bob Campbell, Ruth Dwyer, Sheila Hirtle, Frances Itani, and Ethel Poth.

The main research collection of W.O. Mitchell *fonds* is at the University of Calgary, and we appreciated the assistance given to us by the staff at Special Collections. We are especially indebted to Apollonia Steele, Special Collections librarian, and Marlys Chevrefils, archival assistant, who always showed great interest and enthusiasm in our project and who efficiently and patiently dealt with our requests over many years. Thanks, too, to Jean Tener, who was head of Special Collections at the beginning stages of our research at the University of Calgary. We are grateful, as well, for the help offered by archival services at other university libraries: the University of Alberta Archives; the University of Saskatchewan Archives; the University of Manitoba Archives and Special Collections, especially Dr. Richard E. Bennett, John E.L. Richthammer, and Dr. Gaby Divay; and the Thomas Fisher Rare Book Library, University of Toronto. Thanks to Bruce Whiteman, Dr. Carl Spadoni, and Renu Barrett for their assistance with our research in the Macmillan Archive at the William Ready Division of Archives and Research, Mills Memorial Library, McMaster University. Other archives and records offices to whom we owe thanks are the New York Hospital Archives, St. Petersburg High School Archives, Haig Public School in Weyburn, the former Weyburn Mental Institute, and the Winnipeg Winter Club. Debra Dauk (Calgary Police Service Archives) and Liana Wadsworth (RCMP Archives) kindly conducted some searches for us.

We researched historical background and notices of the Mitchells in numerous newspapers, many of which were made available through inter-library loan at Trent University, and we thank the staff for their assistance. We are grateful as well for the help and facilities made available for our newspaper research at the City of Calgary Public Library and at the Glenbow Museum and Archives in Calgary. Thanks to Pat Molesky, the reference archivist at the Glenbow, for supplying background information on Calgary and High River and for providing photographs of High River. Staff at the Soo Line Historical Museum in Weyburn and the Museum of the Highwood were helpful with information, newspapers, and photographs. Various newspaper offices offered us the opportunity to look through their bound copies of newspapers: the *Castor Advance*, *Weyburn Review*, and *High River Times*.

Macmillan of Canada granted us permission to quote from correspondence in the Macmillan Archive regarding Mitchell's publications, and for permission to quote from the work he published with Macmillan: *Who Has Seen the Wind*, *Jake and the Kid*, *The Kite*, *The Vanishing Point*, and *Since Daisy Creek*. We would like to thank Kim Herter, assistant editor, at Macmillan for her help. Permissions for other materials were gratefully received from the following: Edward Weeks, former editor of the Atlantic Monthly Press, to quote from the correspondence between the press, W.O.

Mitchell, and F.M. Salter; Mrs. F.M. Salter, to quote from correspondence between F.M. Salter and W.O. Mitchell; Michael Benedict, editorial director of *Maclean's*, to quote from correspondence between *Maclean's* and W.O. Mitchell; Madame Justice Low, to quote from Earle Birney's letter to W.O. Mitchell.

We would like to thank Elizabeth Salter for providing a photograph of her father, and to thank Joe and Peter Clark for permission to use as our cover image the photograph of W.O. taken in 1946 by their father, Charles Clark. Thanks also to Courtney Milne, who kindly allowed us to use his photograph of O.S. Mitchell's gravesite plaque.

We are grateful to the Social Sciences and Humanities Research Council of Canada for a two-year research grant (1984-1986), which made possible Barbara's part-time research, and helped with travel and tape-transcription costs. We would also like to thank Trent University and the Department of English Literature, which provided assistance over a number of years through sabbatical leaves, unpaid leaves, and personally funded research grants. Joanne Heath-Menger transcribed many of the taped interviews with W.O. and Merna Mitchell, and we appreciate her thorough job of untangling the oral narrative.

We thank the McClelland & Stewart team which saw our manuscript through to its final book form: Avie Bennett, chairman and president, and Douglas Gibson, publisher, for their encouragement; Jonathan Webb, senior editor, who edited our manuscript with thoughtful and thorough scrutiny and always respected our position; Peter Buck, production editor, who copy-edited the manuscript with meticulous care; and Ingrid Paulson who designed the book and its cover.

We are grateful to our friends, especially Michael and Florence Treadwell, Fred and Annette Tromly, and Frances Itani, who listened patiently, who prompted us with incisive questions and who always responded with interest. We thank our family, too, who, without a doubt, heard more than they cared to hear, but who never flagged in their support and enthusiasm.

NOTES

Frequently Used Names:

WOM   William Ormond Mitchell
MLM   Merna Lynne Mitchell
 FMS   Frederick Millet Salter, University of Alberta
  EW   Edward Weeks, editor, Atlantic Monthly Press
  DC   Dudley Cloud, managing editor, Atlantic Monthly Press

Unpublished Material:

The largest holding of unpublished material is at Special Collections, the University of Calgary Library. The W.O. Mitchell *fonds* are numbered MsC 19. An accession amounting to forty-nine boxes was made in 1976 as noted in the catalogue, *The W.O. Mitchell Papers* (1986). A second accession was begun in 1998, and is in the process of being catalogued. Included in this collection are manuscripts for published and unpublished work, personal letters, scrapbooks (assembled by Mitchell's mother, Mrs. O.S. Mitchell), photographs, and business correspondence.

The William Ready Division of Archives and Research Collections, Mills Memorial Library, McMaster University in Hamilton, holds correspondence between W.O. Mitchell and the Macmillan Company of Canada.

Atlantic Monthly Press in Boston, Massachusetts, holds W.O. Mitchell's and Edward Millet Salter's correspondence with Edward Weeks, Dudley Cloud, and Jeannette Cloud concerning *Who Has Seen the Wind*, some short stories, and "The Alien."

The Family holds material such as W.O. Mitchell Ltd. business correspondence and papers, a few unpublished manuscripts, and personal letters.

The biographers hold approximately sixty hours of taped interviews with W.O. Mitchell and Merna Mitchell. Most often they were interviewed together but we deliberately conducted separate interviews on occasion. The interviews were taped between 1981 and 1995, and these tapes were transcribed or summarized. We also kept private diaries containing information from informal telephone conversations with or about W.O. Mitchell and from our numerous visits with him.

Eighty hours of interviews with relatives, friends, business acquaintances, and students of W.O. Mitchell were taped and transcribed or summarized. In one or two instances interviewees preferred untaped interviews, in which case notes were made. Occasionally we obtained information by letter.

The following abbreviations are used in the Notes:

Atlantic Atlantic Monthly Press, Boston.

Family Manuscripts, letters, papers held by the Mitchell family.

McMaster Macmillan Papers, William Ready Division of Archives and Research Collections, Mills Memorial Library, McMaster University, Hamilton, Ontario.

NFB *W.O. Mitchell: Novelist in Hiding*. Dir. Robert Duncan, National Film Board of Canada, 1980. Video recording, transcripts, and rushes are held at UCalgary. We quote from the unpublished transcripts of the film and the rushes.

PD Personal Diaries includes diaries and informal notes written by the biographers following informal conversations with the subject.

PI Personal Interviews conducted by telephone or without the use of the tape recorder.

PL   Personal Letters to and from the biographers.

PTI   Personal Taped Interviews conducted by the biographers. Unless otherwise noted the interview is with W.O. Mitchell.

UCalgary   W.O. Mitchell *fonds*, Special Collections, University Library, University of Calgary, Calgary, Alberta.

W.O. Mitchell's Major Works (published and unpublished), where quoted, are referred to within the text by the following abbreviations:

A   "The Alien." Ms. (complete) in biographers' files. Unless otherwise indicated, references are to this ms. Other sources: *The Alien* (condensed version of Part III): *Maclean's*, 15 Sept. 1953 to 15 Jan. 1954 (nine instalments semi-monthly). Ms. (incomplete) at UCalgary.

AJK   *According to Jake and the Kid*. Toronto: McClelland & Stewart, 1989.

Art   *For Art's Sake*. Toronto: McClelland & Stewart, 1992.

BBW   *The Black Bonspiel of Willie MacCrimmon*. Toronto: McClelland & Stewart, 1993.

DWO   *Dramatic W.O. Mitchell*. Toronto: Macmillan, 1982.

Eve   *An Evening With W.O. Mitchell*. Toronto: McClelland & Stewart, 1997.

JK   *Jake and the Kid*. Toronto: Macmillan, 1961.

K   *The Kite*. Toronto: Macmillan, 1962.

LL   *Ladybug, Ladybug. . . .* Toronto: McClelland & Stewart, 1988.

RD   *Roses Are Difficult Here*. Toronto: McClelland & Stewart, 1990.

SD   *Since Daisy Creek*. Toronto: Macmillan, 1984.

SH   *How I Spent My Summer Holidays*. Toronto: Macmillan, 1981.

VP   *The Vanishing Point*. Toronto: Macmillan, 1973.

WW   *Who Has Seen the Wind.* Toronto: Macmillan, 1947. Unless otherwise
      indicated this is the edition to which we will refer. In 1947 the novel
      was also published by Little, Brown in an edition that was about
      seven thousand words shorter than the Canadian one. This version
      was used for subsequent editions, including paperback editions.
      In 1991 McClelland & Stewart published an edition illustrated
      by William Kurelek which used the longer text version, and in
      1997 Macmillan published a fiftieth anniversary edition using the
      longer text.

Preface

1. This figure is only an estimate. It is difficult to obtain *all* records prior to
   1980, and some of our records stop at 1997. Statistics have been gathered
   from the following: Sheila Latham ("The Production of W.O. Mitchell's
   Texts: A Bibliographical Study," Diss. Univ. of Leeds, 1997); Rosemary
   Evans at CPC; and Family files.
2. David O'Rourke, "An Interview with W.O. Mitchell," *Essays on
   Canadian Writing*, 20 (Winter 1980-81): 152.
3. Mark Twain, *The Autobiography of Mark Twain*, ed. Charles Neider (New
   York: Harper & Row, 1959) 33.
4. NFB, 64.
5. William Wordsworth, "My Heart Leaps Up," *The Norton Anthology of
   English Literature*, ed. M.H. Abrams (New York: W.W. Norton &
   Company, 1996) 1382.
6. PTI, 18 Apr. 1987.

Chapter 1 (Pages 1-13)

1. PTI, 22 Dec. 1983.
2. NFB, A-15.
3. NFB, roll 3, 1.
4. PTI, 22 Dec. 1983.
5. "BU Convocation: Prairies Have New Look, Graduates Told," *Brandon
   Sun* report of Mitchell's convocation address, 9 Nov. 1974, UCalgary,
   MsC 19.48.4.
6. Wallace Stegner, *Wolf Willow* (New York: Viking, 1966) 8.
7. Stegner, 21.
8. WOM, "Prairies: Poetry of Earth and Sky," *Century, 1867-1967* (*Edmonton
   Journal* and *Calgary Herald*) 13 Feb. 1967: 22.
9. PTI, Dec. 1981.
10. "Prairies: Poetry of Earth and Sky," 22.

11. WOM, "Beginnings: W.O. Mitchell," *Calgary Herald, Today*, 20 Dec. 1980: 3.
12. WOM, "Writers on the Prairie," CBC radio series, broadcast 9 Feb. 1955, ms. notes, UCalgary.
13. NFB, A-15.
14. Couchaching Conference address, ms., 6, Family.
15. "Beginnings: W.O. Mitchell," 3.
16. WOM, "Bridge Over Loneliness," *Western Living*, Oct. 1990. See also earlier version of this argument: Couchaching Conference, ms., 6-7, and NFB.
17. NFB, 64.
18. *WW* (Boston: Little, Brown, 1947) 252. This epitaph is not in the Macmillan 1947 edition.
19. WOM, "Biographical Information," Apr. 1946, Atlantic.
20. NFB, roll 1, 2.
21. NFB, 64.
22. PD, Dec. 1997.

Chapter 2 (Pages 14-33)

1. PTI, 1 Feb. 1986; PL, James Mitchell, 22 Jan. 1986; Mrs. W.A. Mitchell, Ireland, 22 Aug. 1986. In 1997 we searched the Public Records Office of Northern Ireland, the parish records, and visited the family estate, but discovered little concrete evidence. W.A. Maguire, *The Downshire Estates in Ireland 1801-1845* (Oxford: Clarendon Press, 1972) traces the history of three marquises from 1789 to 1845, but there is no mention of a Mitchell, who would have been only a small freeholder.
2. PL, James Mitchell, 22 Jan. 1986. James recalls a family story about John's first days off the *Cultivator*, how he found walking the streets of New York a very strange experience, for his legs continued to compensate for the pitching deck of the ship. PTI, James Mitchell, 27 Jun. 1986.
3. PTI, 1 Feb. 1986. According to WOM, one brother went to the California goldfields, and the other eventually to Australia.
4. PL, James Mitchell, 22 Jan. 1986.
5. PTI, James Mitchell, 27 June 1986.
6. Scrapbook of O.S. Mitchell, UCalgary, MsC 19.1.1.
7. William, 1859; James, 1860; Anna, 1862; Samuel, 1865; Reubena, 1866; John, 1869; Alexander, 1871; Ormond, 1874; Margaret, 1877; Elizabeth, 1879.
8. PTI, Jack Mitchell, 24 Aug. 1984.
9. PL, James Mitchell, 22 Jan. 1986. Includes photocopy of auction advertisement.
10. *Hamilton Spectator*, 12 Sept. 1904.

11. Scrapbook of O.S. Mitchell.
12. The *Hamilton Spectator* printed a notice in 1873 that Bret Harte's reading in Hamilton was cancelled due to a booking conflict.
13. *Hamilton Spectator*, 10 Apr. 1873.
14. Scrapbook of O.S. Mitchell.
15. PTI, 1 Feb. 1986.
16. Scrapbook of O.S. Mitchell.
17. Scrapbook of O.S. Mitchell. Mark Twain often included a version of "Riding a Bronco: Tenderfoot Tells of the Ups and Downs of His Only Attempt" in his repertoire. O.S.'s copy was reprinted from the *Arizona Graphic*. See *Mark Twain Tonight! An Actor's Portrait*, selected, edited, and adapted by Hal Holbrook (New York: Ives Washburn, 1959) 137-38.
18. Laura (Markle) Begg to WOM, Apr. 1977, Family.
19. PTI, Dec. 1981. "Mr. Dooley says . . ." was a continuing series in one of the Boston papers. WOM said, "Mr. Dooley was a folksy Irish philosopher who made political and social observations about the hypocrisies and peccadilloes of the establishment."
20. PTI, 2 Jan. 1986; 14 Oct. 1985.
21. NFB, 44. Just prior to this discussion of the shamrock WOM describes his orchids as "immortal": "These are new growths so it keeps growing across the bark. It dies off at the back. . . . So they are immortal, they will just go on forever and ever. Dying at the back, blooming at the front, blooming each year."
22. PTI, 2 Jan. 1986.
23. O'Rourke, 155.
24. *Huron Expositor*, 1 Jan. 1886.
25. PTI, 2 Jan. 1986.
26. PTI, 14 Oct. 1985.
27. PTI, 14 Oct. 1985.
28. Daddy Johnson first appeared in the CBC "Jake and the Kid" radio series and was later reincarnated as Daddy Sherry in *K*.
29. History Book Committee, *As Far as the Eye Can See* (Weyburn: Focus Publishing, 1986) 64.
30. Isabel Eaglesham, *The Night the Cat Froze in the Oven* (Weyburn: Weyburn Review Ltd., 1982) 21.
31. PTI, 2 Jan. 1986. See *WW* 215, where Brian's grandmother recalls sitting in the buckboard with John and counting the revolutions of the bandana. In *Memories of Early Weyburn* (Weyburn: Weyburn Review Ltd., 1994) 3, R.M. Mitchell implies that John and William arrived by train, as did many of the settlers.
32. R.M. Mitchell, 16, 21.
33. Letter from Margaret McMurray to daughter (Maggie), 4 Jun. 1906, UCalgary, MsC 19.1.3. John's death certificate says that he was in farming

from 1900 to 1912, so perhaps he still owned land which he farmed or managed.

34. Letters from Margaret McMurray to Mr. Ludlam, superintendent of the School of Nursing, New York Hospital, 18 Oct. 1899 and 27 Mar. 1900, New York Hospital Archives.

35. Maggie McMurray's autograph book, 1888-94, UCalgary, MsC 19.1.2.

36. *Bayfield Bugle: Souvenir Edition,* 24 Jun. 1976: 2A, 31B.

37. Margaret McMurray to Mr. Ludlam, 27 Mar. 1900, New York Hospital Archives.

38. She describes herself in a letter of application to the New York Hospital as 5'7½" and 120 pounds. 18 Oct. 1899, New York Hospital Archives.

39. PTI, 2 Jan. 1986.

40. Margaret McMurray, letter of application, 18 Oct. 1899, New York Hospital Archives.

41. Clinton newspaper article, Red family scrapbook, UCalgary, Second Accession.

42. PTI, 2 Jan. 1986.

43. Nurse's Record, New York Hospital Archives.

44. Alumnae form, 18 Feb. 1947, New York Hospital Archives.

45. Letter from Lucia Minturn to Margaret, UCalgary, MsC 19.1.3. The Minturns were one of the greatest ship owners in America and were also recognized for philanthropic work with immigrants and the poor.

46. PTI, 2 Jan. 1986.

47. PTI, 2 Jan. 1986. Jack Mitchell and Dick Mitchell also remember the miniature cotton bale and their mother's story about Twain. See also Justin Kaplan, *Mr. Clemens and Mark Twain* (New York: Simon and Schuster, 1966) 372. Livy was taken to Florence, Italy, in 1903, where she died 5 June 1904. So, if Margaret nursed Livy it would have been before she qualified as an R.N. If she did outside nursing at that time, it is quite possible that she nursed Twain in 1903 when he was suffering from bronchitis and rheumatism or, indeed, during the winter of 1905 when he again suffered from bronchitis. Or, it may have been one of the two daughters whom she nursed. Jean suffered from epilepsy and spent the next five years after her mother's death in and out of sanatoriums, and Clara suffered a breakdown after her mother's death and was placed in a rest home on Sixty-ninth Street in New York.

Chapter 3 (Pages 34-59)

1. Eaglesham, 48.

2. Eaglesham, 62.

3. Scrapbook of O.S. Mitchell. PTI, 2 Jan. 1986.

4. *As Far As the Eye Can See*, 62. According to this item on J.T. Mitchell, he arrived in 1903 and settled on SE 29-7-14 in 1904.

5. Before going West, James Mitchell was known for his concrete work on many silos and barns in the Waterdown area, some of which still bear his initials.

6. PTI, 1 Feb. 1986.

7. Eaglesham, 23.

8. WOM often disputed Jack's remembrances, saying that, though Jack was seven years older, Jack often did not remember as accurately as he did, arguing that very early he had developed a sensitivity to detail that served him well as a writer. PTI, 1 Feb., 1986.

9. Margaret to parents, 27 Apr. 1906, UCalgary, MsC 19.1.3. This letter is written on a New York Hospital "Form 15" for patients' records.

10. Maggie McMurray and John McMurray to Margaret, 10/13 May 1906, UCalgary, MsC 19.1.3.

11. Margaret to parents, 27 Apr. 1906, UCalgary.

12. O.S. to Margaret, 31 May 1906, UCalgary, MsC 19.1.3.

13. Eaglesham, 71.

14. Stegner, 219.

15. PTI, 1 Feb. 1986.

16. PTI, 1 Feb. 1986.

17. PTI, 1 Feb. 1986.

18. PTI, 1 Feb. 1986.

19. PTI, Ruth Dwyer (one of the recent owners of the house), 27 Jun. 1986.

20. PD, 15 Dec. 1983.

21. PTI, Jack Mitchell, 25 Aug. 1984.

22. Eaglesham, 86-98.

23. "Mitchell's Drugstore Changed Ownership Nov. 1," *Weyburn Review*, 4 Nov. 1925: 1.

24. PTI, Jack Mitchell, 24 Aug. 1984.

25. Michael R. Marrus, *Mr Sam: The Life and Times of Samuel Bronfman* (Toronto: Viking, 1991) 68.

26. John Craig, *The Years of Agony: 1910/1920* (Toronto: Canada's Illustrated Heritage, Natural Science of Canada, 1977) 77, 113.

27. PTI, 1 Feb. 1986.

28. PTI, Jack Mitchell, 25 Aug. 1984. Marrus in *Mr Sam* says the "whisky sixes" were large cars in which the rear seats were removed and the motors were souped up (76).

29. PTI, 1 Feb. 1986; 17 Apr. 1987.

30. Eaglesham, 64.

31. NFB, 77. There are only a few extant Weyburn newspapers before 1922 so this cannot be verified.

32. Note to O.S. Mitchell, 10 Dec. 1900, UCalgary, MsC 19.1.1.

33. Gerald Friesen, *The Canadian Prairies* (Toronto: University of Toronto Press, 1984) 341.

34. PTI, Jack Mitchell, 24 Aug. 1984.

35. University of Alberta convocation address, ms., 15 Nov. 1975, UCalgary, MsC 19.19.14. Reworked into "Debts of Innocence," *Saturday Night* Mar. 1976, 36-37.

36. PTI, 1 Feb. 1986.

37. NFB, 76-78.

38. PTI, Monty Adolphe (WOM's second cousin), 15 Aug. 1996.

39. PTI, 1 Feb. 1986.

40. PTI, William "Hodder" McConachie, 15 Aug. 1996; PL, Eleanor McKinnon to WOM, 7 Jul. 1997 and to biographers, 7 Aug. 1997. Family.

41. PTI, 1 Feb. 1986.

42. John Portwood, "Voice of Experience," *Calgary Magazine* X (May 1988): 24.

43. PTI, 1 Feb. 1986.

44. PTI, 1 Feb. 1986.

45. PTI, 17 April 1987.

46. Billie to his parents, Dec. 1919, UCalgary, MsC, 19.1.1.

47. Portwood, 24; *WW* 240-42.

48. Dr. W.J. Mayo to Alex Mitchell, 7 Apr. 1921, UCalgary, MsC 19.1.1.

49. PTI, 1 Feb. 1986.

Chapter 4 (Pages 60-87)

1. The *Weyburn Review* (18 Oct. 1922) reported that "Mrs. M.L. Mitchell accepts a new mortgage for $12,157.50" for the arena.

2. PTI, Jack Andrews, 27 Aug. 1984.

3. PTI, 26 Dec. 1983.

4. NFB, roll 1, 2.

5. *Weyburn Review*, 5 Apr. 1922: 2.

6. *Weyburn Review*, 21 Jun. 1922: 8.

7. PTI, 26 Dec. 1983.

8. PTI, 17 Apr. 1987.

9. PTI, 17 Apr. 1987.

10. PTI, 13 Oct. 1986.

11. PTI, Dec. 1981.

12. PTI, 24 Jun. 1984.

13. PTI, 1 Feb. 1986.

14. PTI, Jack Mitchell, 26 Aug. 1984.

15. PTI, Dick Mitchell, 25 Aug. 1984. "He was a tough kid to handle, nothing bad, just disobedient, and maybe it was a little much for Mother with four boys."
16. PTI, 1 Feb. 1986.
17. PTI, 13 Oct. 1986.
18. PTI, 1 Feb. 1986.
19. NFB, 76.
20. PTI, 13 Oct. 1986.
21. PTI, 13 Oct. 1986.
22. PTI, 1 Feb. 1986.
23. PTI, 13 Oct. 1986.
24. PTI, 13 Oct. 1986; 17 Apr. 1987.
25. PTI, 13 Oct. 1986. Lon Chaney was not, in fact, in this movie.
26. PTI, 13 Oct. 1986.
27. PTI, 17 Apr. 1987.
28. PTI, Dec. 1981.
29. PTI, Dec. 1981.
30. PTI, Dec. 1981.
31. PTI, 26 Dec. 1983; Dick Mitchell, 25 Aug. 1984.
32. PTI, 13 Oct. 1986.
33. PTI, Dec. 1981.
34. PTI, Dec. 1981.
35. PTI, Dec. 1981.
36. PTI, 13 Oct. 1986.
37. NFB, A-20-21.
38. PTI, Dec. 1981.
39. PTI, 1 Feb. 1986.
40. PTI, 1 Feb. 1986.
41. PTI, 1 Feb. 1986.
42. PTI, 1 Feb. 1986.
43. PTI, Bill Cameron, 15 Jun. 1984.
44. WOM, "Debts of Innocence," *Saturday Night* Mar. 1976: 37.
45. PTI, 1 Feb. 1986.
46. PTI, 18 Apr. 1987.
47. NFB, 1.
48. PTI, 18 Dec. 1984; 18 Apr. 1987.
49. PTI, Dick Mitchell, 25 Aug. 1984.
50. PTI, 1 Feb. 1986.
51. PTI, Dec. 1981.
52. PTI, 14 Oct. 1985.
53. PTI, 1 Feb. 1986.
54. PTI, Dec. 1981.
55. See also NFB, 48.

56. The certificate is now in UCalgary.
57. NFB, 48-49.

Chapter 5 (Pages 88-112)

1. PTI, 1 Feb. 1986.
2. "The Ten Thousand Dollar Contest," draft ms., UCalgary, MsC 19.35.17.
3. PTI, 1 Feb. 1986.
4. PTI, 1 Feb. 1986.
5. PTI, 19 Feb. 1985.
6. PTI, 1 Feb. 1986. When WOM returned to Weyburn in 1939 for a visit he had a conversation with one of the town's businessmen which was "an eyeopener" for him. Not only did this man tell him stories about the Prohibition years, including details about WOM's father selling liquor through his drugstore business, but he told him stories about bootlegging, prostitution, and blackmail in Weyburn.
7. PTI, 18 Dec. 1984; see also *SH* 38.
8. PTI, Jack Andrews, 27 Aug. 1984.
9. *Weyburn Review*, 22 Mar. 1922.
10. *Weyburn Review*, 26 Apr. 1922: 5.
11. *Weyburn Review*, 6 Mar. 1920, Soo Line Historical Museum Newspaper archives.
12. WOM first used this childhood experience as the basis for one of the *Jake and the Kid* CBC radio episodes, "Earn Money at Home" (1952). The memoir version was published in *Maclean's* (1964) and later worked into *VP* (1973).
13. PTI, 1 Feb. 1986.
14. PTI, 18 Dec. 1984.
15. *Weyburn Review*, 23 Apr. 1924.
16. PTI, 13 Oct. 1986.
17. *Weyburn Review*, 13 Sept. 1922.
18. PTI, 17 Apr. 1987.
19. PTI, William "Hodder" McConachie, 15 Aug. 1996.
20. PTI, 13 Oct. 1986.
21. *Under the Dome: The Life and Times of Saskatchewan Hospital, Weyburn*, ed. Anne Robillard (Weyburn: Souris Valley History Book Committee, 1986) 3, 5, 7, 29. Opened in December 1921, it had a capacity of 1,800. By 1930, when a new wing was added it was "the largest building in Saskatchewan at that time."
22. *Weyburn Review*, 4 Oct. 1922: 2.
23. PTI, 13 Oct. 1986.
24. *Weyburn Review*, 15 Apr. 1925: 10.
25. *Weyburn Review*, 8 Apr. 1925.

26. PTI, 13 Oct. 1986.

27. "Beginnings: W.O. Mitchell," 3.

28. *Weyburn Review,* 5 Jul. 1922: 4.

29. PL, Eleanor McKinnon to biographers, 10 Sept. 1997.

30. PTI, Dec. 1981.

31. PTI, 28 Dec. 1992.

32. PTI, 13 Oct. 1986; 24 Jun. 1984.

33. PTI, 24 Jun. 1984.

34. PTI, Dec. 1981.

35. PL, Eleanor McKinnon to biographers, 11 Aug. 1997.

36. PTI, Dec. 1981.

37. PTI, Dec. 1981.

38. PTI, Dec. 1981.

39. "Debts of Innocence," 36-37.

40. PTI, Dec. 1981.

41. "Beginnings: W.O. Mitchell," 3.

42. PTI, Jack Mitchell, 26 Aug. 1984.

43. PTI, 6 Jul. 1984.

44. PTI, 6 Jul. 1984.

45. PTI, 6 Jul. 1984.

46. PTI, Jim Frederickson, 13 Aug. 1996; William "Hodder" McConachie, 15 Aug. 1996; PL, Eleanor McKinnon to biographers, 7 Aug. 1997.

47. PTI, 17 Apr. 1987.

48. PTI, 26 Dec. 1983.

49. PTI, 24 Jun. 1984.

50. Mrs. O.S. Mitchell announced in the *Weyburn Review* (20 Apr. 1927: 2) that she and her son Billie would be in Winnipeg "where they will visit for some time."

51. WOM ascribes his wrist condition to Kenneth Lyons in *LL,* 62-66. Lyons recalls how humiliating it was to have his mother or even his brother button up his fly until he learned to do it with his left hand.

52. PTI, 26 Dec. 1983.

53. PTI, Dec. 1981.

54. PTI, 26 Dec. 1983.

55. PTI, 26 Dec. 1983.

Chapter 6 (Pages 113-48)

1. PTI, 26/28 Dec. 1983; PTI, Dec. 1981.

2. PTI, Molly Mitchell, 18 Jun. 1984.

3. PTI, 24 Jun. 1984.

4. PTI, 26/28 Dec. 1983; PTI, Dec. 1981.

5. PTI, Dec. 1981.

6. PTI, Dec. 1981.

7. PTI, Dec. 1981.

8. PTI, 26/28 Dec., 1983.

9. PTI, 26/28 Dec., 1983.

10. PTI, 26 Dec. 1983; Dec. 1981.

11. Stuart Oderman, *Roscoe "Fatty" Arbuckle: A Biography of the Silent Film Comedian, 1887-1933* (Jefferson: McFarlane & Co, 1994) ix.

12. PTI, Dec. 1981; PTI, 26/28 Dec., 1983.

13. PTI, 26/28 Dec., 1983. During September 1921, right after the incident, people would go to Arbuckle's house and "yell obscenities relating to how Virginia had died, the most frequent being that she had been raped with a Coke bottle" (Oderman, 174). Although Arbuckle was eventually acquitted in April 1922, he was still the subject of much controversy and notoriety in 1927 and 1928 when the Mitchells arrived.

14. PTI, 26 Dec., 1983; Dec. 1981.

15. PTI, Dec. 1981.

16. PTI, Dec. 1981.

17. PTI, 6 Jul. 1984.

18. PTI, 6 Jul. 1984.

19. Daniel Epstein, *Sister Aimee: The Life of Aimee Semple McPherson* (New York, Harcourt Brace Jovanovich, 1993).

20. PTI, 6 Jul. 1984.

21. "Social and Personal," *Weyburn Review*, 4 Jul. 1928: 4.

22. PTI, 26 Dec. 1983. WOM recalled that years later, in 1968 when he visited Carlyle Lake, he walked up to Pringle's Point and was shocked to see that it was not very high nor a straight drop and that "all I would have got was a hell of a lot of burrs and spear grass and nettle burns if I had thrown myself off it." See also *Eve* 124; *VP* 329.

23. PTI, 26/28 Dec. 1983.

24. PTI, 26/28 Dec. 1983.

25. PTI, 15 Feb. 1985.

26. PTI, 15 Feb. 1985.

27. "Canadian Tourist Visits Local Club," *St. Petersburg Times*, 5 Feb. 1930: section 2, 2. According to the 1999 *Canadian Encyclopedia*, World Edition ("Martin, William Melville"), Martin was a judge of the Saskatchewan Court of Appeal at this time, and was appointed Chief Justice in 1941.

28. PTI, 15 Feb. 1985.

29. PTI, 15 Feb. 1985.

30. PTI, 15 Feb. 1985.

31. PTI, 18-20 Feb. 1985.

32. PTI, 18-20 Feb. 1985; 13 Oct. 1986.
33. PTI, 15 Feb. 1985.
34. PTI, 18-20 Feb. 1985; 24 Jun. 1984.
35. Originally titled "Lincoln, My Mother and Mendelian Law." It was later used in *LL* 68-78 as part of Kenneth Lyons's childhood experiences.
36. *St. Petersburg Times*, 20 Mar. 1929.
37. "Good Citizens' Club to Seek Funds in Tag Drive Saturday," *St. Petersburg Times*, 21 Feb. 1930: 11.
38. PTI, 18-20 Feb. 1985.
39. "70 Boys Enjoy Trip Over Bay," *St. Petersburg Times*, 7 Oct. 1928: 12.
40. "Youthful Diver Will Help Club with Monday Program," *St Petersburg Times*, 11 Nov. 1928: section 2, 4. Paul McMillen Tippy, better known as Palm Tippy, had a reputation in St. Petersburg and all over the States. In October 1928 he returned to spend the winter with his parents in St. Petersburg after two years in Hollywood working for Fox films and doing a vaudeville tour. When only three years old the "little yellow-haired St. Petersburg lad" twice saved young swimmers in Big Bayou from drowning (*St. Petersburg Times*, 20 Oct. 1928: 1, 11, 12; 13 Nov. 1928).
41. PTI, 18-20 Feb. 1985.
42. PTI, 18-20 Feb. 1985.
43. "Canadians Meet Tuesday," *St. Petersburg Times*, 24 Mar. 1930: section 2, 3.
44. PTI, 18-20 Feb. 1985.
45. PTI, 15 Feb. 1985; 18-20 Feb. 1985.
46. PTI, 18-20 Feb. 1985.
47. PTI, Dec. 1981.
48. PTI, Dec. 1981.
49. *St. Petersburg Times*, 4 Nov. 1928: section 2, 1.
50. PTI, Jack Andrews, 27 Aug. 1984; PL, Eleanor McKinnon to biographers, 10 Sept. 1997.
51. PTI, Harriette (Smith) Blackmar, 21 Feb. 1985.
52. PL, Emma Lee (Burke) Chilton to biographers, 30 Aug. 1984.
53. *St. Petersburg Times*, 14 Oct. 1928: section 5, 3.
54. PTI, 18-20 Feb. 1985.
55. PTI, 15 Feb. 1985.
56. PTI, Dec. 1981.
57. NFB, 21.
58. NFB, 27; PTI, 18 Apr. 1987.
59. PTI, 18 Feb. 1985.
60. PTI, 20 Feb. 1985.
61. PTI, 19 Feb. 1985.
62. PTI, Dec. 1981.

63. PTI, Harriette (Smith) Blackmar, 21 Feb. 1985.
64. PTI, Dec. 1981.
65. PTI, Dec. 1981.
66. PTI, 26 Dec. 1985.
67. PTI, Harriette (Smith) Blackmar, 21 Feb. 1985.
68. PTI, Dec. 1981.
69. PTI, Harriette (Smith) Blackmar, 21 Feb. 1985.
70. PTI, Harriette (Smith) Blackmar, 21 Feb. 1985.
71. "Skidding," *No-So-We-Ea* (The Annual of St. Petersburg High School, 1931) 118.
72. "High School's 'Skidding' Proves Treat to Hundreds," *St. Petersburg Times*, 21 Mar. 1931: section 2, 4.
73. PTI, 18-20 Feb. 1985; Dec. 1981.
74. PTI, 15 Feb. 1985.
75. PTI, Harriette (Smith) Blackmar, 21 Feb. 1985.
76. *No-So-We-Ea*, 40, 141.
77. "Rogue's Gallery," *No-So-We-Ea*, 144.
78. PTI, Harriette (Smith) Blackmar, 21 Feb. 1985.
79. PL, Emma Lee (Burke) Chilton to biographers, 30 Aug. 1984. In his sophomore year at the school he achieved a high general average (over 90%) which put him in the Scholarship Club. He did not quite attain the required 90% average to make the Scholarship Club in his junior and senior years.
80. PTI, 15 Feb. 1985.
81. PTI, 18-20 Feb. 1985.
82. PTI, 18-20 Feb. 1985.
83. PTI, Bill Cameron, 15 Jun. 1984.
84. PTI, 24 Jun. 1984.
85. PTI, 24 Jun. 1984.
86. PTI, 24 Jun. 1984.
87. PTI, 24 Jun. 1984.
88. PTI, 6 Jul. 1984.
89. The records are contradictory. His marks are recorded as 52% in Canadian History and 37% in British History. However, it is also noted that the condition in Canadian History was unremoved, indicating that he failed that subject and not British History.

Chapter 7 (Pages 149-78)

1. PTI, Jim Duncan, 14 Jun. 1984; Peter Lehmann, 16 Jun. 1984.
2. PTI, 26 Dec. 1985.
3. PTI, Dec. 1981.

4. While WOM was being initiated, he probably read an item on hazing in the student newspaper, *The Manitoban*. According to the writer of "The Keyhole" column, hazing on the campus was now exclusively a fraternity practice. He warns about its serious consequences: "Let it be remembered that lives have been lost and life injuries endured. Hazing destroys individuality, embitters youth and causes such bodily discomfort and harm that its abuses are only too self-evident." 6 Oct. 1931: 4.

5. PTI, Jim Duncan, 14 Jun. 1984.

6. Tape recording (response to biographers' letter), Blair Ferguson, 30 Nov. 1984.

7. PTI, Peter Lehmann, 16 Jun. 1984.

8. PTI, Judy (Moss) Kennedy, 2 Feb. 1999.

9. PTI, Peter Lehmann, 16 Jun. 1984; Judy (Moss) Kennedy, 2 Feb. 1999.

10. PTI, 26 Dec. 1985.

11. PTI, 26 Dec. 1985.

12. PTI, Judy (Moss) Kennedy, 2 Feb. 1999.

13. *Winnipeg Free Press*, 24 Nov. 1931: 2.

14. PTI, 26 Apr. 1982.

15. PTI, 26 Dec. 1985.

16. PTI, 26 Dec. 1985. "Dan" is probably Dan Renix.

17. PTI, 26 Dec. 1985.

18. PTI, 26 Dec. 1985.

19. PTI, 26 Dec. 1985.

20. PTI, 26 Apr. 1982.

21. PTI, Wilbur Bowker, May 1984.

22. PTI, Peter Lehmann, 16 Jun. 1984.

23. PTI, 30 Jul. 1996; Stephen Franklin, *A Time of Heroes: 1940/1950* (Toronto: Canada's Illustrated Heritage, Natural Science of Canada Ltd., 1977) 102.

24. PTI, 26 Dec. 1985.

25. "All Westerners Are Snobs," *Maclean's*, 16 May 1964: 7.

26. PTI, Peter Lehmann, 16 Jun. 1984.

27. PTI, 24 Jun. 1984. See *SH* 36, where this is ascribed to Hugh's mother.

28. According to WOM the Mitchells were drinking unpasteurized milk from Uncle Jim's farm. Contamination must have been a common situation, for the veterinarian in the Weyburn area wrote an article (*Weyburn Review*, 8 Feb. 1922: 3) urging farmers to comply with sanitary conditions and have their cattle tested semi-annually.

29. PTI, Dec. 1981; 24 Jun. 1984.

30. PTI, 24 Jun. 1984.

31. Rupert Clendon Lodge (1886-1961) was a member of the Royal Society of Canada and a professor emeritus of the University of Manitoba. He

was the author of thirteen books, among them *Plato's Theory of Ethics* and *The Philosophy of Education.*

32. PTI, 30 Jul. 1996.

33. Prof. Rupert C. Lodge, "Science and Literature," *The Winnipeg Free Press*, 10 Oct. 1931: 11.

34. Hugh Cowan and Gabriel Kampf, "*Acta* Interviews W.O. Mitchell," *Acta Victoriana* (Apr. 1974): 21.

35. PL, WOM to biographers, 19 Apr. 1991.

36. PTI, 25 Aug. 1991.

37. WOM, "Panacea for Panhandlers," *'toba*, Nov. 1933: 22; *Art* 48.

38. "Panacea for Panhandlers," Nov. 1933: 21.

39. PTI, 30 Jul. 1996.

40. PTI, 30 Jul. 1996; *Art* 63-64.

41. PTI, 30 Jul. 1996.

42. "Panacea for Panhandlers," Nov. 1933: 22-23.

43. Tape recording, Blair Ferguson, 30 Nov. 1984.

44. "Panacea for Panhandlers," Mar. 1934: 20.

45. "Panacea for Panhandlers," Mar. 1934: 21.

46. "*Acta* Interviews W.O. Mitchell," 21.

47. "Panacea for Panhandlers," Feb. 1934: 24.

48. "Panacea for Panhandlers," Feb. 1934: 23.

49. PTI, 30 Jul. 1996.

50. PI, Margaret (Beattie) Pickersgill, 28 Mar. 1997.

51. PTI, 30 Jul. 1996.

52. Frank Pickersgill, *The Making of a Secret Agent: The Pickersgill Letters*, ed. George H. Ford (Toronto: McClelland and Stewart, 1978). Frank was born in 1915, the youngest of five children. Jack, ten years older than Frank, was a teacher of history at Wesley College when Frank and Bill were students. Frank became a war journalist, was captured in 1940, escaped and joined the secret service. He was captured again in 1943 and was executed at Buchenwald in September 1944. His older brother, Jack, went on to an illustrious career as a Liberal politician, serving as a cabinet minister under St. Laurent and Pearson.

53. *The Manitoban*, 6 Mar. 1934: 1; PTI, 30 Jul. 1996.

54. Pickersgill, 20.

55. *Brown and Gold* (The University of Manitoba Yearbook, 1934).

56. "Prosperity Turns Corner at Prom Held by Pi Phis," *Winnipeg Free Press*, 30 Sept. 1933: 4.

57. *Winnipeg Free Press*, 10 Oct. 1933: 1.

58. Rosie believed he caught syphilis from a chambermaid at a hotel on the lake where he and his parents spent the summers. See WOM, "The Day I Caught Syphilis," *Eve* 123-25.

59. PTI, 13 Oct. 1986.
60. PTI, 27 Dec. 1985.
61. PTI, 27 Dec. 1985.
62. "Arts Prefers Censorship as in Force Now," *The Manitoban*, 9 Mar. 1934: 1.
63. "Highlights of the Drama, Stage and Screen in Review," *Winnipeg Free Press*, 5 Sept. 1931: 19.
64. *Winnipeg Free Press*, 10 May 1932: 11.
65. Rosemary Cullen and Don B. Wilmeth, *Plays by William Hooker Gillette* (Cambridge: Cambridge University Press, 1983). *Secret Service* was written in 1895 by William Hooker Gillette, a well-known American playwright and actor whose plays were popular for their realism and their technical effects.
66. J. Shield Nicholson, *Principles of Political Economy* (London: A&C Black Ltd., 1925).

Chapter 8 (Pages 179-221)

1. *Winnipeg Free Press*, 7/18 May 1934.
2. *Winnipeg Free Press*, 1 Oct. 1932.
3. PTI, 13 Oct. 1986.
4. PTI, 14 Oct. 1985.
5. PTI, 17 Apr. 1987.
6. PTI, 25 Aug. 1991.
7. University of Washington transcript.
8. PTI, 6 Jul. 1984.
9. PTI, Dec. 1981.
10. PTI, 14 Oct. 1985.
11. PTI, 6 Jul. 1984.
12. PTI, 6 Jul. 1984. Proctor Melquist was in the short-story course with WOM. He later became head of Sunset Publications.
13. PTI, 13 Oct. 1986.
14. PTI, 6 Jul. 1984.
15. PTI, Dec. 1981; 6 Jul. 1984; 25 Aug. 1991.
16. PTI 6 Jul. 1984.
17. PTI, Dec. 1981.
18. PTI, 6 Jul. 1984.
19. PTI, 6 Jul. 1984.
20. PTI, 6 Jul. 1984.
21. James Gray, *The Winter Years* (Toronto: Macmillan, 1990) 86, 110-112.
22. PTI, 6 Jul. 1984.
23. PTI, 6 Jul. 1984.

24. PTI, 6 Jul. 1984.

25. PTI, 13 Oct. 1986.

26. PL, Bill Spencer to biographers, 27 May 1995.

27. PTI, 13 Oct. 1986.

28. PTI, 26 Apr. 1982.

29. PTI, Madeline (Austin) Freeman, 2 Feb. 1997.

30. PTI, 26 Apr. 1982.

31. PTI, 26 Apr. 1982; 6 Jul. 1984.

32. PTI, 6 Jul. 1984.

33. His Turner Valley Royalties struck a new well 16 June 1936, "hailed as the largest producing oil well in Canada." "T.V.R. Well Hits Huge Crude Oil," *Calgary Daily Herald*, 17 Jun. 1936: 1.

34. PTI, 13 Oct. 1986.

35. PTI, 13 Oct. 1986.

36. PTI, Wilbur Bowker, May 1984.

37. "Guild Opens New Season," *Calgary Daily Herald*, 18 Sept. 1936. It was performed on Sept. 17, 18, 19.

38. "Guild Excels Former Hits with 'Naples'" *Calgary Daily Herald*, 29 Oct. 1936. It was performed Oct. 28, 29, 30.

39. PTI, 26 Apr. 1982.

40. PTI, 26 Apr. 1982.

41. Pierre Berton, *The Great Depression 1929-1939* (Toronto: McClelland & Stewart, 1990) 152.

42. PTI, 26 Apr. 1982.

43. PTI, Dick Mitchell, 25 Aug. 1984.

44. "Guild Play Will Open Wednesday," *Calgary Daily Herald*, 15 Nov. 1937. It played November 18-20.

45. *The Well of Loneliness* by Radclyffe Hall was published in 1928 and caused quite a stir in England where it was prosecuted and, in spite of a public campaign which included support from George Bernard Shaw, H.G. Wells, Virginia Woolf, and E.M. Forster, it was pronounced obscene. See P.N. Furbank, *E.M. Forster: A Life* (New York: Harcourt Brace Jovanovich, 1977) vol. 2, 153-55.

46. PTI, 13 Oct. 1986.

47. Twenty-two years later, in 1959, Frank Holroyd was the set designer for *Royalty Is Royalty*, WOM's first major stage play.

48. "Two Plays May Represent Calgary When Provincial Tests Held in February," *Calgary Daily Herald*, 18 Dec. 1937. It played December 17 and 18.

49. "Packed Theatre Hears Praise and Criticism at Dramatic Festival," *Calgary Daily Herald*, 18 Feb. 1938.

50. PTI, 13 Oct. 1986; 24 Jun. 1984; 25 Aug. 1991.

51. PTI, 13 Oct. 1986.

52. PTI, 13 Oct. 1986.

53. WOM to Jeannette Cloud, biographical forms, Apr. 1946, Atlantic.

54. PTI, 26 Apr. 1982.

55. PTI, 1 Jun. 1985.

56. PTI, 24 Jun. 1984.

57. The *Drumheller Review* (13 Jul. 1939) announced that WOM had been hired as a temporary instructor in springboard diving and the 20 July issue announced the names of his twenty-five students.

58. PTI, 26 Apr. 1982.

59. *Drumheller Review*, 17 Aug. 1939. The gala the week before, in which WOM did his "Dumb Swede" act, attracted more than 700 people.

60. PTI, 24 Jun. 1984.

61. WOM, "Grace and Illusion: The Writer's Task," *The English Teacher* (English Council of the Alberta Teachers' Association) 3. 2 (Jun. 1963): 6.

62. PTI, 24 Jun. 1984.

63. PTI, 6 Jul. 1984; 13 Oct. 1986.

64. PTI, 13 Oct. 1986.

65. PTI, Jack and Dick Mitchell, 25 Aug. 1984.

66. PTI, 8 Jun. 1984.

67. PTI, Dick Mitchell, 25 Aug. 1984. The only indication in the *Weyburn Review* of any problems with the carnival is an item that says it was postponed from 8 March to 15 March due to spring-like weather.

68. PTI, 6 Jul. 1984.

69. PTI, Dick Mitchell, 25 Aug. 1984.

70. Linda Lawson, "Ham on Wrye," *Easy Living* XI. 2 (Feb. 27–Mar. 26, 1989): 20.

71. NFB, 70.

72. WOM, "Introduction," *Freefall: An Anthology of the Writing Division* (The Banff Centre, 1976).

73. Virginia (Scott) Bue to WOM, 14 Feb. 1963, Family.

74. "Project '63," interviewer Harry Boyle, CBC, 28 Sept. 1962.

75. PTI, 14 Oct. 1985.

76. PTI, Dec. 1981.

77. PTI, 17 Apr. 1987.

78. NFB, roll 68, 47-49.

79. Jack Danylchuk, "Mitchell," *The Albertan*, 13 Feb. 1965: 16.

Chapter 9 (Pages 222-67)

1. PTI, 26 Apr. 1982.

2. PTI, 24 Jun. 1984.

3. PTI, 24 Jun. 1984; MLM, 2 Jun. 1982.

4. Walter Greenwood and Ronald Gow, *Love on the Dole* (London: Cape, 1935) 77-78.

5. PTI, 24 Jun. 1984; MLM, 2 Jun. 1982.

6. PTI, 24 Jun. 1984.

7. PTI, 24 Jun. 1984.

8. PTI, MLM, 4 Sept. 1983.

9. The envelope is postmarked August 11, UCalgary, MsC. 19.1.5.

10. Dr. A.K. McKinn, "A Tribute to Rev. Spurgeon M. Hirtle," *The Canadian Baptist* 1 Aug. 1955: 4.

11. Citation, Supplement to the *London Gazette*, 4 Oct. 1919: 12359, National Archives of Canada, acc 1992-93/166.

12. PTI, MLM, 15 Jun. 1995.

13. "Dr. Mather Refuses Oath, Bares Revolt," *Boston Globe,* 3 Oct. 1935: 7.

14. *Boston Globe,* 5 Dec. 1935: 24.

15. PTI, MLM, 15 Jun. 1995.

16. PTI, MLM, 15 Jun. 1995.

17. PTI, Betty (McNally) Love, 29 Jul. 1996.

18. David Leighton, *Artists, Builders and Dreamers* (Toronto: McClelland and Stewart, 1982): 55.

19. "1,200 See Little Theatre Problem Play Offering," *Edmonton Journal,* 5 May 1938: 9.

20. "Drama of Woe and Poverty Stirs Little Theatre Crowd," *Edmonton Journal,* 4 Mar. 1939: 13-14.

21. PTI, MLM, 22 Jun. 1984.

22. PI, MLM, 5 Mar. 1998.

23. PTI, MLM, 22 Jun. 1984.

24. PTI, Chet and Lois Lambertson, 17 Jun. 1984.

25. PTI, Betty (McNally) Love, 29 Jul. 1996.

26. PTI, Betty (McNally) Love, 29 Jul. 1996.

27. PTI, MLM, 2 Jun. 1982.

28. PTI, 18 Apr. 1987.

29. PTI, 18 Apr. 1987.

30. PTI, Betty (McNally) Love, 29 Jul. 1996.

31. PTI, MLM, 2 Jun. 1982.

32. N.d. 12 or 19 Aug. 1940, UCalgary, MsC 19.1.5. Translation: "We hope that you do not let your mother work too hard or are we catty in making remarks like that?"

33. PD, May 1989.

34. PTI, 17 Apr. 1987.

35. PTI, 24 Jun. 1984.

36. PTI, 24 Jun. 1984.

37. UCalgary, MsC 19.1.5.

38. PTI, MLM, 2 Jun. 1982.

39. PTI, 24 Jun. 1984.

40. "Introduction," *Freefall*.

41. PTI, 25 Aug. 1991.

42. To complete his B.A., WOM had to take French 2, History 4, and two other arts courses (which were English 53, English 64).

43. UCalgary, MsC 19.2.6.

44. "28th Spring Play Staged by Student Drama Group," *Edmonton Journal* 15 Feb. 1941: 15. It played February 14 and 15 in Convocation Hall and was directed by E. Maldwyn (Casey) Jones, who would later produce and direct WOM's play *Royalty Is Royalty*.

45. "University Spring Play Wins Success on Opening Night," *Edmonton Bulletin*, 15 Feb. 1941: 22.

46. PTI, MLM, 2 Jun. 1982.

47. PTI, 18 Dec. 1984.

48. PTI, 18 Dec. 1984.

49. PTI, Robert Blackburn, 25 Mar. 1999.

50. FMS to DC, 28 Apr. 1945, Atlantic.

51. Robert Blackburn, "Foreword," *The Art of Writing*, by F.M. Salter, ed. H.V. Weekes (Toronto: Ryerson Press, 1971) v. FMS had studied at the University of Chicago and distinguished himself with publications in the field of medieval literature. During his tenure at the University of Alberta (1939 to his retirement in 1960) he published articles on Shakespeare and also, posthumously, *The Art of Writing*.

52. PTI, 18 Dec. 1984.

53. PTI, 18 Dec. 1984.

54. PTI, Dec. 1981.

55. PTI, Chet and Lois Lambertson, 17 Jun. 1984.

56. PTI, 24 Jun. 1984.

57. PTI, 24 Jun. 1984.

58. FMS to Mrs. O.S. Mitchell, 23 Nov. 1941, UCalgary, MsC 19.3.1.

59. PTI, 26 Dec. 1983.

60. Jack Paterson to FMS, 23 Sept. 1941, UCalgary, MsC 19.3.1.

61. PTI, 26 Dec. 1983.

62. PTI, Dec. 1981.

63. FMS to DC, 28 Apr. 1945, Atlantic.

64. WOM, "Elbow Room," *Maclean's*, 12 Feb. 1941: 18-20, 39. See *AJK* 13-27.

65. "Escaping Prisoners Were Members of Working Party," *Edmonton Journal*, 12 Feb. 1941: 2. This report, eight months before "Elbow Room" was accepted, warned people "to watch for these men and not give assistance or lifts in motors to strangers."

66. "Elbow Room," 20. See also *AJK* 21. Mitchell made some changes when he reprinted these stories in 1989, and this speech was toned down.

67. Jack Paterson to WOM, 28 Oct. 1941, UCalgary, MsC 19.3.1.

68. FMS to DC, 28 Apr. 1945, Atlantic.

69. *Queen's Quarterly,* 49 (Summer 1942) 132.

70. FMS to DC, 28 Apr. 1945, Atlantic.

71. PTI, MLM, 2 Jun. 1982.

72. "Pirates of Penzance Performed with Zest," *Calgary Herald,* 7 Feb. 1942: 7.

73. PTI, MLM, 2 Jun. 1982.

74. PTI, 24 Jun. 1984.

75. PTI, 24 Jun. 1984. This research and freefall was the basis for a number of scenes in Part One of *WW.* See, for example, Brian and Forbsie's conversation in the sand pile; the scenes where Brian fantasizes that he is playing with R.W. God; and his "song-one" about God. See also Laurence Ricou's "Notes on Language and Learning in *Who Has Seen the Wind*" for an excellent discussion of Brian's development within the framework of Piaget's theories (*Canadian Children's Literature,* 1977-78, no. 10: 3-17).

76. PTI, 24 Jun. 1984.

77. PTI, 4 Sept. 1983.

78. PTI, 4 Sept. 1983.

Chapter 10 (Pages 268-92)

1. PTI, MLM, 2 Jun. 1982.

2. PTI, Cec and Marg Hewson and Pearl Coppock, 14 Jun. 1984.

3. PTI, 4 Sept. 1983.

4. *Castor Advance,* 2 Dec. 1942.

5. PL, Doris Thomson to biographers, 5 Dec. 1986.

6. PL, Kathleen Davies to biographers, 30 Nov. 1986.

7. PL, Kathleen Davies to biographers, 30 Nov. 1986.

8. PTI, Cec and Marg Hewson and Pearl Coppock, 14 Jan. 1984.

9. PTI, 4 Sept. 1983.

10. PL, Kathleen Davies to biographers, 30 Nov. 1986.

11. PL, Doris Thomson to biographers, 5 Dec. 1986.

12. "Grace and Illusion," 14-15.

13. PL, Doris Thomson to biographers, 5 Dec. 1986. See *WW* 22 where Brian watches the porridge cook: "It went *bup bup,* very slowly at first, then faster; there were old men's mouths opening and closing as it boiled."

14. Two poems by his students appeared in the 18 Nov. and 2 Dec. 1942 issues of the *Castor Advance.*

15. PTI, Eddie Wong, 26 Feb. 1984.

16. PTI, 17 Dec. 1986.

17. PTI, Eddie Wong, 26 Feb. 1984. Forty-seven years later Eddie Wong still plays hockey in the old-timers' league and has been a key player in organizing the Calgary Flames alumni organization's fundraising for various Calgary charities.

18. PTI, MLM, 4 Sept. 1983.

19. WOM was working from memory. The title of the play is *Antony and Cleopatra* and the quotation is: "Age cannot wither her, nor custom stale/Her infinite variety."

20. PL, Jessie Campbell to biographers describing Velma Caddey's impressions of WOM, 21 Mar. 1984.

21. PTI, Eddie Wong, 26 Feb. 1984.

22. DC to FMS, 21 Sept. 1944, Atlantic.

23. Readers' reports, Sept. 1944, Atlantic.

24. "Honored on 90th Birthday," *Edmonton Journal,* 27 Jan. 1960.

25. PTI, MLM, 4 Sept. 1983.

26. PTI, 17 Dec. 1986.

27. "Grace and Illusion," 12-13.

28. PTI, 17 Dec. 1986.

29. "Grace and Illusion," 13.

30. "The Most Unforgettable Character I've Met," unpublished ms., UCalgary, MsC 19.32.8., 5-6. This autobiographical essay was written in the fall of 1948. It may have been written for *Reader's Digest* but was either never submitted or was rejected. It is difficult at times to tell where fiction (i.e., characters and events as depicted in *WW*) bleeds back into WOM's memory of the facts about Pete Stoller and letting him go from school in 1943.

31. "Grace and Illusion," 13.

32. "The Most Unforgettable Character I've Met," 7.

33. PTI, MLM, 4 Sept. 1983.

34. "The Most Unforgettable Character I've Met," 1-2.

35. PTI, 4 Sept. 1983.

36. As recalled by MLM, NFB, 32.

37. PTI, 4 Sept. 1983.

38. PTI, 4 Sept. 1983. MLM recalled the letter as follows: "So W.O. came home and wrote a letter resigning, that at the end of June they could look for another principal. It wasn't a very nice letter because he wrote that they could shove the school up their collective ass!" PTI, MLM, 4 Sept. 1983.

39. F. Tucker to WOM, 13 Mar. 1943, UCalgary, MsC 19.3.1.

40. PTI, 4 Sept. 1983.

41. See also the teacher-schoolboard confrontations in "Frankincents an' Meer" (*JK*) and "Will of the People" (*AJK*).

42. "The Most Unforgettable Character I've Met," 7.
43. "The Most Unforgettable Character I've Met," 7-8.
44. "The Most Unforgettable Character I've Met," 9.
45. PTI, 17 Dec. 1986.
46. PL, Doris Thomson to biographers, 5 Dec. 1986.
47. PTI, 4 Sept. 1983.
48. *Castor Advance*, 7 Jul. 1943.

Chapter 11 (Pages 293-324)

1. PTI, 17 Dec. 1986.
2. PTI, MLM, 2 Jun. 1982.
3. PTI, 17 Dec. 1986.
4. PTI, MLM, 22 Jun. 1984.
5. PTI, 17 Dec. 1986.
6. PTI, Dec. 1981.
7. "Stoney Indians Appealing to Government for Lands Suited for Stock – Gardens," *High River Times*, 12 Aug. 1943. "It is a matter of record that the Stoney Reservation is mainly stone and gravel, 'the most hopeless agriculturally of any Reserve in the province.'"
8. "Eden Valley Sold to Dept. Indian Affairs," *High River Times*, 14 Oct. 1948.
9. Her articles ran from 12 Aug. 1943 to 8 Sept. 1949.
10. The quotations are taken from Hughena McCorquodale's feature article, "The Stoney Indians Petition Federal Government for Land Suited to New Skill" (*High River Times*, 21 Oct. 1943). She gives an account of this meeting summarizing the interpreters' versions of the various speeches.
11. Hughena McCorquodale to WOM, 3 Nov. 1943, UCalgary, MsC 19.8.
12. "Cow Heaven," *Maclean's*, 15 Nov. 1943.
13. "What's Ahead for Billy?" *The Canadian Forum* XXIV, 282 (July 1944): 85.
14. "What's Ahead for Billy?" 86. Hughena McCorquodale draws the same parallel in her 12 Aug. 1943 article: "In setting out to save under privileged people in far parts, we had better try to clean our record at home." See also her 13 Apr. 1944 article cited below.
15. N.O. Bonisteel to WOM, 21 Dec. 1943, UCalgary, MsC 19.3.1.
16. It appeared in the ms. stories "Billy Was a Stoney" (1944) and "Catharsis" (1947) in *A* (1953), and finally in *VP* (1973).
17. "Stoneys Hold Pow Wow on Easter Monday to Renew Prayer to Govt. for Land," *High River Times*, 13 Apr. 1944.
18. *High River Times*, 13 Apr. 1944.
19. "Billy Was a Stoney," UCalgary, MsC 19.18.10.

20. FMS to DC, 29 Aug. 1944, Atlantic.

21. Readers' reports, Sept. 1944, Atlantic.

22. "Eden Valley Sold to Dept. Indian Affairs." The *Times* reported that it was not a large property (1,100 acres of deeded land and about 1,900 acres of lease) but "should go far in meeting the desires of the Stoneys in the foothills area."

23. At a meeting in late February 1944 with Harry Clark, associate editor of *Maclean's*, WOM suggested a story on Mrs. McCorquodale. Clark wanted the story and wrote WOM in March and again in May urging him to finish and submit the story. But WOM did not do a piece on her until 1956 on the occasion of her retirement from the *High River Times*: "Bob Edwards 'Successor,'" *Calgary Herald* (25 Jun. and reprinted in *Regina Leader Post*).

24. WOM to Mrs. O.S. Mitchell, 1 Mar. 1944, UCalgary. Mitchell's salary was $1,650 at Castor and $1,750 at New Dayton. His income was increasingly supplemented with sales of his stories and articles – $85 in 1942, $250 in 1943, $625 in 1944. So he was turning down a stable *Maclean's* salary that was about three times his current income.

25. FMS to WOM, 8 Mar. 1944, UCalgary, MsC 19.3.1.

26. FMS to DC, 28 Apr. 1945, Atlantic.

27. Jack Paterson to Mrs. O.S. Mitchell, 14 Dec. 1942, UCalgary, MsC 19.3.1.

28. FMS to WOM, 8 Mar. 1944, UCalgary, MsC 19.3.1.

29. FMS to DC, 28 Apr. 1945, Atlantic.

30. For a more detailed discussion of WOM's use of the tall-tale tradition, see O.S. Mitchell, "Tall Tales in the Fiction of W.O. Mitchell," *Canadian Literature*, 108 (Spring 1986): 16-35, and Catherine McLay, "Crocus, Saskatchewan: A Country of the Mind," *Journal of Popular Culture*, 14 (Fall 1980): 333-49.

31. Donald Cameron, "W.O. Mitchell: Sea Caves and Creative Partners," *Conversations with Canadian Novelists – 2* (Toronto: Macmillan, 1973), 50.

32. FMS to EW, 10 Jan. 1944, Atlantic.

33. Miss Boyce to FMS, 19 Jan. 1944, Atlantic.

34. FMS to WOM, 8 Mar. 1944, UCalgary. "The Ben" was subsequently reworked and retitled "The Owl and the Bens."

35. FMS to DC, 19 May 1944, Atlantic.

36. DC to FMS, 23 May 1944, Atlantic.

37. "Grace and Illusion," 12-13.

38. PTI, 13 Oct. 1986.

39. FMS to WOM, 8 Mar. 1944, UCalgary.

40. "The Owl and the Bens," *Atlantic Monthly*, Apr. 1945: 83.

41. PTI, 13 Oct. 1986.

42. FMS to WOM, 8 Mar. 1944, UCalgary.

43. DC to FMS, 17 Aug. 1944, Atlantic.

44. FMS to DC, 29 Aug. 1944, Atlantic.

45. EW to DC, 6 Dec. 1944, Atlantic.

46. DC to WOM, 30 Apr. 1945, Atlantic.

47. PTI, 14 Oct. 1985.

48. PTI, MLM, 21 Jun. 1984.

49. "Auction Fever," *Liberty* (New York), 20 Oct. 1945. *Liberty* was one of the top pulp-fiction magazines in the United States and paid top dollar for stories.

50. WOM to DC, 9 [Apr.] 1945, Atlantic.

51. FMS to DC, 28 Apr. 1945, Atlantic.

52. DC to WOM, 30 Apr. 1945, Atlantic.

53. FMS to WOM, 5 May 1945, UCalgary, MsC 19.11.6.

Chapter 12 (Pages 325-66)

1. "Chooses High River as Future Home," *High River Times*, 5 Apr 1945: 10.

2. WOM, notes for "Mrs. McCorquodale Day." Family.

3. MLM to Mrs. Green, 1 Oct. 1962. Family.

4. PTI, MLM, 16 Jun. 1982.

5. "Prairies: Poetry of Earth and Sky," 22-23.

6. WOM "High River: A place to love at first sight," *Star Weekly Magazine*, 22 Sept. 1962: 1.

7. "High River," 2.

8. Historical Committee, *Leaves from the Medical Tree* (Lethbridge: Lethbridge Herald Press, 1960) 11.

9. PTI, MLM, 2 Jun. 1982.

10. "High River," 4.

11. "High River," 4, 1.

12. Tom Primrose, "Personality of the Week," *Calgary Herald*, 4 Feb. 1956: 5.

13. PTI, MLM, 21 Jun. 1984.

14. FMS to WOM, 28 Apr. 1945, UCalgary, MsC 19.11.6.

15. FMS to DC, 28 Apr. 1945, Atlantic.

16. FMS to WOM, 28 Apr. 1945, UCalgary.

17. FMS to WOM, 5 May 1945, UCalgary, MsC 19.11.6

18. FMS to WOM, 9 May 1945, UCalgary, MsC 19.11.6.

19. Reader's report, 16 Apr. 1945, Atlantic.

20. FMS to WOM, 9 May 1945.

21. Primrose, 5.

22. "Houses Come in from T. Valley," *High River Times*, 2 May 1946: 1.

23. PTI, Grace Clark, 28 May 1984.

24. PTI, 14 Oct. 1985.

25. PTI, Grace Clark, 28 May 1984.

26. PTI, MLM, 2 Jun. 1982.

27. "UFWA-UFA Annual Dinner W. Mitchell Guest Speaker," *High River Times*, 19 Dec. 1946.

28. WOM to mother, 11 Mar 1946. UCalgary, MsC 19.3.1.

29. WOM to Jeannette Cloud, 3 Jun. 1946, Atlantic.

30. PTI, MLM, 15 Jun. 1995.

31. PTI, MLM, 16 Jun. 1982.

32. FMS to WOM, 29 Dec. 1945. UCalgary, MsC 19.11.6.

33. EW to WOM, 1 Mar. 1946, Atlantic.

34. FMS to WOM, 28 Apr. 1945, UCalgary, MsC 19.11.6.

35. EW to FMS, 1 May 1945, Atlantic.

36. FMS to DC, 28 Apr. 1945, Atlantic.

37. DC to WOM, 18 May 1945, Atlantic.

38. FMS to WOM, 26 May 1945, UCalgary, MsC 19.11.6.

39. FMS to WOM, 26 May 1945, UCalgary, MsC 19.11.6.

40. "Who Has Seen the Wind" ms., edited by FMS, UCalgary, MsC 19.40.10.

41. FMS to WOM, 27 Jun. 1945, UCalgary, MsC 19.11.6.

42. "Who Has Seen the Wind" ms., UCalgary, MsC 19.40.10.

43. WOM to DC, 31 Aug. 1945, Atlantic.

44. WOM to DC, 13 Sept. 1945, Atlantic.

45. Dan Riley, Tom Primrose, Hugh Dempsey, *The Lost Lemon Mine* (Frontier Publishing Ltd., 1968) 5.

46. DC to WOM, 21 Sept. 1945, Atlantic.

47. PTI, 14 Oct. 1985.

48. EW to WOM, 6 Dec. 1945, Atlantic. This includes a four-page letter accompanied by fourteen pages of editorial suggestions.

49. WOM to EW, 26 Jan. 1946, Atlantic. This includes a four-page letter accompanied by four pages of response to EW's editorial suggestions.

50. EW to WOM, 6 Dec. 1945, Atlantic.

51. FMS to WOM, 29 Dec. 1945, UCalgary, MsC 19.11.6.

52. FMS to WOM, 31 Dec. 1945, UCalgary, MsC 19.11.6.

53. WOM to EW, 26 Jan. 1946, Atlantic.

54. EW to WOM, 6 Dec. 1945, Atlantic.

55. WOM to EW, 26 Jan. 1946, Atlantic.

56. WOM to EW, 26 Jan. 1946, Atlantic.

57. Frederick Philip Grove, "Who Has Seen the Wind by Harry [sic] Mitchell," reader's report, Feb. 1946, UCalgary, MsC 19.11.6.9. Also at McMaster, box 123, file 1.

58. WOM to mother, 11 Mar. 1946, UCalgary, MsC 19.3.1. Enclosed was Grove's reader's report.

59. Frederick Philip Grove, *The Letters of Frederick Philip Grove*, ed. with introduction by Desmond Pacey (Toronto: University of Toronto Press, 1976) 493.

60. WOM to mother, 8 Mar. 1946, UCalgary, MsC 19.3.1.

61. WOM to Ellen Elliott, 11 Mar. 1946, UCalgary, MsC 19.3.1. Also McMaster.

62. WOM to Ellen Elliott, 25 Mar. 1946, McMaster.

63. WOM to Ellen Elliott, 11 Mar. 1946, UCalgary, MsC 19.3.1. Also McMaster.

64. EW to WOM, 1 Mar. 1946, Atlantic.

65. Jeannette Cloud to Ellen Elliott, 18 Mar. 1946, Atlantic.

66. WOM to EW, 4 Mar. 1946, Atlantic.

67. WOM to DC, 11 Apr. 1946, Atlantic.

68. WOM to DC, 14 May 1946, Atlantic.

69. EW to WOM, 1 Mar. 1946, Atlantic.

70. WOM to DC, 11 Apr. 1946, Atlantic.

71. WOM to Jeannette Cloud, 1 Sept. 1946, Atlantic. Included with the one-page letter were three pages of requested reinsertions, a list of additional cuts, a map of the fictional town, four pages of answers to editor's queries, and a two-page outline by chapter of the novel.

72. WOM to Jeannette Cloud, 1 Sept. 1946, Atlantic.

73. WOM to Ellen Elliott, 28 Oct. 1946, McMaster.

74. WOM to Jeannette Cloud, biographical forms, Apr. 1946, Atlantic.

75. PTI, 26 Dec. 1985.

76. William Wordsworth, "Ode: Intimations of Immortality from Recollections of Early Childhood," *The Norton Anthology of English Literature*, 1388.

77. Wordsworth, "Ode: Imitations of Immortality," 1387.

78. Joseph Conrad, "Preface," *The Nigger of the Narcissus* (London: J.M. Dent & Sons, Ltd., 1960) 5.

79. "Grace and Illusion," 14.

80. FMS to WOM, 31 Dec. 1945. UCalgary, MsC 19.11.6.

81. PTI, 26 Dec. 1985.

82. Samuel Marchbanks, "Review of Spring Novels," *Peterborough Examiner*, 12 Mar. 1947.

83. Grove, reader's report, Feb. 1946.

84. "Canada Is Sold Short by Authors: New Yorker," *Globe and Mail*, 12 Jun. 1948: 17.

85. PTI, 13 Oct. 1985.

86. EW to DC, 6 Dec. 1944, Atlantic.

87. "Further Success for W.O. Mitchell," *High River Times*, 26 Sept. 1946: 1.

88. PTI, MLM, 2 Jun. 1982.

89. WOM to Jeannette Cloud, 9 Feb. 1947, Atlantic.

90. Ellen Elliott to John Gray, Feb. 1947, McMaster.

91. WOM to John Gray, 2 Dec. 1947, McMaster.

92. Joseph Henry Jackson, "Review of W.O. Mitchell's *Who Has Seen the Wind,*" *San Francisco Chronicle.* Digest of reviews, Atlantic.

93. "Review of W.O. Mitchell's *Who Has Seen the Wind,*" *Boston Sunday Post,* 30 Mar. 1947. Digest of reviews, Atlantic.

94. Lloyd Wendt, "Review of W.O. Mitchell's *Who Has Seen the Wind,*" *Chicago Sunday Tribune,* 2 Feb. 1947. Digest of reviews, Atlantic.

95. Samuel Roddan, "Review of *Who Has Seen the Wind,*" *Canadian Forum,* Apr. 1947: 22.

96. Earle Birney to WOM, 23 Jul. 1947. Earle Birney Papers, Thomas Fisher Rare Book Library, University of Toronto.

97. Ethel Wilson to Ellen Elliott, Apr. 1947, *Ethel Wilson, Stories, Essays and Letters,* ed. David Stouck (Vancouver: University of British Columbia Press, 1987) 137.

98. William Arthur Deacon, "Novel of Distinction Recalls Saskatchewan's Barren Years," *Globe and Mail,* 1 Mar. 1947. Many of the reviews, both American and Canadian, are collected in UCalgary, MsC 19.42.1 and in MsC 19.3.2., which holds Mrs. O.S. Mitchell's scrapbook relating to *WW.*

99. WOM to William Arthur Deacon, *Dear Bill: The Correspondence of William Arthur Deacon,* ed. John Lennox and Michele Lacombe (Toronto: University of Toronto Press, 1988) 234-35.

100. William Arthur Deacon to WOM, 5 Mar. 1947, *Dear Bill,* 237.

101. "From Manitoba 'U' Cheer Leader to Novelist – By Way of Biarritz," *Winnipeg Tribune,* 15 Mar. 1947, UCalgary, MsC 19.3.2.

102. WOM to DC, 3 Jun. 1947, Atlantic.

103. WOM to DC, 7 Apr. 1947, Atlantic.

104. WOM to John Gray, 2 Dec. 1947, McMaster.

105. The short stories were "The Day Jake Made Her Rain," "Shoparoon for Maggie," and "Air-Nest and the Child Harold." The novella was "The Devil's Instrument" and the article was probably "Flying Rancher."

106. "Macleans Magazine Offers Edit. Post to W. Mitchell," *High River Times,* 10 Jun. 1948.

INDEX